Holy Spirit, and God's continual calling of children and young people to further the gospel.

6. Recognising the need to shape a new generation of leaders with authenticity for mission in a world of diversities in the twenty-first century, we are called to work together in new forms of theological education. Because we are all made in the image of God, these will draw on one another's unique charisms, challenge each other to grow in faith and understanding, share resources equitably worldwide, involve the entire human being and the whole family of God, and respect the wisdom of our elders while also fostering the participation of children.

7. Hearing the call of Jesus to make disciples of all people – poor, wealthy, marginalised, ignored, powerful, living with disability, young, and old – we are called as communities of faith to mission from everywhere to everywhere. In joy we hear the call to receive from one another in our witness by word and action, in streets, fields, offices, homes, and schools, offering reconciliation, showing love, demonstrating grace and speaking out truth.

8. Recalling Christ, the host at the banquet, and committed to that unity for which he lived and prayed, we are called to ongoing co-operation, to deal with controversial issues and to work towards a common vision. We are challenged to welcome one another in our diversity, affirm our membership through baptism in the One Body of Christ, and recognise our need for mutuality, partnership, collaboration and networking in mission, so that the world might believe.

9. Remembering Jesus' way of witness and service, we believe we are called by God to follow this way joyfully, inspired, anointed, sent and empowered by the Holy Spirit, and nurtured by Christian disciplines in community. As we look to Christ's coming in glory and judgment, we experience his presence with us in the Holy Spirit, and we invite all to join with us as we participate in God's transforming and reconciling mission of love to the whole creation.

CONTENTS

ACKNOWLEDGEMENTS

This second volume in the Edinburgh 2010 series contains reports of the work of nine groups working on the main study themes identified for the study process, and two shorter contributions from those working on transversal topics. It is not presented as the final word on any of these topics but represents a stage in the process and provides the raw material from on discussion at the conference in Edinburgh in June 2010 will build. The volume is commended to churches, mission groups and students of mission for study and reflection throughout the Christian world. In particular, it is intended to serve as pre-conference reading material for all those attending in June, who are encouraged to study it and work out their own responses to facilitate informed and stimulating discussion which will help to clarify the main issues and priorities in 'witnessing to Christ today'. It should be clear that material published in this volume, and in the series will generally reflect the diversity of the views and positions of the contributing individuals and groups, and does not necessarily represent those of the series editors or the Edinburgh 2010 General Council.

The editors wish to express their warm appreciation of the work of the conveners of the different study groups, who bore the responsibility for the conduct of each study, their core group members, and those who worked hard to draft and redraft the texts to deadlines. We recognise with hearty thanks the guiding and advisory work of the Study Process Monitoring Group: Maria Aranzazu Aguado, Rosemary Dowsett, Knud Jørgensen, John Kafwanka, Jooseop Keum, Wonsuk Ma and Petros Vassiliadis. We also wish to thank Wonsuk Ma (Regnum) and Tony Gray (Bound Biographies) for their help in making its publication possible.

Daryl Balia
Kirsteen Kim
General Editors

Introduction

Experimenting with a Multi-Regional, Cross-Denominational, Poly-Centric Study Process

Daryl Balia and Kirsteen Kim

The World Missionary Conference, Edinburgh 1910 was motivated by the perception that the Christian gospel is good news for the whole world but it understood that world to be divided into Christian and non-Christian lands. One hundred years later Christianity is recognised as a truly world religion, widely spread across the globe and locally rooted in a huge diversity of cultures and in varied regions. Historic forms of church life which originated in West Asia and Europe are being reconfigured for new situations, and in the context of newly emerging churches and movements, especially in Africa, Asia, Oceania and the Americas. The representatives of churches and mission organisations meeting in 2010 do not see themselves as part of an enterprise of European peoples on a mission to the rest but as participating in the mission of God, which is worldwide and multi-directional. Christian mission today is made up of the witness of countless local churches as well as transnational and cross-cultural flows. It is facilitated by an ever growing variety of organisations and groups, inspired by new and renewed forms of spirituality, and undergirded by academic studies of various kinds.

The context of world Christianity poses new challenges to Christians and churches seeking to be faithful in witnessing to Christ today. Faithfulness in fulfilling the one mission of God implies participating in the one body of Christ and sharing the same Holy Spirit. But this raises the issue: How can we witness faithfully together, and recognise one another's contributions to God's mission, when we belong to so many different denominations, live in such diverse cultures, speak so many different languages, and experience such widely differing socio-economic conditions?

To the challenge of world Christianity is added the challenge of a changed world situation since 1910. In particular, there is a deepening awareness of processes of globalization, of the fragility of the earth which we share, and of the interpenetration of religions and cultures as populations grow and move. These perceptions accentuate the sense that we belong to one world, and bring home to us the significance of human diversity for Christian mission. We ask, what does it mean to witness to Christ in the plurality and pressures of this age?

Preparation for the 1910 conference was by means of eight 'Commissions' which investigated what were considered the most pressing issues facing Western missionaries in their day. So too in 2010 it is considered important to wrestle with the issues of mission, church and world by means of a study process. What is more, the process is collaborative and holistic: as far as possible it is the whole church reflecting together on the triune God's mission in and to the whole world.

The Edinburgh 2010 study process is unique – it is a project of churches worldwide which is multi-regional, cross-denominational and poly-centric. Edinburgh 2010 is sponsored by all the major Christian world bodies covering the five main streams of world Christianity recognised today: Catholic, Orthodox, Protestant, Evangelical and Pentecostal. It is a very large undertaking. There are study events taking place in every continent which involve hundreds of Christians in different parts of the world. At least ten volumes will be published in connection with it, and many articles are expected from it. The project is focused on nine study themes. The conveners of the study groups on these themes are nine women and ten men from Protestant, Orthodox, Evangelical and Pentecostal backgrounds; three are Africans, four Asians, two North Americans and ten Europeans. They have been challenged to do collaborative work which brings together perspectives that are as inclusive as possible of contemporary world Christianity.

In addition to the main studies, Edinburgh 2010 study processes have been organised in all continents – including Latin America and Oceania, by regional and confessional groups, including six Roman Catholic institutions. Furthermore, seven transversal topics have been identified which cut across the main themes, and various bodies are contributing from these perspectives. No one enterprise can capture in full the diversity of Christianity today but the breadth and inclusivity of the Edinburgh 2010 project mark it out as a very special – and almost certainly unparalleled – event in Christian history.

This volume contains the preliminary results of the Edinburgh 2010 study project, which was set up in 2005, and reconstituted in 2007, to mark the centenary of the World Missionary Conference. It is intended to contribute, from a research perspective, to the aim of witnessing together to Christ in the twenty-first century. The goal of the Edinburgh 2010 study process is

> to study the Bible and the world in which we live, and listen to each other across geographical and ecclesial borders on key issues in mission today, in order to bring together insights from academics, mission practitioners and policy makers – with a commitment to produce resources for churches, mission movements, colleges, and so on. The focal point is that a new vision in terms of God's purposes for creation in Christ and a renewed spirituality and mission ethos be developed in the life of churches worldwide.[1]

This volume contains a summary of what has been achieved through the study process up to the end of 2009 and forms the preparatory volume for the centenary conference to be held in Edinburgh on 2-6 June 2010. There it is intended that the material will be subjected to rigorous critique from various transversal perspectives and engaged with by church and mission delegates from around the world. There will be presentations from distinguished guests and reports from regional and confessional events not represented in this volume. So the next volume in this series – the conference report –will move the discussion on further, and other volumes which will form part of the Edinburgh 2010 series will amplify and develop what is in summary here.

As an historic 'first', the Edinburgh 2010 study process is necessarily experimental. Not only the outcomes but also the failures and omissions, and the process itself, will therefore be of interest to future generations. Here we will describe the process to date and discuss in more detail its objectives and current outcomes. We will go on to evaluate what has been achieved at this stage of the project, affirming the value of the work and setting out what remains to be done before, during and after the centenary conference to better meet the goals of the project.

The Edinburgh 2010 Study Process

Edinburgh 2010 was planned very much with the heritage of Edinburgh 1910 in mind and, like its predecessor event, began by setting up a study process. The academic framework of the process has, arguably, changed little, and the discourse in both centuries is in English. However, there are several differences between the study process of 1910 and that of today. The most pronounced is that the leaders in 1910 were all of European descent, of Protestant denominations and overwhelmingly male. A second difference is that the main work done by the eight 'Commissions' of 1910 was gathering information on mission activities in different parts of the world and discussing strategy. This they did primarily by means of questionnaires. Discussion of theology was curtailed because it would make ecumenical cooperation too difficult. Today the facts are largely known, and most of the Edinburgh 2010 discussions relate mission theory and practice to theological issues at the heart of mission. A third difference is that the means of research have changed. The postal systems of today probably do not match up to those of the imperial period but in the era of globalization, email does an even quicker job of linking researchers around the world. In 2010, like 1910, many hard-bound volumes will be produced, but in 2010 the internet makes it possible to expand the published material almost infinitely. Under the 'study process', 'events' and 'resources' links on the project website (www.edinburgh2010.org) you can find programmes, papers, reports, statements and photos of the many different study activities worldwide which have fed into the project and trace some of the interconnections between them. In fact, the multi-faceted, hyper-linked, open-ended worldwide web better represents the content and ethos of Edinburgh 2010 than the bound volumes.

To set up the 2010 process, stakeholders called an international council together in 2005 and 2006 who identified pressing mission themes for our generation. It proved impossible to limit them to just eight, as some wished. In 2010 there are nine main themes:

1. Foundations for mission
2. Christian mission among other faiths
3. Mission and postmodernities
4. Mission and power
5. Forms of missionary engagement
6. Theological education and formation
7. Christian communities in contemporary contexts
8. Mission and unity – ecclesiology and mission
9. Mission spirituality and authentic discipleship

Each theme was further developed by the international council to suggest the scope and issues that could be addressed. The elaborated statement of the themes can be found on the website and in the appendix to this book. The main part of this volume is occupied by nine chapters, which are summary reports of the work done by the core groups working on these main study themes.

A further seven 'transversal' topics were included, which the international council considered important topics in their own right, but which were intended to complement and exercise a critical function with the regard to the main themes. The transversal topics are:

1. Women and mission
2. Youth and mission
3. Healing and reconciliation
4. Bible and mission – mission in the Bible
5. Contextualization, inculturation and dialogue of worldviews
6. Subaltern voices
7. Ecological perspectives on mission

Material relating to these topics has been gathered on the website but core groups were not formed for these topics in the same way. However two groups, representing transversals 1 and 4, have submitted short articles which form the final chapter of this volume. It is expected that the transversal topics will come more to the fore at the 2010 conference itself.

Unlike the first Edinburgh study process, the elaboration of the 2010 themes by the international councils in 2005 and 2006 was explicitly theological. In 2010, unlike 1910, a theological approach is possible partly because the basic data about world Christianity is already known and also because the 2010 member bodies are prepared to engage one another theologically. It is also necessary in 2010 because the main questions about mission are no longer just methodological. Mission is recognised by all the sponsoring bodies as beginning from the initiative of God – the *missio Dei* – and this theological understanding is reflected throughout the detailed statement of the themes (see Appendix II).

For each of the nine main themes, core groups were formed, in most cases in 2008, but in the case of theme 1 not until early 2009. Two conveners (three in the case of theme 8) were appointed for each theme and they gathered a representative core group around them of their own contacts, and others recommended by the Edinburgh 2010 office and stakeholders. The conveners were deliberately chosen to complement one another in terms of denomination, region and gender, and groups were encouraged to be as diverse as possible within the financial constraints of the project. In most cases conveners were geographically far apart – in three cases they were in different continents – and were collaborating for the first time. The conveners and their core groups functioned in order to consolidate the work done by the group and their wider network together with that produced by other 2010-related study processes (of which there are many, as listed under 'events' on the website), collected from existing academic missiological research, strategic organisational mission practice and grassroots experience, and gleaned from contributions from individuals writing in their own capacities.

Keeping focused on the overall themes of Edinburgh 2010,[2] each study group was tasked with doing the following within their particular area of study:

- Identify some *key questions and items* which are of global importance
- Highlight some general *historical achievements and developments* since 1910 till today
- Give some *illuminating and telling regional case studies* and examples which illustrate major trends and challenges
- Identify *key priorities* for global Christianity concerning the future of Christian mission in the twenty-first century
- Propose *strategic recommendations* to consider and communicate
- Find creative ways to meaningfully translate findings into formats that can motivate Christians involved in mission at grassroots level
- Include discussion questions that will facilitate use of the publication in peer discussions[3]

For the most part, conveners and core group members were not full-time academics but informed and reflective church and mission personnel. For the purposes of this book, they were required to produce work that was academically credible but aimed at church and mission leaders rather than academics. Work is in progress to 'translate' this literature still further into 'church-friendly' material suitable for use at a more grassroots level and in varied contexts.

Unlike 1910 when questionnaires were prepared centrally for the Commissions to use, the 2010 process has been much less prescriptive and the methodology has been left largely to the groups. Due to time constraints core groups were expected, to a high degree, to make use of existing knowledge and material and, for the most part, the core groups concentrated on the task of gathering and processing knowledge and perspectives from across the church worldwide. Most groups also issued a call for papers – and sometimes case studies – and organised one or two consultations or group meetings in order to draft the chapter required for this book. There is only one example of questionnaire-base research but there are examples of more grassroots studies contributing to the work on the themes. The conveners and groups have worked hard, and in most cases have also made a larger agenda to produce a substantial publication in addition to the chapter included here. Limited funding was made available from the Edinburgh 2010 budget and the groups have put in their own resources as well. The many organisations represented by the conveners and group members have also contributed to the process by supporting the respective groups.

From early 2009, the research process was brought together by a designated Research Coordinator working with a Study Process Monitoring Group. As much as possible, the Research Coordinator brought the attention of the groups to other significant pieces of work relating to their fields, and to Edinburgh 2010-related regional and confessional conferences and processes working on the same or similar themes. The Study Process Monitoring Group made strategic decisions regarding the work and also commented on drafts of the papers. The work of integrating the different studies and bringing them into engagement with the transversal topics, and with regionally and confessionally based studies, is ongoing as we approach the conference, and will be a major part of the study process there.

Evaluation of the study so far

The main tangible outcome of the study process was intended to be this publication, and to that extent it has succeeded. The editors recognise that this text is more of a working document, raw material for the conference, rather than a finished product. It is not the final word on any of the topics; it merely opens a discussion to be continued at the conference, at many other events in 2010 and in other mission studies in the coming years.

Each of the groups has conducted their research in a distinctive way which represents the leadership and composition of the group and is appropriate to the subject matter. The editors have respected the integrity of each independent study and restricted editorial intervention to what is required for clarity, credibility and to respect basic publishing conventions. They have only intervened in rare cases of obvious weakness or omission, and in order to broaden participation. This editorial approach was partly due to the limited timeframe and a consequence of the geographical distances involved, and as well as to human weakness, but it was also a deliberate policy. The editors had no desire to stamp a uniformity on the texts and outcomes because this would be contrary to the open spirit of Edinburgh 2010 and it would stifle the diversity represented by world Christianity. Furthermore, the integration of the studies and the focusing of them is properly an ecumenical activity, and the conference will be the best forum for that.

The result may be unsatisfactory to those used to more solid and crafted work, or to a more academic genre. It may equally not be found suitable by those looking for worked out mission strategies or material to apply directly in a local church setting. However, we believe it does have value in the context of the Edinburgh 2010 process and for the churches and mission organisations which have sponsored it. We ask the readers to overlook a certain amount of repetition between chapters due to independent working and to respect the varied nature of the material because such an inclusive and global study process cannot have neat and tidy outcomes. All the groups have struggled hard to relate to one another across ecclesial, cultural and other barriers, and many have wrestled with the text to find a form of wording which all can hold in common. The result should be treated as work in progress, to be continued and developed in other forums.

As they stand, the chapters open up mission questions for our day. They affirm the diversity and richness of world Christianity, as well as exposing the complexities and the challenges of witnessing to Christ today. The studies underline many of the enduring questions of mission studies, questions raised a century ago, including the most basic one of all: why mission? They also raise new issues, especially posed by Christian and religious plurality and the context of migration, by new forms of injustice and abuse of power, by contemporary technologies and communications, and by varied and sometimes conflicting worldviews. In different chapters new initiatives in mission are shown and case studies highlight surprising new movements and methods of evangelism and service. For future generations this volume provides a snapshot of the variety of witnessing activities, of understandings of the gospel, and of motivations for mission in the first decade of the twenty-first century. It shows there is a large measure of agreement, mutual recognition and common working, while also revealing some contradictions and significant tensions in mission approaches.

There is something to be learnt also from the different research methods chosen by the different groups and from the way they have approached mission theology in the context of world Christianity. Three chapters – 1, 6 and 8 – take a more traditional ecumenical approach of trying to do justice in one paper to many different viewpoints and as far as possible reconcile them. At the other extreme, chapter 4 focuses on a case study of a very local example of mission and then invites sympathetic responses from other parallel contexts. Groups 5 and 9 have collected a variety of case studies and set them alongside one another as distinct but complementary. Groups 2, 3 and 7 have gone a little further in integrating individual papers and case studies into a particular theoretical framework. Mission studies, as much as mission itself, admits of many different methods. Which method is more appropriate for witnessing to Christ together in today's world remains for further discussion.

Although all the groups were varied and attempted to be representative of world Christianity in terms of their composition, it must be admitted that these preliminary results remain only partially reflective of the realities of world Christianity, and that the study process so far falls short of the kind of mutual engagement across boundaries which those who initiated it had hoped for. There may be several reasons for this. One reason is perhaps a well-meant but excessive willingness to affirm one another and look for commonality and complementarity, and a reluctance to provoke conflict and risk warm relations. Time is needed to build up sufficient trust and strong enough relationships to allow people to challenge one another and express opinions frankly while also maintaining fellowship, and a study process of this kind where people from different backgrounds come together for relatively short periods may not be the forum to achieve this. When deadlines are pressing, people may also restrain themselves from expressing their views for the sake of having an outcome. Another possibility is that the conveners naturally tended to invite those already in their networks – even though from different denominations or regions – and that not enough was done centrally to ensure diverse opinions within the groups. Despite all efforts toward inclusivity, those most involved in the process are still based in the West – so that other continents are represented largely by their diasporas, working in English – and with limited access to discourses in other languages, and mainly Protestant – although of many different denominations. A further reason that deep engagement across confessions and regions is not yet achieved is that once the framework for the study had been set in the initial stages, it proved difficult for conveners and drafters to incorporate material from other perspectives. As pointed out above, each chapter has a governing paradigm and drafting required fitting different contributions within that, even when they challenged the paradigm.

Nevertheless, a great deal has been achieved in this unique experiment with a multi-regional, cross-denominational, poly-centric study process, and much has already been learnt in the doing. There remains a lot of work to be done to really bring out the issues relating to each theme and highlight the priorities implied for mission. In the case of most themes there is also a great deal of material and many perspectives from other study processes related to Edinburgh 2010 – regional and confessional – which will be introduced into the process at the conference. In addition, the perspectives from transversal topics expressed there will challenge some of the assumptions, methods and content of these chapters; and it is hoped that the cross-fertilization between the themes which will happen as part of the conference process will help to further refine the outcomes. Nevertheless, we believe that what is offered here already will help get preparation for the conference off to a meaningful start, and contribute to rethinking mission generally, for the sake of renewed and effective witness to Christ today.

Endnotes

[1] Edinburgh 2010 Study Process Guidelines 2008.

[2] The intended outcomes of Edinburgh 2010 are as follows:

- Churches will be provided with an opportunity to celebrate what God has done in the growth of the Church worldwide over the past century and to prayerfully commit to God the witness of the churches in the twenty-first century
- The biblical call to mission will be affirmed and articulated within our contemporary contexts with particular focus on the meaning of evangelization and relevance of Christian witness today
- A key conversation on mission will be initiated with mission leaders from the older mission movements of the North and the new mission movements from the South and East, with dialogues held among representatives of different Christian traditions
- Guidelines will be developed and studies published to help church and mission leaders evaluate for their own situation models of mission which are proving effective elsewhere
- Networks will be mobilized and alliances formed so as to develop greater strategic collaboration and greater synergy in fulfilling the mission mandate
- Based on a critical assessment of the status of the world, a new vision of God's purposes for creation in Christ and a renewed spirituality and mission ethos will be developed in the life of the churches worldwide.

[3] Edinburgh 2010 Study Process Guidelines 2008.

THEME ONE
FOUNDATIONS FOR MISSION

Preface

Study Theme 1 Foundations for Mission brought together in its conveners two research projects: Canon Janice Price of the Church of England led 'Foundations for Mission in the UK and Ireland: A Study of Language, Theology and Praxis', a joint venture of the British and Irish Association for Mission Studies, the (former) Global Mission Network of Churches Together in Britain and Ireland, and the Global Connections network of Evangelical mission agencies and churches, which examined the altered state of affairs in foundations for mission in Britain and Ireland in 2010. Revd Dr Deenabandhu Manchala leads the Just and Inclusive Communities section of the World Council of Churches which sponsored 'Mission at and from the Margins', an ethnographic study seeking to understand the mission of the church in the South Indian state of Andhra Pradesh in the light of the experiences of Dalit or 'outcaste' communities. Both these projects brought empirical and experiential concerns to the topic and their work was shared at a meeting at the Ecumenical Institute, Bossey on 1-4 May 2009 with a wider group which was brought together by Edinburgh 2010, with the support of the World Council of Churches, expressly to draft this chapter.

In addition to the Conveners, ten others from different continents and churches participated in the meeting which was convened by the Edinburgh 2010 Research Coordinator, Dr Kirsteen Kim. Dr Paul Rolph, Research Supervisor, University of Wales, Bangor, UK attended as a consultant to 'Sinking Foundations'. Revd Dr Peniel Jesudas Rufus Rajkumar, Associate Professor of Systematic and Dalit Theology, United Theological College, Bangalore, India attended as a leader of 'Mission at and from the Margins'. Dr Emma Wild-Wood, Lecturer in Mission Studies, Cambridge Theological Federation, UK had also participated in the Towards 2010 project which looked back at the Commission of Edinburgh 1910. Three people were invited for their expertise in biblical studies: Dr Simanga R. Kumalo, Senior Lecturer in Practical Theology, University of Kwazulu Natal, South Africa, who is heavily involved in the contextual bible study being pioneered there; Rev. Dr Néstor O. Míguez, Professor of New Testament Studies, Instituto Universitario ISEDT, Buenos Aires, Argentina; and Revd Jacques Matthey, Director of the World Council of Churches Programme on Unity, Mission and Spirituality, who had also been deeply involved in 'Mission in the Bible', a project of the Francophone Association for Mission Studies (AFOM). Three others were invited to bring a theological perspective: Dr Edmund Chia, Professor of Doctrinal Theology, Catholic Theological Union, Chicago, USA; Dr Christina

Manohar, Professor of Theology, Union Biblical Seminary, Pune, India; and Dr Petros Vassiliadis, Professor of Theology, Aristotle University of Thessaloniki, Greece. Dr Beverly Mitchell, an African American and member of the American Baptist Church who is on the faculty at Wesley Theological Seminary, Washington, DC, was unable to attend the meeting but commented on the draft document from her expertise in systematic theology.

Having received input from each participant, the May meeting agreed to divide the chapter into experiential, biblical and theological foundations and produced initial drafts of each section. Following the meeting, Dr Rajkumar and Dr Wild-Wood took the drafting work forward, integrating the sections and completing the final draft in consultation by email with the wider group.

1 Introduction

Witnessing to Christ today, the theme of the project to mark the centenary of the Edinburgh World Mission Conference in 1910, implies that our Christian mission relates to Christ's own mission. Such an assertion would have found favour with those gathered in 1910. During the last one hundred years the same point has been restated in different ways. The International Missionary Council's meeting at Tambaram, India, in 1938, entitled 'The World Mission of the Church' declared, 'the essential task of the Church is to be the ambassador for Christ.'[1] In 1958 the same Council, meeting in Ghana, asserted 'The Christian world mission is Christ's not ours.'[2] In contrast to 1910, when the emphasis was on the *missions* of the churches, the emphasis in 2010 is on *God's mission* (*missio Dei*) in which Christians participate.[3] This represents a move from 'A Church-centred mission to a mission-centred church,'[4] and towards an exploration of missionary collaboration beyond the church. In 1910 there was frequent mention of the plurality of 'missions'; in 2010 mission is considered to be singular but, as the plural 'foundations' of this chapter's title suggests, there are many approaches to understanding and participating in mission: 'Mission is complex and multiple: witness, proclamation, catechesis, worship, inculturation, inter-faith dialogue. These activities are carried out…in concrete situations…'[5] In the course of a century many developments have taken place that influence our practice and understanding of mission, not least is the growth of the world Christianity, which is an unanticipated answer to Edinburgh 1910's prayer for the 'Christianisation' of the world. Christians from Africa, Asia, Latin America and the Pacific have since critiqued and enriched the mission tradition of the Western nations represented in 1910. Likewise, Edinburgh 1910 was a largely Protestant affair; the Christian unity that delegates prayed for, whilst still partial, means that Catholics, Orthodox and Pentecostals are part of the Edinburgh 2010 project.

This chapter examines shifts in missiological reflections since 1910 and demonstrates the variety of foundations for mission studies recognised today. It groups the foundations into three categories: experiential, biblical and theological, and assumes that, for holistic missional practice, attention to each category is required. Since there is little space for historical explanation, recent developments are emphasised. It is impossible to be exhaustive; however, the contributors to this chapter come from four continents and several Christian traditions and we hope we have provided a representative introduction that will stimulate readers to further reflection and action.

We begin with experiential foundations because it is in recognition of these that the greatest development in mission studies has occurred. The last century has seen a growing awareness that our history, culture, politics, environmental and economic status (often termed 'context') influence the way in which we read the Bible, theologise and participate in mission. The relationship of these three foundations is, however, reciprocal, and they can be treated in any order.

2 Experiential Foundations for Mission

2.1 Why experience as a foundation for mission?

Mission does not happen in vacuum. It is grounded in and derives from particular contexts. God's mission, expressed through the life of the Trinity, revealed through Exodus, Incarnation and Pentecost, takes place in and impacts upon the concrete realities of history. As Jesus Christ took human form and shared our experience, 'Mission in Christ's way… cannot but be rooted in a certain context concretely addressing the challenges in that specific context'.[6] Further, if we recognise that *reception* of the gospel is embedded in specific human history and experience, it is logical that experience constitutes a foundation for mission. In accepting experience as one of its foundations, mission has the twin-obligations of *being informed by* experience (both past and present) and *seeking to impact* human experience (spiritual, physical, psychological, social, cultural, political, economic) in creative fidelity to the gospel of Christ.

Mission founded on experience is polyvalent. The practitioners of mission are the ones who make decisions about the shape of their local mission. Recognising experience as a foundation for mission fosters a critical engagement with one not-so-obvious aspect of mission thinking, namely the tendency in mission theology to privilege the so-called theoretical above the empirical. It recognises the need to accord epistemic value to those practitioners of mission who have been denied the privilege of theorizing due to the politics of power, and whose only resources are their experiences. It is upon these resources also that contemporary thinking has to be founded for mission to maintain ethical integrity and accountability. These experiences have to be considered critically and dialectically with theological and biblical sources.

The experiential approach also helps us to discern that the so-called theoretical is located in a particular framework of experience. The granting or denying of epistemic value to a particular experience is related to the question of power. Therefore experience as the foundation for mission brings not only a methodological critique to mission but also a moral one. It helps to interrogate the exclusionary nature of mission practice which neglects 'experience' in general and certain experiences in particular. Further this shift offers a normative direction to suggest alternative modes of reorganising the boundaries of the foundations for mission so as to make them more inclusive.

In contexts where biblical interpretations and mission theology have borne bad fruits in practice, communities are placed in critical tension with the received biblical and theological resources. However, mission founded on experience has a Spirit-enabled 'orthopathic' dimension 'which infuses in the oppressed the strength to rise above the dehumanization of their daily conditions'.[7] When this consciousness becomes a hermeneutical premise, people are empowered 'to risk questioning and reinterpreting the Scriptures in the light of their own experiences and insights'.[8] So experiential foundations for mission also enable a critical retrospection of mission from the perspective of those from the 'underside' of mission history. In discerning its mission the global church has to acknowledge that the history of Christian mission was at one time very much aligned with European colonial expansionism. Attentiveness to the experiences of those affected by this agenda of colonial expansionism has prompted a radical rethinking of mission. It is now being recognised that 'especially where Christianity has been dominant and militant, Christians must now be prepared to listen, to wait and to serve' and that 'Christian stewardship of life through the pursuit of justice, peace and the well-being of creation will win the gospel of Jesus Christ a hearing in ways seldom achieved by sheer proclamation.'[9]

An historical critique of past experience which attempts to discover and understand the events and actors of the past on their own terms is also a valid part of an experiential approach to mission and contributes to healing of memories. For instance, it is frequently acknowledged that the interconnections between the modern missionary movement and colonialism damaged the Christian endeavour by presenting a powerful Christendom model of the religion from a Western world view. In isolation such statements rarely explain the growth of confident and independent Christianities in the global South. To appreciate movements in mission today it is important to hear testimony from Christians in different regions of the world of the experiences of conversion, justification, sanctification and new life, of struggles and persecution, and of the formation of Christian community. These are expressed in the burgeoning Christian literature in many languages and parts of the world today. The foundations for mission are also challenged by exploration of the historical dynamics of power in each situation: the agency of indigenous people in contextualizing Christianity from their earliest engagement with it;[10] the changing relationship between Christianity, culture and politics;[11] the different missionary ethos before the age of high imperialism[12] and the entanglements and disentanglements of missions with the colonialist mindset during it;[13] and the changing face of Christianity and the rise of new Christian movements.[14] This form of historical study is enriched by the empirical research techniques of the social sciences and the nuanced understanding of human societies that they bring. An understanding of the 'qualifiers' of mission experiences throughout history can enable proper participation in God's mission today.

Therefore experience as a foundation for mission brings with it a constructive-critical dimension to Christian mission, which enables Christian mission to learn from the past while engaging with the present and envisioning the future.

2.2 Whose experience?

Making experience a foundation for mission raises questions concerning the 'revelatory' nature of experience that makes it a foundation for mission. Though experience can be understood in a generic sense, not all experience can become a foundation for mission. There is need for 'qualifying' experience. It is at this point that differences emerge: Does one set of experiences take priority over all others? Or does the particular context dictate the experiences that influence mission? For example, many Africans look to cultural roots as being the defining set of experiences when arguing for the inseparability of 'evangelisation and inculturation'.[15] Or cultural, economic and political experiences may be brought together to 'interpret the Gospel of Jesus Christ to the contemporary African in the light of the African condition'.[16] In Latin America the qualifier of experience may be the 'just claim' of those at the margins of the human history, the 'others' of the human story of deprivation, exclusion and oppression with whom Jesus Christ, the Crucified God identifies himself (Matt 25:35-46).[17] Ecofeminists understand that 'the *interdependence of all things* is a constitutive reality of the universe'[18] and develop a creation theology in response to the experience of the degradation of the earth.

This chapter is informed by the results of two main research projects which will briefly be introduced here. The first, 'Mission at and from the Margins' was an ethnographic study project sponsored by the World Council of Churches seeking to understand the mission of the church in the South Indian state of Andhra Pradesh in the light of Dalit experiences. (Dalits are 'outcaste' communities previously known as 'untouchables'.) The study was carried out through participant observation and unstructured interviews with individuals and focus groups from Vegeswarapuram, a village in West Godavari district of Andhra Pradesh.

The popular understandings of mission in this context were proclamation (expected to result in numerical church growth) and pastoral care. Simultaneously social justice and resistance to casteism were recognised as God's mission. However, these two aspects of mission were not fully integrated. This is shown by the fact that the Dalit Christian leaders expressed discomfort in using the premises of the church for discussing social justice, especially because of the community's preparedness to take up force as a means of self-defence to resist violence against them.

Regarding the agency for mission it became clear that in the past overseas missionaries with their position of power played the role of primary agents of mission. However as time passed, Dalits became the primary agents of mission and used the *conditions* of mission set up by the missionaries like indiscriminate access to schools, hospitals, hostels and 'holy spaces' like the church, which had symbolic value, to navigate their quest for equality, enhanced self-dignity and social status and further the mission of proclamation and pastoral care. These conditions of mission were seen as a liberative-transformative space by Dalit communities for self-assertion and reclamation of their place in society rather than as components of the colonizing process. Therefore, Dalit entanglements with missionaries are much more complex than patron-client or colonizer-colonized relationships. Dalit communities, which had no stake in local power, viewed those in their own country who had power as 'colonizers'. For them, the conversion experience of which they were the primary agents helped in their quest for freedom from oppression. In this the conditions of mission played and continue to play the role of midwife. Hence proclamation, pastoral care and social justice are all recognised as part of the mission of God. The agency for this mission extends beyond the church.

The second project is a piece of empirical research sponsored by the Churches Together in Britain and Ireland Global Mission Network, Global Connections and the British and Irish Association for Mission Studies. Researchers sought to investigate the contemporary theological understanding, motivation and practice of mission in England, Ireland, Scotland and Wales. Through a questionnaire, website analysis and interviews they gained insight into the public portrayal, corporate and individual understanding of mission today among national churches and agencies and among clergy from all denominations in one English region.[19] The focus of the data gathering process was a Ratings Scale Questionnaire that was sent to the major denominations and mission agencies. Effectively it requires them to critique their own understandings and practice and in so doing has resulted in the development of a powerful learning tool. Areas such as the reasons for doing mission, the place of people from other cultures, understandings of the Trinity form the basis for sets of questions.

The theological models at the heart of this research are broadly mission as *Missio Dei*, as Proclamation, and as Justice and Liberation.[20] In both the local and national research it was found that attitudes to mission reflected an amalgam of all three approaches but did not place great emphasis on *missio Dei*. This is interesting in view of the prevalence of *missio Dei* in contemporary theological treatments of mission foundations. Privileging the experience of the poor in mission was not a popular stance in the survey results from the questionnaire in the UK and Ireland research, except when the questionnaire was completed by missiologists. The response to the question 'The yardstick of mission is concern for the poorest?' resulted in a large number of neutral responses (neither agree nor disagree) and the responses regarding the relationship between mission and justice were the most disagreed with statements. Responses showed some difficulty in thinking about the relationship between mission, justice, development and concern for the poor. It was the responses on proclamation that attracted most agreement, except in perceiving proclamation as acting justly and loving one's neighbours, even though expressing God's love to all carried the highest assent.

These results, therefore, from individuals and agencies in the British Isles portray mission primarily as proclamation. The research highlights a disconnection between those who study and those who practice or support mission in the British Isles and between some contemporary models of mission elsewhere in the world church. In this project 'experience' was understood in the first instance as the empirical process by which data was collected. The analysis of data now raises questions about the way in which the experience of respondents influences their understanding of mission and how conscious they are of their context. Further questions are posed about the effects of these comprehensions when listening to other voices in the world context.

A debate over what experiences take priority emerged when comparing these two research projects. All contributors to this chapter agree that the mission of God as understood from the biblical witness includes affirming the sanctity of life, particularly whenever it is threatened, abused or destroyed. It is this that makes mission an ally of those who are struggling for life – the poor, the oppressed and the excluded. But research showed that this was not a priority for all people involved in mission. In both cases mission as proclamation was the primary model and its relationship to questions of justice and poverty was not always clearly articulated.

For those whose understanding of mission involves a strong concern for the poor, according preference to the experiences of the oppressed ('others') when defining 'experience' becomes imperative if mission has to be 'mission in Christ's way' because these experiences constitute important biblical resources for mission theology. This derives from the biblical conviction that 'God also shares in… the marginalization of non-people, and in the pain of the oppressed', which is 'what brings the Third World together as Christian theologians'.[21] These 'others' are often referred to in the Bible as the 'the poor'. Their experiences can be seen as 'negative contrast experiences' which have special revelatory significance when considered in juxtaposition with biblical witness to God's activity.[22] Negative contrast experiences are occasions of God's revelation, which is not so much in the oppressive situation, but in the resistance which brings it to an end and, in so doing, ushers in God's kingdom of peace and justice. In Christian perspective, the crucifixion of Jesus Christ is the ultimate negative contrast experience. It speaks of solidarity with the oppressed as well as the resistance of the oppressed. In the light of the cross, negative experiences are only regarded as contrast experiences if they evoke the critical protest and resistance to the negative situation which we Christians label as sin. In other words, not all human experience is a valid foundation for mission but only that which resonates with the life, ministry, death and resurrection of Jesus Christ.

3 Biblical Foundations for Mission

Christian mission is grounded in the Scriptures in their entirety.[23] It is impossible to make a complete theology of mission around one particular passage, because not only do we sometimes find biblical passages pointing in different directions but also because the same narrative can be interpreted differently. The reading of the Bible in different mission contexts has demonstrated, biblical criticism notwithstanding, how the changing contexts of our witness bring about new ways of understanding and engaging in God's mission. We realise that the biblical texts are 'polysemic'[24] – that is they contain multiple layers of meaning. The plurality and diversity of our reading of Scriptural texts speak to the plurality and diversity of our human condition, our different histories and cultures, our foreseeable confrontations and the need for wider mutual acceptance and solidarity.[25] We will bring some examples of how some key texts for mission have been read at different times before discussing the implications of this for how Christians can read the Bible together in mission today.

3.1 The Samaritan woman: One story, many readings

The New Testament presents to us, as part of Jesus' ministry, not only Jesus' invitation to his disciples to follow him but also the narratives of many other men and women, who as they encountered Jesus, felt that they had become witnesses and announcers of his redeeming presence and love. One such story – of Jesus' encounter with the Samaritan woman (John 4) – has been interpreted differently by diverse authors in different settings.[26]

Saint Augustine*:* Augustine reflects on this story in his *Treatise on the Gospel of John* written in the early fifth century. Using an allegorical approach, Augustine makes this passage a prophetic instance of the gentile mission: '*A woman came.* She is a symbol of the Church not yet made righteous. Righteousness follows from the conversation. …*a Samaritan woman came to draw water.* The Samaritans did not form part of the Jewish people. The fact that she came from a foreign people is part of the symbolic meaning, for she is a symbol of the Church. The Church was to come from the Gentiles. We must then recognize ourselves in her words and in her person… She found faith in Christ, who was using her as a symbol to teach us what was to come.'[27]

Jean Calvin*:* According to Calvin, 'When He acknowledges to the woman that He is the Messiah, He unquestionably presents Himself as her Teacher in correspondence with the hope she had conceived… He wanted such an example of His grace to be visible in the case of this poor woman that He might testify to all that He never fails in His duty when we want Him to be our Teacher. There is no danger of His disappointing one of these whom He finds ready to be His disciple.'[28] In these words emphasis is laid on the teaching aspect of Jesus.

Modern interpretations adopt different emphases according to different methodologies and perspectives of the interpreting subjects. Some emphasise 'reading the text itself', others reading 'behind the text' (its historical context) or 'in front of' or 'before the text' (reactions provoked by the text).[29]

A classical doctrinal approach: Many churches use a form of what is presented as a literal approach. Jesus would be seen as the Messiah who comes as a merciful saviour to an adulterous and sinful woman who is unable to understand Jesus' spiritual mission. De facto, classical doctrinal positions predominate in such cases, stressing the symbol of the living water and emphasising the woman's 'conversion'. Most traditional commentaries use this approach.

A reading of the text in its original context attempts to understand the history and religion of Samaritans, the intentions of John's gospel and other occurrences of witness among or by Samaritans in the biblical and early Christian tradition. It highlights how Jesus overcomes the cultural and religious boundaries between Jerusalem and Samaria and the barriers between men and women. It could lead to reflections on relationships between Christian, Jewish and other religious communities as well as on the role of women in Christian communities.

A narrative approach pays attention to the change in the sequence, represented by Jesus' request to the woman to go and fetch her husband,[30] at which point two parallel monologues become a dialogue. The question which addressed the real issue for the woman broke the barrier that was building up between the two. Not only had gender and ethnic divisions hindered communication, but so had two languages, that of everyday house duties over against that of the wisdom tradition and allegories. In the narrative approach attention is given to communication issues, the world views reflected in the words of the dialoguing partners, and the point of entry that allowed more profound communication to occur. Mission then is the possibility of establishing contact through overcoming different worldviews.

A cultural reading: In South Africa, where political issues have shifted from racism to ethnicity, the text would clearly be understood with regard to the issue of ethnic conflicts and the way Jesus was able to cross such boundaries. Depending on who is in the group and who is facilitating, the text can be used to encourage the crossing of cultural boundaries, overcoming hatred and violence between ethnic groups, such as Zulus and Xhosas. Mission then would be concerned primarily with intercultural reconciliation and healing.

A feminist approach sees the text affirming Jesus' understanding of the woman's oppression under patriarchy. It uncovers her unfair treatment under patriarchal laws. This reading emphasises Jesus' willingness to break down oppression and act as a liberator who empowers oppressed women. While for many readers the Samaritan woman represents the "sinner" *par excellence*, in a feminist hermeneutical approach she is vindicated for a struggle for equity in gender relations. She is freed from being a victim and regains dignity as one of the first missionaries who calls others to experience the same liberation.[31]

In the latter readings, the story appears as but one example in the New Testament where Jesus carries his mission to those marginalized by society, be it culturally, religiously or socially. Through his engagement with them in their contexts, experiences and narratives, they respond by participating in mission shaped by his example.[32] All the approaches referred to have an interface with systematic and contextual theological traditions leading to different emphases in mission. These are not mutually exclusive but represent overlapping plurality of Christian faith and experience worldwide.

3.2 The Great Commission: One call in four gospel perspectives

Diversity is not only found among readers and interpreters of biblical texts, but within the biblical tradition itself. In a chapter on foundations for mission, it seems necessary to hint at the significance of some of the texts which in history proved of major motivating importance for mission, including oppressive misinterpretations, such as has been the case with the various versions of the 'Great Commission'. The stories which tell of Christ's resurrection and words of sending show significant differences in emphasis in the final stage in which they have been recorded by the four gospels. For Mark and Matthew, Jesus appeared in Galilee, whereas that event happened in Jerusalem according to Luke and John.[33] Mission is thus described as originating in two different places, a rural one at the periphery of Jewish society, the other at the urban centre.

One can also discern variations in the content of the mandates given by the resurrected to his disciples. In **Matthew**, the commissioning location is a mountain as it is for many major events of Jesus' life, including the temptation story, which presents an alternative vision of mission: that of ruling the world in power, a strategy defended by God's enemy. Authentic mission is, however, a long term formation of disciples, with two main characteristics, an ecclesial one and an ethical one. To be disciples involves baptism with a trinitarian formulation, thus linking to a church community. It also implies living according to the teaching contained in the main speeches of Jesus (Matt 28:20).[34] These include the Sermon on the Mount, the chapter on forgiveness (18) and the parables in Matthew 25. Matthew's commission carries the double love commandment ('all I have commanded you'). Finally the text requests the formation of communities across ethnic boundaries ('all nations,' not only the House of Israel). The comparison with Matthew 9:13 indicates that the verb translated by 'go' can imply to live differently where one lives. Matthew shows how the one who received all power promises his presence as Emmanuel to disciples living the life-style of the beatitudes.

Mark's gospel has been transmitted with an uncertain ending. The shorter ending (16:1-8) is abrupt and difficult to interpret. The key actors are the women who are committed to tell the disciples and lead them to Galilee, but who cannot overcome their fear at the incredible event. The gospel seems to indicate that, after the resurrection, discipleship must start again at the same place where the journey of following Jesus to the cross started. Mission after Easter remains a life of discipleship on the way to the cross. The longer ending summarises various traditions of early Christianity, focusing on the unbelief of the disciples, then leading to a specific commission (16:15-20). It is the only version of the great commission carrying the technical terminology of 'preaching the gospel' (v. 15) to the widest possible horizon, 'all creation' and referring to major classical charisms and the spiritual healing ministry, 'signs' (vv.17,20). Reaction to evangelism leads to salvation or judgment. The mission command is addressed to the Eleven (only); the signs however will accompany all future believers.

In **Luke** 24:48,49 and **Acts** 1:8, the sent ones are qualified as 'witnesses' with the promise to be empowered by the Spirit. In Luke there is particular emphasis on the capacity given to the disciples to interpret the Torah, prophets and psalms as announcing Christ's death and resurrection. It is a text with particular significance for work on mission and the Bible. It will form the basis for materials for the Week of Prayer for Christian Unity in 2010.[35] Luke's is the only gospel which includes a strategic formulation as to the successive geographic development of mission from the first centre in Jerusalem to the ends of the world. The plan of the book of Acts is included in the way Christ's speech is edited. To be witnesses means attesting that the Scriptures foresaw preaching of conversion and forgiveness of sins (*aphesis* in v. 47 reiterating 4:18, with qualification) in Christ's name as result of the Easter events. This sending of the disciples as witnesses replaces the establishment of a political entity for Israel, anticipated on the basis of old biblical hermeneutics (Acts 1:7-8).

John's gospel (John 20:21-23) clearly parallels the sending of the Son with the sending of the disciples within a trinitarian movement, involving the Father and the Spirit. Peculiar to John is the simultaneity of Easter and Pentecost: the Spirit is given as a confirmation of the sending word, as power to forgive (or not forgive) sins. The way the commission is formulated identifies the way the church's mission is to be conceived with the trajectory of the mission of the Son. John's gospel has a further specificity insofar as it carries a blessing for Christians of future generations who will not have had the privilege of direct witness of Christ's resurrection. The quality of the life which is promised is not linked to the specific experience of the first apostles.

3.3 The calling of Abraham: One story many New Testament interpretations

The Old Testament is also full of examples of God's calling and sending, of God's blessings through the faith and message, deeds and lives of all the people of Israel and peoples of other nations. Abraham is one of the most prominent witnesses to God's calling and obedient response.

Under the name Abram he receives the calling, the sending, the promise and the blessing (Gen 12:1-4). Using a mission-centred hermeneutic this text becomes a paradigm, for it includes characteristic elements present in many stories of people called to fulfil the different tasks that God's saving love demands. In short, Abram hears God's voice and is sent to the adventure of faith. A promise of abundant life is given; life prolonged through his descendents. There is also a blessing, which reaches to all the families, to all the human family.[36] Thus mission is a relational commitment: the engendering of a new family of faith, to be a blessing for all. Yet, when we follow the story of Abraham and his descendents we find diversity and even conflict, confrontation and distress as much as faith and endurance, solidarity and hope. The promise, the blessing and the faith are not free from the shortcomings of human life and circumstances.

This paradigm is variously raised in both Testaments. In the Hebrew Scriptures Isaiah 51:2 recalling Abraham's mission, says, 'Look to Abraham your father and to Sarah who bore you; for he was but one when I called him, that I might bless him and multiply him.' The New Testament offers several understandings of that promise. In Matthew 1.1 Abraham is mentioned as the forefather of Jesus. The promise of family and blessing is being fulfilled because that lineage allows for the coming of the Messiah into the world. So, Abraham's and Sarah's mission is accomplished, not only in their life-time, but long after death, for they continue to engender children of the promise, and the benediction extends through new generations.

John the Baptist goes one step further: 'And do not presume to say to yourselves, "We have Abraham as our father," for I tell you, God is able from these stones to raise up children for Abraham' (Matt 3:9). In Luke, written for the Gentiles, we find fourteen references to Abraham. Mary's song recalls God's promise to Abraham (Luke 1:55), as does Zachariah's prophetic outburst at the birth of John (Luke 1:75). Another significant example, related to Jesus' ministry, is the description of Zacchaeus' 'conversion' as his re-entering Abraham's family (Luke 19:9-10). Paul's long argument about the mission to the Gentiles in Galatians 3 is based on a new understanding of the promise to Abraham, an argument further expanded in Romans (Rom 4), where the promise and the blessing is the upholding of Abraham's mission through his 'seed', the Christ. Abraham is an example of faith in the letter to the Hebrews (Heb 11:8-12).

Simply by looking at the Abrahamic references we can see how, even within the Scriptures, the mission mandate is reinterpreted in new contexts. The reinterpretation of Abraham's significance for humanity is not limited to the

Bible. Both the Jewish and Islamic hermeneutical traditions provide alternative readings of Abraham's story and of the significance of his descendants, each bearing important impact on mission and interreligious relations in the contemporary world.[37]

3.4 Mission hermeneutical principles

We have offered examples of how biblical texts concerning mission are given different interpretations in different times and situations. We have also shown how a biblical character or episode is presented in different ways throughout Scripture, giving contrasting understandings. The attempt to reduce the multiple voices in the Bible to the 'only correct one', to judge the differing interpretations with the standards of our own understanding, has proved to be at the origin of innumerable conflicts among Christians. It has brought about mutual accusations and unhealthy competition, and, as such, has hindered common mission, fostering proselytism and sectarianism. A theology committed to the fullness of the biblical message must allow the richness of the Word to come alive in many ways and settings. The Bible allows for a rich variety of ways to witness to Christ in each context. Some conflicts over mission since 1910 might have been softened had this been seriously taken into account.

Yet, this does not mean that there are no limits. The variety of biblical testimonies and possible interpretations speak with one voice in affirming Jesus as the crucified and resurrected Messiah. The faith in a God who discloses Godself in saving love to human beings and the whole of creation, that communicates God's Spirit creating community, is a call to unity in mission, a unity that wholly depends on God's grace. The limits are given, not by culturally-related interpretations or by the imposition of power, but by our humble recognition of God's freedom to manifest the Good News of salvation revealed through Jesus Christ to all the people, in ways proper to every context. There is no limit to God's grace and justice, except our human understanding and desire to control the liberating message. Every proclamation of this gospel is valid, as long as it bears witness to God's unconditional love shown in the cross and resurrection of Jesus Christ. This criterion is crucial in a context of competing interpretive claims.

We cannot reduce the biblical canon to our own internal canon. Different trajectories in the Scriptural texts show the multiplicity and even the tensions within God's revelation. Prophetic and priestly traditions both coexist within the same Bible. Together with many others they relate to a complex approach to human life. They challenge and comfort, moving us by the Spirit who makes everything new and assures us of God's presence in our lives and our world. Any attempt to give a partial account of the biblical narrative causes a distortion of mission. The 'plurality of canons' within the canon speaks of the complementarity of the biblical witness, and results in an ecumenical call to mission.[38] There are various emphases in mission, originating in different ways to relate to the biblical text and tradition and to particular situations of the contemporary world. Yet this does not mean that we can avoid taking sides. We cannot be indifferent to the suffering of our world. We need to respond missionally in our contexts.

The Bible inspires us in our response to God's initiative. The inspiration of the Word, notwithstanding the different ways this has been understood in Christian history, is related to the inspiration of the Christian community, receiving from Scriptures guidance and strength for walking the paths of mission. In that sense, the Bible itself is mission, with, besides and beyond the church boundaries. It witnesses to Christ even when we fail to comply with Jesus' invitation to be the continuing presence in his own mission. The Word in the Bible participates in God's redemptive mission.

4 Theological Foundations for Mission

The twentieth century saw the focus of missiology shift from ecclesiology and soteriology (although these remain important) to prioritise trinitarian reflections as being foundational for a proper understanding of and action in mission. Consciously influenced by experience as shaper of theology and aware of the polysemic nature of the theological task, familiar themes in missiology were reworked and we highlight some of them here.

4.1 Trinitiarian missio Dei

Christ's sending out the apostles to proclaim his gospel is rooted in his being sent by God the Father in the Holy Spirit (John 20:21). This classical formulation of *missio Dei,* affirming that mission is God's sending forth, was expanded in ecumenical discussion in the twentieth century to include the participation of the church in the divine mission.[39] This conviction led to a reconsideration of mission as ultimately proceeding from a trinitarian God, [40] the '...epiphany of God's plan and its fulfilment in the world.'[41] The triune God '...is not a kind of intellectual capstone which can be put on to the top of the arch at the very end; it is... the presupposition without which the preaching of the Gospel... cannot begin'[42] The way in which the triune God sends forth has been variously understood in recent years. Placed alongside classical hierarchical formulations has been an emphasis on the relational.[43] Community has been emphasised: the triune God is a '...dynamic, relational community of persons, whose very nature is to be present and active in the world, calling it and persuading it towards the fullness of relationship that Christian tradition calls salvation'[44] and equality and justice are modelled on trinitarian relationships.[45] Other theologians have been wary of comprehending God as simply a model for human relations and demand that Christians *participate* in and practice the relationality of the triune communion.[46] 'To engage in the relationships in God means that we are brought up against the challenge of the alien, the radically different the unlike; but [we experience] a fellowship more intimate than anything we can other wise know.'[47] Whilst there is concern that such close association with the divine is arrogant, many link the participation in God's mission with an active engagement in the sending movement of the threefold Godhead. The language of mutuality and reciprocity that arises from social and participative models demonstrates a 'divine livingness'[48] that enhances our understanding of mission as God's manifestation – in Christ and the Spirit – of love to whole creation, in which we are called to participate.

Trinitarian reflections have been enriched by different cultural perspectives. For example, Chinese culture provides insights in understanding the dynamic of the Trinity: The Chinese phrase for spirit parallels the Hebrew understanding of spirit, *ruach*, in connecting the outer and inner dimensions of a person together as one. This suggests a narrative theological approach, so that '…the conceptual understanding of revelation and the economic Trinity can be "fleshed out" by concrete tangible narrated events in the life, ministry and death of Jesus Christ. The vividness and the power of the story of Jesus can then complement the more reflective conceptual understanding of revelation and the Trinity.'[49] Likewise, from an Indian perspective, there are correspondences between *ruach* and the Hindu concept of *atman* that signify the Spirit as enlivening and vivifying breath and vital energy of all that lives, linking the action of the Spirit to that of the life-giving creator and the life-restoring liberator.[50]

4.2 Mission in and through Christ and the Spirit

The focus on the relational and communal Trinity, however, has encouraged a fresh understanding of the mutuality and reciprocity between Christ and Spirit, 'the principal agent of mission'[51]. From the early church two types of pneumatology developed: the West usually understood the Holy Spirit as the agent of Christ to fulfil the task of mission; the East emphasised the Holy Spirit as the source of Christ and the Church, gathering the people of God in his kingdom and then going forth in mission. The last century has seen an extraordinary rise in Pentecostalism, with its christo-centric orientation and its Spirit practice,[52] and an engagement with primal religions and a desire to inculturate Christianity by including the realm of the spirits. These experiences have influenced missiology, encouraging reflection upon the inseparable relationship between Christ and the Spirit expressed in different ways such as the 'anointing of the Spirit' and the 'accompaniment of the Spirit,' suggesting that there is no part in Jesus that is not touched by the Holy Spirit.[53] Jesus was conscious of God's Spirit working through him. A pneumatological mission theology was expressed in Jesus' inaugural proclamation at Nazareth (Luke 4:8), in which he began, 'The Spirit of the Lord is upon me'. Christo-praxis is repeated in the actions of blessing, confronting, challenging, dialoguing, leading and renewing the mission of God in the contemporary contexts of different people groups and races. Linking christology and pneumatology avoids exclusive christo-centrism in our understanding of the person and work of Christ, neither neglecting the creative activity of the Spirit in creation, mission and redemption, nor emphasising a false autonomy of the Spirit that displaces Christology and the Trinity.[54]

4.3 Mission ecclesiology

The shift towards a Spirit theology has engendered a missiological understanding of the Christian community (church) and its internal work (liturgy). The mission of the church is seen in her search for a spiritual framework that affirms human life, mutual respect and equality by working towards inner and mutual conversion, just community, survival of God's creation, together with church growth. In the symbiosis of Spirit and Christ the institutional element of the church is complemented by the charismatic element; for if Christ *institutes* the church, it is the Holy Spirit that *constitutes* her.[55] The Spirit reminds people of Christ's way of mission and challenges the church to be a community that seeks new ways of actualizing Christ's mission.

Since 1910 there has been a focus on ecumenical unity as 'common Christian witness': 'The mission of the church in the power of the Spirit is to call people into communion with God, with one another and with creation. In so doing, many Christians believe, that the church has a responsibility to live out the unity for which Jesus prayed for his people: "that they may all be one... so that the world may believe" (John 17:21) and that his conviction must be proclaimed and witnessed to in the community into which people are invited'[56] Thus some churches have formally united, whilst others maintain a 'reconciled diversity.' The present context 'of the rapid growth of "emerging" churches worldwide' has also led to theological attempts to delineate a 'reconstructive and reformative ecclesiology that recognizes that followers of the way of Christ are multiple, embedded, particular and hospitable' and seeks to 'mark them as faithfully participating in Jesus' way of knowing, acting and being in the world'.[57] These local forms of church pose new challenges to unity in mission.

An awareness of the liturgical dimension of our Christian self-understanding has developed in postmodernity as a significant element of the Christian witness, '...for the life of the world' (John 6:51). The emphasis of the old mission paradigm on the rational comprehension of truth, and as a result the prioritizing of verbal proclamation in witnessing to Christ, has widened to a more *holistic* understanding of mission in our days, thus adding a more spiritual element to our mission. Prayer is significant – either as the intercessions of Christians which connect God's will and the accomplishment of God's mission, or as silence, understood as a means of accompaniment or resistance. Christians celebrate the Eucharist, not only as a 'thanksgiving', but also as a divine offering *(anaphora)* for the entire creation. The Eucharist is an affirmation of the Church's identity as 'an icon of the eschaton', a foretaste of the kingdom of God.[58] The Lord's Supper, as a remembrance of Christ's reconciling work, is only constituted where the congregation shares (1 Cor 11:20-21) and an important condition for participating in the Lord's Table is a conscious act of *reconciliation* with one's sisters and brothers through the 'kiss of love' (Matt 5:23-24).

Mission is an authentic witness to the Church's eschatological experience (that is, the inclusive reality of God's kingdom) as the Holy Spirit 'blows wherever s/he wills' (John 3:8). The Holy Spirit's 'sending' force lies in the multiplication of the potential witnesses, because the visions and gifts are shared by people of all genders, ages and social categories (cf. Joel 2); and they are brought together in communion by the Spirit. Thus Christian mission is relational more than rational and is not limited to a proselytizing mission, but has become holistic in character; redemption from sin covers all aspects of social, moral, and ecological concerns.

The gifts of the Spirit, in addition to word and sacrament, qualify the wider missionary task of the church. The church does not itself constitute God's reign but anticipates an eschatological fulfilment of God's purposes. If the church participates in God's mission, this is best done when her mission moves out of the corporate Christian life and worship, in what Orthodox Christians call, 'liturgy after the liturgy'[59]. Thus for many Christians the life of the church, expressed dynamically in the Eucharist, is the springboard of the churches' witness to the world. A recognition within ecclesiology that the church is primarily a community of worship, of sacrament and word challenges a secular hierarchical model of church; it reminds us of the priesthood of all believers, who by their baptism are commissioned 'to proclaim God's marvellous acts' to the world (1 Pet 2:10).

4.4 Kingdom and creation

An understanding of mission as God's activity has led to an expectation of its signs throughout God's creation and an emphasis on the kingdom of God as distinct from but overlapping with the church. Though some highlight authentic witness of the kingdom which extends their missionary task and responsibility to all kinds of social, economic and ecological activities as mission, such a holistic understanding does not undermine those who continue to place emphasis upon evangelization through verbal proclamation as the main task of mission: 'To speak of evangelism means to emphasize the proclamation of God's offer of freedom and reconciliation, together with the invitation to join those who follow Christ and work for the reign of God'[60]. Central to Christ's mission was the idea of '…the coming of a Messiah, who in the 'last days' of history would establish his kingdom (Joel 3:1; Isa 2:2, 59:21; Ezek 36:24, etc.) by calling all the dispersed and afflicted people of God *into one place,* reconciled to God and becoming one body united around him'.[61] Therefore, the apostles, and all believers thereafter, were commissioned to witness to the coming kingdom of God through the proclamation of the good news of the resurrection of the crucified Messiah and his inauguration of a new social, spiritual, and cosmic reality, encouraging loving service, the social struggle for justice, peace and the preservation of God's creation. Mission is thus seen in a variety of activities: building relationships in participation, seeking unity but not uniformity, breaking human-made barriers that are oppressive and life-negating. Amidst the current socio-economic crisis Christians cannot stay aloof, or worse, support the current world economic system that threatens the human and environmental existence, but must peacefully struggle for an alternative system, based on the biblical model of the 'economy of the enough' (2 Cor 8:15; Ex 16:18). This moves us beyond the exclusive church-centred mission *(missio ecclesiae)* and enables us to contextualize theologies and missiologies.

St. Paul expressed the eruption of the kingdom in terms of a *new creation* (2 Cor 5:17). Equally significant, therefore, is another development in contemporary missiology, which sees our mission under a Creator God as safeguarding the integrity of God's creation. A sense that God's mission encompasses the whole cosmos suggests that Christian mission includes all of God's created order.[62] Indeed, if 'the heavens declare the glory of God (Ps 19)'and the created order bears witness to God's loving kindness then we may participate in God's mission along with creation as well as to creation. This awareness has stemmed both from a growing awareness of the interconnectedness of all life on planet earth and a trinitarian understanding of God who reconciles all creation and eschatologically brings the new creation into communion (Rom 8:18-25)

5 Conclusion

Recent shifts in missiology, and attention to experience as a foundation for mission, have led to scrutiny of models assumed by missiologists and practitioners.[63] To conclude this chapter we present three models of mission that have gained prominence during the last forty years and which draw upon each of the three sets of foundations we have presented. Our explanations are brief; others will point to different models; but we offer them as examples of ways in which the three foundations cohere.

5.1 Mission as liberation

The paradigm of mission as liberation is one of the most dramatic illustrations of the shift in mission thinking and practice. 'Mission as liberation', which derives its impetus from Liberation Theology, attempts to 'reflect on the experience and meaning of the faith based on the commitment to abolish injustice and to build a new society,'[64] thus enlarging the concept of salvation by understanding Jesus as redeemer from structural evils. Initially arising as a response to systemic inequality in Latin America, it has influenced many across the world to social action and re-reading of Biblical texts for new theological emphases. Christ's baptism and crucifixion are examples of liberative solidarity. Jesus' choice to be baptised instead of to baptise shows Jesus' prophetic identification with the poor. By submitting himself humbly to be baptised, Jesus receives authority and loses identity thus discovering his authentic selfhood as the lamb of God, God's beloved Son, the Messiah.[65] Jesus began his prophetic mission, defending the poor and confronting *mammon.*[66] It was this, especially his challenge of the ruling religious elites and colonial powers, which led to Jesus' death. The journey which began at Jordan in humility was to end on Calvary, in humility and shame: both events described by the same word, 'baptism' (Matt 3:13-15; Mark 10:35-40; Luke 12:50).[67] This baptism is the basis for the church's mission. In exercising its liberative mission the church is guided by the gospel imperative that all will be judged according to whether they fed the hungry, clothed the naked, cared for the sick, or visited the prisoner (Matt 25:15-16). In short, they who inherit God's kingdom are those who give life to others, especially the poor and marginalized.

5.2 Mission as dialogue

In the last decades more and more churches are engaged in inter-faith dialogue as part of their witness. From the 1970s the Orthodox advanced the 'economy of the Holy Spirit' as the theological foundation of a theology of religions.[68] From 1984 the Roman Catholic Church reflected specifically on the relationship of dialogue and mission, asserting that mission includes 'the dialogue in which Christians meet the followers of other religious traditions in order to walk together toward truth and to work together in projects of common concern.'[69] Since the advent of the dialogue approach, it has been common within Christian circles to have either mission *or* dialogue – as if engaging in one excludes, or creates problems for, the other. Yet many Christians living in societies where the majority of the people adhere to religions other than Christianity are daily engaged in dialogical forms of mission.[70] This dialogue is aimed at showing forth the love of God and bearing witness to the virtues of God's kingdom, rather than growing the institutional church. In Knitter's model of mission-as-dialogue conversion remains a goal but it is primarily (although not exclusively) conversion to the service of God's kingdom.

The work of Indian Christian theologians furnishes a pneumatological basis for dialogue which 'recognises the involvement of God through the Spirit in earthly realities'. Therefore mission theology should recognise that 'its starting point can be none other than a particular experience of the Spirit in the world, and that interacts with other contextual theologies.'[71] The result of this approach is a theology of mission as living in the Holy Spirit, rather than accomplishing tasks. Crucial to this theology is the discernment of the Spirit's presence and activity in creation, in contemporary movements, in spiritualities and in individuals by the criterion of the fully human life of Jesus Christ.[72] God's saving love is revealed in Christ and is active throughout the world by the Holy Spirit. Thus dialogue involves seeking to recognise and affirm this presence at work through conversation with others.

5.3 Mission as reconciliation

By his cross and resurrection Jesus Christ brought reconciliation with God and with one another. In a world full of conflict and fractured relationships it is all the more important that the practice of Christian mission should demonstrate a commitment to reconciliation.[73] An awareness of reconciliation has grown through the movement for Christian unity, through a model of being-with-others-in-loving communion,[74] and through the practice of mission as healing, in which Christ's suffering and death '…put an end to the association of the divine with ideals of a perfect, sane, beautiful and un-passionate existence.'[75] The mission of God as reconciliation calls for transformed relationships in all domains: between humans and God; between humans as individuals, communities and cultures; and between humans and the whole of creation. By 2005 the world mission conference in Athens recognised the global interest in reconciliation and healing within churches and societies which prompted a rethinking of what God is calling us to in mission today. Noting that the reconciliation received in Christ is to be shared in the world, the conference acknowledged reconciliation as a key dimension of mission.[76]

Reconciliation is an integrating metaphor which encompasses and draws together a wide range of ideas which are the elements of the one mission of God. The different biblical terms related to reconciliation, such as sacrificial atonement, shalom, justice and peacemaking, suggest five dimensions of Christian mission which illustrate this integrative power of reconciliation: conversion as reconciliation, international peacemaking, reconciliation between indigenous and non-indigenous peoples, reconciliation between Christians and reconciliation with the whole of creation.[77]

These three models of mission demonstrate that, despite their individual distinctiveness, the empirical, biblical and theological foundations for mission are complementary and serve to strengthen and deepen a relevant Christian witness in the twenty-first century.

Endnotes

[1] *The World Mission of the Church: Findings and Recommendations* (London: IMC, 1939), 26-7, quoted in Norman E Thomas, *Classic Texts in Mission & World Christianity,* (Maryknoll, NY: Orbis, 1995), 81.

[2] Excerpt from minutes quoted in Norman E. Thomas, *Classic Texts in Mission and World Christianity* (Maryknoll, NY: Orbis Books, 1995), 88.

[3] For example, Christopher J.H. Wright, *The Mission of God: Unlocking the Bible's Grand Narrative* (Downers Grove, IL: IVP Academic, 2006).

[4] David J. Bosch, *Transforming Mission: Paradigm Shifts in Theology of Mission* (Maryknoll, NY: Orbis, 1991), 370.

[5] Peter C. Phan, *In Our Own Tongues* (Maryknoll, NY: Orbis, 2003), 3.

[6] World Council of Churches, Commission on World Mission and Evangelism, 'Mission and Evangelism in Unity Today' (2000), §48. Published in Jacques Matthey (ed.), *'You*

Are the Light of the World': Statements on Mission by the World Council of Churches (Geneva: WCC Publications, 2005), 59-89. Available at www.oikoumene.org.

7 Samuel Solivan, *The Spirit, Pathos and Liberation: Toward an Hispanic Pentecostal Theology* (Sheffield: Sheffield Academic Press, 1998), 62.

8 Solivan, *The Spirit, Pathos and Liberation*, 145.

9 'Hope from Old Sources for a New Century', a consensus paper in Walter Brueggemann (ed.), *Hope for the World: Mission in a Global Context* (Louisville: Westminster John Knox Press, 2001), 15.

10 For example, John K Thornton, *The Kongolese Saint Anthony: Dona Beatriz Kimpa Vita and the Antonian Movement, 1684-1706* (Cambridge: CUP, 1998), Emma Wild-Wood, 'St Apolo of Europe or What's in a Luganda Name?' *Church History* 77 (2008), 105-127.

11 For example, J.D.Y. Peel, *Religious Encounter and the Making of the Yoruba* (Indiana: Indiana University Press, 2000).

12 For example, Daniel Jayaraj, 'Mission Reports from South India and Their Impact on the Western Mind: The Tranquebar Mission of the Eighteenth Century', in Dana L. Robert (ed.) *Converting Colonialism* (Michigan: Eerdmans, 2008).

13 Andrew Porter, *Religion verses Empire? British Protestant Missionaries and Overseas Expansion, 1700-1914* (Manchester: Manchester University Press, 2004).

14 Ogbu Kalu (ed.) *African Christianity: An African Story* (Pretoria: University of Pretoria, 2005)

15 Laurenti Magesa, *Anatomy of Inculturation: Transforming the Church in Africa* (Maryknoll, NY: Orbis, 2004).

16 Valentin Dedji, *Reconstruction and Renewal in African Christian Theology* (Nairobi: Acton, 2003), 261.

17 Consuelo del Prado, 'I Sense God in Another Way', in Elsa Tamez (ed.), *Through Her Eyes: Women's Theology from Latin America* (Maryknoll, NY: Orbis, 1989), 140.

18 Mary Judith Ress, *Ecofeminism in Latin America* (Maryknoll, NY: Orbis, 2006), 1.

19 John Clark, Martin Lee, Philip Knights, Janice Price, Anne Richards, Paul Rolph, Nigel Rooms (eds), *Foundations for Mission in the UK: A Study of Language, Theology and Praxis* (London: CTBI, 2010).

20 Stephen B. Bevans & Roger P. Schoeder, *Constants in Context: A Theology of Mission for Today* (Maryknoll, NY: Orbis, 2001).

21 John Parratt, *An Introduction to Third World Theologies* (Cambridge: Cambridge University Press, 2004), 11-12.

22 See Edward Schillebeeckx, *The Understanding of Faith: Interpretation and Criticism* (London: Sheed and Ward, 1974), 65.

23 There are many valuable general studies on the interface between biblical scholarship and missiology, for example: Donald Senior & Carroll Stuhlmueller, *The Biblical Foundations for Mission* (Maryknoll, NY: Orbis, 1983); Lucien Legrand, *Mission in the Bible: Unity and Plurality* (Maryknoll, NY: Orbis, 1990); David J. Bosch, *Transforming Mission. Paradigm Shifts in Theology of Mission* (Maryknoll, NY: Orbis, 1991), 15-178; William J. Larkin Jr. & Joel F. Williams (eds) *Mission in the New Testament. An Evangelical Approach* (Maryknoll, NY: Orbis, 1998); Johannes Nissen, *New Testament and Mission, Historical and Hermeneutical Perspectives* (Frankfurt: Peter Lang, 1999); Christopher J.H. Wright, *The Mission of God: Unlocking the Bible's Grand Narrative* (Downers Grove: IVP Academic, 2006); James Chukwuma Okoye, *Israel and the Nations: A Mission Theology of the Old Testament* (Maryknoll, NY: Orbis, 2006). The

Association Francophone Oecuménique de Missiologie AFOM is contributing to the Edinburgh transversal 'Bible and Mission' through Marie-Hélène Robert, Jacques Matthey et Catherine Vialle (eds), *Figures bibliques de la Mission. Exégèse et théologie de la mission, approches catholiques et protestantes* (Paris: Le Cerf, 2010).

[24] Polysemy, '…the feature by which our words have more than one meaning when considered outside of their use in a determinate context.' 'Beyond the polysemy of words in a conversation is the polysemy of a text which invites multiple readings.' Paul Ricoeur, *Hermeneutics and the Human Sciences. Essays on Language, Action and Interpretation* (edited and translated by John B. Thompson; Cambridge: Cambridge University Press and Paris: Editions de la Maison des Sciences de l'Homme, 1981), 44, 108.

[25] A general survey of methods of interpretation (or hermeneutics) can be found in: Raymond E. Brown, *An Introduction to the New Testament* (New York: Doubleday, 1997), 20-47.

[26] For a transcultural evaluation of different readings of this story: H. de Wit, L. Jonker and D. Schipani (eds) *The Eyes of the Other. Intercultural Reading of the Bible* (Amsterdam: Institute of Mennonite Studies, Vrije Universiteit, 2004).

[27] Augustine, Treatise on John (*In Johannis Evangelium Tractus*) 15:10, cited in Joel C. Elowsky (ed.), *Ancient Christian Scripture Commentary on the New Testament* (Downers Grove, IL: InterVarsity Press, 2007), IVa, John 1-10, 146.

[28] *Calvin's New Testament Commentaries John 1-10* (Translation by Oliver and Boyd Ltd; Grand Rapids, MI: Eerdmans and Carlisle: Paternoster, 1995), 102-03.

[29] Gerald West, *Contextual Bible Study Methods* (Pietermaritzburg: Cluster Publications, 1992), 13. See also Brown, *An Introduction*, 28-29.

[30] Néstor Míguez, 'Reading John 4 in the Interface Between Ordinary and Scholarly Interpretation', in de Wit, *The Eyes of the Other*, 334-47.

[31] Such readings are numerous, for example: Teresa Okure, *The Johannine Approach to Mission: A Contextual Study of John 4.1-42* (Tübingen: J.C.B. Mohr, 1988); Vandana, *Waters of Fire* (Bangalore: Asia Trading Corporation, 1989), 76-92; Gail R. O'Day, 'John', in Carol A. Newsom & Sharon H. Ringe (eds), *Women's Bible Commentary* (expanded edition; Louisville: Westminster John Knox Press, 1998), 383-85; Mukti Barton, *Scripture as Empowerment for Liberation and Justice: The Experience of Christian and Muslim Women in Bangladesh* (Bristol: University of Bristol, 1999), 107-118. There is evident interface between these approaches to John 4 and the Edinburgh study transversal on 'women and mission'.

[32] More critical towards the biblical text is Musa W. Dube, 'Reading for Decolonization (John 4.1-42)', in R.S. Sugirtharajah (ed.), *Voices from the Margin: Interpreting the Bible in the Third World* (3rd edition; Maryknoll, NY: Orbis, 2006), 297-318.

[33] John 21 also attests to the Galilean tradition which can be read as emphasising unity in diversity and the importance of Peter and the disciple whom Jesus loved.

[34] David Bosch, 'The Structure of Mission: An Exposition of Matthew 28:16-20, in Wilbert R. Shenk (ed.), *Exploring Church Growth* (Grand Rapids, MI: Eerdmans, 1983), 218-48; Jacques Matthey, 'The Great Commission According to Matthew', *International Review of Mission* 69/274 (April 1980).

[35] The theme of the Week of Prayer for Christian Unity in 2010 is 'You are witnesses of these things' (Luke 24:18), intentionally related to the 2010 Edinburgh celebrations.

[36] The translation of the blessing admits more than one interpretation: 'in you all families will be blessed', or 'in you all family will bless themselves'. The second would indicate that blessing reaches other peoples (only) as they relate to the Abrahamic faith.
[37] For attempts by Jews, Christians and Muslims to read the Hebrew Bible together, visit www.scripturalreasoning.org.
[38] 'Ecumenical' is used here as defined by the WCC Central Committee in 1951: '...everything that relates to the whole task of the whole Church to bring the Gospel to the whole world.' World Council of Churches, *Minutes and Reports of the Fourth Meeting of the Central Committee, Rolle (Switzerland), August 4 – 11, 1951* (Geneva: WCC, 1951), 65. A similar expression is found in § 6 of the 1974 Lausanne Covenant to describe world evangelization: 'World evangelization requires the whole church to take the whole Gospel to the whole world'. The Lausanne Covenant is available at www.lausanne.org
[39] Bosch, *Transforming Mission*, 389-93.
[40] British Council of Churches, *The Forgotten Trinity* (London: The British Council of Churches, 1981-91).
[41] Vatican II, *Ad Gentes* 'Decree on the Mission Activity of the Church' (1965), §9, Available at www.vatican.va.
[42] Lesslie Newbigin, *The Relevance of Trinitarian Doctrine for Today's Mission* (London: Edinburgh House Press, 1963), 84.
[43] Ion Bria, *Go Forth in Peace: Orthodox Perspectives on Mission* (Geneva: WCC 1986), 3.
[44] Stephen Bevans, *Models of Contextual Theology* (2nd edition; Maryknoll, NY: Orbis Books, 2002), 15.
[45] Leonardo Boff, *Trinity and Society* (Tunbridge Wells: Burns & Oates, 1988), 236.
[46] Peniel Jesudason Rufus Rajkumar, 'Making a Difference Together: Prospects for Ecumenism in the Twenty-first Century', *The Ecumenical Review*, 60/3 (2008), 239-253.
[47] Paul Fiddes, *Participation in God* (London: Darton, Longman & Todd, 2000), 55.
[48] Elizabeth A Johnson, *She Who Is: The Mystery of God in Feminist Theological Discourse* (New York: Crossroad, 2000), 205.
[49] Damon So, *Jesus' Revelation of his Father: A Narrative-Conceptual Study of the Trinity with Special Reference to Karl Barth* (Milton Keynes: Paternoster, 2006), 22.
[50] Christina Manohar, *Spirit Christology: An Indian Christian Perspective* (Delhi: ISPCK, 2009), 230-32.
[51] John Paul II, *Redemptoris Missio* 'On the Permanent Validity of the Church's Missionary Mandate' (1990), §21. Available at www.vatican.va.
[52] Wonsuk Ma, 'In Jesus Name... Power Encounter from an Asian Pentecostal Perspective', in *Principalities and Powers: Biblical Reflections in the Asian Context* (Manila: OMF Lit., 2007).
[53] Manohar, *Spirit Christology*, 42-43.
[54] Manohar, *Spirit Christology*, 29.
[55] John Zizioulas, *Being as Communion: Studies in Personhood and the Church* (London: Darton, Longman & Todd, 1985), 140.
[56] World Council of Churches, 'Mission and Evangelism in Unity Today', §66.
[57] F. Leron Shults, 'Reforming Ecclesiology in Emerging Churches', in *Theology Today*, 65, (2009), 425- 438.

[58] Petros Vassiliadis, *Eucharist and Witness: Orthodox Perspectives on the Unity and Mission of the Church* (Brookline, Ma, Holy Cross Orthodox Press, 1998), 54.
[59] This term was first coined by former CWME Moderator Archbishop Anastasios Yannoulatos ('Orthodoxy and Mission', *SVSQ* 8 (1964), 139ff), and further developed by Ion Bria in *Liturgy After the Liturgy: Mission and Witness from an Orthodox Perspective* (Geneva: WCC, 1996).
[60] World Council of Churches, 'Mission and Evangelism in Unity Today', §62.
[61] World Council of Churches' Commission on World Mission and Evangelism, 'Mission as Ministry of Reconciliation' (2005), §28. Published in Jacques Matthey (ed.), *'You Are the Light of the World': Statements on Mission by the World Council of Churches* (Geneva: WCC Publications, 2005), 90-126. Available at www.oikoumene.org.
[62] Cf. Ken Gnanakan, *God's World, A Theology of the Environment* (London: SPCK, 1999).
[63] See Bosch, *Transforming Mission*, 181-89; Bevans and Schoeder, *Constants in Context*, 286-347.
[64] Gustavo Gutiérrez, *A Theology of Liberation: History, Politics and Liberation* (Maryknoll, NY: Orbis Books,1988), 174.
[65] Aloysius Pieris, *An Asian Theology of Liberation* (Edinburgh: T & T Clark, 1988), 46-48.
[66] Aloysius Pieris, *God's Reign for God's Poor: A Return to the Jesus Formula* (Kelaniya: Tulana Research Centre, 1999), 57.
[67] Pieris, *An Asian Theology*, 49.
[68] Georges Khodr, 'Christianity in a Pluralistic World – The Economy of the Holy Spirit', *The Ecumenical Review* 23 (1971), 118-128.
[69] Secretariat for Non-Christians, 'The Attitude of the Church Towards the Followers of Other Religions: Reflections and Orientations on Dialogue and Missions', *AAS* 75 (1984), 816-828.
[70] Paul F. Knitter, 'Mission and Dialogue', *Missiology: An International Review*, 33 (2005), 199-210; see also *Jesus and the Other Names: Christian Mission and Global Responsibility* (Maryknoll, NY: Orbis, 1996).
[71] Kirsteen Kim, *Mission in the Spirit: The Holy Spirit in Indian Christian Theologies*, (New Delhi: ISPCK 2003), 242-3.
[72] Kim, *Mission in the Spirit*.
[73] Robert Schreiter, 'The Theology of Reconcilation and Peacemaking', in Howard Mellor and Timothy Yates (eds), *Mission, Violence and Reconcilation* (Sheffield: Cliff College, 2004), 11-28.
[74] See Harry Sawyerr, *Creative Evangelism: Towards a New Christian Encounter with Africa* (London: Lutterworth Press, 1968), 72.
[75] World Council of Churches, Study group on healing, 'The Healing Mission of the Church' (2005), §25. Published in Jacques Matthey (ed.), *'You Are the Light of the World': Statements on Mission by the World Council of Churches* (Geneva: WCC Publications, 2005), 127-62. Available at www.oikoumene.org.
[76] Jacques Matthey (ed.), *'Come, Holy Spirit, Heal and Reconcile': Report of the World Council of Churches Conference on Mission and Evangelism, Athens, May 2005* (Geneva: WCC Publications, 2008).
[77] Ross Langmead, 'Transformed Relationships: Reconciliation as the Central Model for Mission', *Mission Studies* 25/1 (2008), 5-20.

Theme Two
Christian Mission Among Other Faiths

Preface

This chapter was prepared by a core group led by co-conveners Lalsangkima Pachuau, Asbury Seminary, USA (Presbyterian, India) and Niki Papageorgiou, Aristotle University of Thessaloniki (Orthodox, Greece). Other members of the group were Eunice Irwin, Asbury Seminary (Christian and Missionary Alliance, USA), John Azumah, London School of Theology (Presbyterian, Ghana), Michael Biehl, Missionsakademie, University of Hamburg (Lutheran, Germany) and Knud Jørgensen, Areopagos, Denmark (Lutheran, Denmark/Norway), who acted as secretary to the group. Gwen Bryde (Lutheran, Germany) was associated with the core group as youth representative and took part in its second meeting. Michael Jagessar, United Reformed Church (Guyana/UK) also gave input, first as a member of the core group and then in preparing an extensive bibliography on the study theme. The group met twice (in Hamburg); the first time in January 2009 to gather ideas and gain an overview of the topic, and the second time in August to review and edit the sections of the report.[1]

At an early stage it was decided to collect position papers and case studies from a variety of persons with various backgrounds and experiences. The position papers include reflections on the theme from the following perspectives: Roman Catholic, Greek Orthodox, Ecumenical, Evangelical, Pentecostal, and Adventist. Among the case studies are articles on Christian mission among Muslims, Hindus, Buddhists, Jews, new religious movements and folk religionists. This material has been used as resource material and background for the report of the core group, and also to compensate in some manner for the lack of a broader consultation. The group intends to have all these papers published as a book on theologies of religion. All position papers are placed on the Edinburgh 2010 website.

1 Christian Mission among Other Faiths: A Centennial Historical Background

'How should we relate with and witness to people of other faiths?' This appears to be the most crucial missiological question facing Christians at the end of the twentieth century. While some go to the extent of consultative relations with the adherents of other faiths (under such rubrics as 'wider ecumenism'), others look for peaceful manners of communicating the meaning of Christian faith with the intention of persuading (or converting) them to the faith. We shall identify a few crucial milestone-themes in the development of Christian missiological thought on this topic between Edinburgh 1910 and Edinburgh 2010.

1.1 Edinburgh 1910 and fulfilment theory

Among the eight topics of the commissions in 1910, two of them – Commission I and Commission IV – had 'non-Christian' in the titles. While Commission I does not really deal with 'non-Christian' as such, Commission IV relates the missionary message to non-Christian religions. A questionnaire containing eleven questions was distributed to missionaries working among non-Christians around the world, and 187 responses were received.[2] Among the eight commissions, the responses to the questionnaire generated by Commission IV were considered to be the best and the commission attracted the 'disproportionate attention' of scholars in the succeeding decades. The Continuation Committee of Edinburgh 1910 seriously considered publishing the responses, but abandoned the attempt with 'reluctance', says Brian Stanley.[3] As the commission's report says, the focus was not on non-Christian religions per se, but on studying 'the problems involved in the presentation of Christianity to the minds of the non-Christian peoples.'[4] Though veiled by the reigning Western optimism and victorious spirit, it was one of the early serious empirical works on other faiths. The dominant theology of religions in Commission IV is 'fulfilment theology,' and the missionary task was concluded to be a humble enquiry and identification of '"points of contact" in non-Christian religions', using them 'to draw adherents of other faiths toward the full revelation of truth found in the Christ ....'[5] The fulfilment idea is seen to be apostolic (or biblical) as the report explains:

> We can see how the whole Apostolic view grew out of the twofold endeavour of those first missionaries of the Church to meet what was deep and true in the other religions, and to guard against the perils which arose from the spell which these earlier religions still cast upon the minds of those who had been delivered from them into the larger life of the Gospel.[6]

Since the theology of fulfilment caters more to the so-called 'high religions', other religious traditions, generally categorized as 'animistic', did not fit the theory so much. But the relatively small survey materials on primal (or 'animistic') religious traditions (27 responses, of which 16 were missionaries in Africa[7]) provided helpful material for later scholarship in the field.[8]

1.2 Continuity or discontinuity

The fulfilment theology at Edinburgh 1910 continued to be the dominant approach for much of the first half of the twentieth century. It was largely on the broad basis of the fulfilment idea that the emerging challenge of secularism was responded to in the Jerusalem meeting of the International Missionary Council in 1928, and in the influential 'Laymen's Inquiry' published in 1932 as

Rethinking Missions. The latter proposed a radical departure for missionary motive and stirred much debate. It criticised the missionary denouncement of other religions, invited the missionaries to be co-workers with people of other faiths, and advocated that 'the primary duty' of a missionary should be presentation 'in a positive form his [*sic*] conception of the true way of life and let it speak for itself.'[9] It was this radical redefinition of the missionary's work in relation to other ('non-Christian') religions that set the next major theme in motion – that of continuity or discontinuity – at the Tambaram (Madras, India) meeting of the International Missionary Council in 1938.

A Dutch missiologist and a former missionary to Indonesia, Hendrik Kraemer, wrote a preparatory text for the meeting, *The Christian Message in a Non-Christian World*. Written in seven weeks,[10] this 450-page book was not easy to understand. While the thesis of the book may simply be stated as 'discontinuity' and not 'continuity', the manner by which Kraemer came to the point is complex and easily misunderstood. Against many false allegations later on, Kraemer showed a deep respect for all non-Christian religions saying, 'the non-Christian religions are not merely sets of speculative ideas about the eternal destiny of man,' but are 'inclusive systems and theories of life';[11] and the Christian attitude to them 'has to be essentially [a] *positive* attitude.'[12] However, Kraemer made a great departure from the Edinburgh 1910 search for 'points of contact'. He said that such a search for 'points of contact' is 'a misguided pursuit',[13] and he argued that God's revelation in Jesus Christ was 'absolutely *sui generis*' and could not be related to other religions. As Wesley Ariarajah rightly states, 'The revelation of Christ, in his [Kraemer's] view, directly contradicted all human religious life and wisdom',[14] and thus there cannot be continuity from non-Christian religions to Christianity. O.V. Jathanna summarises Kraemer's view in the words, 'the Christian faith is radically different from all other religions in that it is radically theocentric, even as a soteriological religion'.[15]

Kraemer's book, his presentation in the conference, and the follow-up writings, stirred long debate. So polarized was the discussion that while James Scherer of the United States calls Kraemer's book 'the most famous book about mission theology of all time,'[16] for C.F. Andrews, a missionary in India, it was to be dropped '"unceremoniously" into the waste paper basket'.[17] The conference affirmed Kraemer's main point while opposing his idea of radical discontinuity. It says,

> …we believe that in Him [Christ] alone is the full salvation which man [*sic*] needs…. We do not think that God has left Himself without witness in the world at any time. Men [*sic*] have been seeking Him all through the ages. Often this seeking and longing has been misunderstood. But we see glimpses of God's light in the world of religions, showing that His yearning after His erring children has not been without response.

In the succeeding discussions, it became clear that even those who follow Kraemer's discontinuity position do not necessarily agree with its radical nature. Lesslie Newbigin, for instance, while agreeing with Kraemer's discontinuity theory in general, does not agree that there is total discontinuity.[18]

1.3 Dialogue in the pluralistic context

By 1988, when the World Council of Churches (WCC) organised the fiftieth anniversary of the International Missionary Council's conference in Tambaram, it was clear that the ecumenical church had moved on from Kraemer. The main theme had become dialogue in the pluralistic context. Proponents of dialogue in Protestant ecumenical circles introduced their case by opposing Kraemer's position. In WCC circles, no one did more than Stanley J. Samartha to introduce the concept of inter-religious dialogue as he transformed his position as Study Secretary of the Word of God and Living Faiths of Men into the Director of the sub-unit on Dialogue with People of Living Faiths and Ideologies between 1968 and 1971.[19]

In this movement toward a dialogical approach, the WCC followed Vatican II developments in the Roman Catholic Church. The Vatican Council posited an affirmative posture not only toward non-Catholics, but also to non-Christian religions. In its document *Nostra Aetate*, Vatican II states that the Catholic Church is not opposed to anything 'true and holy' in other religions. This was seen by many as a major departure from its traditional position. Theologies of religions such as Karl Rahner's 'anonymous Christian' theory and Raymond Pannikar's 'unknown Christ of Hinduism' followed up Vatican II in paving the way for a new and positive attitude to other religions. Asian Christian leaders and thinkers in religiously pluralistic neighbourhoods took the lead in this venture.

Interfaith dialogue, as it was introduced from the early 1970s, was a controversial subject matter, or it was treated so. Proponents such as Stanley Samartha insisted that any motive to convert the dialogue partner of another religion is unacceptable. The dialogue partner is to be treated with respect and should be received with openness. Any claim for superiority by Christians is considered an impediment for the practice of dialogue. Interpreted this way, many feared dialogue was a way of compromising their Christian faith, and thought that it rendered Christian mission meaningless. Along with dialogue came a controversial relativistic theology called 'pluralistic theology', which affirmed the salvific validity of different religions. Some pluralists were of the opinion that interfaith dialogue can happen only through pluralistic theology, thus confusing dialogue with pluralistic theology. Mission, for pluralistic theologians, has to be confined to what is morally just, dialogically possible and resulting in the common liberation of humanity, all of which aspects can be shared with people of other faiths.[20] Samartha, for instance, defines mission as 'God's continuing activity through the Spirit to mend the brokenness of creation, to overcome fragmentation of humanity, and to heal the rift between humanity, nature and God'.[21] In a gathering in 1986, pluralist theologians described themselves as those who 'move away from insistence of the superiority or finality of Christ and Christianity toward a recognition of the independent validity of other ways'. They described this as 'the crossing of a theological Rubicon'.[22]

Closely tied to the question of plurality and dialogue is the validity of religious conversion as a change of religion from one to another (inter-religious conversion). While most pluralistic theologians either minimize or question the validity of inter-religious conversion, conversion remains one of the most important self-defining topics for Evangelicals. It was on this issue that dialogue and evangelism or dialogue and mission were often set in tension. The tension has now been largely resolved in most Christian circles. As the ecumenical effort to forge 'a code of conduct on conversion' affirmed in 2006, 'while everyone has a right to invite others to an understanding of their faith, it should not be exercised by violating others' rights and religious sensibilities'.[23]

Dialogue was confused with pluralistic theology, and continued to be treated by some with suspicion for quite some time. Other Christians came to interpret interfaith dialogue differently. As early as in the mid 1970s, Evangelical leader and thinker John R.W. Stott discussed 'dialogue' favourably as a mode of Christian mission. Drawing from the examples of the famous missionary to India E. Stanley Jones, who practised 'roundtable' conference as 'dialogue with Hindus', and Bishop Kenneth Cragg's work 'dialogue with Moslems', as well as Bishop David Sheppard's work on 'dialogue in industrial Britain', Stott advocated a true Christian dialogue as a way of doing Christian mission.[24] In the decades following Stott's work, other Evangelical Christians have spelled out an Evangelical theology of religions. While some have discussed the issue mainly in the new pluralistic context of the West, others such as Timothy Tennent have dealt with the issue in connection with the non-Christian religious faiths.[25] The recent works of Pentecostal theologians such as Veli-Matti Kärkkäinen[26] and Amos Yong[27] have clearly signalled that theology of religions, with dialogue and witness in the pluralistic world as the core subject-matter, has come of age. In the Catholic Church, post-conciliar documents such *Redemptoris Missio* (1990) and *Dialogue and Proclamation* (1991) seek to both correct what are perceived to be theological errors in interreligious issues and to connect the plural context with the church's faith.[28] Since the joining in 1961 of a large number of Orthodox Churches in the WCC, the Orthodox tradition has also contributed significantly in reshaping Christian missiological thought. Its pneumatological perspective of communion of the entire creation with God and theological-anthropological understanding of *theosis* or deification makes the Orthodox missiology a true invitation to the life of the triune God.[29]

The plurality of religions has now been accepted as the fact of life. Christian mission cannot be conceived without acknowledging the plurality of religions and the demand for a dialogical mode of existence and way of witnessing.

Christians must treat people of any faith and no faith with genuine respect in their act of witnessing to the gospel.

2 From Geography to Scenarios

The developments described above occurred in a world which has dramatically changed during these last hundred years. Without using the term, the participants of the Edinburgh conference had envisioned a globalization of Christian faith, but, even more so, of Christendom. Their understanding of 'ecumenical' (*oikumene* – the whole inhabited world) referred to the sphere of Christian domination. The success of Christian mission would be the conquest of the 'non-Christians' in the form of an expansion of the territory of the Christian nations into the whole globe and thus the fulfilment theory for some implied the vision that eventually all other religions should vanish.

During the decades after the Edinburgh conference a multiplication occurred of churches, denominations, movements and confessions, such as Evangelical, charismatic, Pentecostal. In the same period the nascent Ecumenical movement became acutely aware that beyond the Protestant mission movement there were other and often much older churches living and witnessing to Christ in various cultures. Today we realise that among the various dialects of the Christian faiths, there are different understandings and hence different ways of analysing the missionary and religious situation in the world. Some Christians see regions or other religious groups under the shadow of sin or evaluate human activities in the light of the last judgment. Others emphasise the realm of spirits or powers and principalities fighting with or against God. Again others analyze the globe in social, political, economic terms and relate their faith response to what they conceive to be the challenges of the local situations and global tendencies. These are debates among Christians with differing world views which in some cases conflict with each other. For instance, while some Christians fight for liberation,[30] others call for evangelism of individuals. The debates, however, unlike at Edinburgh 1910, today cut across geographical boundaries and occur at the same time in various places and contexts. There they carry with them a former history of relating, as in the case of Christian and Muslim faiths as opposing forces; this lingers in the background of actual relations of Christians and Muslims.[31] The debate on how to perceive the world and how to account for the presence of other faiths was opened towards the close of the twentieth century among Christians. It raises questions as to how we should understand Christian mission among other faiths: as a mission to non-Christians, as a mission among other faiths, or witnessing to Christ in the context of contemporary challenges in the mutually edifying fellowship of 'neighbours of living faiths and ideologies'.[32]

These different Christian attitudes coexist along with those of adherents of other faiths and along with new religious movements which have sprung up after the Edinburgh meeting in 1910 and still continue to come into being.

Although estimates of numbers vary, there is general agreement that the Christian faith globally has the largest number of adherents, followed by the Muslim faith and Hinduism. The next group in size is that of 'non-religious people', by which David Barrett and his team understand persons without formal or organised religious relations, including agnostics, freethinkers, humanists and secularists. Two points however are noteworthy with regard to the numbers relating to Christianity. Firstly, in spite of all the many forms of mission the percentage of Christians in the world population did not significantly change during the last hundred years. Secondly, Christianity – in almost all its forms – has been grown significantly in the global South and this growth has taken place primarily in the postcolonial period.[33]

From a sociological point of view the truly global religions are Christianity and Islam. They cross ethnic and national frontiers and are inculturated in various cultures and peoples. Other world religions like Hinduism and Buddhism are strong and dominant in their regions of origin and among migrating Hindus and Buddhists living in diaspora communities.[34] Buddhism as a missionary religion, and in various forms, has attracted some Westerners, and new religious movements growing out of Hindu traditions have found new adherents.[35] An awareness that the history of religions has not yet come to an end is one aspect of our theme 'Christian mission among other faiths'.

The contexts in which these attitudes towards and conceptions of the others occur is often described with the term *globalization*, which is a complex concept. For the sake of our discussion we focus on globalization as a specific constellation of global relations and strategies affecting or even dominating local circumstances. Goods and international funds move freely around the globe but their trading is concentrated in only a few places in the world[36] and the consequences affect other places in diverse ways. (Bio-)technologies and also military technologies, which have become so threatening in the last decade, are produced in certain countries but put to use or even imposed on the other side of the globe where they are used to create economic or technological domination. Migration is a world-wide phenomenon; migrants move to selected places where only a few (and well educated) are welcomed, whereas the mass of the migrants who have left their homes because of economic threat are searching for a better life which the receiving societies are unwilling or unable to provide.[37] Information technology is globally present but causes a digital divide excluding those who 'have not' more effectively than frontiers. These examples demonstrate that globalization is a power constellation and generates new hierarchies and dependencies or oppression[38] and marginalization, and in some cases offers new opportunities and liberating interrelations.

To sum up, human life in the globalized world is not de-territorialised. Conflicts and violence, military action, famine and floods, affluence and poverty are concentrated in particular places on the globe with a shocking regularity over time. Seen critically in a non-Western perspective, globalization still knows a geography and therefore centres of powers[39]. Most of these are still localised in the global North; the present power centres are, however, no longer so clearly co-extensive with one geographical region since new power centres have come into being in the global South and East. Nor are they any longer co-extensive with the former power centres of Christianity because new power centres have emerged outside the North.

2.1 Scenarios

It is especially at the cross-sections of global and local powers that the questions of identity have become burning issues for national states, ethnicities, cultures, and also for religions. Against this background we shall look at 'Christian mission among other faiths', not by comparing, contrasting, or relating the Christian religion to other religions as was done in the report of Commission IV at Edinburgh 1910. Individuals or groups need to formulate their answers to these challenges. The challenges interact with and influence each other, compete and in many cases clash. To understand 'Christian mission *among other faiths*' means to perceive Christians as believing human beings among other believing and non-believing human beings, sharing, facing, or opposing each other in specific situations in which they live their faith and draw on their respective traditions. This aspect is captured by what the Pontifical Council for Inter-religious Dialogue termed 'dialogue of life',[40] meaning that Christians and churches exist among other believers, among those who oppose religion altogether or feel they have moved beyond it. Christian mission witnesses to the incarnated Christ, and the faith thus finds expression, or is inculturated, in a 'diapraxis' (see below). To become a Christian should not mean to change one's culture and thus to alienate oneself from those among whom one is living.

The dynamics of the meetings of the world religions are not only defined by their faiths, theologies, world views, and spiritualities. Local and/or global factors play an important role: Which faith group constitutes a majority or the marginalized? Are the practitioners allowed to act openly in their societies and is mission permitted? Transgressing the geographical and Protestant vision of Edinburgh, we today include the insights and approaches of churches and traditions which were not present in 1910, including some of the oldest churches in the world and some of the numerically strongest strands of Christianity (Orthodoxy, Roman Catholic, Pentecostal). Their approaches in mission, and more specifically to mission among other faiths, come into view.[41] Mission is the task of the local churches, but what some call 'reverse cross-cultural mission' is going on at a large scale today. The missionaries of today may come from South Korea and work in Afghanistan or China or come from Ghana and work in Germany or Finland. Even where mission is not conceived in an ecumenical manner those who are in mission cannot overlook others being in mission.

Against this background a number of scenarios come to mind which characterize challenges of the present and the near future for 'Christian mission among other faiths' because they call for specific forms of missionary engagement in the contact with members of various faith communities. The way they relate to each other in multi-ethnic or plural situations may reach from opposition, which may eventually lead to violence or oppression of the others, to a dialogue of communities and individuals, or to a relativism in the guise of pluralism which dissolves any faith into a mere personal persuasion. Thus believers of various faith communities are forced to recognise to what extent their own religious perception of the situation and the motivations for their actions or their power aspirations contribute to the local constellation. This means that a dialogue of life is incomplete without a dialogue of faiths. Christian mission among other faiths has to be specific to the context Christians share with believers of other faiths.

2.1.1. Pluralism, multi-ethnicity, multi-cultural societies

Globalization has brought nations and cultures into closer contact, and Christian mission faces pluralism in various forms. Migration is one of the main reasons for the co-existence of different religions and faith groups within one region. The challenge to all faith communities today is to shift from tolerating a factual pluralism to a concept of religious pluralism which transcends earlier concepts like the fulfilment theory or the criteria of difference or continuity. In some regions of Africa and Asia, religious, ethnic, and cultural pluralism has always been a characteristic of society and has fostered concepts of more fluid or multiple identities. Some of the postcolonial societies, however, struggle in this respect. Whereas on a grassroots level believers of different faiths often live peacefully together, the situation changes when in such contexts a religious group identity becomes a political factor, as in some parts of Indonesia where Christians and Muslims clash, or as in India where groups have politicised Hinduism with the result that Christians and Muslims are accused by them of being non-Indians.

Led by politicized or even ethnicized religion, a lack of freedom of religion characterizes many parts of the world today. In some countries Christian believers and their congregations are forced to keep quiet, and any form of mission is judged to be illegal.[42] The main challenge for the Christians in such a situation is probably how to stay faithful and live their faith among other faiths when they are not allowed to become publicly visible, or to receive new believers, and are constantly under suspicion for being 'unsafe' citizens. Pressure leads Christians to leave regions like Iraq, where churches and Christian communities are vanishing. We also note that other faith communities may perceive their existence in predominantly Christian cultures and nominally pluralist cultures along similar lines. Christian mission in such contexts has often been accused of being a colonial force. It is imperative to promote an understanding of mission as witnessing to Christ, meaning that Christians live together with those of other faiths. The fruitfulness of theologies of religion for such contexts will have to be proved by whether they help Christians to interpret the plurality of religion in relation to pluralism in social and political life.[43]

2.1.2. Urbanization

One scenario of growing importance is urbanization. Currently more than fifty percent of the world population and approximately fifty-eight percent of the world's Christians live in urbanized areas. We recognise an urban scenario in the metropolises of what used to be the first world, but the fastest growing cities are in Asia, Africa, and Latin America. It is estimated that in 2050 between 75-80 percent of the world's population will live in urban centres or regions, which also will comprise the majority of the Christians of the world. The hope for (better) economic opportunities will often, for the migrants, result in the loss of supportive community structures, a break-down of relations and of the extended family system, and possibly a weakening of values. Global religions, ideologies, new forms of living one's faith, new religious movements and cults emerge or re-arrange the balances in the communities or influence worship and bring new challenges of syncretism. A loss of identity and search for survival in the new context are also spiritual challenges which force people to reformulate their faith and identity. On the other hand, urban regions offer the possibility to integrate into new networks along old lines of adherence or to radically reformulate one's faith.

Urbanization is one aspect of migration, taking place both within countries and regions as well as being a global phenomenon. Approximately 175 million people, or three percent of the world's population are estimated to be on the move worldwide. Compared to 1910, when migration was mainly of European peoples to their colonies, migration from the North has declined. The countries of origin of people on the move today lie mostly in Asia, Africa, South America and Eastern Europe, and the receiving countries are mostly in the global North,[44] although the countries hosting the highest percentage of migrants are oil-producing countries (Arab Emirates, Kuwait), and Asia hosts the largest refugee population.[45] Migration can be a transitory state in life or a definite change. Although reasons to migrate often are hunger, war, natural catastrophes, and lack of economic opportunities, the vast majority of people affected by these threats stay in the regions struck.[46] Migration is part of globalization but most countries have highly restrictive legislation which places migrants in the receiving countries in a situation of being tolerated but most often considered illegal. Migrants may find in their faith a resource for survival which will strengthen the cultural-linguistic expression of their faith as their identity. Faith, origin, and the search for a future, for identity and dignity blend together, and therefore this scenario is important for our theme.

2.1.3. Marginalized aboriginal and indigenous peoples

At the opposite end of a global map of such scenarios are the aboriginal and indigenous peoples. An estimated 300 million belong to this group and are concentrated in seventy countries on all continents. Despite their unique cultures they share a specific blend of ethnic, cultural, economic, political, and religious identities which distinguish them from the surrounding dominant societies and the national states of which they are considered citizens. Many aboriginal cultures retain stories of being assigned geographical locations on the earth. They respectfully embraced many of the customary laws they inherited from their ancestors who, they believe, received these directly from the Creator. These remain binding upon all descendents as a covenant sign of the group's response to the gifts of the Creator. They mark their right relationship to the cosmic and to one another, and define how they relate to their environment and people beyond the confines of their community. Through these the people live with structure, order and certainty. In the history of mission we see how entire peoples became Christian, and then struggled with how to reconcile their identity with the new faith, and also with how to relate their community sense and constitutive exclusion lines to an understanding of being part of a universal church. Most of the Christians in the global South today originally came from these primal religious and cultural traditions.

The life and environment of aboriginal peoples are endangered today. The traditional religion, or a revitalised version, cannot always help to ensure survival. For instance, where religion is linked to land and the land is taken away in the name of modernization or the development of the nation-state, these groups do not only become homeless or displaced, but also become rootless peoples without a future. The globalized world does not easily tolerate enclaves, and in many cases the dominant societies are not willing to recognise the rights of these communities.[47] Christian mission among aboriginal peoples must ask how Christians and Christian churches will be engaged in fighting for their rights. And how they should relate to them in witnessing to Christ. Are they willing to recognise how aboriginal or indigenous peoples which have become Christian may enrich Christian faith by their ways of inculturation?[48]

2.1.4. Information technology, cyberspace and virtual realities

The advanced electronic communication systems are offering new channels for communication transgressing the medium of written text by including records of spoken word, sound and image. They even offer new forms of co-presence and interaction and thus formulate new challenges and opportunities for mission. Since the last decade of the twentieth century, groups or individuals adhering to different religions have globally and locally been using the internet for propagating their beliefs.[49] Virtual space and communication via the worldwide web can create interactive transnational communities of reference which ensure a presence also where the religion in question is not found. Classic traditions and their institutions, organisations, groups, individuals, and cults populate cyberspace in order to influence individuals. Through the internet, traditions or beliefs reach far beyond the actual region of their presence, and can therefore create a kind of globalized consciousness for their adherents. Such global interaction can affect their perception of the actual situation and influence the actions they take locally. Where access to the internet is available on a broad basis a multitude of presentations of faith and religion coexist separated from the physical church or group in which they are based, which makes it difficult to 'discern the spirits'. Also websites for interreligious dialogue and mutual cooperation have sprung up. This scenario is very influential, especially among youth in the West and in the technologically advanced sectors of Asia.

2.2 Conclusions

The scenarios presented are not the only ones which could be described. But through them we see clearly the global spread of Christian faith, and they help to identify present and future challenges to the global Christian faith community. A hundred years after the Edinburgh conference these scenarios testify to the shift from distinguishing between a Christian and a non-Christian world to recognising a global world. Christians and people of other faiths face an enormous diversity of global and local expressions of Christian faith and ways of witnessing to Christ. In this context we propose to reflect on our theme more from the perspective of the other. A theology which recognises the dignity of human beings as created by the one God cannot deny such dignity and respect to others; it will therefore want to honour their faith. Not religions, but human beings meet and share, ignore or enrich one another, clash and fight. Phenomena like religiously tainted violence and fundamentalism are not best approached as if they were caused by religion or mission. They are better understood as attitudes of human beings engaging in conflicts in which they activate their religious convictions and power aspirations to understand their situation and to search for possibilities to act and to change it.

3 Perspectives and Hermeneutical Reflections

Because Christians believe that what God has done in Jesus Christ is good news for all, Christians are called to share the good news in the power of the Spirit. This is the *raison d'être* for mission. This mission takes the concrete form of witness (*martyria*). Mission is therefore to share one's faith and conviction with other people, inviting them to discipleship, whether they adhere to other religious traditions or not. Such sharing is to take place with confidence and humility.[50] Our faith is about discovering grace in the cross and resurrection of Jesus Christ. Vulnerability is therefore how we encounter the others, without forgetting the faith we are stewards of.

3.1 Dialogue, witness and mission

Mission is what the church is sent to *be* – *koinonia*, community, presence, nearness, worship. Mission is what the church is sent to *do* – *diakonia*, care, service. Mission is what the church is sent to *say* – *kerygma*, proclamation of the gospel, dialogue, apologetics. The overriding concept is that *mission is witness to others about the gospel. Martyria* is the sum of *kerygma*, *koinonia* and *diaconia* – all of which constitute dimensions of witnessing: 'We are using a missiological hermeneutic when we read the New Testament as the testimony (witness) of witnesses, equipping other witnesses for the common mission of the church'.[51]

Dialogue is, in this perspective, part of what we are sent to *say* and thus a key expression of witness. Dialogue means witnessing to our deepest convictions, whilst listening to those of our neighbours in a two-way exchange. Without such commitment to others dialogue becomes mere chatter, in the same manner as it becomes worthless without the presence of the neighbour. This emphasis on 'neighbour' further means that we cannot dialogue with, or witness to, people if we from the outset resent their views. The scenarios presented above describe how all of us live in a multi-religious setting, in situations where coexistence with believers of other faiths is part and parcel of our daily life (even though the power relations among people may be very asymmetric). Christian theology must therefore be a theology of dialogue[52]. And it must be a theology of inculturation and contextualization – in conversation with and listening to the local context and its culture and religion. Contextualization is not an alternative to mission, but a specific way of being in mission. In the same way dialogue is not an alternative to mission, but a specific way of being in mission.

Dialogue is only possible if we proceed from the expectation of meeting God who has preceded us and has been relating to people within the context of their own culture and conviction. God is there before we come (Acts 17) and our task is not to bring God along, but to witness to the God who is already there. We therefore take off our shoes as we approach men and women of other living faiths. Dialogue is a way of taking seriously that all humans are created in God's image. The other is always 'you' – someone that I listen to because there is something valuable to listen to from any human being created in the image of God. In the same manner I too share with others what is on my heart – what I have seen and heard and touched with my own hands (1 John 1:1-2).

Old Testament theologian Walter Brueggemann uses the term 'othering' to remind us of the importance of not seeing the religious other as a counter-object but rather 'the risky, demanding, dynamic process of relating to one that is not us'.[53] In a similar manner some Orthodox theologians advocate making the 'other' a partner.[54] To evolve such a mindset, Kärkkäinen says, Christian churches and congregations should be encouraged and empowered to initiate patient training and education with regard to such issues as:

- Raising the awareness and importance of interfaith engagement, which means venturing outside one's own safety zone and making oneself vulnerable.

- Helping deal with our fears of the other that often include not only the generic fear of the 'stranger' but also the tendency to 'demonize' others' religion and beliefs
- Facilitating the study of another religion in order to gain a more accurate portrayal of another person's beliefs and sensitivities, including the capacity to interpret the meaning of rites and rituals.[55]

Another metaphor for 'othering' is that of 'hospitality', a concept that we know from Scripture as well as in various cultural contexts, and which is used in a WCC document from 2006. The metaphor is here used as the hermeneutical key to a Christian understanding of dialogue with others.[56]

Just as *martyria* expresses itself in dialogue, it also encompasses *diakonia* and *koinonia*. Dialogue aims at joining hands. At a personal and relational level a dialogue relationship carries with it a concern for the welfare of my sister and brother in terms of being a neighbour. In the larger context – in the Christian fellowship with Muslims, Hindus, Buddhists and others – dialogue has to do with reducing the images of hostility of one another, developing relationships across the barriers of faith, race, gender and cultural background, and stimulating common action for the sake of society. This is often called *diapraxis* (bringing together dialogue and praxis). There is a growing need for such diapraxis, especially in the form of community-oriented dialogue. It is important to meet neighbours, colleagues and groups in the community with an attitude of sharing and listening. In that way we can get to know each other better, create friendships and relationships across barriers of ethnic, cultural, social, political and religious differences. Joining with others of different background in community projects for peace, human rights, social activities, health improvement, political freedom and democracy is an important aspect of being in dialogue with others.

Dialogue is *a basic way of life* because Christians share life and contexts with neighbours of other faiths. This implies that they establish dialogical relations so that there is hope of mutual understanding and fruitful co-existence in multi-religious and pluralist societies. If it is a basic way of life, then the arena for dialogue cannot be limited to the media, the public sphere and scholarly discussions and debates. Rather dialogue has to do with family, working place and neighbourhood. A very high percentage of people in the West have never had a conversation about faith with people of another faith. Dialogue here is therefore a matter of creating meeting places and using opportunities.

Dialogue is no a substitute for mission or a hidden form of mission. Mission and dialogue are not identical, neither are they so opposed to one another. One can be committed to dialogue and to Christian witness at the same time: 'We affirm that witness does not preclude dialogue but invites it, and that dialogue does not preclude witness but extends and deepens it'.[57] The Christian faith cannot surrender the conviction that God, in sending Jesus Christ into our midst, has taken a definite course of action and is extending to us forgiveness, justification, and a new life which, in turn, calls for our response in the form of conversion.[58]

3.2 Christian mission in a pluralist world

The scenarios above have described aspects of the pluralist and multi-religious global setting. An essential point of entrance into a Christian view on how to relate to this global context is the WCC statement at San Antonio in 1989: 'We cannot point to any other way of salvation than Jesus Christ. At the same time we cannot set limits to God's saving power.... We appreciate this tension, and do not attempt to resolve it'.[59]

Living in a plural context has for centuries been the daily experience of most of the world. Accepting to live in a pluralist world implies that mission will not attempt to 'conquer' the world in any religious or other sense. Pluralism is the context of Christian mission among other faiths. The claims of rationalism have, in Western culture, left people with a heritage that gives priority to the world of facts in the public realm while faith and values belong to the private sphere. In the private sphere Western culture has accepted pluralism. The Christian faith, together with other religions and religious worldviews, has been relegated to this sphere where pluralism reigns in a growing jungle of religiosity and individualised values. One consequence is that we have lost the concept of Christian faith as *a public truth*; that is, as a truth that relates to all of us and which has importance for society and community.[60] This development may be acceptable for religious views and for new spiritualities which view themselves as attaining to an esoteric *gnosis* in closed circles. For the Christian faith it is different: The Christian faith is a confession of Jesus Christ as Lord, not only my Lord or the Lord of the church, but the Lord of creation. This confession cannot be relegated to the sphere of the individual, and it cannot accept that there is more than this reality – the reality over which Christ is Lord.

Christians do not accept being relegated to the private sphere. However, where Christians express this conviction or act accordingly, they accept that in the public space their voice is one voice among others because they are committed to pluralism. The missionary theologian Lesslie Newbigin calls this *committed pluralism*, in contrast to *agnostic pluralism*.[61] Agnostic pluralism has renounced any talk about knowledge and truth in relation to faith. Committed pluralism, on the other hand, takes other worldviews seriously and dares to raise questions about the other's faith.

We enter the dialogue on the basis of our own belief or confession – and recognise that others will do the same. This stance implies that truth is to be found in a life of discipleship to Jesus Christ as he is known through a life lived in the community of disciples, in faithfulness to the tradition about him, and in openness to all truth which may be discovered in history. Our commitment is to a historic person and to historic deeds. Without these events, our faith would be empty. There need not be any dichotomy between 'confessing Christ' and 'seeking the truth'. As we meet the other, we expect to hear and learn more of truth. Granted, we shall interpret these new truths by means of the truth we have already committed our life to. Our encounter with Christ through Scripture and faith represents our ultimate commitment. And we expect that our neighbour will have his or her faith commitment.

There will be many different answers to the question of Christian understanding of other faiths:

- Other religions and ideologies are wholly false; non-Christian religions are the work of the devil and demonic cunning
- Other religions are a preparation for Christ (which the gospel fulfils; this was the view of Edinburgh 1910; cf. section 1 above); there are essential values in other religions
- An understanding, emphasised by Orthodox theologians, of the presence and work of the Holy Spirit in creation, culture and religions[62]
- The Roman Catholic view of the world religions as concentric circles (with the Catholic Church as the centre)
- Karl Rahner's view of non-Christian religions as the means through which God's salvation in Christ will reach those who have not been reached by the gospel ('anonymous Christians')
- The view that religions are worlds in themselves, with their own structures and worldviews. They face in different directions and ask different questions. The gospel relates differently to Islam than it does to Hinduism or Buddhism. And the differences are for real. Other religions are not a sort of reduced copy of Christianity or simply echoes of Christianity's own voice[63].

The view of those who collaborated to write this paper is that religions are ambiguous responses to divine revelation. Within every religion, also in Christianity, there is a dark side, but Christians will also recognise 'revelation' in all of them, particularly in terms of creation. Christians may cautiously claim that every part of the created world and every human being is already related to Jesus (cf. Paul's speech on Areopagos where the presence of the altar for the unknown God implies that God is already there). Everything was made through the Logos, he is the life of all, and he is the light that gives light to every man. Christians will recognise the presence and work of Jesus not only within the area where he is acknowledged. In every human there is not only a moral consciousness (Rom 2:14-15), but also a religious consciousness.[64] This does not imply that everything is light; both Scripture and experience make it clear that there is also darkness, but the light shines in the darkness. And this light will also shine in the lives of all human beings: The Christian confession does not imply that we should deny the reality of the work of God in the lives and thoughts and prayers of men and women outside the Christian church. Neither do we deny the dark side of religion – every religion including Christianity –

but this dark side does not prevent us from seeing the light of God in the lives of men and women who do not acknowledge him as Lord.

For Christians the cross of Jesus exposes our rejection of God and our sin – *and* God's way of meeting this rejection. The power of God is hidden on the cross *sub contrarie specie*, Luther said; that is, under its contradiction. Christians believe that what looked like defeat turned out to be victory. This historic deed – the turning point of history – 'stands throughout history as witness against all the claims of religion – including the Christian religion – to be the means of salvation....religion is not the means of salvation'[65]. At the same time the cross becomes *the master clue* for Christians in our common search for salvation. And it is along the same way that we wonder whether we who follow Christ, can be saved apart from all who have not yet had the opportunity to respond to the gospel.

> The church, therefore, as it is *in via*, does not face the world as the exclusive possessor of salvation, nor as the fullness of what others have in part, the answer to the questions they ask, or the open revelation of what they are anonymously. The church faces the world, rather as *arrabon* of that salvation – as sign, first fruit, token, witness of that salvation which God purposes for the whole.[66]

There is in the Good News *a scandal of particularity* in the way God relates to the world. It is this scandal of particularity that we meet in the Christ revelation. At the same time we cling to God's 'amazing grace' and the confidence that this grace is sufficient for us and all other creatures. So there is a '*wideness in God's mercy*'[67] where the narrow boundaries of the church are widened through what in Orthodox theology is called, 'the economy of the Spirit'.[68] Down through history we find theologians who have spoken about God's work in the world and the possibility of salvation beyond explicit Christian faith:

- Justin Martyr believed in *logos spermatikos*, or seed-bearing word, by which he affirmed the seed of the revelation in Christ in existing cultures.
- Clement of Alexandria proposed that God had given the law to the Jews and philosophy to the Greeks.
- Irenaeus, like his contemporaries, assumed that the gospel had been taken throughout the world by the apostles. Had he known otherwise, he would still have been optimistic about the salvation of the unevangelized since Christ's incarnation implied for him a recapitulation of the history of fallen humanity, and since people will be judged according to the privilege of revelation that they have received.
- *Lumen Gentium* from Vatican II states that 'those also can attain to everlasting salvation who through no fault of their own do not know the gospel of Christ or His Church, yet sincerely seek

God…'.[69] Even in the more strict declaration *Dominus Iesus* (2000) it is emphasised that 'the salvific action of Jesus Christ…extends beyond the visible boundaries of the Church to all humanity'.[70]

- Martin Luther rarely spoke about the unevangelized. However, in his commentary on Romans (1515), he writes about those who have not heard the gospel that 'all people of this type have been given so much light and grace by an act of prevenient mercy of God as is sufficient for their salvation in their situation, as in the case of Job, Naaman, Jethro and others'[71]
- The Christian apologist J.N.D. Anderson affirmed the uniqueness of Christ but also affirmed that where the God of all grace has been at work in the hearts of individuals, they too may profit from this grace[72]
- Harold A. Netland, an Evangelical missiologist, encourages Evangelicals to explore the implications of trinitarian theology for our understanding of other religions and advocates a 'dynamic tension between the universality of the triune God and the particularity of the incarnate word…'[73]
- Alister McGrath, a contemporary evangelical Anglican[74], states:

> We cannot draw the conclusion….that only those who respond will be saved. God's revelation is not limited to the explicit human preaching of the good news, but extends beyond it. We must be prepared to be surprised at those whom we will meet in the kingdom of God[75].

In the same manner, as in the San Antonio statement of the WCC mission conference in 1989, we affirm the uniqueness of Christ: Anyone who ever has been, is now or ever will be saved is accepted by God on the grounds of the sacrifice of Christ and our identification or union with him. There is no other ground. To this should, however, be added that God gives to every human being a revelation sufficient to elicit saving faith; no one will be condemned because of lack of revelation. In conclusion, we can never solve the creative and dynamic tension between being both missionary and dialogical.

3.3 Pneumatological approach

When the Roman Catholic Church accepted the idea that salvation beyond its own boundaries was possible, yet through Christ, it affirmed the Spirit's work elsewhere, leading to greater interest in dialogical engagement with other religions.[76] Dramatic change in the doctrinal position of Roman Catholics raised difficult questions about where and how to locate the work of the Spirit in the religions. Recently, Pentecostal-charismatic scholars began a conversation to identify God's work through the activity of the Spirit and spirits among non-Christians, bringing them to faith.[77] The Holy Spirit's role in other religions raises two issues of significance for Christian mission among other faiths: (1) the relationship of Spirit and spirits in the religions; and (2) primal religion as the basic structure for understanding spirituality in the religions, with Israel's religion as a foundation for Christian witness.

3.3.1 Pneumatological dimension in a Christian theology of religions

The dialogue movement assumes the Spirit's activity mediating witness of the gospel in conversations with people of other religions. A pneumatological approach goes farther to identify dynamic moments when Spirit-induced phenomena happen in individuals and in religions. Kirstéen Kim calls this new area 'mission pneumatology'.[78] Pentecostal scholar Amos Yong seeks evidence of the (Holy) Spirit and the spirits at work in people of other religions, but holds in theological tension Christian orthodoxy and openness. His approach, probing aspects of 'one-Spirit' and 'many spirit' cosmologies, anticipates God's revelation to be present in areas of: the Ultimate powers, the lesser powers, ancestors, nature, human and other spirits in religions or new spiritualities. This approach is along the lines of what may be broadly termed 'discerning of Spirit(s)'.[79] In his method Yong does fresh exegesis of biblical accounts describing persons of other faiths living in proximity to Jewish or Christian communities. He examines language from texts that describe interactions, suggestive of witness, to detect the dynamics between the (Holy) Spirit and spirits. Believing a spiritual dimension exists in all religions as well as in Christianity, his immediate concern in mission is to become aware of, yet not accept uncritically, accounts of how people in the religions have spiritual relationship with the powers, their community and their world.[80]

This focused investigation across cultures and religions locates patterns of receptivity and response from people in the religions. Like data may be found in similar religious contexts revealing the nature of the Spirit's witness of Christ. Such pursuit is limited by the Christian belief that we may expect but cannot determine absolutely the work of the Holy Spirit whose task it is to 'testify to Christ and make him known so that people will believe' (John 14-16).

3.3.2 Recovery of pneumatological foundations from primal religions and worldviews

Primal and aboriginal religions, as described before, have been recovered as a resource for witness. Edinburgh 1910 participants opined that the Christian gospel was unlikely to be readily accepted into Africa because of its strongly held traditional religious beliefs, in which there were no inherent concepts upon which to build the Christian message.[81] A century later African Christians, missiologists and historians argue the opposite, attributing conversion of more than fifty percent of the population of Africa, and much successful spreading of Christianity in the West, largely to the witness of Pentecostal Christians from the global South.[82] Scholars now ascribe the spread of African Christianity to the fact that it became so well adapted to its base of primal religion.[83] The worldviews of primal people and people of the Old Testament have similarities, and parallels exist between primal religious and Pentecostal groups.

The uniqueness of the primal worldview rests in an inherent belief of indigenous peoples that creation is a living system, a network of spiritual relationships in which they find themselves. Creation is invested with the Spirit that gives life and power to control and guide all things. Amos Yong, writing about the implications of such a worldview to create capacity for a holistic relationship to God, summarises his discussion on the pneumatological theology of creation, speaking of Old Testament scriptures, by saying, 'Most important, the spiritual and the material realms are intertwined both ontologically and epistemologically. Regarding the former, the Spirit both hovers over the waters of creation and gives the breath of life; the human is intimately and intricately connected with the orders of creation'.[84] Both traditional believers and Pentecostals rest their faith on being in relationship with the powers and following the design of creation. This theo-cosmic posture grounds all else. For this reason, pneumatological foundations are basic to Christian witness among other religions, and a starting point is exploring the Spirit(s) dimensions of faith.

The basic religious insight that Christians from primal backgrounds gain is that Christ is Creator God, the Lord of creation. Initially, their worship occurs while encountering the Spirit in creation. Later, after indigenous people accept Jesus Christ as Lord of the new creation, who made salvation possible by restoring harmony to all things through his sacrifice, worship becomes adoring the triune God and pursuing the kingdom of God on earth. If Pentecostal spirituality can be described as a re-emergence of 'primal spirituality' in postmodernity,[85] it is well suited to challenge spiritualities of Western Christianity and theistic or meta-cosmic religions because it relates to the creation and the Spirit. The Pentecost narrative is comprehensive, affirming unity in diversity, engaging many traditions but pointing each to a single reality.[86] The Apostle Paul invited diverse people in Athens to consider Christ on the basis that the Spirit's power in creation was from God who made all things, and present in the Son, the risen Christ, whom God has declared as Lord (Acts 17).

Pentecostalism's apologetic is experiential, not merely rational. Pentecostals participate in a persuasive sharing of life in the Spirit. When Christians from the global South living as immigrants in situations of struggle manifest vibrant faith and tenacious hope in God for daily needs, such evident faith challenges secularists. When Western Christians attempted spiritual warfare to reach people with alternative spiritualities they largely failed, but a constructive pneumatological approach may have succeeded because identities are restored through spiritual relationship—a new self-understanding that they are made in the image of God (*imago Dei)* and belong to the people of God.[87] By healing prayers sin is overcome and harmony brought to the community.[88]

The pneumatological approach arose because Christians needed categories and criteria by which to search out the (Holy) Spirit among the spirits in the religions. In Pentecostal churches, spiritual phenomena abound: worship offers immediate access to divine power; signs and miracles happen in response to faith; personal empowerment flows as tongues and ecstasy strengthen daily life; exhortation comes through words of knowledge and wisdom; the Word is spoken by messengers appointed to guide the community.[89] The blessing of wellbeing is felt, the harmony of all creation, while in mystical communion with nature.

3.3.3 Power encounter

The word pair 'power encounter' is fairly recent, but intends to describe an ancient phenomenon: The powerful encounter when two religious worldviews and two religious groupings clash. The prime examples in the Bible include Elijah and the prophets of Baal on Mount Carmel, and Jesus' battle with Satan and his driving out of evil spirits as signs of the advent of the kingdom. Up through the history of the church there are many examples of such power encounters from situations where the Christian faith was crossing cultural and religious boundaries. Examples are also known from the recent and contemporary history of mission. The phenomenon is widespread among indigenous Christians and charismatic and Pentecostal churches in the global South.

Originally the confession of faith according to the Apostles' Creed was prefaced by renouncing the devil and all his works and all his being. This renouncement is still in use in some churches and is particularly being used at baptism, to ensure and proclaim that the devil has no rights anymore to this infant or adult, who immediately after is marked with the sign of the cross. In this sense baptism is a power encounter, reminding the devil that he has lost the battle on Golgotha on Easter morning. In some settings renouncing the devil also implies the removal and burning of fetishes belonging to the person to be baptised (e.g. in Ethiopia). This biblical image reminds us that faith is God drawing us to himself and thus to turning us away from what can be called demonic in all religions. This reality must follow us into dialogues of religion and particularly in our encounter with religious practices invoking the spirits. The encounter with New Spiritual Movements has again brought this reality home to a Western culture that thought it had got rid of the primitive notion of 'devil'. In the practice of some of these movements, the door to an occult jungle of spirits and 'forces' is made wide open. Often this has resulted in personalities being invaded and in communities being demonized.[90]

Some would say that the matter of power encounter also relates to some of the major destructive forces in the world, such as the use of violence and war to solve conflicts, the oppression of women, discrimination against others (apartheid, casteism, ethno-centrism), and the distortion of sex and sexual abuse.[91]

People of faith must discern and respond to the spirit dimensions of the religions and their environment – although these are conceived in different ways. The new approach widens evidence and introduces vocabulary to facilitate interreligious dialogue on the spiritual level and concerning experience of the Spirit. Mission pneumatology is a helpful and hopeful task.

4 Challenges and Questions for Continuing Discussions:

1. How do we understand mission in the religiously pluralistic context of today, and how has the concept of mission been shaped by our understanding of other religious faiths and our relationship with people of other faiths?
2. What ways of doing mission to and among people of other religious beliefs are respectful to and not hurting the feelings of other faith communities?
3. How may churches in the West gain new insights from churches in the global South about witness and dialogue in a pluralistic setting? What could churches in the global South gain from discussion on pluralism in the North?
4. Does the focus on the Holy Spirit in creation, culture and religion provide new avenues for a Christian theology of religion?
5. Can there be 'un-baptised' and/or 'churchless' Christianity (as some call it)? Should the church encourage un-baptised or churchless Christianity depending on the context?

Endnotes

[1] Two other significant Edinburgh 2010 events feed into this theme: the consultation on 'Mission as Reconciliation in Pluralistic Contexts' organised by Philip Sieuw at the Seminari Theoloji Malaysia consultation on 8-11 June 2009, and the Pre-centenary Edinburgh 2010 Study Conference on Christian inter-religious relations at the United Theological College, Bangalore on 17-19 July 2009, organised by Marina Behara. The results of these will be included in the report of the Edinburgh 2010 conference, June 2010.

[2] Brian Stanley, *The World Missionary Conference, Edinburgh 1910* (Grand Rapids, MI and Cambridge: William B. Eerdmans Publishing Co., 2009), 235. Only three of the 11 questions dealt specifically with the nature and characters of other religions. These are questions 2, 6, and 8.

[3] Stanley, *The World Missionary Conference,* 245.

[4] World Missionary Conference, Edinburgh 1910, *Report of Commission IV: The Missionary Message in Relation to Non-Christian Religions* (Edinburgh and London: Oliphant, Anderson, & Ferrier, 1910), 1.

[5] Stanley, *The World Missionary Conference*, 212.

[6] World Missionary Conference, 1910, *Report of Commission IV*, 215.

[7] Stanley, *The World Missionary Conference*, 235.

[8] See J. Stanley Friesen, *Missionary Responses to Tribal Religions at Edinburgh, 1910* (New York: Peter Lang, 1996).
[9] William Ernest Hocking (ed.), *Rethinking Missions: A Laymen's Inquiry after One Hundred Years* (New York and London: Harper & Brothers Publishers, 1932), 40.
[10] Veli-Matti Kärkäinen, *An Introduction to the Theology of Religions* (Downers Grove, IL: IVP, 2003), 181.
[11] Hendrik Kraemer, *The Christian Message in the Non-Christian World* (London: International Missionary Council, 1938), 102.
[12] Kraemer, *The Christian Message*, 104.
[13] Kraemer, *The Christian Message*, 134.
[14] Wesley Ariarajah, *Hindus and Christians: A Century of Protestant Thoughts* (Grand Rapids, MI: William B. Eerdmans Publishing Co., 1991), 66.
[15] O.V. Jathanna, *The Decisiveness of the Christ-event and the Universality of Christianity in a World of Religious Plurality* (Frankfurt: Peter Lang, 1981), 94.
[16] James A. Scherer, *Gospel, Church, & Kingdom: Comparative Studies in World Mission Theology* (Minneapolis, MN: Augsburg Publishing House), 17.
[17] C.F. Andrews quoted by T.V. Philip, *Edinburgh to Salvador: Twentieth Century Ecumenical Missiology* (Delhi: ISPCK, 1999), 194.
[18] Joe M. Thomas, 'Continuity, Discontinuity, and the Finality of Christ: A Theological Essay on the Thought of Lesslie Newbigin and Hendrik Kraemer', *Dharma Deepika: A South Asian Journal of Missiological Research* 29/1 (January – June, 2009), 28.
[19] See Stanley J. Samartha, *Between Two Cultures: Ecumenical Ministry in a Pluralist World* (Geneva: WCC, 1996), 38-75.
[20] See, *inter alia*, Paul F. Knitter, *Jesus and the Other Names: Christian Mission and Global Responsibility* (Maryknoll, NY: Orbis Books, 1996), 108-153; S. J. Samartha, *One Christ – Many Religions: Toward a Revised Christology* (Maryknoll, NY: Orbis Books, 1992), 162-175.
[21] Samartha, *One Christ – Many Religions*, 170.
[22] John Hick & Paul F. Knitter (eds), *The Myth of Christian Uniqueness: Toward a Pluralistic Theology of Religions* (Maryknoll, NY: Orbis Books, 1987), viii.
[23] World Council of Churches, 'Toward a Code of Conduct on Conversion' (draft), available at www.oikoumene.org (accessed August 5, 2009).
[24] John R.W. Stott, *Christian Mission in the Modern World* (Downers Grove: IVP, 1975), 58-81.
[25] See Timothy C. Tennent, *Christianity at the Religious Roundtable: Evangelicalism in Conversation with Hinduism, Buddhism, and Islam* (Grand Rapids, MI: Baker Academic, 2002).
[26] Kärkäinen, *An Introduction to the Theology of Religions*.
[27] See Amos Yong, *Discerning the Spirit(s): A Pentecostal-Charismatic Contribution to Christian Theology of Religions* (Sheffield: Sheffield Academic Press, 2000).
[28] See William Burrows (ed.), *Redemption and Dialogue: Reading* Redemptoris Missio *and Dialogue and Proclamation* (Maryknoll, NY: Orbis Books, 1994); John Paul II, *Redemptoris Missio* 'On the Permanent Validity of the Church's Missionary Mandate' (1990); Pontifical Council For Inter-Religious Dialogue, 'Dialogue and Proclamation: Reflection and Orientations on Interreligious Dialogue and the Proclamation of the Gospel of Jesus Christ' (1990). Documents available at www.vatican.va.

[29] Petros Vassiliadis, Niki Papageorgiou, George Kondortha & Nikos Dimitriadis, 'Mission among Other Faiths: An Orthodox Perspective', a position paper submitted to Study Group 2, Edinburgh 2010 (2009), available at www.edinburgh2010.org..
[30] The recent consultation on 'Christian mission among other faiths' at Bangalore repeatedly addresses liberation and fighting for justice (2.5.6) and violence (5.6) in the context of mission. 'Report cum Statement of the consultation at the United Theological College, Bangalore, India, 2009. Towards Edinburgh 2010. A Consultation on "Christian Mission among others Faiths"'. Papers available at www.edinburgh2010.org.
[31] J. Azumah, 'Christian Mission and Islam', position paper submitted to Study Group 2, Edinburgh 2010 (2009), 2-3, available at www.edinburgh2010.org.
[32] 'Report cum Statement, Bangalore', 8.
[33] D. B. Barrett *et al.*, 'Missiometrics 2008: Reality Checks for Christian World Communions', *International Bulletin of Missionary Research* 32 (2008), 27-30.
[34] The term 'transnational' names these movements which are crossing frontiers and cultures but are not global in the sense of being present everywhere. In the context of our theme 'transnational' applies especially to local ethnic-religious diaspora communities which are however in constant relation to their home communities. S.L. Pries, *Die Transnationalisierung der sozialen Welt. Sozialräume jenseits von Nationalgesellschaften* (Frankfurt/M.: Suhrkamp Verlag, 2009), 16. P. Aghamkar submitted a position paper on an Indian Christian attempt to relate to Indian migrants residing in the US by revisioning the Hindu Diwali festival. P. Aghamkar , 'A Christian Diwali: Contextualizing Witness as Celebration with the Hindu Community', paper submitted to Study Group 2, Edinburgh 2010 (2009), available at www.edinburgh2010.org.
[35] See Ole Skjerbaek Madsen, 'The Church's Encounter with New Spiritualities', a position paper for Study Group 2, Edinburgh 2010 (2009), available at www.edinburgh2010.org).
[36] Pries, *Transnationalisierung*, 29.
[37] T. Prill, *Global Mission on our Doorstep. Forced Migration and the Future of the Church* (Münster: Monsenstein & Vannerstadt, no year).
[38] The 'Report cum Statement, Bangalore' cautions against the mammonization of structures and relations (6) and greets chances to work together in issues like environmental issues or in fighting HIV/Aids (7).
[39] S. Randeria & A. Eckert (eds), *Vom Imperialismus zum Empire. Nicht-westliche Perspektiven auf Globalisierung* (Frankfurt: Suhrkamp Verlag, 2009).
[40] See Pontifical Council for Inter-Religious Dialogue and the Congregation for the Evangelization of Peoples, 'Dialogue and Proclamation' in Burrows, *Redemption and Mission*, 93-118, especially 104.
[41] See position papers for Study Group 2, Edinburgh 2010 on confessional approaches to mission among other faiths, available at www.edinburgh2010.org: Vassiliadis *et al.*, 'Mission Among Other Faiths. An Orthodox Perspective'; Harold A. Netland, 'Christian Mission among Other Faiths: The Evangelical Tradition', position paper submitted to Study Group 2, Edinburgh 2010 (2009), available at www.edinburgh2010.org.
[42] For some hints to reactions, see Azumah, 'Christian Mission and Islam', 4.
[43] See for instance, H. Ucko, 'Christian Mission among Other Faiths', against V.-M. Kärkkäinen, 'Theologies of Religions. A Position Paper', both papers submitted to Study Group 2, Edinburgh 2010 (2009), available at www.edinburgh2010.org.

[44] Jehu J. Hanciles, 'Migration and Mission: The Religious Significance of the North-South Divide', in Andrew Walls & Cathy Ross (eds.), *Mission in the Twenty-first Century: Exploring the Five Marks of Global Mission* (London: Darton, Longman and Todd, 2008), 118-29

[45] Prill, 'Global Mission', 32, 35.

[46] An estimated overall migration stock of 175 million in 2000 against a figure of 975 million alone suffering from hunger. See www.welthungerhilfe.de/hunger_spezial.html.

[47] An interesting example for a different approach to an originally indigenous religion by W. Abimbola, *Ifá Will Mend Our Broken World: Thoughts on Yoruba Religion and Culture in Africa and the Diaspora* (Roxbury, MA: Aim Books, 2003).

[48] See for instance, M. Vargas, 'A Neopentecostal Experience of Bolivian Aimara people', unpublished paper submitted to Study Group 2, Edinburgh 2010 (2009), available at www.edinburgh2010.org; or G. Chamorro, *Auf dem Weg zur Vollkommenheit. Theologie des Wortes unter den Guaraní in Süd-Amerika* (Exegese in unserer Zeit, 11), (Münster: LIT Verlag, 2003).

[49] See for example, Gary Bunt, *iMuslims: Rewiring the House of Islam* (Chapel Hill: University of North Carolina Press, 2009); J. Kwabena Asamoah-Gyadu, '"Get on the Internet!" Says the LORD': Religion, Cyberspace and Christianity in Contemporary Africa', *Studies in World Christianity* 13 (Dec 2007), 225-242; Kirsteen Kim, 'Ethereal Christianity: Reading Korean Mega-Church Websites', *Studies in World Christianity* 13 (Dec 2007), 208-224.

[50] Notto R. Thelle, 'Mission to Buddhists?', position paper, submitted to Study Group 2, Edinburgh 2010 (2009), 9, available at www.edinburgh2010.org.

[51] Darrell Guder, *The Continuing Conversion of the Church* (Grand Rapids, MI: Wm B. Eerdmans, 2000), 53-55.

[52] David J. Bosch, *Transforming Mission. Paradigm Shifts in Theology of Mission* (Maryknoll, NY: Orbis Books, 1991), 483-84.

[53] Walter Brueggemann, *The Covenanted Self: Explorations in Law and Covenant* (Minneapolis, MN: Augsburg Fortress, 1999), 1.

[54] Vassiliadis, 'Mission among Other Faiths'. Cf. also (Archbishop) Anastasios Yannoulatos, 'Problems and Prospects of Interreligious Dialogue: An Eastern Orthodox Perspective', *Ecumenical Review* 52/3 (July 2000), 351ff.

[55] Veli-Matti Karkkainen, 'Theologies of Religions'.

[56] 'Religious Plurality and Christian Self-understanding', preparatory document for the World Council Of Churches Assembly, Porto Alegre, 2006. See also Ucko, 'Christian Mission among Other Faiths'.

[57] World Council of Churches, *The San Antonio Report* (Geneva: World Council of Churches, 1990).

[58] Bosch, *Transforming Mission*, 1991, 488.

[59] WCC, *The San Antonio Report*.

[60] Lesslie Newbigin, *Foolishness to the Greeks* (Grand Rapids, MI: Wm B. Eerdmans, 1986), 21-41.

[61] Lesslie Newbigin, *The Gospel in a Pluralist Society* (Grand Rapids, MI: Wm B. Eerdmans, 1989).

[62] Kirsteen Kim, *The Holy Spirit in the World. A Global Conversation* (Maryknoll: Orbis, 2007), 51-52.

[63] Bosch, *Transforming Mission*, 485.

[64] Terrance L. Thiessen, *Who Can Be Saved? Reassessing Salvation in Christ and World Religions* (Downers Grove & Leicester: Inter-Varsity Press, 2004), 107-110.
[65] Lesslie Newbigin, *The Open Secret* (Grand Rapids, MI: Wm B. Eerdmans, 1978), 200.
[66] Newbigin, *The Open Secret*, 203-204.
[67] Clark H. Pinnock, *A Wideness in God's Mercy: The Finality of Jesus Christ in a World of Religions* (Grand Rapids, MI: Zondervan, 1992).
[68] Vassiliadis, 'Mission among Other Faiths'.
[69] Vatican II, *Lumen Gentium*, 'Dogmatic Constitution on the Church' (1963), §16. Available at www.vatican.va.
[70] Congregation for the Doctrine of the Faith, *Dominus Iesus* 'Declaration on the Unicity and Salvific Universality of Jesus Christ and the Church (2000), §12. Available at www.vatican.va.
[71] Pelikan, Jaroslav (ed.), *Luther's Works* (St Louis: Concordia, 1972), 25:181, quoted in Thiessen, *Who Can Be Saved?* 57.
[72] J.N.D. Anderson, *Christianity and Comparative Religion* (Downers Grove, IL: InterVarsity Press 1970).
[73] Harold A. Netland, 'Christian Mission among Other Faiths'. See also Timothy Tennent, *Theology in the Context of World Christianity* (Grand Rapids, MI: Zondervan, 2007).
[74] See also Alister McGrath, 'Evangelism and Apologetics' (2009), position paper submitted to Study Group 2, Edinburgh 2010, available at www.edinburgh2010.org.
[75] Alister McGrath, 'A Particularist View: A Post-Enlightenment Approach', in John Hick, *et al.* (eds), *More than One Way? Four Views on Salvation in a Pluralistic World* (Grand Rapids, MI: Zondervan Publishing House, 1995), 65-70.
[76] Vatican II awakened the Church to recognize the wider work of the Holy Spirit in the world, leading to ecumenical openness and restoration of relations with other Christian churches; the documents affirmed the 'pre-eminence' of the Spirit's role as the 'principal agent' of the church mission *ad gentes* (John Paul II, *Redemptoris Missio* 'On the Permanent Validity of the Church's Missionary Mandate' (1990), §§21-30. Available at www.vatican.va). Kim, *The Holy Spirit in the World*, 146-47.
[77] Works of two authors, Amos Yong and Kirsteen Kim, provide a sample of the new approach: Yong, *Discerning the Spirit(s)*; Kim, *The Holy Spirit.*
[78] Kim, *The Holy Spirit*, 140.
[79] Yong, *Discerning the Spirit(s).*
[80] The terms 'One Spirit' and 'many spirits' distinguish cosmological answers to the question of whether power is concentrated in a single Spirit or many spirits? Amos Yong's discerning of the work of God in 'one Spirit' and 'many spirits' cosmologies allows that the Holy Spirit need not be christologically perceived (Yong, *Discerning the Spirit(s)*, 68), but that criteria for discernment of the Spirit cannot be other than Christological (Yong, *Discerning the Spirit(s)*, 167). Yong's project fits with Ole Skjerbaek Madsen's investigation of new spiritualities and new religions, where followers have rejected a personal understanding of the Divine or Source. A point of contact in witness, both would agree, should be initially along the lines of what has been received and experienced as truth; the hope is also that the person might recognize the *logoi spermatikoi* within the new spirituality, at least God's Spirit being still present if only identified in the initial dialogue leading to Christ (Madsen, 'The Church's Encounter with New Spiritualities').

[81] Harold F. Miller, 'Closure for an African Century,' *Occasional Papers* 26 (An oral version of the paper was presented to the annual Mennonite retreat at Limuru, Kenya, Dec 1998); accessed online at: mcc.org/respub/occasional/26closure.html on August 27, 2009.
[82] Philip Jenkins, *The Next Christendom: The Coming of the Global Christianity* (New York/Oxford: Oxford University Press, 2001), 8.
[83] Harold W. Turner, 'The Religious Reactions of Primal Societies to Higher Cultures: A New Field in the History of Religions', a lecture at the Centre for the Study of New Religious Movements in Primal Religions, Birmingham, United Kingdom, 1986; Gillian M. Bediako, '"All Believers Are Primalists Underneath": Towards a New Appreciation of Old Testament Religion as Primal Religion', a lecture at Calvin College, Grand Rapids, MI, Michigan, July 2007; Andrew Walls, 'Primal Religious Traditions in Today's World', in *The Missionary Movement in Christian History: Studies in the Transmission of Faith* (Maryknoll, NY: Orbis Books, 1996), 119-39.
[84] Yong, *Discerning the Spirit(s)*, 300
[85] Harvey Cox, *Fire From Heaven: The Rise of Pentecostalism and the Reshaping of Religion in the Twenty-first Century* (London: Cassell, 1996).
[86] Kirsteen Kim, *The Holy Spirit*, 162, paraphrasing Amos Yong's investigation of a 'unity in diversity' theme in the account of Pentecost, describes how '…on that occasion the Holy Spirit is seen to be the ground of personal encounter and of personal identity in community, establishing eschatological reconciliation'. See Amos Yong, '"As the Spirit Gives Utterance": Pentecost, Intra-Christian Ecumenism and the Wider *Oikumene*', *International Review of Mission* 92/366 (Apr 2003), 299-314.
[87] Madsen, 'The Church's Encounter with New Spiritualities'.
[88] Marcelo Vargas describes indigenous Christian spirituality among the Aimara people in Bolivia as they are nurtured in the Power of God Church in his article, 'A Neopentecostal Experience of Bolivian Aimara People'.
[89] Vargas, 'A Neopentecostal Experience'.
[90] See *inter alia* Madsen, 'The Church's Encounter with New Spiritualities'.
[91] Walter Wink, *Engaging the Powers. Discernment and Resistance in a World of Domination* (Minneapolis, MN: Fortress Press, 1984); Kim, *The Holy Spirit*, 150-6.

Theme Three
Mission and Postmodernities

Preface

The Nordic Institute for Missiological and Ecumenical Research (NIME) agreed to take responsibility for the work on the theme of 'Mission and Postmodernities' for the Edinburgh 2010 study process. The purpose of this theme is to consider issues raised by the new phenomena of postmodernity in its various forms in North and South and its significance for mission. This was to involve an investigation of twenty-first century thought structures, religious beliefs and practices as well as ethical principles in a world of information technology. It also required consideration of the influence of postcolonialism, economic structures, internationalism and engagement (or disengagement) with institutions and particularly with institutional religion. And in addition the group was expected to discern commonalities and particularities in postmodern developments in different regions of the world. As a first stage of this study process, NIME devoted their Study Days in 2007 to the topic. The lectures and responses from the Study Days were published in *Swedish Missionary Themes*.[1] The Egede Institute, Oslo, Norway, was given the administrative responsibility for the further process, with its director Rolv Olsen (Lutheran) appointed coordinator.

Originally, it was intended to follow up the NIME Conference by organising a global consultation on the theme with 15-20 specialists taking part, and with a 'Core Group' editing the results. Due to limited economy and time restraints, this scheme was abandoned, and it was resolved rather to invite missiological scholars and practitioners worldwide to contribute academic articles, case studies, liturgies *et al* to an 'Edinburgh 2010 *Festschrift*', and give the Core Group the task of exploring the theme further on the basis of the received material. Revd Andrew Kirk (Anglican, UK), formerly Dean of the School of Mission, Selly Oak, Birmingham, accepted an invitation to be the group's convenor, together with Dr Kajsa Ahlstrand (Lutheran, Sweden), professor at the University of Uppsala, Sweden and chairperson of NIME, as co-convenor. In addition, the Core Group consisted of (in alphabetical order) Tania Petrova (Pentecostal, Bulgaria), Teresa Francesca Rossi (Roman Catholic, Pontifical University of St. Thomas Aquinas, Rome), J. Jayakiran Sebastian (Church of South India, Professor of Mission and Cultures, Lutheran Theological Seminary, Philadelphia), with the coordinator as secretary of the group.

The core group sent an invitation to a good number of people across the globe to contribute a written piece of work on any aspect of the theme of mission and postmodernities relevant to their particular context. Out of the articles submitted, all of which are published, with the author's permission, on the Edinburgh 2010 website, a representative number will be selected for publishing as a kind of *Festschrift* in honour of Edinburgh 2010. The group looked for contributions from people who share different perspectives on the subject: those attracted by postmodernity, those critical of it and those who may not believe that it exists at all; those who believe that it is relevant to mission, and those who do not; those who think it offers a positive environment for mission and those who believe it undermines mission. Participants to the process were at liberty to interpret the theme as they wish, on the grounds that there is no one way of understanding it. The group is interested in postmodernity's putative effect on mission spirituality, mission action and church life in all its dimensions and on how it may shape an understanding of mission and the nature of the Christian community. There is a particular interest in how postmodernities may influence the interpretation and application of the Bible as the normative story of God's mission in the world.

The group sought to solicit contributions that reflected different styles of writing: reflective essays that seek to grapple with theoretical constructs from an historical, philosophical, theological or human sciences perspective; presentations in the form of case-studies, reports of action groups, conversations about contemporary modes of liturgical life, and others that will emphasise the place and influence of the arts in relation to the theme. The emphasis desired was that of creative engagement, after the analysis and critique of postmodernities had been achieved. Hence, the letter of invitation asked the recipients to bear in mind that the intended outcome of all the study-groups was to provide rich material for thought and action, not so much for the academy as for 'grass-roots' Christian communities in their mission calling. For this reason the language and structure of the essays should reflect the need to communicate with non-specialised audiences. The overall objective was to call for a renewed understanding of mission and renewed ways of being in mission that address in concrete ways the urgent issues of concrete situations.

The core group met for initial deliberations during the 2008 International Association of Mission Studies (IAMS) Conference in Balatonfüred, Hungary, and convened in Prague from 22-26 June 2009 to assess the contributions received so far and to prepare the statement of the group. Kirk Sandvig (Lutheran, USA, and doctoral student at the University of Edinburgh), the Edinburgh 2010 Youth Coordinator, also participated in the Prague conference. Sadly, due to visa problems, Sebastian was prevented from attending.

The core group was intended to be as representative as possible of the worldwide church, in gender, age, ethnic background, denominational affiliation and geographical spread. In this, we did not entirely succeed. European nations are heavily over-represented. We acknowledge this as a serious shortcoming. Two things, however, may be said to mitigate this unwanted bias. Firstly, the problem is not so much the presence of Scandinavians and other Westerners, but rather the relative paucity of voices from the global South. Secondly, it may be that the challenge of postmodernities is felt more strongly and perceived as more urgent in the

Western world than in societies where the impact of modernity has been less thorough. Nevertheless, it cannot be denied that the imbalance in core group membership as well as in the sample of contributions received constitutes a weakness. It is to be hoped that the bias will be counterbalanced by other voices taking part in the continued conversation.

1 Introduction: The Process

What is meant by postmodernities, and where is the relevance for Christian mission? Isn't postmodernity rather a matter of architecture and philosophy; a game with words in academic circles, having little or no relation to the actual life of the Christian church? Also, are not the concepts and tenets of postmodernities inevitably at odds with the church, negating the validity of its mission – or of any mission at all – leaving Christians with the option of caving in to its demands or of firmly rejecting its tenets? Or does a possibility remain for constructive interaction between mission and postmodernities? Does postmodernity perhaps offer some new and valuable insights, viewpoints and lessons; might its approaches even enhance the understanding and practice of Christian mission?

The study theme with the title 'Mission and Postmodernities' deals with issues raised by the new phenomenon of postmodernity and their significance for mission. This involves an investigation of twenty-first century thought structures and institutions, the impact of information technology, religious and ideological beliefs and practices and ethical values. It requires consideration of the influence of postcolonial realities, economic structures, globalization and engagement (or disengagement) with institutions, and particularly with institutional religion; it should also try to discern commonalties and particularities in postmodern developments in different regions of the world. Eight so-called 'key issues and questions' were defined at the outset (see Appendix I). While the received contributions can be seen to directly address these questions only to a very limited degree, they still formed a framework for the discussion. The purpose of this survey is to try to point towards some tentative answers to these issues and to the specific questions suggested for the study.

In the following, we will first try to delineate how we understand the term 'postmodernities' and give an indication of important features and challenges. From there, we will give a brief survey of salient points in the historical development since Edinburgh 1910. From the solicited material we will describe different ways of engaging with the subject, including case studies, and show examples of attempts at creative translations of the gospel in the contexts in question. Finally, we will try to indicate some implications for contemporary mission and suggest some key priorities. In general, but not in every particular, the report commands the assent of the group.

2 Mission and Postmodernities: Our Understanding

What is meant by 'mission' and by 'postmodernity/ies'? The terms are complex in nature and might be understood in different ways. The core group did not seek to impose a uniform understanding of the terms on the contributors or writers. Nevertheless, it found it necessary to try to reach some common ground on how to understand the concepts, in order to avoid misunderstandings. The following is not intended to be read as if it represented an exhaustive definition or the final word on the subject; it is a summary of how the group understood and approached the matters at hand in this particular context.[2]

2.1 Postmodernism and postmodernity/ies

The term 'postmodernities' is an ambiguous and elusive concept, in this perhaps mirroring the nature of what it is used to describe. The ambiguity is underscored by the lack of consensus on which term it is proper to use: should we talk of 'postmodernity', or does the multifaceted nature of the phenomenon demand the use of the plural, 'postmodernities', or perhaps it is better simply to use 'postmodernism'? Admittedly such linguistic questions have their value, and may sometimes be crucial, but this is not the place for entering into the matter in depth. For our purposes here, a brief survey of the background of the term, together with the rationale for our choice of usage, should suffice.

By using the prefix 'post-', it is understood that postmodernity relates to and follows in the wake of modernity, either as a further development of or as a reaction against it. Contrary to what one might expect, the origin of the concept is to be found, not within the realm of philosophy, but rather in the field of architecture. Postmodernism is the revolt against the constraints of modernism with its focus on functionalism and stylicism, signalling the return of wit, ornamentation and the combination of elements that seemingly do not fit together, in a way that could often be described as provocative, and at times even perceived as outrageous.[3] Later, the term was adopted by philosophers and other academics, and used to characterize a broader cultural trend, a paradigm shift caused by the apparent loss of trust in, in some instances perhaps even the collapse of, modernity in terms of an overrated confidence in the power of reason and grand, objective narratives, purporting to be all-inclusive explanations of reality.

As to the terms 'postmodernism', 'postmodernity' and 'postmodernities', they basically refer to the same general trend and could thus be used interchangeably. However, in order to obtain more precision, we recommend that two different main aspects of the trend be distinguished. Thus, we suggest 'postmodernism' be used to signify the original sphere of architecture, and by extension, the different fields of art, and reserve 'postmodernity' for use within areas such as philosophy, the political/social sphere and ethical matters, such as human rights, denoting a way of thought, practice and existential orientation.

Further, facing the multifaceted nature of postmodernity as it appears in its manifold contexts, and realising that it might be difficult to determine whether it is advisable to speak of postmodernities or perhaps rather merely of different degrees of postmodernity, we suggest differentiating between speaking of 'postmodernity' as a general cultural trend and 'postmodernities' as the various expressions of that trend. In this, we believe that we also reflect the deep scepticism towards single entities and single answers inherent in the whole idea of postmodern existence.

2.2 Modernity and postmodernity

Postmodernism in the arts and postmodernity as a philosophical and cultural term signify a reaction against, and alternative to, modernity and its tenets. The term 'modernity' is used to denote the period of history beginning, roughly speaking, with 'the Enlightenment', the industrial revolution and European colonialism, and is characterized by belief in the power of reason, progress and the potential of the scientific method to solve hitherto intractable human dilemmas. Typical for modernity is the grand narrative, a project designed to convince everyone of the truth of a particular vision or theory about historical development, as for example the cases of the Social Darwinist belief in the superiority of the white race, the nation state as the sole legitimate foundation for a political framework, Liberalism, Communism or Nazism as superior political ideologies, Deism or Atheism as the most rational worldview, or perhaps even the assumptions of some variations of Christian mission that the Christian faith is the most advanced creed and has produced the highest civilisation so it needs to be spread throughout the whole world. The catastrophic political events of the twentieth century, predominately the two World Wars, shattered Western optimism and self-confidence, and thus the pillars of modernity were shaken. The abuse of science and reason, not to mention the destructive force of the predominant ideologies, left in their wake a profound distrust towards grand, universal solutions.

Together with this, we witness a crisis of authority, a profound suspicion of all *a priori* claims to truth and knowledge, a disillusionment towards the grand narratives of modernity. In postmodernity, everybody has a voice; there is not necessarily any 'right' or 'wrong' voice; it all depends on the point of view. Thus everybody contributes, and everybody is free to pick what is preferred from the patchwork of many voices; eclecticism is fundamental to postmodernities. Power and the wielders of power are likewise viewed with suspicion, as are any authoritarian and hierarchical structures. In view of this inherent suspicion towards power and wielders of power, postmodernity may be described as a subaltern approach. In many ways, although limited to affluent society, postmodernity represents the voice of marginalized people insisting on equal treatment, on their angle of approach and point of view being as valid as those traditionally favoured.

Briefly, modernity is characterized by belief in the power of rationality and scientific ingenuity to solve human problems. Therefore it engenders optimism about the future. Admittedly, there might be occasional setbacks, but eventually, they will be overcome. A new day is always dawning; the best is yet to come. In contrast, postmodernities conceive of change without any necessary progress, having no belief that the future will be better than the present. Unlike modernist optimists, somebody who has imbibed postmodernity does not regard change as good or bad in itself – it is just the way it is.

While authority is taken for granted in pre-modern societies, and supported by the grand narratives of modernity, in postmodernity authority is fragmented, should be debated and probably be challenged. As a result of the manifold abuses of power, the whole concept of power and obedience is made problematical. Thus, postmodernity in the West appears on the one hand to be a revolt against modernity. On the other hand, it may appear to form a kind of symbiosis with that which it critiques, as its premises do not allow it to posit a clear alternative. Thus, a number of observers characterize the change of mood as 'late modernity'.

Two previous movements, romanticism and existentialism, both highly critical towards modernity, have had a profound influence on postmodernity. The first in relativizing the excessive emphasis on the rational part of human nature, and by exploring the deep currents of the emotions and the feelings; the second, in stressing the priority of becoming over being, and therefore the inevitability of rejecting the patterns of life that others have chosen for us and choosing only those which are completely authentic for us. Likewise, postmodernity relies more on personal experience than on external authority, on emotional instincts than on doctrine. It does not believe in a static given-ness to life, and is therefore always exploring and experimenting with new forms of living.

2.3 Salient characteristics of postmodernity

Postmodernity is a fluid, impressionistic concept; it is not 'cut and dried'. What is characteristic for one brand of postmodernity may be of less relevance for others. This notwithstanding, we find certain core themes and values common to the various impressions. For example, plurality, construction and change are pivotal. A multitude of cultural, linguistic, political, religious and other options exist simultaneously, and the individual may choose the understanding of things and the way of life as preferred at the moment. The world is constantly changing; reality is not so much given as constantly being (re)negotiated. Hence, identity is liquid, not static. Postmodernity is a subjective, relational and dialectical approach to life; rather than seeking objective truth outside of ourselves, emphasis is given to relationships with 'the other'.

Contextuality is pivotal to postmodernities. Notions of objectivity and universality are frowned upon; the subjectivity and conditioned-ness of all experiences and opinions are emphasised: 'Where you stand depends on where you sit'. The answers to questions of correct or false, right or wrong depend on the perspective, the context, and therefore will always be partial and biased. Although it might be logical to talk of postmodernity as a general cultural trend, in view of the multifaceted nature of the phenomenon and in accordance with postmodern scepticism towards singular entities, we find it equally natural to speak of postmodernities. If it is possible to speak of the existence of multiple, or multifaceted, modernities, there should be no insurmountable obstacle to the concept of multiple postmodernities. In a postmodern environment, it is natural to use both the singular and the plural. There will be differences of opinion, however, as to whether postmodernity really is a new phenomenon, and just how countercultural it is. Is it not, in reality, just another part of the tradition of revolt against the excessive pretensions of those who have put so much emphasis on reason as a neutral tool for understanding existence that they have ignored other, more fundamental aspects of human experience?

The postmodern trend is no marginal phenomenon, not something happening on the fringe of society. Rather, it is penetrating whole cultures, a paradigm shift consciously and subconsciously transforming commonly accepted habits, notions and patterns of thought in its wake. Thus, one need not consciously consider oneself postmodern to be deeply influenced by its views and values. Even the concept of time and history has been vastly altered in postmodernity, perhaps as fundamentally as with the outset of modernity. In pre-modern societies, time was viewed primarily in the context of the religious belief in the far more important horizon of eternity and in the context of the seasons, so vital to an agrarian society, thus emphasising its circular or repetitive nature. This perspective tended to stress a golden age in the past, so that any change needed to be the restoration of the same. Modernity, on the other hand, instituted a shift against tradition, a profound transformation in the way people were regarding time and space. It is said that modernity and the Enlightenment, as its intellectual expression, invented the concept of history, so that from then on people conceived of the past as actually being fundamentally different from the present and the future. To the modern mind, time moves in a unilateral direction, inexorably and gloriously moving from past to the present and further on towards the future. This march of time frequently is perceived as moving dialectically through historical epochs. Hegel and Marx were two notable examples of those who built systems around the notion of epochs negating each other in a process of ever higher (or more progressive) syntheses, until an ultimate synthesis was achieved, when history marked by contradictions would end.

While pre-modern humans believed in authority and tradition, and modern people put their trust in reason and objective, scientific truth, the postmodern tendency is to rely on the subjective emotions and experiences. Thus, simplified, when being asked how they know the truth, pre-moderns would answer 'I've been told'; moderns reply 'I think'; while postmoderns would say

'I feel'. From this comes postmodernity's reluctance towards any notion of preferred views or angles of approach: What makes your point of view more valid than mine? Rather than listening to and relying on specialists, humbly taking notes, it allows many voices to speak, challenging hierarchical truths. Similarly, the postmodern approach to tradition is eclectic. Of the many options available, one chooses what best suits the situation. Faithfulness towards tradition is of less importance. So is inner consistency; even apparently contradictory positions may be reconciled and combined, as with Christians believing in the Hindu doctrine of reincarnation. Even within aesthetics, there is the same revolt against elitism. With postmodernity comes a breakdown of the barrier between 'high' and 'popular' art; what is valuable is entirely up to the subject. Thus, postmodernity may be said to have truly taken the slogan 'beauty is in the eye of the beholder' to heart.

Postmodernity also marks a shift in how we view the determining factors of our existence, such as the notions of ultimate authority and the question of who is 'the author of life'. In pre-modern society, God, the gods or the spirits, were the author of life, and religion and religious authorities were crucial in transmitting the divine will and the response of the faithful. In modernity the pride of place was taken over by universal truths, which were deducible from reasoning about the forces of nature or the flow of history. Religion was required by society to conform to the demands of established truth or else be relegated to the private sphere, as revelation was perceived to be inferior to reason. In postmodernity, however, the individual is the author of his or her own life. Authority rests no longer outside of one's reach, with God or with the forces of nature, but inside, and woe to those who presume to override an individual's right to authorship. But the individual's 'I' is not immediately given. The 'I' is constructed; the author of the subject is re-authored all the time by the same subject. Contrary to modernity, such an authorship may easily embrace the tenets of revelation and/or tradition. However, unlike an unquestioning acceptance of these sources of knowledge in pre-modernity, in postmodernity this is entirely dependent on the will of the author.

2.4 Limitations of postmodernity

Some will question, however, not only whether we have truly entered a postmodern society, but whether our current state is postmodern or maybe even post-postmodern. Perhaps, postmodernity ended on 11 September 2001 (9/11)? The signs pointing towards religious awakening might also be taken to imply that what we now witness is a post-postmodern return to traditional views and values. Even if such an analysis is correct, however, it only captures part of the overall picture. The return to traditional values, even to what often is labelled as 'fundamentalist' opinions and practices, is a matter of choice, a conscious – or subconscious – rejection of dominant notions and habits, and as such in itself a postmodern reaction. Other external factors, notably the effects of climate change and the ongoing, periodic crises in the world economic system influence the way we think of the world and ourselves. The acceptance of the concept of having moved into a post-postmodern era largely depends on our understanding of postmodernity, whether the postmodern is seen as opposite to, or at least a reaction to, the modern, or basically as a continuation of the same.

As far as we can see, postmodernities are hardly resonating with people living in poverty. Their appeal seems largely limited to the more affluent and urbanized segments of affluent societies. The reason behind this may be that postmodernity is connected with a shift in capitalist production, from an emphasis on the industrial output of goods designed to meet real needs to the production of services for those who can afford to pay for them. Having this in mind, it is hardly surprising to find neo-Marxists such as Habermas and Eagleson among the strongest critics of postmodernity. So, there are serious limits to the postmodern account of reality. Most people accept the view of meteorologists regarding climate change, regardless of how they *feel* about it, economic crises cannot just be *negotiated* away, and authoritarian fundamentalist religious beliefs have not disappeared because some declare that we are now living after modernity. Postmodern, modern and pre-modern realities are not just shackles to be cast off at leisure. To cite Richard Dawkins' memorable aphorism, 'show me a cultural relativist at 30,000 feet and I'll show you a hypocrite.'[4]

3 Case Studies

Here, eight of the contributions received by the study group are given a brief survey, indicating possible answers to at least some of the initially stated 'key issues and questions'. It should be kept in mind, however, that each of the articles in question may address more than one of the given topics, and that the submitted reviews give a far from exhaustive indication of the contents of the papers.[5]

Several authors explore ways in which postmodernity affects understandings of the basis of Christian faith, and hence of Christian mission, addressing these particularly in and from Europe.

Jan-Olav Henriksen[6] reflects on challenges to churches in the northern hemisphere, advising an accommodationist rather than a confrontational approach. Although he writes with a special view to the Scandinavian context, his analysis and reasoning is readily translatable to other contexts. On the other hand, **Andrew Kirk**[7] advises that it is part of the study of mission to take note in any and every situation of the counter-cultural force of the gospel. The latter has its own criteria for deciding the nature and extent of its contextual relevance; passing cultural trends or fashions should never determine its ultimate validity and cogency.

Jayakiran Sebastian[8] follows up Henriksen's essay by reflecting on challenges to churches on the Indian subcontinent. Sebastian points out that the concept of *missio Dei* has been a dominant missiological paradigm for several decades and has come to govern missiological thinking and theological self-understanding. In this sense it has functioned as an underlying motif over against which all discussion of missiology has had to contend. His contribution questions this way of thinking and posits an understanding of mission as mission 'to' God which opens up new and fresh ways of thinking, belief, and praxis.

Postmodern patterns of community, including virtual communities on the internet, are discussed in a manner fitting to the subject. Unlike the more academic character of the majority of the contributions, **Andrew Jones**[9] submitted a blog on the constructive aspects of the virtual church, arguing that the vital question is not whether virtual communities are true churches, but how the church may utilise the possibilities of the internet to fulfil its mission. Jones emphasises that virtual is not unreal, that the virtual merely has not yet actualized its potential, that the church by its very nature is a virtual community, awaiting its consummation in the New Jerusalem. He refers to how, in the letter to the Hebrews, the visible is portrayed as being preceded and legitimized by the invisible, not the other way around.

The effects of postmodernity on Christian mission and the implications for Christian mission are discussed by two German scholars with respect to the Central European situation, and are amplified with reflections from a Russian and a Chinese perspective.

Michael Herbst[10] reflects on the ultra-secular condition of the 'post-*Volkskirche*' situation[11] in the Eastern German province of Pomerania, in the former German Democratic Republic (GDR). His findings are relevant for large parts of Central and Eastern Europe, for example Bulgaria and the Czech Republic. Although the context might be described as post-socialist or ultra-secular rather than postmodern, his description and analysis of people who 'have forgotten that they have forgotten God' sounds familiar at least to Scandinavians, almost as an eerie prophecy of a not-too-distant future. Even in such ultra-secular, or perhaps post-secular, contexts, people may be looking for wider reality; though, as a rising interest in the paranormal shows, a re-enchantment of the world may indeed be taking place. Although people do not trust the institutions, some connection with the past is still sought for; church buildings are still needed, their connection with the transcendent cherished. A postmodern society, in so far as it exists, is a fragmented society. Perhaps, we are witnessing simultaneously a search for the transcendent and a memory loss, a society that is definitely not at ease with itself.

The realisation that Europe can no more be regarded as Christian territory forms the starting point of the investigation of **Friedemann Walldorf**[12] into missiological models for postmodern Europe. He maintains that churches need to overcome their Eurocentric perspective, viewing their task through the lens of *missio Dei* and their sister churches in the global South, exploring the missiological quest for understanding and Christian revival in contemporary Europe. Three possible missiological models are introduced: the inculturational model, regarding the church as the soul of Europe; the dialogical model, endeavouring to discover God in Europe; and the translation model, searching for ways to share the gospel with today's Europeans. Considering the claims of reconciled diversity, regionalization and critical postmodernism, and acknowledging the need to appreciate perspectivity and the creativity of human knowledge, while admitting the existence of universally valid expressions of empirical reality and theological truth, Walldorf concludes that from an Evangelical perspective due concern must be taken both to context, text and community. Finally, he claims that Europeans have not abandoned the search for truth for the experience of relationships, but that they seek relationships *and* a truth to carry those.

Speaking from a Chinese perspective, **Jieren Li**[13] points out that, although postmodernity is rooted in Western post-industrial society, it might still be relevant for the Third World. He starts from a description of the contemporary Chinese church landscape with three main currents: First, institutional Christianity – a post-denominational body in a situation that might be seen as pre-denominational. Second, autonomous Christianity, frowned upon by the authorities but no real threat to society. And third, intellectual Christianity – scholars fascinated by Christian thinking, but with virtually no contact with organised church. He goes on to discuss the implications for mission in postmodern China, analysing the strengths and weaknesses of various approaches.

Olga Zaprometova,[14] writing from a Russian perspective, gives a creative response to the question of emotions and their potential as a way towards seeking union between Christians. While centuries of different doctrines and practices constitute formidable obstacles on the way towards communion, through mutual recognition of the traditions and the imperatives imposed on Christians from the contemporary world, she suggests ways by which some degree of understanding and cooperation can be achieved. No Christian tradition is sufficient by itself; encounters between the 'enthusiasm' of Pentecostals and the struggle for *theosis* and salvation of the Orthodox may prove fruitful for both parts, as well as the other Christian denominations.

Challenges related to telling the biblical story to those who embrace postmodern relativism and are suspicious of all metanarratives are addressed from two widely different perspectives.

David Kettle[15] gives an original, interdisciplinary approach to the question of hope, giving much food for thought, although it might be argued that the context of his analysis is as much modern as postmodern. Kettle maintains that one major shortcoming of postmodernity is its lack of hope. Hope is not the same as optimism; one of the main differences being that it is open to the grounds of despair, while, unlike pessimism, facing them without despairing. Western culture, though, is heavily infested by narcissism, turning away from the world in despair, constructing a 'self' to become the focus of life. For the church to meaningfully communicate the gospel of hope in a narcissistic culture, it needs to be characterized by authentic spirituality, hospitality, participation, and prophecy.

Speaking in a sub-Saharan African context, **Jim Harries**[16] discusses challenges to Bible translation, creatively using mathematical language to that purpose. His essay points to the crucial topic of the role of language within postmodernity, as well as suggesting that witchcraft and magic are issues well worthy of further consideration, even in a postmodern European context.

4 Key Questions

The following issues and questions relating to mission in postmodernity have been raised by these papers and in group consultations.

4.1 Hope

Is hope a key category for Christians in mission? If so, how do Christians live out hope, in communities as well as individuals? Facing poverty, the environmental crisis and similar, how may hope become more than an empty sounding slogan? How is hope in the Christian sense inserted into cultural contexts? Is it valid to claim that hope is absent from postmodern worldviews, as it emphasises change without progress? If not, where is the element of hope in postmodernities?

4.2 Otherness

Postmodernity may have contributed to contemporary awareness of otherness. There is a danger, however, that the encounter with the other leads to fear of the otherness of the other, rather than to enhanced understanding. Actually, this otherness may be experienced even concerning oneself. When relations with the other often fail, how should we respond to the other and overcome the fear of the other? Through recent communication developments, such as Facebook, virtual communities are created, simultaneously providing closeness and distance. There is a certain ambiguity in such relations, mirroring the mobility of current society, relations becoming virtual, but still real. May this provide means to overcome obstacles in facing the other? Virtual churches appear, even to the point of virtual eucharist, as for instance at 'Post the Host'. [17] Are virtual communities a viable alternative to traditional congregations, or should bodily presence still be regarded as indispensible for worship?

4.3 Believing and belonging

In recent years a good deal of sociological research has been done, most notably by Grace Davie, on the relationship of the general populace of post-Christian countries to the churches.[18] Some have proposed that the position of the majority is that they still believe in the essentials of the faith, but do not find it necessary to belong to the institutional structures of religion. Others, particularly in those parts of Europe where the majority are still baptised in infancy and, perhaps, contribute to taxes that go to the churches, suggest that the majority still belong to the institution in a sense, but do not really believe in the fundamental claims of the gospel as proclaimed by the churches. In the first case, it can be said that they believe without belonging; in the second case, that they belong without believing. In both cases, perhaps, underlying postmodern attitudes are being displayed in relation to religion.

4.4 Conversion in a postmodern context

Although the possibility, and even legitimacy, of converting others is being questioned and even denied, it remains entirely possible to convert, perhaps even to make more radical conversions in a postmodern climate than previously. One of our group members had encountered and related one such conversion story: a journey from white, male Baptist pastor to veiled Muslim woman. Conversions are not necessarily regarded as conclusive, for it is quite possible to convert several times.

4.5 Ethical values and rights in a relativistic culture

Current secular Western cultures are a curious mixture of the absolute and the relative. On the one hand, some people go beyond the valid, if sometimes ambiguous, notion of human rights, by seeking to impose through legislation certain 'correct' views, currently held by strong lobbying groups, of what constitutes acceptable and unacceptable human behaviour. Thus, there is pending in some societies legislation that would make the criticism of different lifestyles and beliefs into the offence of harassment. At the same time, the right of religious believers to dissent from certain practices on the grounds of conscience is being denied. In this way, both freedom of religion and freedom of speech, two fundamental rights upheld in the Universal Declaration of Human Rights, are in danger of being taken away. The notion of being abused or oppressed is prevalent in postmodernity. The question remains, though, who determines whether abuse has taken place or not, and by which criteria? The fact that something is perceived by someone or some group as abusive does not make it abusive. The claim of being abused might it itself be the cause for abuse. Accusations of oppression can be made into a tool for oppression. So, the suspicion of an abuse of power or privilege ought not to lead to uncritical acceptance of any protest. On the other hand, discrimination on the grounds of belief, as well as ethnic identity, gender and so on, is considered a grave assault on individual liberty; whilst tolerance of others' beliefs and practices is exalted into one of the supreme virtues of a liberal society. It is almost inevitable that in societies that have lost any solid grounds for asserting particular ethical values there should be so much ambiguity and confusion. At one and the same time, absolute ethical norms are being both affirmed and denied. Christians are called to witness to truth, as revealed in Jesus Christ, within the turmoil and muddle of inconsistent ethical stances and contradictory interpretations of human rights.

5 Mission in Relation to Postmodernity

To claim that the concept and practice of mission has changed dramatically in the last decades is hardly controversial. More arguable is whether this has taken place as a result of postmodernity, or just happens to have occurred in parallel with its emergence, due to other reasons, to be found in the broader context of recent history. The familiar stereotypical image of Western Christian mission as an imperialistic, colonial enterprise, although still embarrassingly accurate at times, is less typical than often alleged. With some few, if notorious, current exceptions, the image fits poorly with the actual reality of mission, which is marked by a far more humble and egalitarian approach. Today, Western mission may actually be accused of having gone so far in the opposite direction, in its shift from proclamation to dialogue and from evangelism to witness, that the message has been diluted and mission become mute.

Christian mission is no longer predominantly Western. The churches of the global South, now representing the overwhelming majority among the world's Christians, have to a large extent taken over the missionary mantle. Korean, Brazilian and Nigerian missions, for example, reveal a confidence the West may have lost, although it might be argued that their mission practice exhibits some of the alleged imperialistic traits shown by Westerners in history. One major difference, though, is that their mission is less likely to be backed or accompanied by overt political motivations or influence. Thus, although sentiments, vocabulary and methods may be similar, one of the key characteristics of imperialistic mission is largely absent.

In this context, the group discussed the following points regarding mission in postmodernity.[19]

5.1 Truth and evangelism

Mission in the New Testament may be summarised as movement and mandate. In the words of Remi Emiel Hoeckman, O.P.:

> Basically, Christian mission is a movement – not wild and uncontrolled but, paradoxical as it may sound, a movement anchored in love, originated in love, originating love. Christian mission is love... seeking. It is movement anchored in the mystery of God creating and in the mystery of God redeeming, God reaching out to send (Wisdom 11:12; 1 Tim 2:4).
>
> Christian movement is movement anchored indeed in the mission of Jesus, who totally transcends the Old Testament missionary horizon. Jesus did not sit at the gate of the temple like the prophet, waiting for the people to come to hear his message. Nor did he stay in the thinly-populated regions of the river Jordan like the Baptist. No, he moved across the length and breadth of Palestine – always on his way. 'Let us move on to the neighbouring villages so that I may proclaim the good news there also. That is what I have come to do' (Mark 1:38). This purposeful movement is particularly clear in Luke's gospel, where through ten chapters Jesus is quite ostensibly on his way to Jerusalem (9:51 – 19:41).

> Geographically, Jesus was moving towards Jerusalem, but missiologically speaking he was on his way to all men, for it was on the cross that his blood would be poured out for salvation of many, i.e. of all.[20]

Such an understanding of mission may be said to show a basic commonality with postmodernities in their emphasis on flexibility and movement. Still, Christian mission is also concerned with passing on the Christian tradition, something less appreciated in postmodernities. Several influential theological trends reveal close affinities with postmodernity. Whereas historical Christianity, not least in its Lutheran version, has put much emphasis on doctrinal questions, newer theological thanking and practice tends towards focus on practice and downplays the importance of doctrinal differences. Even when contemplating the multifaceted nature of Christianity, the tendency often is to leave doctrine aside and focus on event and experience.

During the last decades, the church in the West has undergone a significant shift towards what might be termed a 'softer' Christianity, emphasising life and ethics rather than faith and doctrine. Although far from being a uniform trend, one may easily spot, especially in traditional Protestant churches, a tendency towards downplaying, ignoring or even outrightly rejecting the traditional concept of eternal damnation in hell, focusing less on proclamation than on co-existence and dialogue, moving from traditional exclusivist positions towards more inclusivity or even pluralist notions of the relation between Christianity and other religions and worldviews. Such a shift is clearly in tune with postmodern subjectivity and scepticism towards established truth.

Is it possible, though, to continue affirming belief in the existence of absolute truth, pivotal not only to historical Christianity, but possibly to most religions, and simultaneously to acknowledge the postmodern claim that it is inherently impossible in all human striving to obtain this truth? One biblical icon that may prove helpful, indeed to have a special affinity with a postmodern setting, is Paul's assertion that now we can only see in a glass darkly (1 Cor 13:9-13). The face when seen reflected in a hammered copper plate (the nature of the mirrors of that time) is real, but the reflection is distorted and at times almost unrecognisable. Reality is real, but our perceptions are always limited, fragmented and often even misleading. In a similar vein, the Buddha is credited with having said that his teaching is like a finger pointing towards the moon; it is not the moon itself.

Many contemporary societies witness to the proliferation of different messages, propaganda and publicity within the media; and then there is the ubiquitous presence of the worldwide web. This diversity reflects in part a deep distrust in the hegemonic aspiration of any one message that claims exclusivity or superior knowledge. There is a real problem with truth claims as a starting-point for conversation and a much greater preference for a mutual dialogue in which the participants start out to search together for truth. This climate of opinion has undoubtedly affected Christian mission, with a number of leading

Christians in the West, and elsewhere, saying that evangelism in the sense of proclamation is no longer a legitimate activity, only dialogue in which each side, as an equal partner, listens to the beliefs and values of the other, with the hope of resolving misunderstandings and conflict and working together for commonly shared social goals.

Nevertheless, the judgements we make on others' beliefs are made on the basis of our beliefs. This is as much the case within postmodernity as anywhere else. Christian postmoderns, however, have shifted the emphasis away from belief and propositional truths towards the aesthetic and empirical dimensions of Christianity. The truth claims of Christianity may be perceived as less important, and consequently given less concern, than beauty of thought in an open theological process, and the visceral impact that may be made by high quality music and other art forms. Accordingly, the presence of other religions is not perceived as a theological problem. The postmodern attitude is that others have the same right to choose their way as I have to choose to mine, and their choice may be as honest and relevant for them as mine is to me.

It is important to point out that a critique and rejection of others' beliefs need not be disrespectful. On the contrary, provided that the critique is done in a sensitive and considerate way, not deteriorating into personal attacks, by disagreeing with someone and taking the trouble to point out why something should be considered mistaken, the other is acknowledged as an equal, responsible like me for his or her acts and opinions and their consequences. One corollary to this is that Christian mission must be performed in humility, equality and mutuality, values that are highly appreciated in postmodernity.

5.2 Salvation and the church

Is it possible still to adhere to the traditional notion of *extra ecclesiam nulla salus* ('outside the church there is no salvation') – a concept diametrically opposite to current attitudes and a postmodern worldview, because it is seen as unfair and illogical? The fear of being unpopular should not prevent the church from adhering to its beliefs. It is highly questionable, though, whether common perceptions of the slogan really are in tune with biblical understandings. It is arguable that the relation between church membership and salvation is hardly an issue in the New Testament. As is natural with emerging movements, the organisational structure of the church in New Testament times is still fluid; there is not even yet a clearly defined borderline between Jews and Christians. Perhaps postmodernity, with its emphasis on life and experience rather than on structures and membership, is in many ways closer to New Testament ecclesiology than what can be said of some of the more traditional Christian positions?

What definitely is an issue in the New Testament, however, is the relation between baptism, faith and salvation. The normal way of being a Christian is in and through the church; the prescribed way to salvation is through faith and baptism. That does not necessarily imply, however, that no other options exist.

Admittedly, the church is frequently described as the body of Christ. Still, it is not necessary to equate Christ with the earthly church; the weeds are to be allowed to grow alongside the wheat. The church is not only a gathering of likeminded people, but the communion of saints who are also sinners. Thus, being a Christian is not a solitary venture, involving me and my God only. To belong to the church is a necessary part of being a Christian. From a theological point of view, I did not choose to be a member of the church. Rather, by choosing Christ, I accept that Christ chose me to be part of his body. The church is a family, comprising all who belong to Christ, not a club.

The parish church, all its limitations and contradictions notwithstanding, at its best still reflects the nature of church, as a family, a community; a fellowship I do not choose myself, but nevertheless belong to, regardless of my feelings at any given moment, not depending on my ability to conceive of its being the case, welcoming me with all my shortcomings and providing a haven, a training ground and a lifelong partnership. The church originated in pre-modern times, and most churches have had problems in coming to terms with modernity. Pentecostalism, on the contrary, although having strong pre-modern characteristics, might be said to be in part a postmodern phenomenon, insofar as it has existed on the fringe of modernity, frowned upon by the established church as well as secular society. Nevertheless, it proved adaptable, not the least due to its fluid or plastic nature, antedating the whole discussion around postmodernities. It may, therefore, be more successful than most churches in addressing postmodern concerns.

One of the most pressing challenges of a postmodern culture is to respond to the privatization of faith. Should the tendency be combated, and if so, how, when the notion of religion as a strictly private matter seems to have become the 'default' position in Western society? What is an alternative? Perhaps the larger openness for spiritual matters shown in postmodernities even allows for a greater understanding for religion and spirituality in the public arena.

Although God has limited our options, he has not limited himself. Though the church may speak with confidence on what God has revealed through Christ, it can never claim to have complete, exhaustive knowledge of the thoughts and ways of its Lord. The final word on who belongs to the kingdom of God has not been revealed to the church; God has reserved for himself the final judgement of who is inside and outside the boundaries of his realm. Thus, we can never conclude with certainty whether those not acknowledging Christ as saviour still may be saved by his grace. Nevertheless, whether our positions on final salvation are exclusivist, inclusivist, pluralist, or any other, all Christians should, like God, earnestly desire all to be saved and come to a knowledge of the truth (1 Tim 2:4).

5.3 Evangelism and witness

Postmodernity harbours a deep felt scepticism towards mission of any kind, but it appears that the suspicion of Christian mission runs especially deep. Attempts at trying to *persuade* others to accept the implications of the story of Jesus may be confused with the notion that Christians are trying to impose their viewpoints on others. For postmodernity, after all, one view may be as good as another; there are no fixed criteria by which to measure validity. One may wonder why mission attempts are felt to be so disturbing in postmodernity. Are they perceived as an invasion of an inviolate privacy? Is the message viewed as propaganda? Or are there other reasons? For the Christian church, some reflection on Scripture passages such as Acts 10 and 15, where conversion followed experiences rather than argument, may be helpful.

We need to distinguish between legitimate and illegitimate proclamation, between the respectful sharing of the received and experienced while pointing towards what has merely been glimpsed, and the condescending imposition of doctrines and practices without regard to the wishes of the recipients. While the latter should be condemned, and no less when practised by fellow Christians – or even oneself, the former should be applauded and encouraged, even though the message might be contrary to one's own convictions.

Although being a Christian is to be a believer in and a witness for the word of God, actual witness need not always be verbal. The witness of a life inspired by love and charity may not only be more authentic, but more effective proclamation as well. The old adage: 'Witness! If necessary use words' needs pondering by all who want to share their faith. Christian service and issues of justice are integral to the gospel. A church that forgets its prophetic role, struggling for peace and the integrity of creation and combating injustice, is not only losing its credibility, but betraying its calling. In postmodernity, an essential aspect of mission has become that of physical, emotional and spiritual healing. New Age teachings, with their appeal to physical wellbeing, psychic healing, therapy and holism may be a useful reminder that humans recognise deep down that they do not live by bread alone.

The Chinese character '*sheng*', signifying 'holy', consists of three parts: there is a large ear and a small mouth, posing above the character for 'responsibility'. Could this be a fruitful metaphor for Christian mission in a postmodern environment, the large ear and small mouth signifying responsible, respectful proclamation and intellectually honest dialogue, combined with earnest efforts to listen and to understand? Witness is bold because it is about sharing amazing good news; it is to be undertaken in humility, for the witness is not to oneself, one's church or 'superior' way of life, but to the risen Lord of all. There is nothing to be ashamed of in confessing one's faith in the crucified and risen Christ as the saviour for all humanity. Everything is to be gained in communication by listening attentively to the questions, doubts and criticisms of those whom we wish to introduce to Jesus.

5.4 Theology of mission

We suggest a *via media* between what are probably two caricatures of mission: on the one hand, the traditional notions of winning souls and establishing the church, and on the other the radical version, which identifies the work of the Spirit in current world events. We confess our belief in the church as the work of the Holy Spirit and the communion of saints. Nevertheless, that does not imply that the kingdom of God is limited to the church. Traditional mission has been eager to fulfil God's calling. While the zeal should be applauded, the methods are not necessarily to be recommended. It is more important that mission is done with – rather than for – God.

The tension between differing views on church and mission is evident within the articles and our group. We will not here presume to give an answer to whether different parts of the church are over-emphasising some aspects of mission to the detriment of others. We would like to point out, however, that Christian mission needs to be holistic to be perceived as valid and relevant. It is always proclamation, dialogue and action in service and for justice; it is always word and deed.

As to the biblical basis for mission, naturally we find not only differences of opinion between the more evangelically and ecumenically minded, but a tendency to root the understanding in different Scripture passages and to use the texts in different ways, pointing at different lessons. The relative prominence of John 3:16, let us say among those who adhere to the Lausanne movement, compared to the fondness for Luke 14:18-19 in circles allied to the World Council of Churches may serve as an example of this trend. Whatever our positions, we need to acknowledge the limitations of our understanding and the inherent danger of abusing Scripture in our arguments.

6 Key Priorities and Suggestions for Further Consideration

Postmodernity appears to be a facet of current life; it will not simply vanish if ignored or completely denied. Hence, it is imperative that the church moves beyond pure denunciation and reflects on how constructively to relate to postmodernity, welcoming its contributions, assessing its impact on individuals and society, and discerning its less constructive elements, in order to reach a deeper understanding of both the gospel and contemporary human beings. Such a task will enable Christians to be valid and relevant witnesses to Christ. In a time when modernity is given much of the blame for the current state of affairs, Christians ought to give modernity due credit for its accomplishments, not only scientific and technical, but even in the social realm. The main problem of modernity for Christians is not the emphasis on rationality and the achievements of the scientific method, but the claims made by some that these by themselves, in a universe closed in on itself, are sufficient to explain human life and nurture human flourishing.

6.1 The exercise of leadership

Within postmodern culture, one may spot a reluctance to take on power, with its responsibilities. It is arguable whether this is the result of a worthy suspicion of power and those who wield it, or merely reveals an immature fear of obligations. Nevertheless, this reluctance is not easily harmonized with images of leadership and power apparently favoured in many church traditions. Neither the formally authorized mono-pastor of the traditional parish congregation nor the allegedly divinely appointed charismatic leader of faith fellowships seem sufficiently attuned to the postmodern distrust of power. In a world where established authority is challenged and distrusted, claims of unique revelation will naturally be perceived as unfair. The prevailing attitude towards notions of uniqueness may be expressed as: 'What makes your god so special; aren't all gods alike?' Perhaps, through postmodernity, the church may rediscover what it means to emulate the Servant King. Churches and theological institutions need to encourage and enable servant leadership, which is so beautiful when transformed from a slogan into a reality.

6.2 Theological education

Probably tensions in the church between academic theology and practised church life will always be there. Whereas in the Western theological tradition, the former has tended to have had more influence, the latter becomes more important for the postmodern conscience. Credibility comes not so much from well thought out and reasoned opinions, but from a life consistent with one's convictions and the ability to encourage, enrich and guide others.

Many postmodern-style churches do not emphasise strong formal theological training. They prefer to stress more informal, practical training. At a time when people are searching for authentic models for living rather than for disconnected propositional truths, it is crucial that theological training is not limited to a theoretical exercise, but that theory and practice interact with each other. This does not invalidate theology as an academic discipline, but academic proficiency is not, and never has been, the sole requirement for pastoral service.

The radical change in the way of thinking and of looking at life represented by postmodernity cannot but influence theological reflection and education. The key question for churches to answer may not be so much 'where can I find a graceful God', but rather 'where do I find an authentic spirituality'? To address this need, it appears that theological education should be conversational rather than authoritarian, focusing more on encouraging students to reflect on their own experiences, form their own opinions and discern spiritual insight than to transmit propositional truth. Although the latter will remain pivotal, to train spiritually mature leaders is likely to be even more crucial.

6.3 Postmodernity and hope for the future

Postmodernity, arguably lacking a real belief in the possibility of progress, does not have any good stories for the future in relation to the alarming facts of global economic mismanagement, the ecological crisis, proper human dignity and rights, nor as a counterbalance to totalitarian religions and worldviews. We find much validity, therefore, in the claim that hope is absent within postmodernities. Admittedly, the contrary claim that hope is a delusion is perhaps not sufficiently explored. We suggest, though, that hope is necessary for transformation. By not settling for the world as it is, keeping hope as a permanent motivating force over against the paralysis that fatalism induces, the possibility of radical and substantial change remains. To us, it appears that this perceived lack of a vision for transformation in the future is a weakness or deficiency in postmodernism and a danger for mission in postmodernity.

It is true, however, that totalitarian systems may come up with appealing – but false – stories of the future. The more simplified the answers that they give the more chance they have of making a broad appeal. This is partly why it is valuable to listen attentively to some of the most valuable contributions of postmodernity; for example, its egalitarian idealism, awareness of the contingencies of life, suspicion of the corrupting influence of power and over-emphasis on the value of rational organisation to the exclusion of the non-negotiable value of the other person.

6.4 The Bible

Postmodern use of biblical texts may differ from the previously established. The primary use of the traditionally privileged biblical texts may be less evident than before, the freedom to choose is stressed, and the patchwork technique is gaining more credence than previously.

The postmodern suspicion of power is clearly shown in postcolonial as well as in feminist hermeneutics. As opposed to liberation theology, whose proponents were inherently trusting the biblical texts to be on side of the poor, feminist and postcolonial readers, such as Musa Dube, Tinyiko Maluleke and Rasiah S. Sugirtharajah, not only realise that these texts have been used to oppress people. Rather, they suspect that such oppression is not only due to abuse of the biblical texts, but is inherent in the texts themselves. Thus, the Bible is no longer seen as an infallible guide, even Christians do not necessarily presuppose that biblical texts are always good for the reader; to postmodern and postcolonial minds, their validity as spiritual guidance remains a question of hermeneutics.

6.5 Environmental crisis and ecology

The ecological movement might be described as a postmodern challenge to modernity. As the grim consequences of the exploitation of the earth's resources become ever more visible, the realisation that these resources are not unlimited, ours to exploit with impunity, slowly begins to sink in. The rather instrumental and utilitarian view of nature in modernity is commonly viewed as part of the problem, needing to be replaced by more holistic approaches, seeing everything as part of the whole and thus being more sympathetic to the natural order. Thus, it appears that postmodernity is more in tune with environmental concerns than is the case with modernity.

Environmental theology follows up this concern, castigating churches for having done little or nothing to prevent this poor management of what has been entrusted us, solely focusing on individual salvation to the detriment of concern for those coming after us. Other Christians seem to regard the environmental crisis as being of less consequence for the church, though. Because they believe that this earth and all within it eventually will perish, they advocate concentrating on the unique tasks of the church rather than being involved in everyday political struggles.

To let the eschatological vision of a new heaven and a new earth obscure the gravity of the crisis would not only be counterfactual, however, it would also be a rejection of the biblical message of stewardship for the earth and its resources. The postmodern emphasis on ecological concern is a highly due reminder for the church as well as for society as a whole, and a necessary corrective to the seemingly more prevalent thinking of nature as a menace to be subdued or a machine to be mastered.

6.6 Reconciliation and healing

What does reconciliation and healing mean in a situation with opposing and irreconcilable views? During the core group discussion, the matter was discussed through a case study on a (fictional) destruction of a Bosnian mosque. What would be the proper Christian response? The consensus clearly was that Christians ought to help the victims of assault, and thus to help rebuilding the mosque would be a true expression of Christian love for the neighbour. However, it was readily admitted that such an act might be perceived as naive from the point of view of Christians suffering under similar measures from Muslim communities, and that it might be difficult to explain to oppressed Christians that their fellow Christians take up such a collection for Muslims. Admittedly, it may be easy for, for example, comfortable Christians in Scandinavia to be generous, and it might easily be perceived as just another instance of apologetic penitence for past misdeeds, real or imagined. On the other hand, by helping oppressed Muslims, it may be demonstrated to those willing to see that not all Christians are crusaders.

7 Postscript

Reflecting on the topic of postmodernities, we have realised how complex a subject it is and how different, even among among a few people, our approaches can be. This fact shows the variety and diversity of positions of different Christian traditions, and even the different theological trends within the same tradition. Postmodernity is a kind of 'boundaries topic', which means not only that churches look at it in a different ways, and with divergent theologies, but also that postmodern thinking addresses the churches, Christianity and religion in a wide range of diverse ways. Our topic can be considered as an *ad extra* topic, calling the churches to interact with various geo-political-cultural contexts, religious milieus and different theological standpoints and ecumenical approaches. Other themes in the Edinburgh 2010 study project are *ad intra* topics, in the sense that they may be dealt with and shaped within a common and shared Christian standpoint: the Bible, the mission of the church, the Christian call and the ecumenical imperative. The theme of postmodernities, in contrast, if we want to be faithful to its very nature, has no 'Christian-oriented counterpart'.

In hindsight it would seem we decided – though we did not make it explicit – that in such a situation we would not attempt to produce an exhaustive presentation, or even a structured presentation; rather we would aim to give flashes and glimpses of the issues, whose aim was simply to point out some of their problematic aspects. In retrospect, one real weakness of our study overall is the relative lack of voices from different cultural contexts and diverse groups (e.g. the global South, women and young people). We were aware of this, and tried to deal with the problem by inviting both women and contacts outside the Western world to contribute, but with only limited success.

Beside practical difficulties, there is also a delicate methodological aspect, which is that the topic of postmodernities, while pointing out a reality of a globalized world, is still basically a Western category. It is used by theologians, philosophers, sociologists and others from countries which have experienced modernity and secularization and, in some sense, bear the marks of a post-Christian environment. To have included voices from the global South would have meant opening the way to very different understandings, which, in turn, might have given contrasting meanings to the concept, and even, perhaps, called into it into question. Although this would have been an extraordinary enrichment, it would probably have broadened the discussion too far to be dealt with in just one chapter.

Endnotes

[1] *Swedish Missionary Themes*, Vol. 95, No. 4, 2007. Papers are also available online at www.missionsresearch.org.

[2] Some sources for the study of postmodernity include: Z. Bauman, *Postmodernity and its Discontents* (Cambridge: Polity Press, 1997); Hans Bertens, *The Idea of the Postmodern: A History* (London: Routledge, 1995); Lawrence Cahoone (ed.), *From Modernism to Postmodernism: An Anthology* (Oxford: Blackwell, 1996); Terry Eagleton, *The Illusions of Postmodernism* (Oxford: Blackwell, 1996); Frederic Jameson, *Postmodernism, Or, The Cultural Logic of Late Capitalism* (Durham: Duke University Press, 1991); J. Andrew Kirk & Kevin J. Vanhoozer (eds), *To Stake a Claim: Mission and the Western Crisis of Knowledge* (Maryknoll, NY: Orbis Books, 1999); David Lyon, *Postmodernity* (Buckingham: Open University Press, 1994); François Lyotard, *The Postmodern Condition: A Report on Knowledge* (Minneapolis, MN: University of Minnesota Press, 1984).

[3] See, Stuart Sim (ed.), *Postmodern Thought* (Duxford: Icon Books, 1998), 86-88.

[4] Richard Dawkins, *River out of Eden* (London: Weidenfeld and Nicolson, 1995), 32.
[5] The papers submitted to the study group are available on the Edinburgh 2010 website, www.edinburgh2010.org.
[6] Jan-Olav Henriksen, 'Multifaceted Christianity and the Postmodern Religious Condition: Reflections on its Challenges to Churches in the Northern Hemisphere' (2009), paper presented to Edinburgh 2010 Study Group 3 and available at www.edinburgh2010.org.
[7] J. Andrew Kirk, 'The Post-Modern Condition and the Churches' (Co)Mission' (2009), paper presented to Edinburgh 2010 Study Group 3 and available at www.edinburgh2010.org.
[8] J. Jayakiran Sebastian, 'Interrogating *Missio Dei*: From the Mission of God Towards Appreciating Our Mission to God in India Today' (2009), paper presented to Edinburgh 2010 Study Group 3 and available at www.edinburgh2010.org.
[9] Andrew Jones, 'The Virtual Church – Keeping It Real' (2009), http://tallskinnykiwi.typepad.com/tallskinnykiwi/2009/07/the-virtual-church-keeping-it-real.html.
[10] Michael Herbst, 'Plural Mission and Missionary Plural in a Post-Socialist Context: The Example of a Post-*Volkskirche*, East German Region'(2009), paper presented to Edinburgh 2010 Study Group 3 and available at www.edinburgh2010.org.
[11] *Volkskirche,* literal translation 'folk church', is a German and Scandinavian equivalent of the English term 'Christendom', in the sense that the boundaries of church and nation coincide.
[12] Friedemann Walldorf, 'Searching for the Soul(s) of Europe: Missiological Models in the Ecumenical Debate on Mission in Postmodern Europe'(2009), paper presented to Edinburgh 2010 Study Group 3 and available at www.edinburgh2010.org.
[13] Jieren Li, 'Multi-identity of the Chinese Christianity in Post-Olympic China: From Pre-modernity towards Postmodernity'(2009), paper presented to Edinburgh 2010 Study Group 3 and available at www.edinburgh2010.org.
[14] Olga Zaprometova, 'Bitter and Sweet Tears: Exploring the Spirituality of the Eastern Church Fathers in the Light of Post-modern Pentecostalism in Russia'(2009), paper presented to Edinburgh 2010 Study Group 3 and available at www.edinburgh2010.org.
[15] David Kettle, 'The Gospel of Hope in a Postmodern Setting' (2009), paper presented to Edinburgh 2010 Study Group 3 and available at www.edinburgh2010.org.
[16] Jim Harries, 'An 'Impact Model' of Language, and Mission and Development in East Africa'(2009), paper presented to Edinburgh 2010 Study Group 3 and available at www.edinburgh2010.org.
[17] www.postthehost.net/index2.html.
[18] See, e.g., Grace Davie, 'Religion in Europe in the 21st Century: The Factors to Take into Account', in *Religion in Late Modernity: Essays in Honour of Pål Repstad* (Trondheim: Tapir Academic Press, 2007), 37-53; *Religion in Britain since 1945: Believing Without Belonging* (Oxford: Blackwell, 1994).
[19] For further reading on mission and postmodernities, see, Grace Davie, *Europe the Exceptional Case: Parameters of Faith in the Modern World* (London: Darton, Longman and Todd, 2002); John Drane, *Jesus and the Gods of the New Age: Communicating Christ in Today's Spiritual Supermarket* (Oxford: Lion Publishing, 2001); George G. Hunter, *The Celtic Way of Evangelism* (Nashville: Abingdon Press, 2000); J. Andrew Kirk, *What is Mission? Theological Explorations* (London: Darton, Longman and Todd, 1999); Milfred Minatrea, *Shaped by God's Heart: The Passion and*

Practices of Missional Churches (San Francisco: John Wiley, 2004); David Smith, *Mission after Christendom* (London: Darton, Longman and Todd, 2003); Andrew Walls, *The Cross-Cultural Process in Christian History* (Edinburgh: T and T Clark, 2002); J. Andrew Kirk, *Mission under Scrutiny: Confronting Current Challenges* (London: Darton, Longman and Todd, 2006); J. Andrew Kirk, *The Future of Reason, Science and Faith:Following Modernity and Postmodernity* (Basingstoke: Ashgate Publishing, 2007).

[20] Remi Emiel Hoeckman, O.P., 'Christian Mission. God Moving to All Men, Transcending All Boundaries', in *Angelicum* 58/3 (1981), 312-322, at 313, 316.

THEME FOUR
MISSION AND POWER

The hand of the Lord came upon me, and he brought me out by the spirit of the Lord and set me down in the middle of a valley; it was full of bones. He said to me, 'Mortal, can these bones live?' Then he said to me, 'Prophesy to these bones, and say to them: O dry bones, hear the word of the Lord. [Then I, the Lord,] will put my spirit within you, and you shall live, and I will place you on your own soil; then you will know that I, the Lord, have spoken and will act.' Ezekiel 37:1,3a,4,14 (NRSV)

Preface

In 2008, representatives from approximately twenty Christian organisations in Canada met to identify a Canadian contribution to Edinburgh 2010. An interest emerged in the theme of Mission and Power as expressed in the churches' relations with indigenous peoples.

An eight-member study team began meeting in December 2008. Challenged by a mandate to reflect on power relations in mission since 1910, the co-chairs proposed an approach featuring information and reflections on Canadian residential schools: a century and a half of Christian mission which has had profound effects on First Nation, Inuit and Métis peoples – the Aboriginal peoples of Canada[1] – and their continuing relations with the rest of Canadian society.

The study team wrestled with the subject of the 'power' of the pen, recognising that in choosing writers, power would be given to some over the many others who could have contributed. Since indigenous peoples' voices are underrepresented in the literature, the team invited three indigenous authors to write their stories drawing on material from their personal and families' experiences of residential schools.

We are grateful to our writers. Terry Leblanc, Eileen Antone and Andrew Wesley submitted thoughtful and deeply moving accounts, illuminating a complex and often difficult history. Ian Morrison, a Canadian of European origin, also wrote from the heart – one voice from the churches which ran the schools. The team received insightful, timely responses to these stories from these individuals from different regions and churches: J. Kwabena Asamoah-Gyadu, Ghana; Dorcas Gordon, Canada; Dewi Hughes, Wales; Hanna Massad, Gaza; Stan McKay, Canada; Edley J. Moodley, South Africa and USA; Débora García Morales, Nicaragua; Philomena N. Mwaura, Kenya; Dorottya Nagy, Romania and The Netherlands; Tito Paredes, Peru; Philip Siew, Malaysia; and Philip Wingeier-Rayo, Cuba and USA.

These writers compared and contrasted experiences of mission and power in their contexts in rich and revealing ways. Wendy Fletcher produced an instructive theological reflection pointing to lessons learned by the Canadian faith community, and lessons still to be learned. We regret the absence of voices from the Canadian Roman Catholic tradition and francophone community. This is a significant gap: over seventy per cent of residential schools were administered by Roman Catholic entities.

Space constraints demanded that stories be edited and international responses be summarised. The unedited four-part case study, complete international responses – including responses not reflected in this chapter – and full biographical information for writers and study team members are available on the Edinburgh 2010 website.[2]

Finally, we acknowledge the work of the Mission and Power study team. The co-conveners were Dr Jonathan J. Bonk, Executive Director, Overseas Ministries Study Center, USA and Lori Ransom, Healing and Reconciliation Animator, Justice Ministries, Presbyterian Church in Canada. The members of the group (all in Canada) were Gail Allan, Bob Faris, Charles Fensham, John Franklin, Maylanne Maybee, Thomas Reynolds; and Editor – Anne Saunders.[3]

1 Introduction*

Christian *mission* has always been associated with *power*. The promise of the risen Christ was that his followers would receive *power* when the Holy Spirit came on them, and that this power would infuse and animate their proclamation of the good news in Jerusalem, Judaea, Samaria, and throughout the entire world (Acts 1:8). In the calculus of Roman *realpolitik*, the laughably parochial audience for these words represented the lowest social strata of a thoroughly subjugated populace inhabiting one of the empire's back eddies. Powerless, even against the slack measure of their nation's own powerlessness, the notion that these rag-tag followers of a crucified faith healer could be of political or religious significance would have seemed ludicrous.[4]

But history is full of surprises. In its first three centuries, the early church grew at an estimated forty percent per decade. By the time of Constantine's public accord with Christianity in AD 312, Christians already constituted a demographically significant proportion of the imperial population – perhaps as much as ten percent. This growth, furthermore, occurred in the face of formidable disincentives. Anyone converting to this faith risked social marginalization at best, and extinction at worst.

With the conversion of powerful political leaders – for whom Constantine may serve as a convenient marker of a prolonged, complex and extraordinarily violent process – *Christianity* evolved into *Christendom*, the great-grandsire of what is today known as 'The West'. Between the Edict of Milan in AD 313 and

*By Lori Ransom and Jonathan Bonk.

Justinian's edict of AD 529, Christianity's status in the Empire evolved from being *one religion among several* legitimate options to being *the only* legal public cult in AD 392. With Charlemagne's ascent to power several centuries later, Christendom emerged full-blown, infusing the West's social institutions and self-perception in its violent, five-hundred-year ascent to global hegemony.[5]

The conversion of peoples to Christianity was achieved by a combination of voluntary, social, legal, and violent compulsions. The incumbent populations of North and South America, Australia, Southern Africa, and most recently, Palestine, were overwhelmed, subjugated, and frequently destroyed. Missionaries applied themselves to winning subjugated peoples over to the religion that would set them on the path to 'civilization', now touted as 'development'. This noble end was used to justify almost any means of persuasion and inducement, including military conquest, genocide, assimilation, and proclamation. In the implicit, and sometimes explicit, thinking of missionaries, Christianity was the actual inner élan of Western civilization's lust and will to dominate.

It was the senseless carnage of World War I that applied the final *coup de grace* to Christendom's five-hundred-year claim to moral superiority. The scales fell off. The witness of millions of 'colonized' Africans and Asians pressed into duty as front line cannon fodder proved that such claims merely shrouded a terrifying pathological reality.

This was the 'Christian' world that made possible and even inevitable the Canadian residential schools described in this study. Ecclesiastical complicity in the clumsy application of state power did not occur in a vacuum. Missionaries and churches then, as now, were susceptible to the self-serving myopias of the powerful. Hailed as enlightened in their genesis, the boarding schools turned out to have been savagely effective instruments in the destruction of the very people they purported to save.

Missionaries from Europe came to North America with the first explorers. So the story of Christian mission with the indigenous people of the continent is over five hundred years long. From the earliest days, Christians were interested in providing a European-style education to indigenous children. The idea of taking indigenous children from their home communities to be educated in boarding schools dates back to seventeenth century New France. This first effort was abandoned until after 1828, when Christians opened boarding, or residential schools, for indigenous children in Upper Canada, having learned from watching similar efforts in the United States of America that removing children from parental influence was helpful in the process of 'civilizing' these children.[6]

A political process of treaty making between European powers and indigenous peoples parallels the mission story. The treaties sought to define the "relationship" between these peoples. The indigenous worldview celebrates the sacredness of all of God's Creation, and the inter-relationships between created beings as sacred. Hence, the treaties have come to be viewed by indigenous peoples as being sacred, as having spirit, the Spirit of the Creator's presence that exists between related beings, because the treaties represent their relationship with the newcomers to their lands.

However, the promise of treaty-making could not compete with colonialism: the drive to acquire power in the 'New World' led to the development of systematic efforts to eradicate the existence of indigenous peoples and cultures. Wendy Fletcher notes[7] that the Royal Proclamation of 1763 'announced a relationship based on friendship.' But 'a shift' occurred over the ensuing century, as immigration accelerated, and newcomers sought greater access to and ownership of land, both for settlement and economic development. The British colonial government 'announced the need to "civilize the Indian", with the introduction of the Gradual Civilization Act of 1857.' This began the process of creating a legal framework for assimilating indigenous peoples. 'In 1869, Canada's first Prime Minister, Sir John A. MacDonald, announced the abolition of Native self-government, which had been promised in earlier agreements.'

Treaty-making continued but with the clear object of resolving land issues. Together, with the *Indian Act* of 1876, a policy of segregating indigenous peoples on small reserve land bases was pursued, which led to the further dissolution of once thriving indigenous nations. Wendy Fletcher continues,

> By 1875 the assimilation project of the new Canadian government took this one step further with the introduction of the residential school policy based on the belief that, 'Aboriginal people were sunk in ignorance and superstitious blindness', and that 'only children taken at an early enough age can be liberated from the depravity of their natural state.'
>
> The result was the development of a residential school model of education which would remove children from their families, forcibly if necessary, such that the 'influence of the wigwam' could not interrupt a process of cultural assimilation. The partnership between government and churches in actualizing this programme led to decades of trauma for indigenous communities. As early as 1907 the Government of Canada received reports depicting the gross neglect of basic sanitation, medical care, nutrition and protection which was running rampant in the schools, even in relation to the standards of the day. This extreme neglect was largely the product of government under-funding. However, despite evidence that significant harm was being done in the schools, the Parliament did not reconsider its support of this assimilationist plan until another half a century had passed. The last school was closed in 1998. The rest, as they say, is history.[8]

While the indigenous peoples of Canada survived these assaults on their very existence, the stories that follow reveal the profound effects on their well-being and sense of identity – as individuals, as communities and as nations. And so, indigenous peoples have found in Ezekiel's prophecy of dry bones returning to life, a metaphor for their journey of recovering a strong and healthy identity.

Canadian philosopher, John Ralston Saul argues in his book *A Fair Country*[9] that over the five-hundred-year history of relations, indigenous peoples have deeply and significantly shaped the collective Canadian consciousness in positive ways that are not generally acknowledged. Ralston Saul invites Canadians to deepen their own sense of identity as a people by deepening their knowledge of the influence of indigenous peoples on Canadian society.

The question now is what we – beneficiaries or victims of this destructive power – do? What *should* we do? Neither the case studies nor the responses in this document provide any easy answers. These raw stories raise serious questions about the nature and means of Christian mission, about missionary complicity with power and privilege, about complicated issues of restitution, justice, legality, and forgiveness across generations to the descendents of both victims and beneficiaries of misused power.

2 Canadian Residential Schools Case Study

2.1 Residential schools: Policy, power and mission·

Culture, faith, mission and evangelism have been at the heart of countless disputes dealing with issues of human identity, the purposes and revelation of God, and church polity and doctrine since the church's inception. This discussion centres on the impact of European culture and faith in its expression of mission to Native North America, as represented in the Canadian residential school policy.

Two myths have tended to polarize this discussion. One is the belief that the indigenous peoples of North America lived in an Edenic state prior to the coming of the Europeans, leading to the logical conclusion that the ensuing social, spiritual and moral destruction was almost entirely a consequence of the encounter with 'the other'. We must reject the suggestion that indigenous peoples were without agency, ignorant and devoid of the capacity to engage and decide for themselves, in light of the lives of people like Membertou or Ohiyesa.[10] As Thomas Giles clarifies, at least in the early days of mission in North America,

> Christianity was not simply thrust on an uncritical indigenous population. Native Americans viewed Christianity through a variety of experiences. They compared it to their own beliefs…They then made crucial decisions whether to accept the new faith…The fact that Native Americans came to know the Christian

· By Terry LeBlanc, a *Mi'kmaq*/Acadian, from *Listuguj* First Nation, who has served in vocational ministry since 1979 and been active in Native North American affairs for many years.

> God...shows...the power of a faith that was able to reach people despite tremendous obstacles – not the least of which were produced by Christians.[11]

At the other extreme is the myth predicated on European dualistic worldviews like the concepts of *terra nullius* and Manifest Destiny.[12] Dualism created the impression that the land of our forbears was a godless, heathen place, unvisited by the One (i.e. God, *Nisgam*, *Maheo*, *Manitou*) who made all things and gave breath to all creation.

Reality lay somewhere between the two extremes, shifting depending upon the specific issue. What weight did these notions have in defining the nature of power in mission in Native North America? What are the implications of these concepts for contemporary mission – Native North American or otherwise?

By 1969 the residential school pact between the Canadian government and four of its churches ended. However, the journey from 'the middle of a valley'[13] of despair, created by assimilative mission practice, was just beginning. Residential schools were a sample of 'the massive changes that indigenous peoples underwent in the century between 1850 and 1950 – years also marked by the creation of the numbered treaties and of reserves.'[14] The schools gave expression to the two-pronged approach felt necessary to deal with the Native problem – Christianization by the churches and civilization by the Canadian government. As the then Archbishop of St. Boniface noted, Aboriginal children were to be 'caught young to be saved from what is on the whole the degenerating influence of their home environment'.[15] Few in the churches are recorded as having challenged the school policy. The same was true of the government of the day with one noteworthy exception. Indian Affairs official Frank Oliver pointed out the essentially un-Christian implication of the Archbishop's formative conclusion:

> ...one of the most important commandments laid upon the human by the divine is love and respect by children for parents. It seems strange that in the name of religion a system of education should have been instituted, the foundation principle of which not only ignored but contradicted this command.[16]

Years later, it was observed that for the children who were taken, 'their parents were, by the light of the [residential school] vision's compelling logic, unfit'.[17] *Mi'kmaq* elder Isabelle Knockwood described the experience of life at the *Shubenacadie* Indian Residential School in Nova Scotia as, in part, a place where '[w]e were being forcibly disconnected from everything our parents and elders had taught us ...'.[18] Stout and Kipling take this one step further as they note that,

> In effect, students were made to feel ashamed of their ancestry, while teachers and other authority figures constantly sought to reinforce the innate superiority of 'white' society and values. On the one hand, this indoctrination involved the devaluing of parents and all aspects of Aboriginal culture. On the other hand,

> schools attempted to disconnect children from their background by prohibiting communication in an Aboriginal language.[19]

While the most severe punishments were usually reserved for children who attempted to run away,[20] the capricious nature of the discipline administered in residential schools contributed to a generalized climate of fear for students. Further exacerbating this situation was the fact that many punishments were either explicitly or implicitly sexual in nature.

Over the years following the end of church-state collusion, schools were transferred to First Nation control. But when the last school finally closed in 1998,[21] the end of the era of cultural and social genocide, as Riediger[22] made clear, was in actuality far from visible. For as Richardson and Nelson note, 'Residential schools... provid[ed] intensive and systemic re-socialization and cultural deprogramming for Aboriginal children while inflicting endless grief onto Aboriginal communities.'[23] Making the case even more emphatic, Reidiger says that, '...residential schools assaulted the Native's individual and cultural identity, and left alcoholism, suicide, violence, and ongoing sexual abuse in their wake'.[24]

The outcome has been decades of continuing social trauma leading to social and cultural degradation. Only handfuls of foresighted, some would say prophetic, traditional Elders managed to keep their cultures from complete annihilation. Stout and Kipling wrote about the profound impact on Canadian Aboriginal peoples that Canadian Prime Minister Stephen Harper acknowledged on 11 June 2008:

> Like a pebble dropped in a pond, the effects of trauma tend to ripple outwards from victims to touch all those who surround them, whether parents, spouses, children or friends. There is ample evidence to support this view among residential school survivors, where the consequences of emotional, physical and sexual abuse continue to be felt in each subsequent generation.[25]

While residential schools have long since closed, the after-effects continue to be experienced – and will be for generations to come.

Seemingly in this approach to mission, without conscious assent, the ideas of *terra nullius* and Manifest Destiny had become firmly entrenched, and a sense of the rightness of these actions toward Native peoples had become incontrovertible. Native peoples, in this conception, represented a less-than-civilized aspect of creation that needed to be fully reworked. As a part of the wild, untamed creation,[26] Native peoples were subject to manipulation according to European ideas about their best interests. As if Native peoples entirely lacked the image of God, redemption looked like remaking them in the image of Europeans.

Clearly the commodified approach to the land and its resources supported the thinking that Native peoples could be easily assimilated into the mainstream of the emerging North American nations – including into churches. Centuries before contact, Western Europeans had developed a dualistic understanding of creation, including land. Since physical, material creation was not understood to be spiritual, it was not redeemable; human souls became the essential and only focus of Jesus' work on the cross. In contrast, for Native peoples, the whole of the creation was possessed of a spiritual nature. In keeping with the text of Genesis 1:28-30, they had intuited that the Creator would, by reason of the activity of creation, deposit something of the Creator's self in all of the creation.

Mission to Native peoples necessitated that Native peoples do three things:

1. Adopt European ideas of material value and wealth connected to resources of the land;
2. Accept the growing social-liberal way of life with autonomous personal well-being and individual competitiveness;
3. Sever connection to belief that the totality of creation is possessed of a spiritual nature.

These behaviours became the focus of the application of power in mission – the government's and the churches' – in operating residential schools. In studying the implications of these continued policies, Wade[27] describes the existence of 'a very close and mutually supportive relationship between colonialism and the so-called "helping professions"' with the following colonial code of relationship:

- You are deficient. I am proficient;
- I have the right to perform prescribed operations upon you, with or without your consent;
- These operations are undertaken for your own good.

While this colonially-based mission practice had, according to many of the day, 'the best interests of the Native population at heart', it was ignorant of the profound differences in perspective of Native peoples and Europeans. Most significantly, it failed to consider the deep connectedness of Native peoples to the land of their forefathers and mothers, and the understanding that the land was possessed of a spiritual essence.

Mission among Native peoples had little to do with the gospel or the scriptures. Native peoples have historically had little argument with either. In fact, on 24 June 2010, we commemorate the first conversion recorded – of Membertou. His own agency in that decision is indisputable. The imposition of power in historic mission was not rooted in the uniqueness or singularity of the person of Jesus or the message of the gospel. It came from the church's worldview of material and spiritual separation which made the gospel about the salvation of the human soul.

In the historic expressions of the wider mainstream Christian tradition, the focus of the church's work has consistently been in an either/or mission – hardly consistent with the teaching in scripture that all creation is to be redeemed. Even today many people experience a dichotomy in the church's mission: souls and/or service. This continues to apply levers of power in inappropriate ways to the lives of people who understand the world in more holistic terms. Native peoples assert that we are whole beings, dwelling in lands that are spiritual in essence, living in interconnected contexts and communities.

Therefore, the issue of mission and power confronting us is how do we discuss the nature of the spiritual? Do we continue to embrace forms of dualism as the foundation of our theologies, and therefore, our missiology? Or do we view the world, and our mission in it, in more clearly holistic terms? In light of the nature of creation and its Creator, can we begin to conceive that there is something more spiritually intrinsic to all of creation that frames the lives of the people and, therefore, the conversation about conversion and redemption?

For those of us on the Jesus Way, we encourage others to understand the fullest expression of Native spirituality as being in right relationship with the Creator, with other human beings and with the rest of creation – in the tradition of our ancestors, but only fully embraced in the person, work, life, teaching, death and resurrection of Jesus. I believe this to be an extension of, not a replacement for, who we are and the direction in which we have been journeying. As Jesus claimed to be the fulfilment, not replacement of the Law, Jesus becomes our way of journeying from past-validated, authentic experiences of our people, through present challenges following a devastating period of encounter, to the future fulfilment of our journey.

In the Native context, a complexity in the issues has developed from what have become compound worldviews and convoluted family and social settings. This will be true in most, if not all, of the places a gospel predicated in a dualistic worldview was or is presented. Our challenge for the coming century is to make our worldview comport with the one in scriptures. Such a worldview reflects the *shalom* of the Creator and the desire that all creation be in balance and harmony, as in the opening days of creation in the Genesis narrative when the Creator announced, 'It is very good!'

2.2 Reflections on intergenerational effects of residential schools·

Residential schools have played a major role in the lives of the Original people in what is now known as Canada. This paper focuses on my experience as a member of the *Onyota'a:ka* Nation, or the *Oneida* Nation of the Thames, located in southwestern Ontario.

The *Onyota'a:ka* people were introduced to the residential school system after settling along the Thames River banks in 1840. During the mid 1840s, *Ojibwa* Methodist minister The Rev. Peter Jones moved to the *Muncey* and *Chippewa* communities across the river from the *Onyota'a:ka*. He had a vision: an educational system teaching Native children to survive as Native people. Rev. Jones wanted all Native children to develop skills for dealing with Europeans to protect what land they had left.[28] In a letter to the churches he

· By Eileen Antone, *Oneida* of the Thames First Nation, Director of Aboriginal Studies/Centre for Aboriginal Initiatives, at the University of Toronto.

wrote, 'It is also our intention to select from these schools the most promising boys and girls, with a view to giving them superior advantages, so as to qualify them for missionaries and school teachers among their brethren.'[29] Believing a formal institute run by Native people would give Native children a chance of survival, in 1849 he opened Mt. Elgin Residential School on the *Chippewa* of the Thames reserve. But, due to failing health, Rev. Jones was unable to continue. The school was taken over by non-Native Rev. Samuel Rose who had administrative problems because of his 'ignorance of Indians'.[30] Instead of Rev. Jones' vision, 'White people fed, clothed, trained, and preached to the students in English'.[31] Without apology Principal Rose stated, 'they are never left alone, but are constantly under the eye of some of those engaged in this arduous work'.[32] Reported a failure in 1858, the school closed in 1864, reopened three years later,[33] but never fulfilled the original vision.

Although Mt. Elgin Residential School was near to the *Onyota'a:ka* community, children were also sent to the *Mohawk* Institute residential school in Brantford in central Ontario which operated from 1834 to1970.[34] After 1892 *Onyota'a:ka* children were also sent to Sault Ste. Marie in northern Ontario, and Brandon in Manitoba.

When collecting data for my doctoral thesis, I interviewed members of the *Onyota'a:ka* community. One participant, an elderly lady, had attended residential school in Brandon during the 1920s. The Indian agent who spoke to her Dad about sending his children to the school had said it was run by Christian people and, therefore, they would be well fed, clothed and educated. 'There was nothing Christian about the school', she commented in the interview; the children were often hungry and punished for speaking their traditional language. She was proud she had not lost her language. She said, 'You know I didn't know how to speak English until I went to that Brandon Manitoba [residential] school. There was E.S. [a friend]. We talked *Oneida*. And if we got caught talking to each other in *Oneida* we would get a strapping.'[35] The prevailing belief was that by removing the language, Native children would more easily assimilate into the dominant society. She said she and her friend hid and spoke to each other in *Oneida*. Therefore, when she returned home she was able to speak her mother tongue.

After 1969,[36] there was a reclamation of the *Onyota'a:ka* language and culture. Many young *Onyota'a:ka* parents went to this elderly lady for *Onyota'a:ka* names for their babies. Sharing this information she asked me, 'What is your Indian name?' I admitted I did not have one. Both my parents attended residential school at Mt. Elgin and witnessed the violence that many children experienced there. They loved me too much to have me experience punishment for speaking my own language. Teaching me only English, they did not bestow upon me an Indian name. Both my parents, having passed to the spirit world, the woman offered to give me an Indian name. She said, 'Your name will be *Kaliwisaks*', meaning 'She who gathers information'. I use this name because that is what I do: I gather information to enhance the learning of Aboriginal people and non-Aboriginal peoples.

After 1925 the United Church of Canada (UCC) administered the Mt. Elgin Residential School and continued Christianizing the Native students in their care, coercing them to get rid of their traditions including the use of their languages, songs and dances which were part of their spirituality. This process of disconnecting Aboriginal peoples from their way of life had a detrimental effect on the identity of many Aboriginal people in Canada. In my journey I have learned that a society's traditional culture ensures its unity and survival. The values, beliefs, history and customs form the basis for attitudes, behaviours and understandings of the heritage that individuals learn. Although a living culture constantly changes and adapts, it still contains principles intrinsic to a particular group of people and to their identity. I have also learned that the relationship to Mother Earth is one manifestation of spirituality. Regardless of what our faith system is, the relationship to everything around us is important to our spiritual well-being and the way we reveal that relationship.

At the 1984 UCC General Council, an Aboriginal woman from British Columbia named Alberta Billy called for an apology from the church for using the Christian message to strip Aboriginal peoples of their traditional way of being. At the next General Council in 1986, moderator Robert Smith made an apology to the Aboriginal peoples of Canada. It was a powerful event to witness. Rev. Stan McKay, a *Cree* minister, began with a teaching from the pulpit. He said words to this effect,

> Once there was this little old woman and this little old man living in a beautiful house. One day a person from another place came to visit and they welcomed him into their home. He stayed and stayed until one day some of his relatives came also. They stayed. These visitors kept inviting more people to the house until finally the old man and woman were living on the veranda because there was no more room inside. The visitors occupied the whole house. The old man and woman kept saying to themselves 'when are these people going to leave so we can move back into our house?' Then another group of relatives of the first visitors arrived and the old man and woman were pushed off the veranda into the bog surrounding the house.[37]

Rev. McKay then stated, 'We will go down to the bog to wait.' One by one the Aboriginal people got up, left the gathered assembly, following him to the bog. On the bog was a tepee where the Elders waited for the apology. In the centre of the bog was a sacred fire and beside were the drummers. The atmosphere was quiet. The evening sunset turned to the dark of night. Eventually we saw hundreds of candle lights coming down the hillside to the bog. This contingent of General Council representatives from across Canada, led by the Moderator, proceeded to the tepee and waiting Elders. Then the Moderator read the following communication:

Long before my people journeyed to this land your people were here, and you received from your elders an understanding of creation, and of the Mystery that surrounds us all that was deep, and rich and to be treasured.

We did not hear you when you shared your vision. In our zeal to tell you the good news of Jesus Christ we were closed to the value of your spirituality.

We confused western ways and culture with the depth and breadth and length and height of the Gospel of Christ.

We imposed our civilization as a condition of accepting the Gospel.

We tried to make you like us and in doing so we helped to destroy the vision that made you what you were. As a result, you, and we, are poorer and the image of the Creator in us is twisted, blurred and we are not what we are meant by God to be.

We ask you to forgive us and to walk together with us in the spirit of Christ so that our peoples may be blessed and God's creation healed.[38]

The Elders and the Moderator came out of the tepee where the apology was again read to the Original people. There was joyfulness. Our people, suppressed by the church for so many years, pulled out their shawls and button blankets and danced, crying and singing, around the sacred fire to the beat of the drums. They invited the other people to join in the release from suffocating oppression. Witnessing this event had a powerful influence on me. I had been raised with the belief that our ceremonies, language, stories, songs, dances, and ways of being were the ways of the devil. Hearing this apology released me to learn about our spiritual ways.

Although the last residential school was closed in 1998, the effects of these schools still ripple through the Aboriginal communities. There is still much work to be done to bring healing and reconciliation to both Aboriginal and non-Aboriginal peoples in Canada.

2.3 A survivor's story: O Ke che manido·

In my early age I grew up in the hunting ground of my ancestors, the *Omuskagowuk* Nation. My life was good – we lived off the land and everything was provided for us. The hunting ground was located in northern Ontario, about 150 miles southeast of James Bay. In the summer months the family would move to the community of Fort Albany on James Bay until it was time to leave in the fall.

· By Andrew Wesley of *Mushkagowuk* ancestry, who recovered from residential school abuse enabled by traditional elders, and works as an Aboriginal priest for Toronto Anglican Diocese. The unedited version of this article first appeared in the Canadian Council of Church's resource, *Suffering and Hope*.

One fall I never made it back to the hunting ground with my family. Instead I was put on a supply ship going back to Moosonee. This was my first trip away from my family and I didn't even know I was being sent far away to a residential school. I don't remember the trip. I was only about six years old, and there were ten other children on that boat. We left at six in the morning and arrived at Moosonee thirteen hours later and were hustled to the school.

I don't even remember my first day at the school. I must have broken down crying all the way, wanting to be with my parents and grandmother. I must have wondered why I had to be in this place, separated from them and from my home. When I think about it now, I was deprived of the right to a normal family upbringing – the right to have my parents and grandmother to love and enjoy, and be nurtured by.

My number at the residential school was 56 and I was known by that number for many years. I was not considered to be a human being, just a number.

Shortly after I arrived at St. Anne's residential school, I remember being in the dining room having a meal. I got sick and threw up on the floor. Sister Mary Immaculate slapped me many times before she made me eat my vomit. So I did, I ate all of it. And then I threw up again, for the second time. Sister Mary Immaculate slapped me and told me again to eat my vomit. I ate it, half of it, and then I was told to go to the dorm. I felt humiliated, being slapped around in front of my friends and being treated worse than a dog, except you wouldn't even treat a dog like that. I was sick for a few days after that. I managed to eat a little here and there because I was afraid it might happen again, so I used to watch how I ate my food. (This incident today reminds me of Isaiah 50.)

Again I remember being in the dining room when I was twelve years old. I was sitting across the table from my friend who was kicking me under the table to tease me. I caught his leg and pulled off his shoe. Sister Mary Immaculate caught me. She took the shoe, which was a heavy shoe (not like the running shoes of today that children wear), and she hit me on my head with the heavy shoe. She hit me about fifty times. I passed out for a while. I was not allowed to report the incident, and I was not allowed to go to the clinic. The beating left a large lump on the back of my neck, at the top of my spine (which has never gone away). For many, many days I had a hard time walking or playing because it hurt. I had a regular, severe nose bleed that kept coming back for months. (Was this person working for the church and Jesus?)

Seeking sources of hope, I revisited the traditional spiritual teachings of my Elders, especially the Prayer on Wisdom my father used. I would like to share it.

> O *Ke che manido*, give me wisdom....
>
> Help me to understand that life on earth is part of your gift, inspiring to our patterns of life, with man the chief steward. Teach me to appreciate the delicate relationship of all things on earth. The majestic flight of Canada geese. The spring

time promise of the wonderful smell of flowers in bloom. The crystal purity of a dew drop and all that it contains.

O *Ke che manido*, teach me the proper respect of my place. Guide me in doing my part to help solve the many problems that beset us. Let me be dedicated to this task, as a bee gathering pollen.

O *Ke che manido*, show me how to utilize the inspiration from the daily miracles that I witness on my walk in your created earth. Help me to remember that nature's songs and laughter are more in tune with life than any wail or frown. Make me realise that in nature there is both tranquility and power; knowing that makes harmony reside also in me.

O *Ke che manido*, make me humble; please give me humility to see how crude the most spectacular man-made thing is compared with a baby rabbit, the wondrous perfection of a snowflake, or the grandeur of your sculptured tamarack trees in the muskeg. Give me wisdom and knowledge to know that if our environment fails because of our over exploitations, I too am doomed.

O *Ke che manido*, open our eyes.

Help us to understand that we are indeed all God's creatures.

That we are all brothers and sisters after all. So be it.[39]

2.4 My healing journey in relationship to Aboriginal peoples·

The period from March 1990 to June 1991 was the turning point for me in my relationship with the Aboriginal peoples of Canada. Recently appointed Associate Secretary for Canada Ministries[40] of The Presbyterian Church in Canada (PCC), I had responsibility for Native Ministries. Three events precipitated a crisis of faith and a reconsideration of my relationship with Aboriginal peoples – indeed, with all people.

The first event began when the mayor of Oka, in Quebec, proposed the extension of a golf course onto land that *Mohawks* claimed was ancestral land. The *Mohawks* responded with a barricade to the land in question. The situation escalated when police attacked and an officer was killed. Only with the involvement of the Canadian Armed Forces did negotiations begin. Finally after almost six months, the stand-off ended.[41]

The second event was the Canadian Conference of Catholic Bishops (CCCB) Consultation in Saskatchewan, held because of breaking awareness of abuses at residential schools run by Roman Catholic Church entities. Aboriginal people at that meeting were invited to tell their stories; I heard, first-hand and for the first time, stories of sexual and physical abuse.[42]

Lastly, I visited two residential schools run by the PCC: Birtle in Winnipeg, Manitoba and Cecilia Jeffrey in northern Ontario. Having naïvely believed that

· By J.P. Ian Morrison, formerly General Secretary in The Presbyterian Church in Canada, who is the church's representative in the Independent Assessment Process for residential school survivors.

abuses did not happen at Presbyterian schools, I listened to former students detail the abuses they had suffered.

All three experiences, particularly the last, were traumatic. In all my years of ministry, I had never realised how cultural dominance had been so devastating to Aboriginal peoples. And an education model sponsored by my church had led to one of the most horrendous events in Canadian history. This realisation forever changed my life.

Born and raised in Glasgow, Scotland, I grew up with little exposure to Aboriginal peoples (the term used was 'Indian', or 'red Indian', to avoid confusion with people from India). In cowboy movies, Indians were portrayed as bad guys, with white settlers being good guys to whom, by right of conquest, North America belonged. Any good Indians were supporting whites in their conquest. In history class, good Indians supported the British conquest of Canada. A major cultural image was the world map with the 'pink bits' representing countries that were parts of the British Empire.

After immigrating to Canada (Montreal) in 1957, my image of Aboriginal peoples remained unchanged. As a draughtsman, I worked with an Indian who was deemed to have 'made it' since he was in a white collar job. At seminary there was one Aboriginal student whose enrolment indicated successful integration into Canadian society. Consistent with the prevailing understanding of Aboriginal peoples in Montreal society in the 1960s, I had a concept of Aboriginal peoples being in the lower Canadian social stratification. As an ordained PCC minister, this concept was juxtaposed with the church's ministry to Aboriginal peoples, like the work at two residential schools – wonderful Christian charity being done there and on the reserves through the dedication of ordained missionaries sent to their first ministerial charge. As a minister in rural British Columbia, helping those who came to the church in need, I learned of the white community's prejudice against Aboriginal peoples: a local hotel room I booked was no longer available when staff saw that the person was Aboriginal. I could not fight this prejudice since I did not yet understand the underlying trauma, caused by residential schooling, which contributed to alcoholism. After moving to Vancouver, I saw the high proportion of homeless Aboriginal people in the poor downtown east side, no more than two kilometres from my middle-class congregation.

My growing awareness of Native situations was shaken by the three events in the early 1990s. Suddenly I could not remember those 'pink' bits on the world map without thinking how a European understanding of colonial conquest had been imposed on indigenous people on every continent. No longer did I believe that my way was the only way. Learning about the pain and struggle of the Aboriginal peoples of Canada broadened my life and forever changed my worldview.

How did the PCC respond? Despite continuing assertions about good work at residential schools, the church set up a review committee. It recommended how the church should work with Aboriginal peoples, and that the church adopt a confession to God and Aboriginal peoples, acknowledging the church's complicity in an assimilation policy and recognising that the residential school system was systemically flawed, allowing the possibility of abuse.[43] While a confession needed further work, Assembly agreed with recommendations 'That the Church commit itself to listen to the issues as they are named and described by Aboriginal peoples ...support healing processes that arise from Aboriginal peoples themselves...[and] commit itself to seeking ways to work with Aboriginal peoples in calling the Government of Canada to acknowledge that its policies were harmful...'.[44]

Two years later the church adopted *The Confession*[45] with Moderator the Reverend George Vais presenting it to Grand Chief Phil Fontaine of the Assembly of Manitoba Chiefs in the fall of 1994 at 'the Forks' in Winnipeg, Manitoba. Accepting the apology, the Grand Chief said he could not yet forgive the church (he attended and was abused in a school run by an order in the Roman Catholic Church).[46]

By this time a growing number of claims made against the Government of Canada and the churches required resolution. Participating in the challenge of trying to resolve the impact of these claims included working with colleagues from the United Church of Canada, the Anglican Church and the Roman Catholic Church, as well as Government of Canada representatives and Aboriginal people. The ecumenical effort was frustrating as we dealt with each denomination's structure. The greatest challenge came with recognition that the Roman Catholic Church had more than fifty different entities involved in running residential schools, and each bore their own responsibility according to their mandate.

Equally challenging were the meetings with Canadian government representatives. More than once, government negotiators disappointed church and Aboriginal representatives, despite efforts to have a common understanding and promise that we were part of a shared enterprise. For healing and reconciliation to succeed, the Government of Canada must accept that Canadians share this land with Aboriginal peoples who were here long before us.

The many meetings with Aboriginal people gave us opportunities to become acquainted and to know each other by name.[47] While anger was often expressed, there was also forgiveness as the church recognised its complicity in the government's assimilation policy. From Aboriginal people, I have learned that there is another way of thinking about life and its challenges. I am eternally grateful to them for teaching me.

My most difficult and rewarding responsibility has been as PCC representative at the individual assessment programme hearings.[48] The claimant, their lawyer, the adjudicator, a government representative, a health worker if the claimant desires, and a church representative (*if* the claimant agrees) attend. The adjudicator invites the claimant to tell their story – often a difficult task (sometimes this is the first time the person has told anyone of the abuse suffered). A skilful adjudicator elicits the information required to assess the level of abuse and to decide the compensation. After the claimant's lawyer and the government representative speak, the church representative addresses the claimant. I speak of how I became involved with the PCC, how I learned only of the good things that happened at the schools, and how shocked I was to learn that my church was no different from the others. Then I speak of my healing journey and the church's struggle to adopt a confession to God and Aboriginal peoples. I usually read aloud *The Confession*, sections 5–7 and say that the church asked me to share this confession, to apologise for any hurt that the claimant has experienced through the neglect of The Presbyterian Church in Canada, and to ask for the claimant's forgiveness.

At one hearing after I spoke, the claimant stood up opposite me, walked around the table, passed his lawyer and the health worker until he reached me. He reached out and gave me a firm handshake and hug, saying that the church was forgiven. He returned to his seat and stated, with tears in his eyes, 'this is the happiest day of my life' because the church admitted what it did was wrong. At another hearing when something similar happened, in closing, the adjudicator asked the elder accompanying the claimant if he had anything to say. He replied that he was moved by what had happened, that he was sorry he had not had the same opportunity at his hearing. It is a reminder that healing and reconciliation cannot take place without personal contact.

Where do we go from here? The church must be involved wherever and whenever it can in the work of the Truth and Reconciliation Commission. The church must continue to pressure the Canadian government to deal with outstanding issues about land and indigenous rights, and revive the recommendations in the *Report of the Royal Commission on Aboriginal Peoples*.[49] The hardest job will be convincing the people of Canada to accept that the Aboriginal peoples of Canada have a unique relationship with those of us who have come to these shores, regardless of how long ago or how recent.

3 International Responses to Canadian Case Study

Moved by the power of the Canadian stories, international readers expressed heartfelt sorrow. For some these stories were new; for all they resonated with personal experiences and the global perspective. The following edited extracts provide a glimpse of how the misuse of power has touched, and continues to affect, the lives of people and communities worldwide.

Dewi Hughes, Wales: While I was not beaten for speaking Welsh, my high school education left me in no doubt about the inferiority of my native culture... Abuse of power in our case...was English imperial power not wanting to be inconvenienced by linguistic diversity. There was collusion from the Church of England in Wales in the nineteenth century ... Christian faith has played a very important part in our resistance to the abuse of power – in leading us to adopt pacifist methods and in giving us a strong intellectual foundation to persevere.

Hanna Massad, Gaza: What makes the Palestinian story and this conflict more complicated [is that] many Jews, Christians and Muslims cover it with the clothes of religion and in the name of religion we oppress people and persecute each other. [And] as Terry LeBlanc said '[the Europeans] failed…to consider the deep connectedness of Native people to the land of their forefathers and mothers; the understanding that the land was possessed of a spiritual essence.' …We see this where the British government…did not understand how much the land meant to the Muslims and to the Christian…where the land is part of their faith tradition and belonging…

Stan McKay, Canada: There is complexity in conversations about mission because the church is tempted to declare that it possesses 'the truth'. …studies at theological schools often programme students to assume the church has resolved historic injustice. …Many churches and the government have made apologies… Statements of apology do not change the impact of historic injustice when there is not significant change in the society and its institutions.

Philomena N. Mwaura, Kenya: I have come to understand that the way churches interpret scripture and understand social dynamics influences the way power is exercised in church and society. Images of a 'powerful' God have been utilised…to justify colonisation, oppression and marginalisation. …My faith has convinced me that cherishing such notions in contexts where the majority of people are victims of power is a theological aberration. I also see the need to redefine power and reclaim the images of God in the scriptures that affirm the life-enhancing attributes of God... These are the resources that provide sites for resisting abusive power and reconstructing liberating perspectives.

Philip Wingeier-Rayo, Cuba and USA: One result of the European colonization methods in…South America was the creation of the *mestizo* race – neither purely European, nor purely indigenous – due to the conquest strategy…of sending mostly single men soldiers. … Upon reflecting on the Canadian stories and the growth of the US Hispanic population and the conquest of the Incas in Peru, I find…culture is a battle ground. There is a struggle over who has the power to educate… Will young people [e.g., Latino children in the US, *mestizo* children in Peru] be raised into the dominant culture or will they learn their native language, history, foods and culture? This is not a new question in the history of conquest.

Débora García Morales, Nicaragua: To read these texts…from my Nicaraguan reality, suggests reflection on the relations of equity from difference. The reflection on power that is made from conditions of subalternity[50] can help. …Faith is the expression of the commitment with God who is in solidarity with those who are subordinated… This criterion has helped me: What does God demand of those who have power? (Micah 6:8) In reading the text, and its context…I find an attempt to justify themselves by those who have not done what God asks.

J. Kwabena Asamoah-Gyadu, Ghana: A majority of African leaders…received their education …through missionary schools… Indeed the former Secretary General of the United Nations, Kofi Annan and one of Africa's most illustrious theologians, Kwame Bediako, were both educated at the oldest Wesleyan mission residential school in Ghana, Mfantsipim School in Cape Coast. …Unfortunately the strong link between education and mission led to cerebral Christianity devoid of the experiential aspects of the encounter with the Spirit of God…familiar in African religion.

Dorottya Nagy, Romania and The Netherlands: Both the cases – the Aboriginal peoples of Canada and Hungarians in Romania – provide examples of how the land is being viewed as the sacred creature of the Creator. The idea of the sacredness of the land is relevant for the emerging theologies of environment. Yet, there is one mistake…in the Hungarian discourses on land. Land is still being viewed as the property of the community; and it is thought that being first on a given territory…gives the right to own the land. …How rich the myths on settlement, God-given guidance to the land… How they all sustain the idea of the property! When influenced by Christianity this idea can develop in much positive direction but it can also shape negative and destructive ideologies...

Philip Siew, Malaysia: In reading the case studies, my heart is saddened by the destructive nature of power being misused, especially in the context of mission endeavour. I have come across the alarming mistakes of power being wrongly used in abusive manner, especially in the context of doing mission. This has caused me to be extra careful of how I hold and use power. …All cultures can be redeemed to manifest God's glory!

Dorcas Gordon, Canada: Antone's case study reminds me how easily a vision, perfect yet imperfect at the same time, can be subverted into something more flawed. ... LeBlanc calls us to view the world as one of balance and harmony in which all are brothers and sisters. I see this as the essence of a sacred living out of power. It is a reminder that not only are we made by our culture, but that the potential is within us to transform culture.

Edley J. Moodley, South Africa and USA: The psychological trauma and damage that occurred as a result of apartheid…cannot be overstated. The Truth and Reconciliation Committee…exposed atrocities experienced by those opposed to apartheid in South Africa, but…more empirical evidence of apartheid crimes surfaces each day… The counterpoint to the abuse of power…came for me via a measured response by people in the Colored, Indian, and African churches. Not least among them was the minority ethnic group of Indian Christians affiliated with the Bethesda Movement.[51] … This group, suffering disenfranchisement at the hands of [both] the black majority and the minority white race…, actively participated in the Bethseda Temple where all races were welcome...

Tito Paredes, Peru: It resonates with our historical and present situation of indigenous peoples of the Andean Countries. Although we did not have the…widespread practice of the residential schools for native peoples, the

> attitudes toward native cultures and peoples were similar. LeBlanc does a good job in describing the problem of Western missions among indigenous peoples as one of confusing culture with the Gospel… The Western church, in our case the Spanish-speaking churches, would do well in siding with the indigenous peoples…

4 Theological Reflection: A Time for Healing*

Reading the stories of Aboriginal people journeying through the residential school experience moves us deeply toward the suffering of the other. The mission of the church, conceived as a colonial undertaking, caused harm. The marriage of political and economic colonization with religion formed a socialization project that devastated generations of indigenous people from many communities across Canada. For decades, no corner of the nation was left untouched by the colonizing reach of the residential school experiment.

Despite the intention to promote well-being, partnering the gospel with the imposition of culture meant stripping away the culture of the other. The assumption of the racial and cultural inferiority of Aboriginal peoples, set in juxtaposition to the presumed superiority of European culture, meant the practical dehumanization of the other. When Christian leaders of an earlier generation formed a partnership with the government based on the view that only the assimilated indigenous person was worthy of citizenship and recognition as a person under the law, a trajectory of harm unfolded that wrapped countless children and their families in trauma and dislocation. To replace one culture with another meant that the 'inferior' culture must be stripped away. To accomplish that goal, children were forcibly removed from their families, severed from their kinship groups and the traditional wisdoms which had sustained them as a people.

The structure of the residential school system meant that children taken into care by the government were subject to both structural and capricious harm. Grossly under-funded by the Canadian government, schools often providing inadequate nutrition, housing, clothing and care were even less likely to provide effective education. It also meant that, in many circumstances, poorly supervised children were left vulnerable to the abuses of violence and humiliation by their caregivers. By its very structure, the residential school system created a world in which its own objectives could never be achieved. Rather than empowering children to fully engage the opportunities of European culture, residential schools left countless children emotionally crippled, effectively illiterate, and sitting on the sidelines of Canadian society. Yet, a Canadian Anglican Bishop writing in 1967 protested to the Department of

---

* By Wendy Fletcher, Principal and Dean, and Professor of Church History at Vancouver School of Theology, a researcher of ecclesiastical and women's history.

Indian Affairs (DIA) that residential schools, even as the department prepared to close them as a failed experiment, should be left open:

> We must continue our efforts among the Indians. Although there is no hope for this generation, if we persist, perhaps we will be able to raise up their grandchildren to the level of a servant class.[52]

The missiology underpinning the residential school system was malformed. It assumed that the good news of the gospel could be shared through force and coercion. In the context of triumphalist, liberal Christianity, the church enthusiastically embraced social reconstruction as religious work. In our effort to remake the world in our own image, we fell. We know from the lessons of history that North American colonization is just another configuration of the relationship between gospel and power which has led to acts of enormous evil perpetrated against the innocent. We know that in every instance the use of power for forcible conversion has given way to destructive outcomes; force does not teach a gospel of love.

In response to these stories, partners from around the globe sound a similar note. In each case, the writers move to their own context, where the misuse of power – power over the other – has led to harm, sin and alienation. All can readily identify the effects of such abuse in their own worlds. Several name the devastating effects which eradication of culture left behind, like loss of ethnic identity, social cohesion and meaning. All resonate with the implicit harm that a legacy of colonization (whether based on race, gender or class) leaves behind for the next generation to clean up.

That's us. We are the generation who must formulate our own theory of mission and its right relation to power. We are the ones asked to move forward after the fall. Where do we go from here? The stories point the way. In each case, the place of moving forward is rooted in mutual release. As joint actors in the residential school drama, each name their story, one of harm and the other of repentance, and a stark truth becomes palpable: no justice is possible in this situation. There is no compensation which can adequately make right the loss of childhood, culture and freedom for several generations and multiple cultures. A childhood cannot be given back.

If not justice, then what can make sense of, and move beyond, the harm of colonization? The stories shared lend themselves to the motif of reconciliation woven from a genuine accounting of the harm and a sincere plea of repentance. Release of harms received by those injured is the next movement in the unfolding dance of reconciliation, as those injured literally open their arms wide in an embrace of welcome, very like the embrace of the cross. As kinship-based cultures, indigenous communities, prior to our government's assimilation policies, welcomed the gospel as communities. Now as communities, indigenous people are beginning the journey of communal forgiveness and release. There is no reason why such welcome and forgiveness should be possible. For some, it may be inconceivable to imagine; and yet, the generosity of spirit expressed by many of those harmed, as they move toward the other in welcome, is opening the way for a transfiguration of this old story into a new day. Perhaps if I had not experienced this opening into transfiguration, I would not understand.

On 9 October 2008, I travelled to the *Nisga'a* village of *Laxgalts'ap*. I made the journey to attend the funeral of Bradley Martin, son of Willard Martin, Vancouver School of Theology alumnus and *Nisga'a* hereditary chief. Bradley had ended his own life. Over a century before, Christian missionaries, bringing their own worldview to this community, had insisted there be no proper burials when death is by suicide. The *Nisga'a* adopted and followed that teaching ever since, even as the church changed its thinking and practice. Willard insisted on giving his son the dignity of a Christian burial and settlement feast; I went to support him in his courage and his wisdom, and to honour the life of his son. Willard, as with many of his people, has survived the trauma of residential schooling and all the dislocation it engendered for so many. I carried with me the weight of our history, a colonizing church, a legacy of harm. I felt shame.

When I arrived, Willard cautioned that likely very few would attend the funeral, as it was breaking with cultural practice. He then asked me to participate in the liturgy which would honour his son. Surprisingly, hundreds of *Nisga'a* came. When the Eucharist was celebrated, every single person came forward to receive. When the *Nisga'a* priest, James, asked me to walk with him ahead of the casket to the graveside, I looked back. Ten young *Nisga'a* men carried their friend, refusing to put him down until the grave was reached. With tears streaming down their faces they walked and walked; behind them hundreds of Bradley's people walked with him his last mile. We stood around the open grave and then James turned and handed me his prayer book, 'You commit him to God for us', he said. As I said the words of committal, and we all stood there suffering and hoping together past the stain of an incredibly wounding history, I saw the healing of God begin. I saw the healing water of God's grace pour out to all corners of the earth and understood that nothing was beyond its reach.

With such moments, a beginning place is framed. By grace and the opportunity which repentance and release offers, we are invited to reformulate our understanding of mission and its relationship to power. If we are able to deconstruct our earlier assumptions about the relationship between gospel and culture, we can begin again. While apparently we have understood that religion always reflects culture, we have not always understood that transposing our assumptions about normative culture onto the other, as a necessary dimension of transmission of the gospel, destroys the gospel's intent. If there is no space for cultural accommodation of the other, then the gospel becomes an agent of hegemonic discourse rather than the liberating word of God's welcome and mercy. A gospel engaged with, but not normalizing, culture is an appropriate vehicle for the transmission of a unitive vision of community which empowers rather than disempowers the other.

Perhaps in the final instance we in this generation are invited to see that the gospel we carry to the world is itself an act of mercy and reconciliation enfleshed. We are disciples of a Reconciler who came to bind up the wounds of all those who have been hurt – perhaps firstly by those who have been hurt at the hands of those who thought they were right. A missiology which will carry us forward onto new ground is not the proclamation of any dogmatism, any set of moral imperatives, or any culturally embedded values as necessary companions to the gospel. It is not a project grounded in a notion of power over another. Rather it is the enfleshment of radical love, which by its practice encircles rather than divides, lifts up rather than steps on, and heals rather than harms.

As we attempt to live into new partnerships in church and world, 1 Corinthians 12:14-26 is a suitable companion for us. With his image of the body, Paul speaks to the community at Corinth drawing on an ancient wisdom of how communities configure themselves. However, Paul takes Aristotle's image of the body and literally turns it on its head. In this passage he insists that the members of the body which are least honoured should be the most honoured; that the least valued be the most cherished. Such an inversion of the power images familiar in Paul's day clarifies his intention for the early community of the followers of Jesus. The least among us, the children, will lead us.

When Paul addressed the community at Corinth, his message was radical. In the face of all our hopes of glory, the glory the world might give, or even the church – in its own limited way, Paul speaks. He says each member of the body is most beloved, and the least among us most beloved of all. He summons us to see ourselves in a new way, not as neo-empire rebuilding wannabes, not as saviours who will fix the world or save the church, but as committed disciples of the Word of Life who will love the world, who will live as love in the world by seeing, by understanding that we, beloved children of God, community of the faithful, we are a community of diverse people. Blessed be. By a gospel of humility and compassion, and only by grace, we will renew the world.

It appears that the witness of the Canadian church in this generation is that there is no harm beyond the reach of God's healing grace. All around us in these hours, the signs of a new world struggling to be born paint themselves across the backdrop of former desolations. Perhaps struggle is another word for hope. Mercy abounds and deliverance remakes us.

5 Afterword: The Story of Residential Schools Continues*

The Anglican Church of Canada, The United Church of Canada, and The Presbyterian Church in Canada, in the late twentieth century, issued apologies and confessions to God and to the First Nation, Inuit and Métis peoples concerning the churches' complicity in the residential school system.[53] Some Canadian Roman Catholic entities and individual bishops have made similar apologies. His Holiness, Pope Benedict XVI, issued an important statement of regret over residential schools in April 2009.

These four denominations entered into a settlement agreement with the Government of Canada, the Assembly of First Nations, and representatives of residential school survivors who had sought legal redress for the physical, sexual, psychological and spiritual abuse suffered as a result of their experience in residential schools. The agreement provides financial compensation to the over 80,000 survivors still living in Canada, and an independent adjudicative process for awarding compensation for substantiated physical and sexual abuse claims. Some 13,000 such claims have already been filed.

The Agreement, effective September 2007, also provides for a Canadian Truth and Reconciliation Commission. The Commission, which began its work in July 2009, has a five-year mandate to examine the legacy of residential schools; document and preserve the story for future generations; and make recommendations to the churches, the government, the indigenous community, and Canadian society at large – recommendations to support the journey of healing and the building of healthy relationships in communities throughout Canada. Significant funding will be available to support community-level events that bring people together on the road towards reconciliation.

More than twenty years ago, a more broadly representative Canadian Christian community committed to supporting the indigenous community's struggle for justice by issuing a pastoral statement called *A New Covenant*,[54] to which they re-committed themselves in 2007. Partnerships between the churches and the indigenous community are growing. The road ahead is long. As some Aboriginal people have said, 'We walk backwards on the long road into the future together, looking to our past to shape our journey forward.'[55]

6 Study Questions

1. It is difficult to understand why we must repent for the sins of a previous generation.
   i. What calls us into repentance and reconciliation?
   ii. How could living out confession/apology (accepted or not) shape the way the church does mission?

---

* By Lori Ransom.

iii. What would 'reconciliation' mean in the contexts described in the case study?
iv. What does 'repentance' look like, practically and theologically, in such contexts?
v. What will sustain journeys of repentance and reconciliation?

2. Power has generally been understood as power *over*.
   i. What alternative models of power are in scripture?
   ii. What strategies could move the power relationships in mission from domination/submission to relationships of mutuality and justice?
   iii. How do we resist moving back into relationships of power *over*?

3. The residential school case study exposes the damaging impact when one culture imposes itself on another. Despite *cross*-cultural and *multi*-cultural approaches, a hierarchical understanding of cultural differences persists in mission praxis.
   i. How can we move to inter-cultural relationship models where power with gives people the capacity to accept from and to embrace the other; to be transformed in relationship with the other; to receive the gift of the Holy Spirit in the gift of the other?

4. Political, economic and religious powers perpetrate evil and seek to redress evil within legal structures which the powers themselves have defined. As a result legal remedies often do not meet the demands of justice in the biblical sense of building right relationship.
   i. What theologies move us beyond legal frameworks to practices of justice?
   ii. What is justice to those whose lives have been deeply scarred and lost through injustice? How can we support victims of injustice in claiming their rightful role in determining what is just?

5. Indigenous Christians suggest that a biblical metaphor for the restoration of the identities destroyed by colonization experiences is the prophetic call of Ezekiel 37, the restoration to life of dry bones.
   i. How can indigenous theologies and biblical scholarship inform journeys of justice and reconciliation and practices of mission?
   ii. What is the role of the recovery of indigenous spiritualities in transforming abusive relations of power?
   iii. How does Ezekiel 37 speak to you concerning issues of mission and power?

7 Priorities

1. Repentance and atonement involve the powerful…

…listening and learning, giving up place of power, giving power
to those harmed by past mission
to tell us how they feel, to help us see the impact of past actions;
to offer, or not offer, as they see fit, suggestions

for where we go from here,
or what needs to happen,
before we can move forward together.
...learning patience in waiting for forgiveness,
which is *not* the first step;
neither is reconciliation work linear.
…recognising these stages:
opening oneself to the other,
confession, repentance,
atonement, forgiveness, reconciliation;
stages that go back and forth
and recur as relationships deepen.

2. Restorative justice involves processes…
…upholding alternative ways
to seek justice and reconciliation.
…emphasising truth telling and restoring relationship,
and *not* attributing guilt and assigning punishment.
…seeking justice between churches and communities
that have been abused by them
or that seek restoration of relationship
between an individual and a community.
…used in criminal justice systems and formal commissions of truth and reconciliation.
…of learning from restorative justice traditions in indigenous communities.

3. Anti-racism and inter-culturalism involve…
...recognising how our understanding of the gospel
has been culturally informed.
…learning ways to avoid giving power and authority
to Christianity as expressed by some cultures,
over Christianity as expressed by others.
…challenging cultural dominance that brings opportunity
to see God's truth revealed
by sharing insights across cultures.
…embracing *inter*-culturality in mission as
openness to engaging differences,
being transformed in encounters with the other.

4. Lifting up the voices of marginalized and subjugated peoples means…
…those with monetary power and relational power can support the powerless
in documenting, recording,
sharing their stories, experiences, insights, knowledge, arts.
…integrating the voices of the powerless in all aspects of mission and ministry,
including decision-making structures
and theological education and formation.
…requiring the powerful to maintain a self-critical stance

about continuing complicity in empire
and structures of domination in church and society.

5. Transforming the meaning of mission means that...
...God's mission calls all people
to work together for healing and justice
in partnerships of mutuality and respect.
...we need new models of mission
emphasising
sharing the work of defining mission
and sharing the exercise of power.
...God's mission is
a gift to all those engaged in that mission,
an opportunity to be transformed by others,
to receive their gifts,
and to become a witness to the gifts of others.

Endnotes

[1] 'Aboriginal peoples' is a collective name used in Canada for the original peoples of North America and their descendants. The Canadian constitution recognizes three groups of Aboriginal people: Indians (commonly referred to as First Nation peoples), Métis and Inuit. These are three distinct peoples with unique histories, languages, cultural practices and spiritual beliefs. More than one million people in Canada (almost four percent of the population) identify themselves as an Aboriginal person, according to the 2006 Census. Fifty-three percent are registered Indians, thirty percent are Métis, eleven percent are non-status Indians and four percent are Inuit. Over half (54 percent) of Aboriginal peoples live in urban areas.
'First Nation peoples' typically refers to what are still described in Canadian law as the 'Indian' peoples of Canada. The term 'Indian', applied to these people by European explorers, is no longer favoured among indigenous peoples who prefer to be identified by their indigenous nationality, e.g. *Cree, Iroquois, Haida, Mik'maw*. Many communities of indigenous peoples also use the term 'First Nation' in the name of their community, e.g. the Fort Albany First Nation. Currently, there are 615 First Nation communities, which represent more than fifty nations or cultural groups, where fifty Aboriginal languages are spoken.
'Inuit' are the Aboriginal people of Arctic Canada. About 45,000 Inuit live in 53 communities in: *Nunatsiavut* (Labrador), *Nunavik* (Quebec), *Nunavut*, and the *Inuvialuit* Settlement Region of the Northwest Territories. The word Inuit means 'the people' in their language (Inuktitut) and is the term by which they refer to themselves. The term 'Eskimo', applied to Inuit by European explorers, is no longer used in Canada.
'Métis' are officially recognized as among the indigenous peoples of Canada. They developed a unique culture as a people who lived in distinct communities as descendants of French settlers and various First Nation peoples, located particularly in western Canada.

[2] Significant work on the theme of 'Mission and Power' relating to Edinburgh 2010 is also being done in Latin America by the Latin American Theological Fellowship which

held conferences in the Dominican Republic, Costa Rica and Chile on 2009. This will be included in the report of the Edinburgh 2010 conference, June 2010.

[3] Jon and Lori wish to express their delight at this opportunity to work with Bob, Charles, Gail, John, Maylanne and Tom whose knowledge, experience, judgment and good humour guided every step of the work.

[4] We are aware that the themes of power and powerlessness alluded to in this paragraph, and so integral to our identities as followers of Jesus and as members of the Community that he referred to as his body, cannot be adequately dealt with in this short chapter. A slightly more fulsome exploration of the theme may be found in chapter seven of Jonathan Bonk's book, *Missions and Money: Affluence as a Missionary Problem ... Revisited* (in the revised and expanded edition, New York: Orbis Books, 2006, 182–188). An adaptation of this material may be found on the Edinburgh 2010 website: www.edinburgh2010.org. It must be noted that many of the most potent and spiritually dynamic churches in the world today are identified as 'Pentecostal' or 'charismatic – comprised of men and women who experience, acknowledge, and celebrate the power of the Holy Spirit in their lives and congregations. That these dynamic congregations tend to thrive among the so-called 'wretched of the earth' is no surprise to any student of the New Testament or mission history.

[5] A majority of merchants, armies, and migrants to the Americas, South Africa, and Macronesia represented the theological posterity of Latin Christendom. Christendom remains deeply divided into six parts: Roman Catholic and Arian in the West; Syrian or Assyrian (Nestorian) of the East and the Coptic Orthodox with the Greek or Melkite, and the Syrian Orthodox or Antiochene or Jacobite or Monophysite. See Peter Brown, *The Rise of Western Christendom: Triumph and Diversity, A.D. 200–1000* (Oxford: Blackwell, 2003), 279–285.

[6] J. R. Miller, *Shingwauk's Vision: A History of Native Residential Schools* (Toronto: University of Toronto Press, 2000).

[7] For the detailed story see John Milloy, *A National Crime: The Canadian Government and the Residential School System, 1879-1986* (Winnipeg: University of Manitoba Press, 1999).

[8] Milloy, *A National Crime*.

[9] John Ralston Saul, *A Fair Country: Telling Truths About Canada* (Toronto: Viking Canada, 2008).

[10] Henri Membertou (1510-1611), a *Mi'kmaq* sagamou in Acadia (Nova Scotia), defended French colonists from other threatening Indians. Charles Eastman Ohiyesa (1858-1939), a *Lakota* raised in Manitoba, attended university and became a physician, storyteller, historian.

[11] Thomas S. Giles in *Christian History*, 35, Vol. XI, No. 3 (1992). I strongly disagree with much the author writes that upholds the stereotypical history of mission bringing civilization to the Indians, devoid of harm. But his comments here on agency are accurate.

[12] In international law, *terra nullius* refers to land never subjected to the sovereignty of any state; and sovereignty may be acquired through occupation. While 'Manifest Destiny' was birthed in the 1800s in America, its philosophical roots were evident in the actions of colonial powers from the earliest point of modernity. I believe churches understood this to be true.

[13] From Ezekiel 37:1b (NRSV).

[14] *Report of the Royal Commission on Aboriginal Peoples* (Ottawa: Canada Communications Group Publishing 1996), 171.
[15] Milloy, A *National Crime*, 27.
[16] From 1905 until 1911 Frank Oliver was appointed and served as the Minister of the Interior and Superintendent-General of Indian Affairs.
[17] *Report of the Royal Commission*, 231.
[18] I. Knockwood, *Out of the Depths: The Experiences of Mi'kmaw Children at the Indian Residential School at Shubenacadie, Nova Scotia* (Lockeport: Roseway, 1992), 50.
[19] Knockwood, *Out of the Depths*, 31.
[20] Knockwood, *Out of the Depths*, 33.
[21] The exact dating of school closures varies depending on what is used for the benchmark. 1998 is the date on which the last facility, originally constructed as a residential school, closed.
[22] J. McDonald, 'The Schools that Failed', *The Edmonton Journal* (2 June 1991), G1–G3, 23.
[23] Cathy Richardson and Bill Nelson, 'A Change of Residence: Government Schools and Foster Homes as Sites of Forced Aboriginal Assimilation – A paper Designed to Provoke Thought and Systemic Change', *First People's Child and Family Review*, 3/2 (2007; Special Issue), 78.
[24] McDonald, 'The Schools that Failed', 22.
[25] Madeleine Dion Stout and Gregory Kipling, *Aboriginal People, Resilience and the Residential School Legacy* (Ottawa: Aboriginal Healing Foundation, 2003), 33.
[26] John Gast's famous painting, *American Progress* makes clear that all that lay before the advance of civilization, including Indians and wild creatures, was to be expunged or brought under subjugation.
[27] A. Wade, 'Resistance Knowledges: Therapy with Aboriginal Persons Who Have Experienced Violence', *Canadian Western Geographical Series*, 31 (1995), 167-206.
[28] D.B. Smith, *Sacred Feathers: The Reverend Peter Jones (Kahkeweaquonaby) and the Mississauga Indians* (Toronto: University of Toronto Press, 1987), 193.
[29] S.R. McVitty, 'The Story of Seventy Years of Progress', *The Missionary Bulletin* 16/2 (1920), 160-208.
[30] Smith, *Sacred Feathers*, 214.
[31] Smith, *Sacred Feathers*, 214.
[32] Smith, *Sacred Feathers*, 214.
[33] McVitty, *The Missionary Bulletin*, 176.
[34] E. Graham, *The Mush Hole: Life at Two Indian Residential Schools* (Waterloo, ON: Heffle Publishing, 1997).
[35] E. Antone, *In Search of Voice: A Collaborative Investigation on Learning Experiences of All Onyota'a:ka*, unpublished thesis (Toronto, ON: University of Toronto, 1997).
[36] The 1969 White Paper was a government policy proposal to abolish the Indian Act, reject land claims and assimilate Native people with the status of other ethnic minorities rather than as a distinct group. It was strongly opposed by Native people and never implemented.
[37] E. Antone, 'A Citizenship Dilemma: Aboriginal Peoples and Identity Questions', in Karsten Mundel and Daniel Schugurensky (eds), *Lifelong Citizenship Learning,*

Participatory Democracy and Social Change (Toronto: Transformative Learning Centre, OISE/University of Toronto), 2004.
[38] Antone, 'A Citizenship Dilemma'.
[39] Translated from *Omushkago Cree* of James Bay.
[40] Canada Ministries was a department of the Board of World Missions which was amalgamated in 1992 with other boards to become the Life and Mission Agency.
[41] For a summary of the *Oka* crisis see www.histori.ca/peace/page.do?pageID=343.
[42] The CCCB decided that local entities would be responsible for responding to the claims. This decision became significant in dealing with the Government of Canada around the matter of legal liability since the CCCB indicated it was the individual entities that ran the schools that were responsible.
[43] *Acts and Proceedings*, The Presbyterian Church in Canada, Toronto, 1992, 562-565.
[44] *Acts and Proceedings*, 1992, 562-565.
[45] *Acts and Proceedings*, The Presbyterian Church in Canada, Toronto, 1994, 365-377, www.presbyterian.ca/webfm_send/1510.
[46] It was heartening to learn that at a recent meeting between the Grand Chief and the Pope in Rome that the Grand Chief forgave his church for the abuse he had experienced.
[47] People like Maggie, Bobby, TJ, Mike, Bob, Yvonne, Phil, Ted, Garnett, Margaret, Vivian and numerous other Aboriginal people, too many to name individually.
[48] Formerly known as the alternate dispute resolution hearings.
[49] *Report of the Royal Commission*.
[50] This is a theme in postcolonial studies: from subaltern (subordinate, marginal, or 'sub-otherness').
[51] John Francis Rowlands, son of a British Quaker turned Pentecostal who came to South Africa in 1925, led the Bethesda Movement.
[52] Bishop of Huron to the Secretary of the Department of Indian Affairs, 1967.
[53] For apologies from the churches see www.rememberingthechildren.ca/partners/documents/ApologiesfromChurches.pdf.
[54] *A New Covenant: Towards the Constitutional Recognition and Protection of Aboriginal Self-Government in Canada*, www.presbyterian.ca/ministry/justice/healing/newcovenant.
[55] Terry Leblanc, at a Mission and Power study group meeting, September 2009.

THEME FIVE
FORMS OF MISSIONARY ENGAGEMENT

Preface

The core group for the theme 'Forms of Missionary Engagement' began work electronically through the Faith2Share website (www.faith2share.net), identifying and discussing key themes before meeting face-to-face in Oxford, UK on 12-13 January 2009 and again on 15-17 June. The group's conveners were Mark Oxbrow (Anglican, British) of the Church Mission Society (CMS) and Faith2Share, Oxford, UK and Genevieve James (Pentecostal, South African) of the University of South Africa (UNISA). Knud Jorgensen (Lutheran, Denmark/Norway) of Areopagos, Denmark acted as secretary to the group. The core group also included: Olga Oleinik (Orthodox, Belarus), Bambang Budijanto (Lutheran, Indonesia/USA), Hun Kim (Presbyterian, South Korea/UK), Monica Melanchthon (Lutheran, India), Jan Lenssen (Catholic, Belgium and Kenya), Joy Mindo (African Initiated Churches, Kenya) and Lazarus Phiri (Evangelical, Zambia). Members of the group contributed papers, solicited other articles, and also received some un-solicited articles, which are posted on the Edinburgh 2010 website. These include papers from Solomon Christian, Joon-Sik Park, Peter Fischer-Neilsen, Jacob S. Dharmaraj, Mary Lederleitner, Jean-Paul A. Heldt. Many of these are referenced in this chapter.

This article is the result of a study process among several contributors across the world. The authors not only hail from different countries but also come from differing ethnic groups, generations and faith traditions. This being the case, there has been a unanimous understanding that 'Forms of Missionary Engagement' is simply too vast a research area to adequately explore in one article. The study group has therefore decided on producing further material in multiple formats in the near future.

1 Introduction

This article explores the varieties, manifestations and strategies of missionary engagement in our world today. We begin by studying the theological underpinnings regarding the role of the local church in mission and move on to examine and describe specific areas of strategy that are salient to the mission endeavour in the twenty-first century. These forms of missionary engagement include mission with the vulnerable, partnership, mission with children, 'receiving' mission, and the mission of the media. These specific themes are emphasised since they bear significant consequences for missionary engagement in our time. This article will conclude with urgent areas for strategic consideration in our mission engagement.

The present context of mission engagement takes places amidst globalization, neo-liberalism, multiculturalism, unprecedented urbanization, religious fundamentalism, widespread poverty and injustice, a growing yearning for new forms of spirituality and the 'shift of the centre of gravity' of Christianity from global North to global South. In some respects this contextual plethora does mirror the scenario of Edinburgh 1910 yet in other respects, today, the world is essentially a different place. The infinite diversities of contexts yield a multitude of focused and creative mission strategies

The Roots of Mission Strategy

As indicated above mission strategy is rooted in a specific spirituality and historical expression of faith. It is formulated in response to a specific social context and carried out with the available resources. The exploration of mission engagement typologies is an unending endeavour as change banishes the conventional and is the only constant.

2 The Primary Role of the Local Church in Mission: The Local Church in Many Forms

Since God is a missionary God (*missio Dei*), God's people are a missionary people (John 17:18-21) and they await 'the life of the age to come'. Edinburgh 1910 talked about 'church *and* mission'; today we must talk about 'the church *of* the mission' and 'the mission *of* the church'[1].

2.1 The local church as the church-in-mission

The local church is the people of God in the local context. This context and church are part of the Church universal; we may therefore use the term *glocal* (the local and global). In each local context the people of God are the footprint of the Church universal. It seems the early churches had no authority over one another, from the very beginning each was a *complete* church. Roland Allen suggests that their success was due to the fact that they trusted both the Lord and the people to whom they had gone.[2] It took decades before mission took the views and advice of Allen to heart but slowly the Edinburgh 1910 concept of 'older' and 'younger' churches has been replaced and the church-for-others has become the church-with-others.[3] This applies to both Protestants and Catholics. The Roman Catholic Church has affirmed that the universal church finds its true existence in each local church and that the universal church only exists where there are local churches.[4]

In the past, local churches often had a parish structure. In many places this remains an appropriate structure, especially in countries with so called 'majority' (state or 'established') churches. The parish structure, however, grew alongside the notion of *Corpus Christianum* where the church was wedded to the holders of power. The church became a pastoral institution adopting the shape of society's structure with parochial churches and a division between *clerici* (priest) and *idiotes* (lay people).[5] Even whilst the parish structure remained dominant, there have always been alternate models with greater focus on the small community (*ecclesiola* within the *ecclesia*), the monastic community, the fellowship of believers, and on being *missionary bands*.

Today the people of God creates and experiments with new forms and structures. One such model is *the house church* which exemplifies the characteristics of the early church; that is: it has no church building, often no professional form of leadership, and is sometimes considered an illegal religion. Using the images of *clan, synagogue and temple*,[6] the house church is the clan living together in a small 'hamlet'; the synagogue is a community where the smaller groups gather regularly; and the temple is the site of larger scale celebration – where the many come together.

Other models are called *emerging churches*[7] – new forms that try to bind together the original apostolic core with new imaginative, less structured forms, gathering in cafes, dance clubs, on riverbanks, etc. These emerging churches live as communities that transform secular space and live out a spirituality similar to that of the desert fathers.

We may also consider what are called *independent* churches (or African indigenous or initiated churches) encompassing a total of 400 million people worldwide – churches that reject historical denominationalism and seek a more effective and contextual missionary lifestyle.

All these new forms signal more *fluid* communities, providing multiple strategic options depending on context and target group. Despite these new models emerging, with growing dissatisfaction with traditional forms of church, more Christians, primarily in the West, live without a local church, alienated from current expressions of church. It is worth noting, however, that fluidity of form can weaken the sense of belonging and responsibility within community

(Heb 10:25; 13:1), particularly when churches mirror the consumer society (e.g. market driven churches). Membership in such a community may not lead to any lasting changes in the life of a person; thus people could miss such essential things in Christian life as accountability, sacrifice, and ministry.

The twentieth century has seen the rise and growth of various spiritual/ecclesial movements and non-monastic religious communities, such as the Focolare and St. Egidio communities in the Roman Catholic Church; Vineyard and the Alpha course in Protestant/non-denominational churches; the Lord's Army (Romania) and the Transfiguration Fellowship (Russia) within the Orthodox Church. Such communities came into being as a reaction to the institutionalization of churches. Being movements of ecclesial renewal they also have a strong mission impetus.

2.2 Mission, revival and renewal

Renewal of the local church begins when the Holy Spirit calls a congregation or group back to their true identity and source (Luke 15:17). This identity is found in God, God's coming kingdom, in the Word made flesh, the Bible and the Tradition of the Church universal. Local church renewal occurs when the Holy Spirit transforms the people and the community into the likeness of Christ through repentance (*metanoia*) and openness of hearts to God. This renewal of spiritual power comes often as the community creates space for prayer and when it worships in 'spirit and truth' (John 4:23). *Worship, community and mission* signify the three-dimensional life of the local church.[8]

2.3 The witnessing church

The primary task of local Christians is to be witnesses. The church's call, according to the New Testament, is to witness. *Mission is witness*. *Martyria* is the sum of *kerygma, koinonia* and *diaconia* – all three of which constitute important dimensions of the witness for which the church is called and sent. We read the New Testament as the testimony (witness) of witnesses, equipping other witnesses for the common mission of the church.[9] *Testimony* in this way becomes a demonstration, through the lives and actions of God's people, to the fact that the kingdom of God is present in the disciples of Jesus Christ. This understanding of mission as the witnessing life of the body of Christ is crucial today when in many cases mission has become a private affair with little or no accountability to the local church.

In some new models of local church *witness* is viewed as a missional vocation and as part and parcel of being incarnational and relational. Is not one of the most important explanations of growth among churches in the South that they are witnessing churches, not only in a theoretical and theological sense, but also in practice? Do they not, more than the churches in the North, *do and practise* what they *are* ecclesiologically, that is: God's witnessing people in mission? Is not this in turn a major reason both for their own growth and for the growing missionary activity that emerges from these churches? And if so, *what may the churches in the North learn from the churches in the South with regard to mission?*

Witness and disciple-making go hand in hand.[10] Discipleship and disciple-making are the critical point in the life and being of the local church. If discipleship fails at this point, it will fail at all others. The basis for the founding of a movement that has extended itself into the twenty-first century was Jesus' investing his life and embedding his teachings in his followers and developing them into authentic disciples. Do local churches today need to find their way back to the *catechisms* of the early church and to a vigorous discipleship that in some parts of the church today has drowned in consumerism and in making discipleship too easy? We mention in this context *consumerism* because in various parts of the world this has become a driving ideology of the ministry of the local church.

Witness and discipleship will break down the traditional division between priest and lay people. One result of this is a dramatic change in the role and work of the priest/pastor. The people of God are the true priesthood (1 Pet 2:9), and therefore, all who confess Christ are 'priests'. We still need priests and pastors, as we need other leadership functions (teacher, evangelist, apostle, prophet – Eph 4:11), but the basic structure of the local church and for mission is the priesthood of all believers. The church must again become a community in which all members, equally, encourage each other to discover and develop their gifts and ministries in the countless areas of human existence where transformation and renewal are needed.

2.4 A missional church

The word *missionary* refers to the specific mission activities of the church, whereas the word *missional* is related to the nature of the church, as being sent by God to the world. A focus on the local church in mission reflects a desire to see congregations in both the North and the South become missional. Impacting the world begins with local congregations giving up Christendom assumptions and adopting a missionary stance both within their own culture and cross-culturally. Missional congregations pray for renewal both within their community and in the market place. In local congregations, missional structures are created that go beyond the hierarchies of the past and provide a balance between worship, community and mission at all levels of church life – in cells, local and trans-local expressions of church. Every member is motivated and equipped to take his/her role in inspiring, encouraging and equipping local leaders. Missional leaders fan into flame a vision that both builds on and sparks excitement and directs the church toward imaginative *diakonia*. Missional congregations partner with other communities, both congregational and those specifically ministry-focused. Activities and strategies are created that embody the way of Christ on the way to new people.[11]

2.5 The two structures of the church

It was in Antioch that the first missionary band came into being after the resurrection (Acts 13:1-3). The local church was growing among different people groups. When this local church wanted to move beyond its own borders, they prayed and the Holy Spirit told them to send out a *missionary team* of Paul and Barnabas. This model is paradigmatic for the relationship between 'come' and 'go' structures. Both are needed, both together constitute *ecclesia.* In the history of the church we find illustrations of this paradigm in the itinerant evangelists from Ireland and Scotland (*perigrini*), the monastic movement, the Nestorian church moving east, the Jesuits in India, Japan and China, the Moravian brethren, and eventually from 1792 in what we have called 'mission societies'.

This basic go-structure is needed when the local church wants to go beyond its own borders; and accountability and participation of all the community are essential here. The problem arises when the two structures are separated. The reasons for such a separation vary:

- When the church has no structure for going beyond; for example, the Reformation churches, which lacked the missionary orders of the Roman Catholic Church.
- When the church does not take up the call to go; for example, so-called 'state churches', which are defined by national boundaries.
- When individuals or small groups of Christians, fuelled by revival, search for new, more 'effective' ways; for example, the voluntary movements in the wake of the Great Awakenings.
- When mission is split into 'foreign' and 'home' missions, as at Edinburgh 1910 where the main players were 'foreign' mission societies.

The result is the emergence of so-called 'para-church' organisations, separated from the parish structure. (As both together constitute 'church', the word 'para-church' is a misnomer.)

Today the two structures are searching for ways of joining hands. Mission societies link up with the local church in new concrete ways, and local churches see themselves as 'missional' in their own context. The missionary band remains an integral part of being church, but must always find new expressions in new contexts. To better understand the nature of this shared mission, it is necessary to turn our attention to the area of vulnerability in mission.

3 Vulnerability in Mission – Mission without Power

Meet Mwizero,[12] an elderly Batwa woman from Burundi in eastern Africa. She lives with a group of widows in a makeshift grass hut. She represents the poorest people living in one of the poorest regions of the world. She has no food, no home and cannot read or write. She has no country; she is a pygmy and her neighbours do not consider her a human being. If she falls sick she cannot visit a hospital nor can she register a marriage. If someone would kill her, it would not be murder; she is, after all, not a human being. She has no church though she knows and believes that there is a God who will remember her.

Nirma Rani, a Dalit girl student from India was slapped for saying *Namaste* to a Brahmin teacher and her father was beaten up later for questioning such an act. Caste is practiced in schools where Dalit children occupy separate seats given to them. Dhanam lost her eye when she was beaten up by her teacher for helping herself to drinking water from a pot without waiting to be served by a caste person. She had polluted the water by her touch.[13] These stories of abject poverty represent many poor people. These stories must be shared.[14] The world must listen to them and allow their voices to be heard.

3.1 Human and divine vulnerability

The concept of 'vulnerable missions' is used to refer both to mission in contexts of poverty and mission by the powerless. 'Mission is an exercise in vulnerability as we share in God's reconciling purpose which was achieved by God becoming weak and helpless, particularly in the sacrifice of Jesus of Nazareth. Mission is the place of identification with the marginalized'.[15]

In an age when the majority of Christians live in more vulnerable life situations, we ask ourselves whether vulnerability contains the potential, the capacity and power that can be employed for the purposes of mission. How might a posture or position of vulnerability on the part of the church equip it for effective mission? Should vulnerability be recognised as an enabling condition for mission?

At one level mission is about communicating the faith in order that the reign of God may become a reality, making possible liberation and life in all its fullness for all vulnerable peoples, for all children of God irrespective of caste, race, religion or gender. The Bible shows special concern for the poor, the vulnerable, the forgotten and the oppressed. The heritage of the Christian faith, although filled with a myriad of injustices from colonialism, slavery, apartheid, environmental irresponsibility and mistreatment of women, also bears witness to communities who have been at the forefront in looking for ways to alleviate poverty through simple acts of kindness.

Vulnerability is also a condition of divine mission. The Christian scriptures are replete with images of the vulnerable mission of God (Isa 53: 4-5,12); of the God who identifies with the most vulnerable in society, thereby setting this God apart from all other Gods. Hence Israel asks, 'Who is like you among the gods?' (Ex 15: 11). This God is both transcendent and immanent, enmeshed in God's creation, open to being hurt and bruised by God's own creation, who suffers insults and humiliation, rejection and derision, and endures suffering in love. This vulnerability of God is driven to the limit: when in Christ God makes Godself vulnerable. The patriarchal ideal of invulnerability is opposed, in fact distorted by the Crucified, who was and is experienced by his friends as the Son of God. Jesus Christ is God's wound in the world.[16] In the suffering Jesus, God embraces the suffering of the world for the sake of humanity. Christ suffers when we suffer. The pain people suffer is the pain of Christ himself.[17] We need to be vulnerable if we want to live in an intimate relationship with one another, with God and Jesus Christ.

3.2 Vulnerability as an enabling condition for mission

We have been called to be wounded for the sake of the world. We are marked with the sign of the cross which identifies us as having been placed in the world to be wounded. Where are the wounds of the church? What type or kinds of wounds are we willing to bear and endure in and through our participation in God's mission of liberation?

There are agencies that admit to being engaged in 'vulnerable mission'. The *Alliance for Vulnerable Mission*, for example, understands vulnerable mission as 'the use of local languages in ministry combined with "missionary poverty"' as the tools required for vulnerable mission since they enforce 'humility and operation on a "level playing field" with local people'.[18] Yet, one needs to be cognisant of the difference between choosing to be vulnerable, which allows you to find ways to exploit your vulnerability, and the vulnerability of those without the choice to exploit it.[19] If we not among the vulnerable, we have the option to choose vulnerability out of love and solidarity with those who are vulnerable without the choice to exploit it.

Our vulnerable God also calls us—the church in mission—to liberate the vulnerable and heal the pain in and of the world. Our identity as church and our existence as church, finds meaning in the prolongation of God's vulnerability in service to all women and men, particularly to the despised, the humiliated, the discriminated against, and the rejected of our history. The vulnerability of the church that is engaged in mission is a sign of relationship, receptivity, and communication.

In a 1994 article, David Bosch discusses this vulnerable nature of mission by recalling the history of the many missionaries who became martyrs for the sake of their faith in mission fields far from home. With their deaths these missionaries entered a communication process not as 'models' but as 'victims', says Bosch. Their total identification with their mission resulted in martyrdom, which became 'the seed of the church'.[20] This is vulnerable mission; mission that involves being victimized, the laying down of life for the sake of the gospel. Such a missionary model that embraces sacrifice for the sake of others leads people to freedom and community and is sustained by the belief that God suffers along with the suffering peoples of this world. 'It is this dimension, more than any other that distinguishes the Christian faith from other faiths.' The distinctiveness of Christianity is to 'be looked for in its weakness, in its inability to prove itself or to force its way'.[21]

Those who are vulnerable have little to lose and are therefore prone to take more risks and be more open to others and other conditions. There is therefore a certain potential in vulnerability. By keeping windows of vulnerability we might experience new things, gain new insights for our lives and our understanding of God, the world and humanity. When someone who has no need to be vulnerable becomes vulnerable in order to identify with those who are, and together with them struggles to be resilient against all death-dealing forces, structures and systems, and thus together with them moves towards a society transformed—of justice and communion, then he or she participates in the vulnerable mission of God. The kind of mission that is required here is not of contemplative theologizing but of liberative action in solidarity with the oppressed. It is a solidarity that is built on a relationship of complete vulnerability and identification with the oppressed community; sustained by a process of mutual giving and receiving, and nurtured by seeing in the other the ethical demand of responsibility.

Mwizero and Dhanam are not just a statistic; they want to hear of the kingdom of God which will transform their world and ours. Martin Luther King Jr. wrote in his last book, *The Trumpet of Conscience*, that the rich cannot remain secure in the midst of seething poverty set beside the glaring contrast of the wealthy.[22] Brain McLaren suggests we should confront poverty by changing the dominant suicidal systems that propagate poverty in the economic sphere through stark economic injustices (prosperity), the increasing gap between the rich and the poor (equity) and a lack of peaceful coexistence (security). He says that we cannot give a little to the poor without asking the question of why they are poor. He mentions seven categories in which the church must be engaged including trade, aid, debt, limits, wages, justice and community.[23] John Stott advises the church to approach poverty in our times in three main ways: rationally, as we understand the realities given to us by statisticians; emotionally, as we see, hear, and feel the poor all around us; and biblically, in order to know the mind of God concerning poverty.[24]

Vulnerable mission begins from below, amongst downtrodden people. Samuel Escobar writes about 'mission from below' in reference to the heart-beat and the thrust of missions today. He states that 'there is an element of mystery when the dynamism of mission does not come from the people in positions of power or privilege… but from below, from the little ones, those who have few material financial or technical resources'.[25] Philip Jenkins reminds us that 'Christianity is flourishing wonderfully among the poor and the persecuted while it atrophies among the rich and secure'.[26] Perhaps the future of mission lies with the vulnerable, the powerless, and the 'small people' of our world.

4 Children: The 'New' Energy for Twenty-first Century Mission

The past decade has seen a significant awakening among some Christians to the biblical and strategic importance and potential of children and youth as both objects of and agents for world transformation. Churches are being challenged to engage with children both inside and outside the walls of the church, especially those who live in poverty, oppression, abuse and exploitation. Increasing numbers of books and other resources offer new insights into the theme of children and childhood in the Bible, child theology, children and mission, and children and leadership.[27]

The last part of the 1990s and early 2000s witnessed the birth of several major initiatives, commitments and movements for and on behalf of children, especially those who are at high risk. Among them were Viva Networks for Children at Risk and their Cutting Edges Conferences, the Oxford Statement of Children at Risk in 1997, the Godly Play Initiative (1997), the Holistic Child Development Program in Penang, Malaysia begun in 2001, the Child Theology Movement, the Children's Church Movement, Children's Prayer Movements, the Children's Spirituality Conference in 2009, the Transform World 4/14 window initiative, the Council for World Mission's Welcome Children – Welcome Jesus project and more.

Of course, there is nothing new about Christians caring for children in poverty and orphans. The Roman Catholic Church, Salvation Army and organisations such Compassion International and World Vision have been caring for children for a long time. What is new though is a clearer understanding of the biblical significance of children and of God's heart for children, including their role as 'signs' of the kingdom. There is also a much greater awareness of the receptivity of children and youth, and of their potential as a force for mission and transformation.

4.1 Children welcomed and deployed for service

Reading Scripture with the child in focus shows vividly that God values children, accepts their worship, and does not hesitate to deploy them to stimulate faith and obedience in children and adults alike. For example:

- The story of Samuel gives a picture of God speaking directly to a child (1 Sam 3).
- Jesus' own spiritual growth as a boy of twelve years involved participation including interacting, listening and asking questions among the teachers in the temple courts in Jerusalem.
- Jesus rebuked the chief priests and teachers of the law for questioning children's participation in worship and their perceptive recognition of Jesus as they sang 'Hosanna to the Son of David', quoting from Psalm 8, 'From the lips of children and infants you have ordained praise' (Matt 21:16, cf. Ps 8:2).

Children are prominent throughout Scripture as a part of God's redeeming plan. While many people view children from a future perspective as if they are persons in the making, the Bible sees them as full and complete persons both now and in the future. God relates, engages and uses children in many of the same ways as God uses adults. It may be argued that children have even better capacity than adults to relate to and engage with God. Indeed, Jesus asked the disciples to learn from children on how to relate to the truth (Luke 18:17).

4.2 Children as agents of transformation

Throughout Christian history God has used children as his willing instruments. In the great historical revivals of John Wesley, Jonathan Edwards, D.L. Moody, the French Huguenots and others, children played significant roles as active participants. The role and form of their engagement varies over time but, even today, God continues to use children in significant ways. The following stories illustrate the significant roles children and youth play today in mission and transformation.

Patricia of Santa Mesa (12 years): making disciples[28]

Patricia is a twelve-year-old girl living in the slum community of Santa Mesa in the Philippines. This community is known as a breeding ground for thieves, criminals, and sex workers. Patricia saw how the children of her neighbourhood were dishevelled, and deprived, so she started teaching five- to ten-year-olds the Bible. She gathers them together once a week, tells them about Jesus, and says she does not want them to grow up to be criminals, but to know about Jesus.

Moko and Selfin of Poso (8 years): preaching reconciliation[29]

Terrorist bombings, beheadings, and raids on villages by Islamic jihadists have plagued the people of central Sulawesi, Indonesia in recent years. After winning a preaching contest last December, eight-year-old Moko travelled to nearby towns to preach God's word to the people. While the people worship, Moko's friend Selfin prays for a touch from God. Aside from physical healing, Moko also preaches about the healing of his homeland, and his hometown of Poso. In his sermons Moko speaks of peace, reconciliation and forgiveness based on Jesus' command that people should love one another.

Pronchai, the Hmong (15 years): environmental ambassador[30]

Pronchai is a fifteen-year-old boy from an isolated minority tribal group in Thailand. For schooling, he moved to the city, where drugs are far too familiar to children and around which bad environmental practices are used, such as forest-burning. Pronchai has shown himself to be a leader, and became the initiator of several community activities, such as environmental care and drug prevention initiatives. As a result, his school received the 'clean school without drugs' award from the Princess of Thailand.

4.3 Children: The untapped force for mission

Both the biblical and contemporary case studies illustrate the timeless principle of biblical wisdom: 'Train a child in the way he should go, and when he is old he will not turn from it' (Prov 22:6). The human mind, personality, and identity are mostly formed during early childhood so that faith formation and faith decisions are also most often made in early years.[31] In the mid-nineties, Bryant L. Myers published research which reveals that nearly eighty-five percent of people who make a decision for Christ do so between the age of four and fourteen.[32] Dan Brewster and others began in 1996 referring to that 'window of receptivity' as the '4/14 Window'.[33] During the twentieth century, children and early teenagers in this age bracket represented the single largest source of new believers for the American church.[34]

The journal *Ministry Today* (January-February 2008) extensively reported a new movement of church engagement with children in the US and abroad. Globally an increasing number of local churches are recognising that children have far more spiritual potential than church leaders had realised. This new awareness is igniting a spiritual revolution in these churches. Many children and young people are no longer coming to church only to be entertained. Rather, given an opportunity and a challenge, they come to worship, contribute and become equipped for the ministry. Children are no longer seen as primarily the 'mission field' but as effective agents of mission.[35]

In the Roman Catholic mission tradition children are invited into a real involvement in mission by the *Pontifical Society of Missionary Childhood*.[36] Every year children are integrated into the mission awareness and activity of local communities. Children are invited to become locally the bearers of mission, and to collaborate in prayer and collecting funds for mission. In some countries they organise, what they call 'star-singing': on the feast of Epiphany, when clothed as the Magi, they sing and witness and encourage local communities and families to participate in their mission.

Research shows that seventy percent of young people from non-Christian backgrounds who made decisions to be Christ's followers acknowledge that Christian friend(s) were the most significant factor in that process.[37] As mission is for the whole church and the significant majority of the church are children and young people, the greatest asset and the best chance the church has to fulfil its mission is through children. Children and young people are in the best position to relate positively to non-Christians, as well as to people of all ages, race and social status, and thus, they have the greatest opportunity to make a difference in the lives of people and community. Sadly, the church has not seriously considered children as co-bearers and partners for mission and has not adequately equipped them for the work of service. In the context of mission and transformation, children and young people have either been invisible or made to stand on the sideline. Now Christians worldwide must place children where they belong, namely 'in the midst' of the church and its mission (Matt 18:2).[38] Children are the bearers, participants and partners in twenty-first century mission.

5 Better Together: Partnership and Collaboration in Mission

Christian missions do not have a good track record in cooperation. In the earliest days in Uganda, Cedric Pulford records that, 'The Catholics felt it their duty to counter the heretics. The Protestants felt a parallel duty to correct the errors of the Church of Rome',[39] and a few years later bitter rivalry broke out between competing missions in Zanzibar, rivalry which played into the hands of local Muslim rulers.[40] In the nineteenth century the best that could be achieved were a series of 'comity agreements'[41] which at least preserved the peace between rival bands of missionaries. The negative effects, however, of these agreements on Christian unity sadly continue to this day with a high degree of territorialism still evident in inter- and indeed intra-denominational relations in many parts of the world. The World Missionary Conference of 1910 in Edinburgh can be seen as a significant milestone in missionary cooperation, providing the opportunity and impetus for subsequent ecumenical, as well as missionary, developments. In preparation for the 1910 conference the Commission on Co-operation and the Promotion of Unity wrote, 'Without hearty alliance among the many Missionary Societies employed in carrying the Gospel to non-Christian peoples, and without the recognition of co-operative effort as the normal condition of missionary work, the most copious supply of workers and of means that could be hoped for, would still be ineffectual'.[42] This same report ends with the optimistic words, 'the Divine guidance that has led us already… in the direction of co-operation and the promotion of unity, will lead us further still'.[43] A century later we can look back on much progress but with an acute awareness also of our continued short comings in 'common mission'.[44]

5.1 Theological principles for partnership

The implications of trinitarian theology for collaborative discipleship and mission have not always been readily understood, but in recent decades Jürgen Moltmann,[45] Leonardo Boff,[46] Miroslav Volf,[47] and others have reminded us of the corporate, collaborative nature of the being and life of God in Trinity and its implications for those who find themselves created in God's image. The *missio Dei* is by definition a collaborative action by Father, Son and Holy Spirit (John 14:26) and also a divine action which invites human participation, if not collaboration: 'As the Father sent me so I send you.' (John 20:21). God has no necessity to engage humanity as agents of God's own mission but chooses the risky course of partnership. This point is further underlined by Jesus' own calling of disciples as co-workers to whom he eventually entrusts the task of global mission (Matt 28:18-20). It is perhaps also significant that Jesus seems to have chosen as his co-workers a group of disciples with quite different theological and social outlooks.

Paul is often portrayed as the great pioneer of mission, which he was, but he was not a 'David Livingstone, go-it-alone' pioneer. Careful examination of the text shows that he was in fact an accomplished collaborator, building networks of shared ministry.[48] He counted among his co-workers[49] local ministers such as Aquila and Priscilla (1 Cor 16:19), fellow itinerant preachers such as Barnabas (Acts 13:2) and Silas (Acts 15:40), young recruits like Timothy (Acts 16:3), and many more (see, for example, Rom 16:21-24), and took to task churches who sought to create division within the growing missional network (1 Cor 1:12-17), the church of Christ.

5.2 Partnership in historical perspective

In the post-apostolic period and through to the twentieth century we have very little evidence of Christians from different traditions or locations partnering together in mission. Stephen Neill and others cited several examples of inter-agency cooperation and boldly claimed, 'Co-operation marks Protestant missions from the beginning',[50] but the picture has actually been much more one of fragmentation. David Barrett, in his statistical overview shows 'foreign mission sending agencies' rising from 200 globally in 1800, to 600 by 1900, and 4,000 by 2000,[51] a significant part of this 'growth' resulting from fragmentation and failure to collaborate rather than completely new work.

Real partnership and collaborative ministry have however taken place in recent years, often in adverse contexts. Four examples will suffice. In 1949 Dr. Bob Fleming gained permission to enter the closed kingdom of Nepal with two colleagues. Struck by the medical needs of the people they determined to meet these needs in the name of Christ. When, in 1953, permission was eventually granted to open a hospital in Tansen, Fleming, a Methodist, extended an invitation to all who would, to join him in this challenging country where conversion was illegal. So the United Mission to Nepal was born in 1954.[52] The International Assistance Mission began is a similar way in Afghanistan in 1966, with a focus on eye care, and has remained in the war-torn country ever since, currently bringing together workers from around forty different agencies.[53] In Europe, when Albania first became accessible to Christian mission in 1991, a group of Evangelicals formed the Albanian Encouragement Project which now brings together over seventy mission agencies for collaborative work within that country.[54] Also in 1991 a number of workers associated with Interdev[55] began the Central Asian Consultation which today continues to foster collaboration in mission in that region and has spawned numerous regional partnerships.[56]

5.3 Mission in a network age

Mission always has its context and so does partnership. The context of the 1820s, when the Church Mission Society (CMS), London gave birth to an autonomous CMS in Australia, provided very little opportunity for these two agencies to collaborate in mission. Partnership in those days was limited to very local forms of collaboration. Today our global context is very different.

In Figure 2, Lipnack and Stamps[57] divide human history into four 'ages of organisation' as follows:

Small Groups	Hierarchy	Bureaucracy	Networks
Nomadic cultures	Agrarian cultures	Industrial cultures	Information cultures
to 10,000 BC	*10,000BC to 18th C*	*18th – 20th C*	*1945 onwards*
Members	Levels	Purpose	Links

Figure 2

This persuasive analysis forces us to ask whether models for mission devised in the seventeenth century (in an agrarian culture) or in the nineteenth century (in an industrial culture) will serve us at all well in the information age of the twenty-first century when what is valued is not our membership of the group, our place in the hierarchy, or whether our skill set fits the purpose of the bureaucracy, but what links we have, how connected we are. It is not only Western young people who come alive in the virtual space of *Facebook* and *Bebo*; across the world a new generation, sometimes with little access to technology, are learning that if you are not connected you are ignored.

In the academic world studies of cybernetics, systemics[58] and chaos theory, and their philosophical implications, multiply year on year and many large companies are adopting approaches to management which play to the strengths of 'whole system' thinking and network dynamics. The popularized classic in this sphere has become Bradman and Beckstrom's *The Starfish and the Spider*,[59] in which the authors argue that in a networked world maximum participation leads to the maximum and most creative output. They cite not just virtual community projects such as *Wikipedia* and open source software such as *Open Office* but also movements like *Alcoholics Anonymous* and *Al Qaeda*, and companies like *Amazon, Napster* and *eBay*.

All of this talk of connecting, maximum participation, and systemic development should be very welcome to a mission community seeking disciples, who discover renewed relationship with God through Christ and envision the day when 'a great multitude that no one could count, from every nation, tribe, people and language, stands before the throne and in front of the Lamb' (Rev 7:9). In many ways the *missio Dei* seems to accord much more readily with the network culture we inhabit today than with the earlier group, hierarchical and bureaucratic cultures. We could point to many biblical images of the missional *ecclesia* which are of a networking nature, such as the Body (Rom 12; 1 Cor 12; Eph 4:12; etc)[60] and the vine (John 15), but each of these also brings new challenges to our understanding of mission and church.

At the close of the last millennium, in 1996 a consultation of missiologists was held in Brazil at the invitation of the World Evangelical Fellowship Missions Commission. Amongst the papers emerging from this Iguassu Consultation was one by Robert Bryjolfson in which he writes, 'Organisational and denominational language continues to detract from the greater realities of unity in mission'.[61] He then goes on to offer eighteen principles for national mission movements which will build consensus and collaboration in mission. Since that date considerable progress has been made in building networks and real collaboration in mission which to a greater or lesser degree reflect these principles. Examples of such new trans-denominational networks for collaborative mission would be, in Africa, *MANI* (The Movement of African National Initiatives),[62] in Latin America, *COMIBAM* (Cooperación Missionera Iberoamericana),[63] in Asia, the Philippine Missions Association,[64] and across continents the Faith2Share network.[65]

Phil Butler, one of the leading thinkers in missional collaboration, writes,

> Effective partnerships and networks … are crucial to this new world order – to identifying the assets and effectively allocating them. Committed to Christ and the holistic proclamation of his love and power, these new, inclusive forms of kingdom collaboration provide options for effective connection that are simply impossible with the old organisational paradigms.[66]

5.4 Building effective partnerships

As our churches engage in mission locally and around the world we can be well networked, enthusiastic about partnership, looking for collaboration and yet still struggle to get going. Partnerships, like all relationships, are fraught with difficulties, and the temptation is still to 'go it alone'. In *Body Matters*, Ernie Addicott records the fifteen principles for effective partnership in mission developed by *Interdev* in the 1990s.[67] In a clearer way than the Iguassu principles (see above), these point to the key role played by vision, clear purpose, high levels of participation and ownership, trust, openness and mutual concern.

'People work together because they trust one another', say Lipnack and Stamps. 'They make deals, undertake projects, set goals, and lend one another resources. Teams with trust converge more easily, organise their work more quickly, and manage themselves better.'[68] Daniel Rickett, author of several books on missional partnerships adds, 'Communication is only as rich as trust is deep. Close contact and high levels of interaction are important ingredients for building understanding and trust.'[69] While trust is recognised as a primary ingredient for effective collaboration within missional networks, this can be difficult to establish when cross-cultural miscommunication threatens to undermine good intentions. Lianne Roembke[70] has undertaken considerable study in the building of trusting relationships within multi-cultural teams and Duane Elmer[71] brings needed wisdom to the challenges of leadership within multi-cultural networks. At an international level the *World Evangelical Alliance Mission Commission* meeting in Pattaya in 2008 initiated a Global Dialogue Task Group to address many of the continuing tensions, misunderstandings and complex partnership issues between churches and missions in different continents.

5.5 Money, power and neo-colonialism

Just as financial tensions rank high amongst precipitating causes for marriage breakdown so does the power exerted by money in international mission partnerships. Mary Lederleitner writes,

> A concern in missiology is how there can be effective cross-cultural partnerships, with vast sums of wealth coming from affluent donors and nations, without fostering a new form of colonialism now known as 'neo-colonialism'. Neo-colonialism implies that although there is no physical occupation by a foreign power, wealth and resources are given in ways that still dominate others. Some on the receiving end of mission funding feel demeaned and controlled by the process. For these partners there is a sense that they are losing their right to make their own decisions and they are losing their voice. Because of this there is a concern whether true partnership, the kind that models genuine mutuality, can ever take place given such a vast disparity of wealth.[72]

Her paper argues that if we can listen cross-culturally, contextualize processes and apply biblical standards and values, then we might begin to address some of these complex issues. Two other missiologists who have worked on these same issues are Jonathan Bonk who speaks of Western missionary affluence as the primary problem,[73] and John Rowell, whose approach is more practical than missiological, addressing the challenge of dependency and suggesting that sustainability might be a more useful concept that the well worn 'three-selfs' principle which puts too much emphasis on independence and looses sight of the biblical pattern of interdependence.[74]

We live in a network world, our God exists in trinitarian partnership, and God's mission into which we are drawn is inevitably characterized by collaboration and partnership, as Christ 'reconciles to himself all things, whether on earth or in heaven' (Col 1:20).

5.6 North-South mission cooperation

> Through all the ages to come, the Indian Church will rise up in gratitude to attest the heroism and self-denying labours of the missionary body. You have given your goods to feed the poor. You have given your bodies to be burned. We also ask for love. Give us FRIENDS![75]

These words, from one of the very few global South participants at Edinburgh 1910, have become one of its most memorable statements. One hundred years later we continue to struggle with friendships strained by postcolonialism, dependency, paternalism and poverty.[76]

The shifting centre of gravity for Christian witness sees Christians in the South achieving rising demographic advantage marked by spiritual zeal and commitment to the unfinished missionary task, whilst in the North a context of consumerism and pluralism brings a depletion of missionary efforts, yet Northern churches and mission agencies retain hegemony in mission leadership. The shift of the centre of growth for Christian witness has resulted in evident changes in the global mission landscape and must shape mission strategy for the twenty-first century. These changing realities have led to a careful reflection on past realities, present dynamics and future aspirations and paradigms through formal and informal consultation within regional and international mission bodies.

The maturing church of the South has begun to reproduce itself in a variety of ways including the sending of mission workers locally and globally. As the field is shared by mission movements from South and North, they are compelled to seek for space and hegemony in leadership. The inevitable question of mutual partnership rears its troublesome head, seeking honest and sincere responses. Mission agencies from the North are discovering how to move from being lead players to becoming team players. This process can be painful for both partners. Northern movements face the temptation to hand pick, groom and 'direct at a distance' their Southern successors, whilst Southern leaders too easily succumb to a craving for power and an unhealthy adoption of Northern values, strategies and relationships.

The demographically advantaged missioners of the South, despite economic challenges evidenced by their exclusion from 'financial clubs' such as the 'G8', agitate for space to still be counted for the cause of God's mission. They desire more palatable and respectable financial support structures. If there is one single dynamic that splits the mission agencies into opposing camps, it is the question of finances. New, less financially dependent, strategies in mission are, however, emerging as witnessed by migration mission movements such as the 'Filipino phenomenon' and the mission of the 'African diaspora'.

5.7 Global collaboration in mission

In recent decades a number of mission agencies or movements have, to a degree successfully, created global structures that enable more effective South-North collaboration. World Vision and Food for the Hungry have both adopted federal structures whilst others have developed a network approach to global cooperation.[77] Within such structures both Northern and Southern agencies can then explore what particular gifts they can bring to the joint mission enterprise. The careful management of organisational culture and leadership succession in such federations and networks is crucial. It is these new structures for mission that are beginning to shape the multi-centred future for mission in the twenty-first century.

6 Receiving Mission: Mission by Migrant Workers from South to North

There has been some controversy over the terminology used to describe 'receiving' or 'reverse' mission but its reality cannot be denied. As we study this growing phenomenon, we become aware of God's plan to shift what we have taken for granted, in our traditional 'sending' view of mission, through a 'radical dislocation' of his people and bringing them together as his 'new work' as a consequence.

6.1 Historical review

In contemporary mission the role of 'diaspora' has been a critical factor. According to Jehu Hanciles,[78] 'since the 1960s in the post-colonial era, migrant movement has been predominantly from areas with weak economic and political systems to the centres of global dominance and advanced industrial growth'. Christians and Christian workers have constituted a significant part of the migration. Afe Adogame[79] notes that 'the reverse-mission agenda is becoming a very popular feature among African churches'. He illustrates this by reference to Tanzanian pastors commissioned in Lutheran parishes in Germany in the early 1980s. Since the Korean War, Korean Christians have migrated to North America and Europe with various motivations, spontaneous, by invitation or under pressure. They settled among other ethnic communities and began to thrive and impact local churches in their regions. There are estimated to be more than 4,500 Korean churches in North America and Europe at present.[80]

'Reverse mission' (from what were traditionally called 'mission fields' into former 'Christian heartlands') positions the 'West as a site of new religious interactions which portend long-term transformations of Western societies'.[81] Some affirmative movements related to 'reverse mission' have been launched in Western churches. The Mission in Western Culture Project (MiWCP) reflected on Western society that has become a mission field[82] and in 1996 the United Evangelical Mission (UEM)[83] conducted a programme for cooperation between German and immigrant congregations in order to 'help German churches to understand and appreciate the movement of reverse mission'.[84] Recently many traditional churches in Europe have made great efforts to establish a relevant policy for 'reverse mission' in partnership with their counterparts in the non-Western world.

6.2 Defining reverse mission

'Receiving mission' is, in a sense, Northern rhetoric as they conceive the idea that they 'foster the welcome of non-European mission workers into Europe to join with us in our mandate to evangelistic vision'.[85] However, the term is now interchangeable with 'reverse mission' which has become more 'multi-lateral rather than unilateral',[86] as non-Western churches return with the gospel to the societies to which they have been greatly indebted for the purpose of building capacity for world mission together. However, these two terms can be seen to imply a deeper divergence of perception as Northern 'receiving mission' anticipates efficiency through partnership in mission, while Southern 'reverse mission' is more focused on the intrinsic mission mandate for the whole world, including Western society. Grace Davie reflects on 'how "mission in reverse" would turn the traditional relationship between Africa and Europe on its head', commenting that 'this has not happened yet'.[87] C. Barbour views 'mission-in-reverse' differently as a way of ministry which does not teach but learns from people ministered to.[88] This view is endorsed by those engaged in the area of international social work, for whom a reverse mission approach, instead of teaching, preaching, and trying to convert others, emphasises 'learning, consciousness-raising, and advocating for changes'.[89]

6.3 Implications of 'reverse mission'

The reverse wave of migration and waning Christianity in Western society have far-reaching social, political and human implications, particularly for Christian history. God's radical dislocation of his people always brought missional implications throughout the Bible. The following are some of the missionary implications of the influx of Christian migrants into Western society.[90]

- New Christian immigrants come from centres of vibrant Christian growth and embody a brand of Christianity that is strongly evangelistic or conversionist. Many of them naturally come to see themselves as 'missionaries'.
- Immigrant congregations are more attuned to religious plurality than Western Christians are and so are able to maintain effective Christian witness in the face of religious pluralism.
- The secularized societies of Europe and North America are redefined as 'mission fields' requiring re-evangelization.
- Migrations provide an impetus for missionary mobilization.
- There is a call for a structural reform of the church to grapple with the challenges of migration.
- There is a major shift in mission understanding with a greater understanding and appreciation of the multi-cultural nature of Christianity in the twenty-first century.

6.4 Western churches receiving non-Western missional Christians

There are two opposite attitudes to migrant churches exhibited by local churches in Europe: the colonial attitude and the cooperative attitude. In many cases, a healthy relationship has not been established between local churches and migrant churches because the local church authorities have not developed policy on relationships with migrant churches. However, the European Evangelical Missionary Alliance (EEMA) have introduced guide-lines, *Receiving Mission Workers to Europe: What Every Church Should Know* for improving the current situation through a proactive response to migrant Christian workers in Europe.[91] Their suggestions include:

- Collecting background information on the sending country
- Being aware of who in your church has cross-cultural experience and an understanding of culture shock
- Supporting the mission workers in transition with cultural mentors, family support, fellowship, links to home church, partnership in ministry
- Preparing the mission worker for re-entry

With these measures proposed by EEMA, the European Evangelical Alliance formulated a call for awareness of cultural diversity and of the poor welcome often offered to 'the foreigner in our midst'.[92]

6.5 Case study: Impact of Korean-European church partnerships

Korean churches have been planted in Germany and in the UK since the early 1970s, with about two hundred churches now ministering in major cities in Germany, the UK, and France. Historically migrant churches grow from mono-ethnic congregations, becoming bicultural, and finally multi-ethnic or locally mono-cultural churches. Following this pattern many Korean migrant churches have grown and now contribute to mission in Europe in partnership with local churches. In this way Koreans have not only planted ethnic churches but have also contributed to the renewal of indigenous European churches.

An outstanding example is the Korean church partnership with the International Presbyterian church (IPC) in the UK since the 1980s. This consists of two presbyteries (groups of churches): the IPC First European Presbytery and the Korean Presbytery. The Korean Presbytery is made up of six Korean speaking churches. Each June the European and Korean Presbyteries meet together for synod. Another example is the partnership programme for cooperation between German and immigrant congregations run by the United Evangelical Mission (UEM) in Germany since 1998. Through this partnership relationship, Korean churches are making many positive contributions to local partner churches, both financial and spiritual. The Korean church in Germany is a typical example of how an ethnic/migrant church progresses from being a locally dependent community to a self-sufficient and self-generative Christian body characterized by fervent worship, prayer, fellowship and theological education.[93]

6.6 Migrant and local churches partner in diaspora ministry

Migrant churches can evolve into multi-ethnic churches that become a platform for incubating other ethnic churches within the diaspora environment. For example, one of the largest Korean churches in London is facilitating the birth of other Asian ethnic churches as they believe God has given them a heart for church planting, fervent intercession and financial resources for mission. Korean churches and a local Baptist church in London also supported the translation of the New Testament into Iranian Azeri, while working with Azeri diaspora Christians in Europe.[94]

If similar partnerships could be encouraged, with a mutual understanding of the significance of migration,[95] there would be many opportunities for European churches and mission organisations to be involved in cross-cultural mission in their own 'backyard'. Rebecca Catto writes, 'So, even though I do not see mission as having been reversed as yet, ...the notion of "reverse mission" is not completely invalidated: it captures an observable and growing trend'.[96]

7 Mission and the Challenge of the Media

The media is often treated in a mission perspective merely as a question of tools. Media enthusiasts tend to see the different media as nothing more than neutral communication channels, which can be controlled by the church and used to serve its purposes. Media sceptics, on the other hand, see the media primarily as channels of sin and immorality, or as a threat to the genuine community of the church. Both groups seem, however, to have too narrow an understanding of the media and to be underestimating its power.

7.1 The power of the media

In seeking to engage with the media in mission, the first task on our agenda is to realise the power of the media today. In the West secularization has led to a significant drop in church affiliation and attendance, particularly in Europe. At the same time people spend still more hours in front of televisions or computer screens, and their understanding of religion is therefore increasingly being shaped by the media rather than by the church.[97] In the non-Western world, media products such as satellite television and the internet become still more available, though access is much more limited than in the West. It has been argued that the entry of modern media to these places has led to a kind of cultural imperialism, where Western values are being forced on the local populations. This has been modified by recent studies, showing that the mediated foreign cultures do not replace the local culture but are critically received and evaluated within the framework of a dynamic local context.[98] For the church this means that it is not possible – even if some would like it so – to inject the Christianity of the West into non-Western populations through the media. The context of the local people is important to bear in mind and the best result is therefore reached when the local church is included in the process of media production.[99] This is, for instance, reflected in 'the ethos' of the television company Sat-7, where the value of local culture and language, among many other elements, are mentioned as important when producing Christian programmes for the Arab world.[100]

7.2 The blessing of the media

The second task is to acknowledge the blessings of the media. From the very beginning the church has used various media such as letters, liturgy and art to spread its message. The advantage of the new media is that they enable the church to do the same faster, across larger distances, and to a potentially much bigger audience. Especially in places where the church is small and the entry of foreign missionaries is difficult, the media have offered a new way to reach non-believers and given local Christians a chance to grow in their understanding of the Christian faith. Also in a Western secularized context, where people can be hard to reach with traditional mission initiatives, the anonymous and home-based reception of media products offers the church new entries to people it has lost. With the appearance of the internet this contact is increasingly interactive, and more dialogical ways of media mission are now possible. One such example is the Danish website www.religion.dk, which attracts more than fifty thousand unique visitors each month for dialogue on religion.

7.3 The media and mission

The third task is to face the fact that, despite the many advantages of the media, it also has consequences for the church which uses it. When the printing press was introduced by Gutenberg in the fifteenth century, the church first encouraged its use but later changed its position as it became clear that the printing industry could not be controlled.[101] Today, the church must live with the fact that no media can be controlled. When the church enters into the media world, it is just one participant among many others, and in order to be heard or seen it must adapt to the rules of the media.[102] Different studies have shown that at least in the Western world mission initiatives by means of the media have had limited effect. Few people watch the Christian television channels, and those who do are often already churchgoers.[103] The poor results can partly be explained with reference to the overall secularization of society, but a lack of competitive resources and willingness to let go and adapt to the media logic are other possible explanatory factors. In the non-Western world there seem to be more stories of success with media mission. For instance Knud Jørgensen reports from West Africa how the use of radio, audio cassettes and literature have resulted in an openness towards the gospel among the Fulani people of West Africa.[104] On the internet, which must be characterized as the most global mission field, there also seem to be stories of effective mission. On the website www.godrev.com/joy-in-heaven, a map shows where people have 'made a decision for Christ' and counts around 1,500 decisions a day. Although from a missional perspective this may seem positive, critical questions must also be raised: What does it mean to accept Jesus in cyberspace? Is it a long term commitment or just a momentary impulse soon to be forgotten? And are there local congregations for these new Christians to join?

7.4 Theological reflection on the media

This leads to the fourth task, which is conscious theological reflection on the media. If it is true that the media play a central role in modern society and therefore are unavoidable for a church in mission, and if it is impossible to use the media without to some degree subordinating to their logic, then what should the church do? The media seem to go against firm dogma as well as institutional authority and celebrate individual choice, experience and the mix of traditions. How can mission with integrity be carried out under those circumstances in such a way that the church does not lose itself, yet can still appeal to the modern world? This includes a discussion of institution, dogma and authority versus individual freedom, experience and personal responsibility, as well as the physical aspects of congregation and mission versus the virtual character of the media world. Working with these and other questions will pave the way for a more pro-active media approach where the church neither excludes the use of media in mission on the basis of traditionalism or fear, nor just follows the media unconsciously and lets them set the agenda for the mission of the church.

The final task is to act. Depending on the result of the theological reflections, the strategically best way ahead must be sought. Some have the technical and financial resources to create and distribute professional and appealing media products to audiences in traditional mission fields or in the Western world. Others will prefer seeking influence on the secular media, trying to introduce the voice of the church as one among many other voices presented there. There are different paths for the church to follow, and since the media world is constantly changing, the church must also once in a while consider its steps. A continual reflection, experimentation and evaluation of the specific actions is therefore needed.

To engage with it effectively in mission, the media, rather than being treated as a specialist matter or a question of tools, should be fruitfully integrated into the overall missiological thinking; not least because the media are responsible for many of those trends and tendencies which occupy the work of the modern missionary.

8 Strategic Priorities for the Twenty-first Century

To conclude this article it is necessary to consider a few areas of urgent attention in mission strategy for our time.

8.1 Urban mission: The city of God or the city of goods

The turn of the century has brought with it a global population explosion that has never before been experienced by any other generation. In addition to this, for the first time the world is now more urban than rural. Over half of the world's six billion people now live in cities. We must acknowledge the urban realities of our world. Our cities have become home to individualism, consumerism[105] and unbridled greed. In the recent financial crises that have crippled national economies, our cities and their seats of economic power, have shown their vulnerability and fragility. We need to pursue strategies that embody an *oikos*-theology[106] that seeks to establish an urban environment of justice and shalom[107].

8.2 Youth agency in mission engagement: The silence of the lambs?

Young people are still inadequately represented in the decision-making bodies of mission organisations and in missiology at large. The fact that young people have to be featured through quotas at major mission events shows the marginality of the youth voice. This is a tragic and disturbing oversight of mission strategy. The fact that young people are the overwhelming majority in many contexts of the world should show the clear need for the consideration of the youth voice. The custodians of mission are not the founding fathers, the grand dames of the world mission movement, or the platinum-haired missiologists. It is perplexing to see the number of obituaries and 'in memoriam' articles published in mission journals; the intentional mentorship of the young is a strategic imperative. The custodians of mission are the young practitioners, lay people and mission scholars who, in dialogue with God and the generations before, engage the challenges of the world and live out the call of God. The urgent tasks below would facilitate the agency of the youth voice:

- Create space for young people to discuss and dialogue on contemporary mission issues.
- Support and facilitate youth dialogue, theological and missiological study through interdenominational encounters and ecumenical partnerships.
- Encourage young leaders to develop their own contextual theologies and strategies to deal with the challenges in their own communities.
- Amplify and disseminate mission knowledge from among the ranks of young people.
- Encourage North-South exchanges where young leaders learn from, and analyze, mission strategies in both the new and old centres of Christianity.
- Call for seasoned missiologists and mission practitioners to seriously and intentionally mentor younger mission scholars and practitioners.

8.3 Mission methods: Aggressive or defensive?

In this century it is crucial to redeem mission from its contentious and often distasteful past. While the offensive mission position is hardly an option given the unrestrained excesses of the past, the defensive posture of mission appears to be a default position. Mission organisations find themselves treading on thin ice as secular governments and interfaith organisations demand more accountability and justification of a faith orientation. The apprehensive and reticent bearing of mission is in stark contrast to the authority and supremacy strategy. It would appear that mission in the world today is bipolar; aggressive, triumphal and arrogant, or, defensive, deflated and apologetic. More exploration and discussion needs to take place with regard to the twenty-first century attitude and posture of mission and its agents.

8.4 Conservative ecumenism versus true ecumenism

'Ecumenical' can no longer be a term that describes a group of mainline affiliated churches, but must reflect the household of God and the wealth of its range. Current mission strategies still lack ecumenical integrity. The reinvention of the mission strategy wheel continues unabated, as there is still a failure to recognise and appreciate talents and resources across the boundaries of denomination, context, gender and age. The true merit of mission strategy must be found in the willingness of the strategists to be ecumenical, that is, truly ecumenical.[108]

9 Conclusion

In this article we have journeyed through time and place to explore forms of mission engagement. We discovered that the God of the Mission calls us to vulnerability, creativity, pliability and integrity in our engagement. As an ensemble study group from differing contexts we marvelled at the dazzling array of the forms of mission engagement, we stood amazed at the diverse agents of mission strategy, and we were in awe that the Mission continues despite the challenges and changes that face our enterprise. The twenty-first century has only just begun, and so, the story of the forms of mission engagement will continue to be told.

10 Questions

1. The main difference between 1910 and 2010 as regards forms of missionary engagement is the change in focus from 'mission societies' to 'local churches'. What are the implications for mission endeavours in the twenty-first century?
2. In what sense do you understand vulnerability to be powerful? What is the difference between enforced and elected vulnerability? How could the mission of my church or community be more effective if it was less powerful and embraced vulnerability?
3. What place do children and young people have in the mission of your church – as agents as well as recipients of mission? How do you respond to the '4/14 window' as a focus for global mission?

4. Is the mission of your church or community collaborative? If not what are the primary barriers to effective collaboration with other Christians (locally and globally) and how will you overcome these?
5. Do you know what migrant Christians have moved into your district in recent years? Do you see them as competitors, a threat, irrelevant or a resource for your own mission? How would you build partnerships for mission (local and global) with Christians arriving from a different country?
6. What is your church or community's mission to the media? What would a 'kingdom of God' approach to the media in your region look like? Who in your community has a missional vocation to work within the media with the support of the church?

Endnotes

[1] See for example, 'Just as Christ carried out the work of redemption in poverty and persecution, so the Church is called to follow the same route that it might communicate the fruits of salvation to men', Second Vatican Council, *Lumen Gentium*, 'Dogmatic Constitution on the Church' (1963), §8 – a theme which is taken up much more strongly in the later documents: Vatican II, *Ad Gentes* 'Decree on the Mission Activity of the Church' (1965) and John Paul II, *Redemptoris Missio*, 'On the Permanent Validity of the Church's Missionary Mandate' (1990). All documents available at www.vatican.va.

[2] Roland Allen, Missionary *Methods: St. Paul's or Ours?* (London: World Dominion Press, 1956 [1912], 183-190.

[3] David Bosch, *Transforming Mission: Paradigm Shifts in Theology of Mission* (Maryknoll, NY: Orbis Books, 1991), 379.

[4] See *inter alia* Robrecht Michiels, 'The Self-understanding of the Church after Vatican II', *Louvain Studies* 14 (1989), 83-107.

[5] See *inter alia* Darrell L. Guder, *The Continuing Conversion of the Church* (Grand Rapids, MI: Eerdmans, 2000), 113ff, 140.

[6] Ryan Bolger *et al.* (eds), 'The Local Church in Mission: Becoming a Missional Congregation in the Twenty-first Century Global Context' (Lausanne Occasional Paper 40), in David Claydon (ed.), *A New Vision, A New Heart, A Renewed Call*, Volume I (Pasadena: William Carey Library, 2004), 565-606. Also available at www.lausanne.org.

[7] Eddie Gibbs & Ryan K. Bolger, *Emerging Churches. Creating Christian Community in Postmodern Culture* (Grand Rapids, MI: Baker Academic, 2006).

[8] Ryan Bolger *et al.* (eds), 'The Local Church in Mission'.

[9] Guder, *The Continuing Conversion*, 53-55.

[10] For the concept of the local church and disciple making, see Alan Hirsch, *The Forgotten Ways* (Grand Rapids, MI: Baker Publishing House, 2006).

[11] Ryan Bolger *et al.* (eds), 'The Local Church in Mission'.

[12] I met an elderly lady at a makeshift internally displaced persons camp for the Batwa people 30 km ride to the east of Bujumbura, the capital of Burundi on 29 April 2009. I have used a common Burundi name for a woman that means 'hope' to represent her. I asked her if I could share her story and she accepted.

[13] Tamil Nadu Women's Forum, *Unheard Voices: Dalit Women*—An Alternative Report for the 15th-19th Periodic Report on India submitted by the Government of Republic of India for the 70th Session of Committee on the Elimination of Racial Discrimination, Geneva, Switzerland (January 2007), 4 . Cf. www.Imadr.org/en/pdf/CERD-India.pdf (accessed February 2008).
[14] See B.J. de Klerk, 'Worship, Prayers and Poverty', *Ecumenical Review* 57/3 (July 2005), 342-357, which offers strategic 'guidelines for worship-service prayers focusing on poverty'.
[15] Graham A. Duncan, 'Towards Partnership in Mission: The Church of Scotland's World Mission Council Policy, 1929–2006', *Missionalia* 35/1 (April 2007), 54-79, at 55.
[16] D. Soelle, *The Window of Vulnerability* (Minneapolis: Fortress Press, 1990), xi.
[17] D.J. Bosch, 'The Vulnerability of Mission', in J.A. Scherer & S.B. Bevans (eds), *New Directions in Mission and Evangelization 2: Theological Foundations* (Maryknoll, NY: Orbis Books, 1994), 73-86, at 79.
[18] See www.vulnerablemission.com:80.
[19] R. Reim, *Power and Vulnerability: Reflections on Mark 9* (Nottingham, Grove Books, 1994), 8.
[20] Bosch, 'The Vulnerability of Mission', 75.
[21] Bosch, 'The Vulnerability of Mission', 77.
[22] Quoted in Brian McLaren, *Everything Must Change* (Nashville, TN: Thomas Nelson, 2007), 254.
[23] McLaren, *Everything Must Change*, 254.
[24] John Stott, *Authentic Christianity* (Downer's Grove, IL: InterVarsity Press, 1995), 363-364.
[25] Samuel Escobar, *A Time for Mission* (Leicester: IVP, 2003), 17.
[26] Philip Jenkins, *The Next Christendom: The Coming of the Global Christianity* (New York/Oxford: Oxford University Press, 2001), 220.
[27] David Sims produced an extensive 67-page bibliography on 'The Child and American Evangelicalism' for the Houston Child Theology Consultation in 2004, see http://childfaith.net/theology/simsbibliography.pdf. Also, Don Ratcliff of Wheaton College, USA, has a very impressive and rich database on 'Children's Religion and Spirituality Research' (www.childfaith.net/books.htm). Jennifer Orona of Fuller Theological Seminary, USA expanded this significant database with a newer collection (www.childfaith.net/newbooks.htm).
[28] Edwin Estioko, Compassion Philippines staff, captured this story in March 2009.
[29] The story is extracted from Lucille Talusan, 'Childlike Faith Transforms Indonesian Village', *Christian World News*, 11 Dec 2007, www.cbn.com/CBNnews/214912.aspx.
[30] Arada Polawat, Compassion Thailand staff, captured this story in March 2009.
[31] Among others, Paul D. Meier, *Christian Child Rearing and Personality Development*, 2nd ed. (Grand Rapids, MI: Baker Publishing Group, 1995); Susan Greener, *Celebrating Children* (Kingstown Broadway, Carlisle, UK: Paternoster Press, 2003); George Barna, *Transforming Your Children into Spiritual Champions* (Ventura, CA: Regal Publications, 2003).
[32] Bryant L. Myers, 'State of the World's Children: Critical Challenge to Christian Mission', *International Bulletin of Missionary Research* 18/3 (1994), 98-102.

[33] Dan Brewster, 'The 4/14 Window: Child Ministries and Mission Strategies', in Phyllis Kilbourn (ed.), *Children in Crisis: A New Commitment* (Monrovia, CA: MARC 1996), 125-139, at 126.
[34] Myers, 'State of the World's Children'.
[35] www.ministrytodaymag.com
[36] For further information see www.vatican.va/roman_curia/congregations/cevang/p_missionary_works/infantia/documents/rc_ic_infantia_pro_20011106_gen-index-profile_en.html.
[37] L. Singlehurst, *Sowing, Reaping, Keeping* (Leicester: Crossway Books, 1995), 36.
[38] Keith White proposed the 'child in the midst' theme as the foundation for the Child Theology Movement. For more information, see www.childtheology.org.
[39] Cedric Pulford, *Eating Uganda: From Christianity to Conquest* (Woodford Halse, Northants, UK: Ituri Publications, 1999), 44.
[40] See P.V. Kollman, *The Evangelisation of Slaves: And Catholic Origins in Eastern Africa* (Maryknoll, NY: Orbis Books, 2005), 84-138.
[41] See A.D. Falconer, 'The Future of Protestantism: Ecumenism and the Mainline Denominations', in A.E. McGrath & D.C. Marks (eds), *The Blackwell Companion to Protestantism* (Oxford: Blackwell, 2004), 405-420.
[42] World Missionary Conference, 1910, *Report of Commission VIII, Cooperation and the Promotion of Unity* (Edinburgh: Oliphant, Anderson & Ferrier, 1910), 5.
[43] World Missionary Conference, 1910, *Report of Commission VIII*, 148.
[44] 'Common mission' is a phrase used aspirationally in many ecumenical documents over the past 30 years. See for example the *Porvoo Common Statement* 1992, Section 1C (available at www.porvoochurches.org/statements/en.htm) and *Called to Common Mission* 1998 (a statement of the Lutherans and Episcopalians in the USA available at www.elca.org). See also, 'common witness': WCC Central Committee, 'Towards Common Witness: A Call to Adopt Responsible Relationships in Mission and to Renounce Proselytism' (1997), §2, par.3. Published in Jacques Matthey (ed.), *'You Are the Light of the World' Statements on Mission by the World Council of Churches 1980-2005* (Geneva: WCC, 2005), 39-58. Available at www.oikoumene.org
[45] J. Moltmann, *Theology of Hope* (London: SCM Press, 1969).
[46] L. Boff, *Trinity and Society* (Tunbridge Wells: Burnes & Oates, 1988).
[47] M. Volf, 'Being as God Is: Trinity and Generosity', in M. Volf & M. Welker, *God's Life in Trinity* (Minneapolis, MN: Fortress Press 2006), 3-12.
[48] See E.J. Schabel, *Paul the Missionary: Realities, Strategies and Methods* (Nottingham: Apollos, 2008).
[49] See Schabel, *Paul the Missionary*, 249-255.
[50] S. Neill, G. Anderson, J. Goodwin (eds), *Concise Dictionary of the Christian World Mission* (Cambridge: Lutterworth Press, 1970), 149.
[51] D. Barrett, 'Christian World Communions: Five Overviews of Global Christianity, AD 1800-2025', *International Bulletin of Missionary Research* 33/1 (January 2009), 25-32, at 32.
[52] United Mission to Nepal, *Fifty Years in God's Hand* (Kathmandu: UMN, 2003), 13-14.
[53] www.iam-afghanistan.org/our-history, accessed 22 May 2009.
[54] www.aepfoundation.org/aboutus.php, accessed 22 May 2009.
[55] www.interdev.org/ZWP10D5.htm, accessed 22 May 2009.

[56] See R. Wood, 'What Is it like to be a Partnership Facilitator?' in *Mission Frontiers: Bulletin of the US Center for World Missions* (Sept-Dec 1999), which edition also contains much other useful material on partnership in mission.
[57] J. Lipnack & J. Stamps, *Virtual Teams: People Working across Boundaries with Technology* (New York: John Wiley & Sons, 2000), 35-6.
[58] For a historical understanding of the rise of cybernetics and systemics, see C. Francois, 'Systemics and Cybernetics in a Historical Perspective' in *Systems Research and Behavioral Science* 16 (1999), 203-219.
[59] O. Bradman, & R.A. Beckstrom, *The Starfish and the Spider* (London: Penguin Group, 2006).
[60] See also the classic study by J.A.T. Robinson, *The Body: A Study in Pauline Theology* (London: SCM, 1952).
[61] R. Brynjolfson, 'From Synthesis to Synergy: The Iguassu Think Tanks', in W.D. Taylor (ed.), *Global Missiology for the 21st Century: The Iguassu Dialogue* (Grand Rapids, MI: Baker Academic, 2000), 477-88.
[62] www.maniafrica.com.
[63] www.comibam.org.
[64] http://philippinemissions.net.
[65] www.faith2share.net.
[66] P. Butler, *Well Connected: Releasing Power, Restoring Hope through Kingdom Partnerships* (Milton Keynes, UK: Authentic Media, 2005), 303.
[67] E. Addicott, *Body Matters: A Guide to Partnership in Christian Mission* (Edmonds, WA: Interdev Partnership Associates, 2005), 169-173.
[68] Lipnack & J. Stamps, *Virtual Teams*, 69-70.
[69] D. Rickett, *Building Strategic Relationships* (Minneapolis, MN: Stem Press, 2008), 17.
[70] L. Roembke, *Building Credible Multicultural Teams* (Pasadena, CA: William Carey Library, 2000).
[71] D. Elmer, *Cross-cultural Servanthood: Serving the World in Christlike Humility* (Downer's Grove, IL: InterVarsity Press, 2006).
[72] M. Lederleitner, 'Is it possible to adhere to Western ethical and cultural standards regarding financial accountability without fostering neo-colonialism in this next era of global mission partnerships? Thoughts and reflections for broader dialogue', paper submitted to Edinburgh 2010 study group 5, 2009. See J. Rieger, 'Theology and Mission between Neo-colonialism and Postcolonialism', *Mission Studies* 21/2 (2004), 201-227; M.T. Cooper, 'Colonialism, Neo-colonialism and Forgotten Missiological Lessons', *Global Missiology*, no. 1 (2005), 1-14; G. Schwartz, *When Charity Destroys Dignity: Overcoming Unhealthy Dependency in the Christian Movement* (Bloomington, IN: Author House, 2006). It was partly these concerns which led to the WCC inspited 'moratorium' on the sending of western missionaries in the late twentieth century. See for example G.H. Anderson, 'A Moratorium on Missionaries?', *Christian Century* 16 (January 1974).
[73] Jonathan J. Bonk, *Missions and Money: Affluence as a Missionary Problem ... Revisited* (Revised and expanded edition; New York: Orbis Books, 2006).
[74] J. Rowell, *To Give or Not to Give? Rethinking Dependency, Restoring Generosity, and Redefining Sustainability* (Milton Keynes, UK: Authentic Media, 2006).
[75] World Missionary Conference, Edinburgh 1910, *Volume IX: The History and Records of the Conference* (Edinburgh & London: Oliphant, Anderson and Ferrier, 1910), 315.

[76] See J. Kwabena Asamoah-Gyadu, 'Listening with African Ears – Reflections on the 2005 World Mission Conference in Athens', *International Review of Mission* 94/374 (July 2005), 343-353, for an interesting perspective on the African presence from Edinburgh 1910 to Athens 2005.
[77] See for example, www.faith2share.net.
[78] J. Hanciles, 'Migration and Mission: The Religious Significance of the North-South Divide', in A.F. Walls A. and C. Ross (eds), *Mission in the Twenty-first Century* (London: Darton, Longman & Todd, 2008), 118-29, at 123.
[79] A. Adogame, 'The Rhetoric of Reverse Mission: African Christianity and the Changing Dynamics of Religious Expansion in Europe', outline of a lecture presented at the conference, 'South Moving North: Revised Mission and its Implications', Protestant Landelijk Dienstencentrum, Utrecht, 26 September 2007.
[80] Refer to www.koreanchurchyp.com. Total numbers of Korean churches worldwide (outside Korea) are estimated at 5174 in 2009.
[81] Hanciles, 'Migration and Mission', 127.
[82] The Mission in Western Culture Project 'is designed as a global initiative to address the question of a missional engagement in Western culture from the perspective of the local church in order to understand the critical issues facing leadership development, discipleship, formation and witness in modern Western culture'. See http://allelon.org/index.php?option=com_content&view=article&id=95&Itemid=94.
[83] UEM, which was formerly the joint mission board of six German mainline churches (Landeskirchen) and the von Bodelschwingh Institutions Bethel, restructured to become a communion of 33 churches in three continents engaged in a common mission. See www.vemission.org/en/.
[84] C. Währisch-Oblau, 'From reverse mission to common mission … we hope', *International Review of Mission* 89/353 (July 2000), 467.
[85] European Evangelical Missionary Alliance, 'Receiving Mission Workers to Europe: What Every Church Should Know', available at www.europeanema.org/.
[86] Adogame, 'The Rhetoric of Reverse Mission'.
[87] G. Davie, *Europe: The Exceptional Case. Parameters for Faith in the Modern World* (London: Darton, Longman & Todd, 2002), 110, quoted in R. Catto, 'Non-Western Christian Missionaries in England: Has Mission Been Reversed?', in S. Spencer (ed.), *Mission and Migration* (Sheffield: Cliff College Publishing, 2008), 109-118.
[88] C.M. Barbour, 'Seeking Justice and Shalom in the City', *International Review of Mission* 73/291 (1984), 303-309.
[89] Hun Kim, 'Receiving Mission: Reflection on Reversed Phenomena in Mission by Migrant Workers from Global Churches to the Western Society', paper submitted to Edinburgh 2010, study group 5, 2009.
[90] For more information, refer to Hanciles, 'Migration and Mission' and Adogame, 'The Rhetoric of Reverse Mission'.
[91] See www.europeanema.org/.
[92] The article was excerpted from EEA, 'The Foreigner in Our Midst'. Available at www.europeanea.org/documents/Foreignersinourmidst.pdf.
[93] Kim, 'Receiving Mission'
[94] The Bible translation for Southern Azerbaijani in Iran started in 1991 and was completed in 2003. The New Testament was published in June 2009. Now a translation of the Old Testament is in progress in partnership with many constituents in London.
[95] On issues of partnership between South and North, particularly in the context of

Europe, see the Kang-San Tan, 'Who Is in the Driver's Seat? A Critique of Mission Partnership Models between Western Missions and East Asian Mission Movements', *Encounters Mission Ezine*, 24, article 3, www.redcliffe.org/uploads/documents/Who_is_in_the_Driver's_Seat_24.pdf.

[96] Catto, 'Non-Western Christian Missionaries in England', 117.

[97] Stig Hjarvard, 'The Mediatization of Religion: A Theory of the Media as Agents of Religious Change', *Northern Lights* 6 (2008), 11.

[98] Lynn Scofield Clark & Stewart M. Hoover, 'At the Intersection of Media, Culture, and Religion: A Bibliographic Essay', in Stewart M. Hoover and Knut Lundby (eds), *Rethinking Media, Religion, and Culture* (Thousand Oaks, CA: Sage Publications, 1997), 20; Lyn Gorman & David McLean, *Media and Society in the Twentieth Century* (Oxford: Blackwell Publishing, 2003), 221.

[99] Knud Jørgensen, *Åpen kanal – Misjon og medier* (Oslo: Luther Forlag, 1987), 50.

[100] For the whole list, see www.sat7.org/en/sat7/ethos.

[101] John B. Thompson, *The Media and Modernity* (Stanford, CA: Stanford University Press, 1995), 56.

[102] Viggo Søgaard, *Media in Church and Mission: Communicating the Gospel* (Pasadena, CA: William Carey Library, 1993), 118-119.

[103] Quentin J. Schultze, 'Evangelicals' Uneasy Alliance With the Media', in Daniel A. Stout & Judith M. Buddenbaum (eds). *Religion and Mass Media: Audiences and Adaptions* (Thousand Oaks, CA: SAGE Publications, 1996), 64.

[104] Knud Jørgensen, *Åpen kanal*, 43.

[105] See David Field, 'Journey Beyond The Gate: The Reign of God and the Response Ability of the Globalised Middle Class' in the *Journal of Theology for Southern Africa* 123 (November 2005), for a discussion on global capitalism and the reign of God.

[106] See A. E Warmback, 'The Journey Continues: Oikotheology and Urban Ministry', *Missionalia* 36/2-3, 165-179.

[107] See Stephan de Beer, 'Contesting Inner-city Space: Global Trends, Local Exclusion/s and an Alternative Christian Spatial Praxis', *Missionalia* 36/2-3, 180-206.

[108] See Rudolf von Sinner, 'Trust and *Convivencia*', *The Ecumenical Review* 57/3 (July 2005), 322-41, for an interesting look at 'trust and *convivencia* in ecumenical communion'.

THEME SIX

THEOLOGICAL EDUCATION AND FORMATION

Preface

The following report discusses the challenges and opportunities of theological education in the twenty-first century and points toward a new international debate. It was developed as part of the Edinburgh 2010 study process by an international group of theological educators representing the Orthodox, Roman Catholic, Reformed, Lutheran, Methodist, Baptist, and Pentecostal traditions. They were led by co-conveners Revd Dr Dietrich Werner, Ecumenical Institute, Bossey, Switzerland, Coordinator of the Ecumenical Theological Education programme of the World Council of Churches, and Dr Namsoon Kang, Brite Divinity School, Texas Christian University, USA, and President of the World Conference of Associations of Theological Institutions (WOCATI).

Group members (corresponding and participating) included: Clare Amos (Anglican Communion Office, UK), Steven Bevans (Catholic Theological Union, Chicago) Nico Botha (University of South Africa), Rob Brynjolfson (International Missionary Training Network/World Evangelical Alliance), Daniel Chiquete (Pentecostal Church, Mexico), Jose Duque (UBL, Costa Rica/Columbia), David Esterline (McCormick Theological Seminary/Institute for Cross-Cultural Theological Education, USA), Tharcisse Gatwa (Rwanda Christian Council of Churches/Butare Theological Seminary), Jet den Hollander (WARC, Switzerland), Afrie Songco Joye (Union Theological Seminary, Philippines), Pantelis Kalaitzides (Volos Academy, Greece), Atola Longkumer (Leonard Theological College, India), Joshva Raja (Queen's Foundation, Birmingham, UK), Israel Selvanayagam (United Theological College, Bangalore, India), Randolph Tuner (Council for World Mission), Douwe Visser (World Alliance of Reformed Churches), Des van der Water (Council for World Mission), and Henry Wilson (Foundation for Theological Education).

Participants met on 30 November – 3 December 2008 and on 13-15 August 2009 at the Ecumenical Institute, Bossey, Switzerland, and the editorial group met in Princeton, USA on 20-21 March 2009. Two other events also fed into discussion on this topic: the consultation on 'Feminist Perspectives on Mission and Theological Education' at the Ecumenical Institute, Bossey on 24-28 November 2008, and the 'Ivory Towers, Muddy Grounds' consultation at the Queen's Foundation in Birmingham, UK on 27-29 March 2009. The group worked between November 2008 and August 2009 to produce this summary report on theological education in world Christianity.[1] In addition to this chapter the group has been working to produce a global handbook on theological education. The primary author of this final version was Dietrich Werner and the editor was David Esterline.

1 Foundations and Clarifications

1.1 Christianity as a religion committed to education – the missionary impulse of theological education

Christianity is about remembering in gratitude and celebrating in community God's act in Jesus Christ in redeeming and renewing the whole of creation. In the task of remembering and celebrating, education has played a major role from the inception of Christianity for the sake of handing over the tradition of Christian faith. When Christianity emerged as a new faith, it embarked on appropriate education to ensure that its faithful were soundly rooted in their faith, equipped to share it, and prepared to defend it when challenged by adversaries. Early Christianity, being deeply rooted in the Judeo-Palestinian tradition, had an intrinsic commitment to education from the very beginning.[2]

The conference in Edinburgh 1910 was marked by a strong commitment to Christian education.[3] This can be seen (a) in the interest in establishing a policy for *general education*, (b) in the concern for common approaches to higher *theological education of missionaries* in particular, and (c) in the specific concern for the theological *training of indigenous church leaders* in vernacular languages.

a) It was clearly an unchallenged assumption at Edinburgh 1910 that countries in the East and South must grow into the systems of civilization, Christianization, and education which had been developed in the 'Christian West' – note the two different messages which were issued, one to the 'Christian nations', and one to the non-Christian nations. However, there was also a sense of the ambivalent character of Christianity as it worked hand-in-hand with modernization and Westernization. There were voices in Edinburgh warning of a one-sided, technical way of exporting Western achievements and standards to other countries. It was against this dominant technological and culturally destructive side of Westernization that participants at Edinburgh hoped for a counter movement consisting of what they called '*moral education of the people of the South*', by which they meant the religious and spiritual education of the masses, education which would safeguard them against the negative side-effects of the encounter with Western modernization and technology.

b) Edinburgh 1910 also dealt (in Commission V) with the methods, places, and principles of the *theological preparation of missionaries*. Until 1910 the majority of missionaries were not trained at an academic level (though there were exceptional cases, such as the Danish-Halle Mission). In reviewing the existing facilities for training, Edinburgh 1910 came to the conclusion that the education of missionaries needed to be drastically improved in terms of (i) language studies, (ii) history of religions and sociology of mission territories, and (iii) general principles of missionary work. Interdenominational cooperation of mission agencies for common training programmes was seen as a priority, with central institutions foreseen in Shanghai, Madras, Calcutta, Beirut, and Cairo. These plans were revolutionary in their understanding of theological education in particular. Without using the terminology, this can be seen as the beginning of (i) theological education of missionaries outside the traditional centres of the West, (ii) a globally coordinated policy and development of theological education in the South, (iii) centralized and interdenominational institutions of theological education in the South, and (iv) theological education on an advanced academic level.

c) Edinburgh 1910 took up the demands of earlier world mission conferences and focused on the *development of indigenous leadership in the younger churches*. The report of Commission III concluded: 'We believe that the primary purpose to be served by the educational work of missionaries is that of training of the native Church to bear its own proper witness.... We believe that the most important of all ends which missionary education ought to set itself to serve, is that of training those who are to be spiritual leaders and teachers of their own.'[4]

One of the more provocative recommendations of Edinburgh 1910 (and one which still pertains today) refers to the urgent need to develop models of theological education beyond the colonial languages: 'The greatest possible care will have to be taken to avoid the risk of denationalizing those who are being trained. In particular, we desire to lay the greatest emphasis on the importance of giving religious teaching, not only of the elementary kind, but as far as possible throughout, in the vernacular.'[5] Although terms like 'indigenization' or 'contextualization' were not yet used, Edinburgh 1910 paved the way for these commitments.

The Second World War delayed the International Missionary Council (IMC) from developing and implementing the Edinburgh 1910 recommendations and those of the subsequent IMC assembly in Tambaram (1938) on theological education. This was to some extent rectified at the IMC Accra Conference (1958) when the Theological Education Fund (TEF) was launched.[6] The three decisive marks of TEF's concern for theological education in the South were specified as (i) *quality* combining intellectual rigor, spiritual maturity, and commitment; (ii) *authenticity* involving critical encounter with each cultural context in the design, purpose, and shape of theological education; and (iii) *creativity*, understood as promoting new approaches in mission. In its three mandate periods, TEF has promoted different goals but all related to the major aim of an indigenous or contextualized theological education in the churches of the South.

In conclusion: (i) The concern for the promotion of theological education has been and should remain a priority area of joint witness and cooperation. (ii) While several indigenous models of theological education were initiated in the nineteenth and twentieth centuries, Western patterns, methodologies, and frameworks were exported throughout the world. It is only in 1970s and 1980s that Western dominance has begun (gradually and partially) to be challenged by contextualized patterns of theological education. (iii) The Protestant missionary movement indirectly (but powerfully) promoted the English language and English forms of teaching and learning as the dominant educational model. In much of world Christianity there is still an urgent need for culturally and linguistically diverse education programmes and resources.

1.2 Theological education and ministerial formation – clarification of terms

A number of key convictions have emerged in the dialogue on theological education in world Christianity which correspond to terms used in this report. We offer the following definitions, bearing in mind that many terms have overlapping meanings or connotations and that usage varies in different ecclesial and cultural contexts.

There is widespread consensus that every member of the people of God has the right to understand Christian faith and tradition in their fullness and should have access to basic education, faith nurture, and empowerment for mission. **Christian education** in most Christian traditions is the general umbrella term which refers to every aspect of education which contributes to the nurture or sustenance of individuals and groups in their being or becoming Christian. 'Christian education' in North America refers to lay education for children and adults, but not to formal seminary or university programmes. This report does not attempt to deal with general Christian education, though we are certainly aware of its scope and significance.

There is also a common conviction that there is no contradiction between immersing oneself into the mystery and personal reality of Christian faith and deepening a critical reflection on its meaning, its foundations, and inner rationality. **Theological education** is another broad term, including in its meaning the reflection of Christian faith and praxis (*fides quaerens intellectum*). In some contexts (like North America) the term 'theological education' is used almost exclusively for ministerial formation, often referring to graduate level degree programmes designed to prepare people for ministry of one form or another. Theological education in a broader understanding – as in the discourse of WCC Ecumenical Theological Education (ETE) – however, is not the prerogative only of those becoming ordained ministers and priests but a fundamental right of every Christian adult. Theological education in this broad understanding aims at developing reflective Christian identity and practice, an informed and spiritually enriched access to biblical tradition, and empowering people for participating in the mission of God in this world. It enables people to reflect critically on the relation between their own Christian identity, their church tradition and other Christian traditions, their relation to the world, and the tasks of God's mission today.

All churches need to prepare some of their members for an ordered form of ministry, be this full- or part-time ordained ministry, sacramental ministry, or educational ministry. The term **ministerial formation** refers to degree programmes (often at graduate level) and other formal courses which provide for the preparation of women and men for different kinds of ordained or non-ordained church ministries in congregations, in mission, in community and parish life, in diaconical services, or in education. In some contexts this term is nearly identical to theological education.

Many churches have **lay formation** programmes which focus on theological training for lay people. These programmes make explicit the understanding that theology should not be regarded as the prerequisite or exclusive property of ordained ministers. This term defines a particular target group; methodologies can be similar to those used in other forms of theological education.

Many churches have realised that theological education in residential or centralized institutions is not viable or not appropriate in their context. **Theological education by extension** (TEE) refers to forms of alternative theological training which allow for a high degree of involvement in the local context and provide opportunities for study (often in the evening) and participation in regional working groups in order to be equipped for the mission and social ministries of the church.

Various attempts have been made to categorize the different models of theological education by mode of delivery, method of funding, and church or state relationship. There are residential and non-residential models, distance education and short term courses, church funded, interdenominational and ecumenical partner-funded, and state-funded programmes, and courses of study leading to degrees at all levels – which are offered in almost all delivery modes, from residential to internet-based. Some of these categories seem to fit well in particular denominations, faith traditions, and parts of the world, but generalizations are difficult to sustain as theological education is offered in almost every form in every part of the world and exceptions to generalized categorization can almost always be found. All forms have legitimate roles to play, and all have deep, abiding value for the church and the world.

1.3 Theological education and Christian mission

There is widespread consensus that theological education is part of the holistic mission of the Christian church.[7] As expressed by the global conference on theological education enabled by WCC/ETE in Oslo in 1996:

> There is consensus among us on the holistic character of theological education and ministerial formation, which is grounded in worship, and combines and interrelates spirituality, academic excellence, mission and evangelism, justice and

peace, pastoral sensitivity and competence, and the formation of character. For it brings together education of:

> the ear to hear God's word and the cry of God's people;
> the heart to heed and respond to the suffering;
> the tongue to speak to both the weary and the arrogant;
> the hands to work with the lowly;
> the mind to reflect on the good news of the gospel;
> the will to respond to God's call;
> the spirit to wait on God in prayer, to struggle and wrestle with God, to be silent in penitence and humility and to intercede for the church and the world;
> the body to be the temple of the Holy Spirit.[8]

Missiology was for a long time marginalized in theological education and in the understanding of theology as a discipline. As many have recognised, much of Western theological formation was shaped when Christendom in Europe did not feel the need for Christian mission because it knew only itself, it was insular and isolated from other parts of the world. This condition resulted in an ecclesiology and a theological education programme without missiological perspective. 'A missionless church saw no necessity for the inclusion of missiology in the theological curriculum'.[9] The Protestant missionary movement exported this reductionist understanding of theology along with the pattern of theological education with the traditional four disciplines. Thus missiology was *incorporated* into a pre-existent curriculum, without making the missionary perspective the overarching dimension of theological education as a whole. David Bosch lamented in an early essay (1982):

> If mission was studied at all, it was usually as part of practical theology, as if it were largely a matter of technique or practical application; or it was offered as a totally separate subject, as if it had little to do with the other "streams", or it was an optional subject, competing with preaching, pastoral counselling, or liturgics for the learners attention.[10]

The rediscovery of the missionary nature of the church in the conciliar ecumenical movement in the 1960s, the evangelical renewal of the Lausanne movement in the 1970s, and the post-Vatican II encyclicals on the missionary nature of the church have had a profound impact on redefining the missionary task and perspectives of theological education.[11] Many have confirmed David Bosch's proposal that missiology needs to be both *dimensional* (that is integrated into, and in close dialogue with biblical studies, church history, systematic theology, and practical theology) and *intentional* in maintaining a critical distance from the other disciplines, bringing its own distinctive perspectives to bear on the theological task.[12]

To summarise the multifaceted debate on mission and theological education, it can be affirmed: (i) that theological education as a whole participates in the task of equipping people for God's mission in today's world; (ii) that all theological education is contextual in its nature and no particular context (or special Western inheritance) should exercise dominant influence over the church and theological education; (iii) that a missionary ecclesiology requires the teaching of broadly understood missiology, intercultural theology, ecumenics, and world Christianity; and (iv) that students and faculty should have the opportunity to experience different social and political realities in other parts of the world church in order to understand the key questions of the mission of the church today.

1.4 Theological education and the church – a relationship of service, ownership, and critical distance

The following points provide a summary of the main convictions in the ongoing debate on the relation between theological education and the church:

a) There is no fundamental contradiction between the principles of academic learning or intellectual discipline on one hand and a church-related faith commitment on the other, although at times there may be tension between the two. It is the task of theological education to strengthen the commitment to Christian faith and to develop a proper understanding and practice of it, which may include liberating faith from narrow-minded or uninformed concepts and/or practices.

b) Theological education has a critical and liberating function in relation to the existing church; with reference to both biblical and Christian tradition, theological education can remind Christian communities of their proper tasks and key mandates.

c) The church has a critical and alerting function over against theological education and the forms of cultural captivity and blindedness in which it can find itself in due to its particular environment and internal value systems. Serious complaints are being heard that the theological academy in the West has lost its world-wide, ecumenical perspective and its missionary impact, and that it is not sufficiently cognizant of emerging shifts in world Christianity today.

d) Theological education therefore needs regular contact with the existing realities of church life, involvement and close touch with the challenges of mission, ministry and life witness of churches today, but it also needs critical distance and a certain degree of autonomy from the daily pressures of church work and from the direct governing processes and power interests of church institutions.

e) Theological institutions and churches have constantly faced the challenge of meeting each others' expectations. On the one hand theological institutions expect churches to send the most qualified seminarians; primary qualifications include dedication, academic competence, and good character. On the other hand, churches expect theological institutions to produce dynamic preachers with wholesome values who have administrative as well as spiritual strengths and pastoral counselling skills. A creative tension here exists in many contexts. One of the key questions has to do with the standards applied to candidates in the selection processes and the way in which the values of academic excellence and formation for ministry are balanced.

f) Churches should regard the support for theological education as one of their most important obligations. A church without qualified theological education systems tends to diminish itself or tends toward fundamentalism. A church with well developed theological education prepares itself for greater interaction with and outreach to the challenges in its society, and deeper commitment to holistic Christian mission.

g) In situations where accountability, transparency, and patterns of governance in church leadership are low, questions are raised about the way theological education may have contributed to these problems. While not all failures in the performance of church leaders can be attributed to the shortcomings in theological education, a valid question is raised: what emphasis should be given to character and spiritual formation, good governance and management principles, and appropriate codes of conduct for church leadership in theological education curricula?

1.5 Theological education and different understandings of the Bible

There is widespread debate today on the different cultural ways of reading and understanding the Bible. The missionary work of some two hundred years has made a remarkable impact on providing the ground for different cultural readings of the Bible by making bible translations available for a majority of languages around the world – a work which is still going on and which cannot be overestimated in its missiological and hermeneutical relevance. The availability of bible translations in different vernacular languages however does not necessarily entail that the ways of reading and interpreting the Bible have changed and become directly related to the methodologies applied in theological education. There is an emerging international debate with regard to intercultural dialogue and hermeneutics; however, the predominance of Western styles of biblical interpretation in theological education still remains unchallenged in major parts of theological education in the South.

At the same time theological controversies in many churches around issues like homosexuality, the ordination of women, or the understanding of creation which are giving rise to tensions within denominational families as well as between them (in the Anglican World Communion, for instance) are very often closely intertwined with different hermeneutical approaches and different ways of understanding and interpreting biblical tradition. Ultimately any serious engagement with theological education is forced 'back to the Bible' – and conversely attitudes to the Bible influence other dimensions of theological education, both in their content and their methodology.

Differences in biblical hermeneutics today are contributing to some of the root causes for ongoing splits within denominations and within world Christianity, and between some seminaries and institutions of theological education in mainline Protestant seminaries, Evangelical and Pentecostal seminaries. It should be mentioned however, that these tensions are not just between some denominational traditions, but many of these reoccur within some world Christian families (like the Anglican Communion, Baptist churches, Orthodox churches, Pentecostal churches).

It belongs to the key convictions of this study paper: (i) that the different hermeneutical approaches to biblical tradition (historic-sociological, charismatic, feminist, Asian and African contextual approaches) need each other and can complement each other in the journey towards a holistic and comprehensive understanding of biblical tradition in theological education today; (ii) that *common* theological education is possible even with divergence and variety in the understanding of biblical tradition and hermeneutics, provided that there is an open and attentive dialogue within the theological curriculum; (iii) that there should be much more input in theological education on the different concepts of contemporary biblical hermeneutics; and (iv) that there is much more in common between theological education institutions in the Ecumenical, Evangelical, and Pentecostal worlds than is often realised. Increased cooperation is not only a biblical imperative; it also holds great potential for the enrichment and strengthening of theological education as a whole.

1.6 Theological education and the unity of the church – interdenominational cooperation and ecumenical learning

Nearly all theological education institutions are expected to meet the following three objectives: (i) they should strengthen the denominational identity of future pastors and church workers, so that graduates will have a very clear understanding of the church to which they belong (*theological education as denominational initiation*); (ii) they should introduce students to the wider horizons of the worldwide church so that they will understand that they also belong to the ecumenical fellowship of churches (*theological education as discovery of catholicity*); (iii) they should prepare candidates to engage models of church unity, to reflect theologically on 'unity in diversity' and to ask how the relation between local or denominational identity and the ecumenical worldwide fellowship can be lived out (*theological education as enabling for ecumenical learning*).

There is a resurgence of denominationalism in theological education today. Many denominations, even smaller churches, tend to develop and maintain their own theological colleges. The denominational fragmentation of theological education is one of the root causes for the continuation of the ecumenical divide.

The writers of this report are convinced that theological education is the seedbed for the renewal of churches, their ministries, and their commitment to the unity of the church. If theological education systems are neglected or not given their due prominence, over the following decades the church will experience a decline in the competence of church leadership and in their capacity for ecumenical and interfaith dialogue and for dialogue between church and society. It has become clear that ecumenical learning is not just the addition of elements of ecumenical theology into the curriculum, but the key question is whether and to what extent the basic orientation of theological education reflects the fundamental relational nature of being the church, its vocation to live with other Christian communities and with the wider human community. A renewal of ecumenical perspectives in theological education is required, as spelled out in the 'Magna Charta on Ecumenical Formation in Theological Education': 'If theological education fails to be guided by an ecumenical vision of a church renewed in mission and service to the whole of humankind there will be a serious shortage in terms of a new generation of Christian leaders, pastors and theological teachers carrying on the ecumenical vision and commitment into the twenty-first century'.[13]

1.7 Diversity in theological education and different forms of ministry in the church

In the midst of the journey from Edinburgh 1910 to today,[14] many different forms of ministry have been affirmed, and it has been realised that the dominant form (full-time ordained) may not be appropriate or adaptable for the ministry needs in some contexts. The need for diversified ministry calls for new forms of theological education. The old assumption that theological education should be structured for those studying full-time and preparing for full-time professional ministry has changed and is being replaced in some areas with forms more appropriate, both in terms of context and ministry.

In many churches of the South, the predominant form of theological education accessible to people in poorer sectors is theological education by extension (TEE). Case studies from TEE projects in several countries[15] underline the indispensable function of these programmes and challenge traditional institutions of theological education to add TEE programmes and to help train the trainers for regional and local TEE programmes. It is likely that decentralized TEE programmes will prove to be the most effective and most widely spread models of theological education in the twenty-first century for many churches in the South. In the North, many theological education institutions offer degree and certificate programmes in alternative formats, including part-time (evening, weekend, or occasional intensive courses) and on-line programmes, some of which serve as formal preparation for ordination. Many more institutions are offering 'hybrid courses', in which some classes take place in traditional face-to-face classrooms while others involve interaction via the internet. The rationale for these new formats has to do with providing increased access, new approaches to pedagogy, and availability of on-line resources.

There is consensus that shaping the future of theological education in support of a diversified spectrum of ministries in the North and in the South is a fundamental issue of **justice**. It is a matter of *access—so that everyone, irrespective of physical or social location or other forms of marginalization will have full access to theological education—as well as the openness of the curricula.* Access to theological education is still extremely unbalanced between North and South, within regions between rural and urban areas, between women and men, between lay people and candidates for ministry. Full access to theological education is one of the key issues for shaping theological education in the twenty-first century.[16]

1.8 Theological education and missionary spirituality – spiritual formation and missionary training in TE

For many networks and churches involved in cross-cultural missionary work the key question for the future of theological education is: Which models of theological education can prepare and equip people for a commitment to integral mission and a deeper missionary spirituality? An impressive amount of work has been done recently on pre-field mission training programmes from denominational and independent agencies, mission networks, and scholars working in the field.[17] *Integral Mission Training: Design and Evaluation*[18] brings together a wealth of resources and new models for training for cross-cultural mission and nurturing mission spirituality both in short-term courses as well as in life-long learning perspective.

The field of missionary training and spiritual formation is widely divergent, with courses offered in preparation for short-term mission, exposure trips which have potential for intercultural learning and firsthand experience, and traditional theological education programmes. There are also Christian groups which send out 'missionaries' with little formation and only rudimentary biblical and theological training. There is a clear need to develop common standards on missionary formation and training and to define the main points in a curriculum designed to form women and men for holistic mission. Modules for missionary training might be standardized, made available for accreditation, and offered across existing denominational and faith tradition lines.

1.9 Women in theological education and new approaches in women's theological networks

It is probable that nothing has changed theological education in the past one hundred years more than the increased presence of women—both in theological study programmes and as theological educators. Women theologians have challenged and renewed methodology, orientation, and the content of the curriculum across theological education. It is often forgotten in the patriarchal perspective of mission history that there was an extensive network of women in mission prior to 1910; it has been estimated that some fifty-five percent of all denominational missionaries sent by Western agencies were women at that stage.[19] The contribution of women to education in this early period cannot be overestimated, even though it has taken a long time to be recognised.

As the result of efforts by women theologians, often working in cooperation with programmes like the WCC Programme for Theological Education, the Foundation for Theological Education, the Program for Theology and Cultures in Asia and others, networks have been formed in several parts of the world: in Asia, the Asian Women's Resource Center for Culture and Theology and the Association of Theologically Trained Women of India (ATTWI)[20] constituted in 1979 in Chennai; the Association of Women in Theology in the Philippines (AWIT)[21]; in Africa (CIRCLE), in the Pacific (Weavers / SPATS)[22]; and on the world level The Women's Commission of the Ecumenical Association of Third World Theologians (EATWOT),[23] the new Anglican Women Theological Educators Network[24] and the Asian/Asian American Association of Women Theologians in the USA.

While we can celebrate the significant changes that have occurred in some contexts during the past decades with regard to women in theological studies and teaching, it should be emphasised that continuing efforts are needed. In most regions of the world there is still an overwhelming task to be accomplished in terms of encouraging, equipping, and enabling young women theologians to gain access to degree programs, teaching positions, and leadership in churches and educational institutions. As there is a backlash in many regions regarding the presence of women in church leadership and positions in higher education in general, it is very important that women receive strong support at every stage in theological education.

1.10 Interfaith learning in theological education

One of the major challenges facing theological education at the start of the twenty-first century is that of helping to equip the churches to respond to religious plurality.[25] The societal and cultural contexts within which this challenge is to be addressed are very varied – one particularly significant difference being between theological education in the historic heartlands of 'Christendom', where religious plurality is being experienced as a relatively new phenomenon, and theological education in societies where the churches have throughout recent history lived as minorities among other faith communities. In any context, though, there are at least three interrelated dimensions of theological education which will need to be developed in the interfaith area: namely, learning about other faiths; equipping the church's ministry with the pastoral capacity to engage positively interfaith relations; and exploring the fundamental theological presuppositions and implications of interfaith encounter.

Firstly, a knowledge of the beliefs, practices and attitudes of other faith communities is an important prerequisite for theological education in contexts where people's lives have been shaped by different religious traditions. Those being educated theologically need first to hear what Islam means to a Muslim, and then they need to reflect on that in the light of their own Christian faith. Without the former, theological education remains an introspective exercise without the challenge of the other; without the latter, it does not go beyond religious phenomenology.

Secondly, insofar as theological education is designed to equip men and women for pastoral ministry and leadership in mission in the churches, it has to develop within them the ability to navigate the complexities of interfaith relations with confidence, sensitivity and integrity. Such navigational ability is not merely a matter of acquiring a set of skills; at a more fundamental level, it is the formation of a set of attitudes arising from a Christian orientation towards the other.

Thirdly, theological education in and for the interfaith arena must include theology. This may seem a truism, but in fact it is easy for engagement with other religions to be kept apart from the core matter of developing credible ways to believe the faith today. Serious recent theological reflection in this area links interfaith engagement to the heartlands of Christian theology – it is in the core affirmations of Christian faith that motivations for inter-religious encounter are to be found, and that encounter in turn reflects back on the churches' understanding of that faith.

In summary: (i) inter-religious dialogue for theological education in the twenty-first century is not an arbitrary option, but a necessary pre-condition and obligatory and basic dimension; (ii) interfaith-concerns should be integrated into all disciplines of theology and not delegated just to one branch or special module and seminar; (iii) inter-faith learning cannot take place without sharing (and/or further deepening) one's own personal journey of direct encounters with people of other living faiths; (iv) sharing appropriate resources for innovative models on interfaith-learning is of extreme importance for the future of theological education.

1.11 Youth, theological education, and ecumenical formation

The majority of Christians in the South are below the age of forty, a fact that theological educators need to keep in mind with regard to every aspect of their work. Educating youth means equipping future generations theologically so that they will be able to face the challenges of their time. Ecumenical formation should be approached as an ongoing educational process, whose coherent aim through its different stages, beginning in early childhood, is to build up the body of Christ, that is, the unity of the church.

Youth have different needs depending on their age group and on their different cultural, ethnic and religious contexts—including multi-religious or atheistic contexts, minority churches, ethnic churches, etc. Young people can never be treated as a homogenous group. Theological education of youth cannot disregard these different needs, but it should respond to and satisfy them using interdisciplinary and inter-religious approaches.

Ecumenical theological education can be a way to raise up a strong new generation of Christian leaders for whom the vision of Christian unity is an integral part of their identity and understanding of the church's mission. Through ecumenical formation, young people discover that they are part of something bigger and deeper than they could ever imagine, and they will develop a commitment to transform and reinvigorate the church.

2 Changing Context of Theological Education

2.1 Unequal allocation of resources and the continuing movement of theological scholars from the South to the North

Several advances have been made with regard to theological education since 1910, namely the creation of independent institutions of theological education in the churches of the southern hemisphere and the development of indigenous and contextualized models of theological education in many parts of the world. At the same time, we are convinced that new (and old) challenges continue to hamper both the relevance and the accessibility of theological education. Some of these challenges seem to be even more dramatic than a hundred years ago. Thus it is urgent that efforts for coordinating international networking and solidarity in promoting theological education be increased. It is the intention of this part of the report to highlight some of the challenges facing theological education and to identify signs of an emerging crisis in theological education in the twenty-first century.

The absolute majority of resources for theological education – in terms of teaching staff, scholarship funds, theological libraries, and publications – are still located in the global North, while the majority of the needs for theological education (recognising the remarkable southward shift of the centre of gravity of world Christianity) are in the South. The Association of Theological Schools has more than 250 member institutions in the United States and Canada, while in the whole of South East Asia there are only 104 theological education institutions (related to ATESEA), and in the whole of South and Central Africa there are only some twenty institutions (with membership in ATISCA). The average full cost for one student place per year at Princeton Theological Seminary is approximately 60,000 USD, while the average cost for a BTh student place in an institution of theological education in Nepal is just 1,000 USD per year. Access to PhD scholarships, to theological library resources, and to research visits for theological students from churches in the South to countries of the northern hemisphere has become ever more difficult, not least due to the restriction of visas and increased health insurance costs.

We continue to observe a tangible *brain drain of highly trained theologians from countries of the South to countries of the North.* Colleges in the South are simply not able to pay adequate salaries. South-South exchange in theological education is demanded but not sufficiently developed or funded. Serious *discrepancies in terms of availability and accessibility of higher theological education* can be observed between countries (compare, for instance, South India and Nepal, Bhutan, Bangladesh or Vietnam and Cambodia) and between different regions within one country. The implications of *global migration* for the landscape of theological education have not yet been fully examined or understood. Related to these phenomena is the *unbalanced system of transfer of theological knowledge between the churches of the North and the churches of the South*: while much of the theological knowledge produced by the theological faculties in the Anglophone North is forwarded to theological colleges in the South, there seem to be blockages to movement in the other direction. New theological knowledge produced in the institutions and churches of the South does not, in general, make its way to the seminaries and churches of the North. (Nor is there easy movement of new knowledge between, for instance, Africa and Asia.) Many European books can be found in the theological libraries of Africa, but comparatively very few books of African origin or relating to African theological developments can be found in the libraries of Europe.

2.2 Explosion in the demand for higher education

According to the UNESCO Report on Higher Education in 2007, the twenty-first century has begun with an explosion in the number of higher education students. Enrolment has increased from approximately 72 million in 1999 to 133 million in 2004. Excluding North America and Western Europe, enrolment in the rest of the world has more than doubled in these five years, with an increase from 41.1 million to 99.1 million. China alone increased its share from 6.4 million in 1999 to 19.4 million in 2004, giving it the largest higher education enrolment in the world at more than 23 million in 2005. This dramatic growth is reflected in the growing demand for theological education in many countries in the South. However, the capacity for theological education in many regions is far from keeping pace with church growth—and this picture is worsening; just as the Christian populations in the West are shrinking, those in Africa and Asia are young and growing very fast.

2.3 Constantinian models of theological education for pre-Constantinian contexts

It can be argued that the predominant trend for the past one hundred years has been to export models and curricula of theological education from the West – and its Constantinian or post-Constantinian church setting –into contexts in the South, which in most cases have a pre-Constantinian setting.[26] Many of the problems and unsolved challenges related to the contextualization of theological education in the churches of the South are related to this background. Much of what is happening in Evangelical or Pentecostal theological education can be regarded as reflecting a pre-Constantinian church situation, whereas much of what has been developed in mainline Protestantism and other established churches reflects the predicaments of a post-Constantinian setting. One of the fundamental tasks today is to strengthen the self-reliance and independence of theological education institutions and curricula in the churches of the South which have to adapt themselves to pre-Constantinian settings.

2.4 Proliferation of new colleges and bible schools

The increasing demand for theological education in the global South has given rise to a *mushrooming of new colleges and bible schools.* While this proliferation reflects a genuine desire for access to theological education, the rapid growth and commercialization of theological education has led to negative side-effects. Many of these new schools offer only light or 'fast food style education'; they have no libraries, no developed curriculum, and no consistent educational framework. Many of the new schools do not have developed relationships with the indigenous churches which exist in their contexts or connections with the established associations of theological schools. This fragmentation, lack of cooperative relationships and common standards, and general lack of integration in the theological education landscape in some regions has reached an unprecedented level.

2.5 Lack of financial viability and quality governance of theological colleges

Mainline theological education institutions are having financial difficulty in some areas *due to shrinking membership and financial setbacks in the related church bodies.* Interdenominational colleges are under similar pressure. The increasing shortage of ministers in some churches is related to this lack of financial support for theological education. Observers have noted problems in governance and management in some institutions of theological education. Leaders may have been appointed for the wrong reasons or may not bring the needed competence in academic administration or financial management. Many associations of theological schools in Africa (and to a certain extent in Asia) remain fragile due to lack of continuous funding, one-sided dependency on outside resources, lack of commitment from individual member schools, or shifts in accreditation processes to government related agencies. Thus commitment to common curriculum development, common training of theological educators and common institutional support is low.

2.6 Shift towards state-funded departments for religious education

As church funds are dwindling and financial support for church-based theological education has become unreliable in the North as well as the South, there is *a trend in certain contexts to state-funded departments of religious education.* In several cases theological faculties which were closely related to churches and served both ministerial formation programmes as well as general religious education programmes have been transformed into departments of religious studies which are integrated into larger faculties of humanities (for example in UNISA, South Africa). This can imply new chances, such as more openness and potential for interdisciplinary research and academic recognition, more financial stability, overcoming dependency on one major denominational tradition. However, this development also poses some questions: How is the inner coherence and church-related responsibility of theological education exercised if the structural framework does not emphasise ministerial formation? How are churches able to formulate their own priorities and directives if they are not structurally related to the institutional framework of theological education?

2.7 Changes in the composition and background of student communities

The age, gender, and denominational backgrounds of students entering theological education continue to change. Fewer students enter theological education with the explicit aim of pursuing ordained ministry. Students tend to be older, with settled families, and from more diverse backgrounds. Some come without foundational Christian formation, and an increasing number come from charismatic and Pentecostal backgrounds. Many come with a job or profession to be maintained along with formal study. Many churches have developed 'multiple paths of preparation for ordination', some of which do not require a seminary degree. Some of these alternative patterns of preparation follow models common to the Pentecostal traditions which have not required formal seminary education for the majority of their ministers.[27]

2.8 Lack of theological education and the growth of Christian fundamentalism

There is a worldwide resurgence of religious fundamentalism and confessionalism, both in churches and in the related theological education institutions. Anti-ecumenical sentiments are on the increase in Latin America and in some countries in Asia and Africa. Many argue that this situation is related to the lack of theological research, that is, to the gap between academic theological knowledge production and popular Christian perceptions, publications, religious literature, hymns, and sermons which inspire the daily realities of life. In many cases what is missing is a popularized theology which can communicate to Christians at the grassroots. Instead populist theological idioms tend to dominate which are not informed by sound contextualized theology.[28] In many theological faculties and seminaries in the South, resources are so limited that lecturers can be supported only on a part time basis, thus reducing the possibilities for extended research and the development of contextual theological resources that might be used in local theological education and inform all aspects of the practice of ministry.

2.9 Weakening of interdenominational cooperation and joint programmes in theological education

There is a trend toward *cutting financial support for interdenominational, intercultural, and ecumenical programmes in theological education.* The number of chairs and institutes for missiology, world Christianity and/or ecumenism courses has been reduced in some regions (for instance, in Western Europe and India) and the financial situation has made it more difficult than ever for interdenominational and joint programmes to remain financially viable. Many denominations, even smaller churches and dioceses, seem to prefer their own small college or seminary rather than joining existing interdenominational institutions. *International financial support for promoting ecumenical theological education has become very limited.*

While the Theological Education Fund (TEF) of the WCC had a keen interest in promoting United Theological Colleges and contributed significantly to a number of institutions which are now well established (United Theological College of the West Indies, founded 1966; United Theological College Harare, founded 1954; United Theological College in Bangalore, founded 1910), we see today that the expectations aligned with this model were met only partly. Recent experiences have shown that United Theological Colleges can provide a viable basis for theological education only if there is a balanced relation between the supporting member churches and the interdenominational college; that institutional instability can occur for such institutions where minority churches feel dominated by majority churches; that for many churches the dominant expectation continues to be that theological education should benefit their own church and denominational identity; and that the number of United Theological Colleges has not increased much in the last fifty years.

2.10 Migration and theological education – new needs for theological training programmes for migrant churches

In the past one hundred years we have witnessed the end of colonial rule, enormous vitality in local ministry, the birth of a polycentric world church, and a new shape altogether with the shift to the global South. We have also seen in the North the emergence of new immigrant churches originating in the South. From the sixteenth through to the middle of the twentieth century, Europeans migrated south, taking with them European models of theological education. Since the middle of the twentieth century the trend has reversed, with massive migration to Europe, North America, Australia and New Zealand. African,

Asian, Latin American and Pacific Islanders have now become part of Christianity in the western hemisphere. While the legacy of European Christendom and its patterns continues to influence many churches in Asia and Africa and the theological thinking and ministerial formation there, forms of non-Western Christianity, including new models of theological education, are spreading in pockets of the West.

3 Affirmations and Recommendations

The following affirmations and recommendations have been identified by the study group as having strategic importance for the future of theological education in world Christianity.

3.1 Christian mission and theological education

We *affirm* that theological education is vital for the transmission of Christian tradition from one generation to the next and for integral Christian mission in today's world. Theological education is essential for the renewal and continuity of the church and its leadership. Theological education is a matter of survival for an authentic and contextual mission of the church in all contemporary contexts.

We *recommend* that churches and partner organisations increase their efforts to strengthen, to accompany, and to enhance theological education – particularly in Africa. Courses on Christian mission, world Christianity, church unity and ecumenism should be given a prominent place and be strengthened in theological education institutions around the world in the coming decades.

3.2 Global and regional forum on theological education

We *affirm* the broad-based dialogue process which is underway with Edinburgh 2010 and recommend that it continue with involvement of representatives from all historical and new Christian churches which are part of world Christianity today. This dialogue process on goals and common cooperation in theological education is needed more urgently now than ever before, in order to avoid isolation and fragmentation in theological education and to enhance cooperation and common responsibility.

In the light of the very few opportunities for dialogue between historical, Evangelical, charismatic, Pentecostal, and independent churches on theological education, we *recommend* that a continuous global forum (a working group) on cooperation in theological education be created. This Global Forum could serve as a continuation committee within the Edinburgh 2010 process to take up some of the challenges identified in this report by bringing together representatives from major associations of theological schools, networks for theological education, and partner organisations supporting theological education. It should cooperate with the WCC's programme on Ecumenical Theological Education and can function as an enlarged framework of WOCATI

(World Conference of Associations of Theological Schools). At the same time the regional ecumenical organisations (such as CCA in Asia, AACC in Africa, CLAI in Latin America) might play a new role in strengthening and supporting networks, fundraising and grant-giving for theological education within their regions.

3.3 Bridging the divide of unequal accessibility of theological education

We *affirm* that access to theological education should be available to all segments of the Christian family, the churches in South and North, East and West, women and men, people from poor and affluent backgrounds (see categories of access to theological education as mentioned in section 7). The fast-growing churches in the South have a right and an essential need to have better facilities for theological education.

In the face of glaring discrepancies in terms of availability and accessibility of theological education we *recommend* that adequate attention be given by churches, ecumenical partner organisations, and Regional Ecumenical Organisations for strengthening theological education programmes and institutions, particularly in those areas where the enormous demand for theological education is not being adequately met at present.

3.4 Theological education between church and university settings

We *affirm* that there are legitimate and different historical reasons for some church contexts to opt primarily for church-related theological education and for others to opt primarily for university-related institutional settings of theological education.

While each context has to be looked at within its own right, we *recommend* that churches consider the following questions as they evaluate related priorities concerning the institutional setting of theological education. (i) What church model (church vision) informs theological education? (ii) What is the balance between the different types of theological education in a given context? (iii) What kind of theological education is most appropriate for nurturing and inspiring a missionary church, engaged in public theology, social witness and global solidarity? (iv) Who are the primary subjects of theological learning? For whom and with whom are students learning theology? (v) Do university settings provide for free and genuine academic exchange of values, ideas, and research? Or are universities driven by business agendas and so tend to devalue the relevance of humanities? Does the university setting safeguard the integrity and identity of Christian theology, ministerial and spiritual formation, and the relationship with the existing churches?

3.5 Innovative forms of theological education and formation for ministry

We *affirm* that churches in both the North and the South need to explore new forms of theological education in order to allow for the full participation of all God's people in mission in today's world. Alternative and creative ways of doing theology and theological education have been developed in churches in both the northern and southern hemispheres, within local and regional theological training centres and ordination programmes as well as in alternative programmes in college- and university-based institutions of theological education. We now have the great opportunity (and challenge) to learn from each other, from the innovative, creative, mission-minded models of theological education which are providing formation, discipleship, and preparation for leadership for both lay people and those preparing for ordained ministry. The primary concern in some areas has to do with overcoming detached and decontextualized styles of doing theology and the predominance of the university paradigm of preparation for ministry. These concerns are being addressed through recognising the increasing diversification of theological education both in the West and in those areas that have inherited Western traditions and, especially, through listening to and learning from those who are developing new or alternative formation and education programmes that are focused directly on God's mission and ministry in the world.

We *recommend* that churches and institutions of theological education develop processes of genuine mutual listening with their respective partners in other parts of the world in order to learn about the innovative patterns of education and formation which exist in many contexts and so move beyond traditional patterns of theological education and the stereotypes often used in viewing other models that tend to simplify complex and demanding situations.

3.6 Church support and ownership of institutions of theological education

We *affirm* that churches, mission organisations and ecumenical partners have a key responsibility for supporting and enabling high quality institutions of theological education while respecting a certain degree of autonomy in their operating and academic research. There are different models by which ownership of theological education is expressed in different contexts. Theological education not only serves the building up of the church from the perspective of the reign of God, but it also creates social awareness, political discernment, social involvement, and Christian participation in the transformation processes of society. Investment in theological education is a direct investment into social and political development and the raising of educational levels.

We *recommend* that churches and agencies (development, mission, and others) reconsider their priorities in terms of making more regular support available for institutions of theological education. As there is no existing standard for the amount that churches should make available to theological education, we recommend that the UNESCO recommendation—that nation states should make available at least six percent of their annual gross national product for higher education—be applied to the churches' support for theological education.[29]

We also *recommend* that consideration be given to means of strengthening theological education in those countries in which Christianity is just emerging in a way which does not impose the fragmented forms of denominational Christianity inherited from the West.

3.7 New forms of global and regional solidarity in theological education

We *affirm* the ongoing obligation of developing new forms of global and regional solidarity in theological education. As many mainline churches in the United States and Western Europe face decline in membership and financial resources, new and financially gifted churches in countries like South Korea, Taiwan, Singapore and other parts of the world should be encouraged to explore a new system of global solidarity for promoting ecumenical theological education worldwide. It is time to review the old one-sided system of funding grants and scholarships and consider whether the WCC or another central organisation should be remobilized for this work, whether primary responsibility should rest with regional bodies, or whether a new approach altogether is needed.

One of the most important forms of developing solidarity and networking in theological education has been the establishment of regional associations of theological schools—which now exist in many parts of the world. Their viability and relevance, however, varies widely, with some providing strong support for the schools in their region while others are dormant. Regional associations should have able and committed leadership and a stable office location; regular contributions from member institutions to establish financial self-reliance; a focused programme for the production of contextual theological textbooks, a common curriculum, and continued education for faculty; a system of assessment and institutional enhancement; working relations with ecumenical partners and the maintenance of communication with all schools in the region; diversity among the member schools in terms of denominational affiliation and faith tradition.

We *recommend* therefore that a round table of ecumenical partners be established for sharing financial, human, and material resources and to coordinate international support for theological education in the South. It is also recommended that joint efforts be made to revive existing associations of theological schools to serve as an instrument for ecumenical regional cooperation, common project planning, and quality enhancement.

3.8 The relevance of theological education for the unity of the church

We *affirm* that theological education is a task common to all Christian churches and that efforts should be made, as much as possible, to do everything in common in fulfilling the Christian mandate of theological education without violating ecclesial or denominational identities in a given setting. The increasing fragmentation and denominational isolation of institutions of theological education is harmful to the very nature of the mission of theological education, which is to introduce people to what it means to be the whole body of Christ in today's world.

We *recommend* that efforts should be taken to increase interdenominational cooperation, that synergies be sought between different denominational institutions of theological education, and that wherever possible interdenominational settings of theological education be developed and strengthened.

3.9 New models of online-education and e-learning in theological education

Recognising the profound impact that information and communication technologies (ICTs—or simply IT in some contexts) have had on education, we *affirm* that theological education is about communicating God's good news and creating new abilities to communicate this good news in today's world. Therefore new information and communication technologies should be explored and developed for use in theological education, including web-based courses of study, research groups working via the internet, distance degree courses at all levels using digital formats, and electronic library and other data resources.

We *recommend* that deliberate attention should be given to issues relating specifically to theological education, such as: what kinds of theological curricula and individual courses can be easily and appropriately provided electronically (i.e., online, via CD-ROM, or other electronic memory device)? What diversified forms of theological education in non-residential patterns (such as TEE programmes) can benefit from the use of the new ICTs? There is widespread use of ICTs in theological education around the world, in Evangelical, Pentecostal, and some mainline institutions, but common understandings of transferability and assessment of learning are still to be developed.

3.10 Financial viability of theological education

We *affirm* the cooperation of church and theological education leaders in the development of improved strategies for the financial viability of theological education and the establishment of common regional standards of financial viability for theological colleges in the southern hemisphere. How to finance theological education in the South? This question is of vital importance for the future of world Christianity. Studies show that deep problems with regard to financial viability are also known in the North.

Although issues of financial stewardship and sustainability are urgent throughout theological education in the South, there has not been a comprehensive study on the topic since 1975.[30] We *recommend* therefore that a major international study be done on the financial viability of theological education both in the North and in the South.

3.11 Innovative models of engaging with persons of other faiths through theological education

We *affirm* that engaging with people of other faiths is an essential component in theological education. This engagement should take seriously the following four forms of dialogue: (i) the dialogue of life, where people naturally relate to each other across religious boundaries in the course of their daily living; (ii) social dialogue, where people of various faiths collaborate with one another in the cause of peace and justice; (iii) intellectual dialogue, which can explore different beliefs and their claims to truth; (iv) spiritual dialogue, where people open themselves to the force of one another's religious experiences.

We also *affirm*: 'Dialogue does not require people to relinquish or alter their beliefs before entering into it; on the contrary, genuine dialogue demands that each partner brings to it the fullness of themselves and the tradition in which they stand. As they grow in mutual understanding they will be able to share more and more of what they bring with the other. Inevitably, both partners to the dialogue will be affected and changed by this process, for it is a mutual sharing'.[31]

In order to engage appropriately in such dialogue Christians, both laity and clergy, need to be well-trained and secure in their understanding of their own Christian tradition and theology. We are aware of the growing importance (and number) of highly equipped and well-funded Muslim institutions of higher and academic education worldwide, and believe that it is vital for the Christian family not to renounce its own tradition of a strong commitment to higher theological education. Although Christians need to be equipped to engage in dialogue with people of all world faiths—as well as the 'faith' of secularism—we believe that given the contemporary world situation it is vital for Christians to be able to engage constructively and confidently with Muslims. The future of Christian-Muslim dialogue needs well-educated pastors and well-trained lecturers of theology and religions in institutions of theological education. The future of many Christian minority churches in Muslim countries also depends to a considerable extend on the educational level of their leadership and their ability to enter into qualified dialogue with Muslim neighbours. We also believe, given both the tragedy but also the renewal of Christian-Jewish relations during the past a hundred years, that theological education needs to encourage exploration of the unique aspects of the Christian-Jewish relationship.

We therefore *recommend* that a collection of innovative models and curriculum proposals for dialogue with people of other faiths should be made available on the internet site of ETE and related bodies.

3.12 Diversity of human languages and the dominance of English in global theological education

We *affirm* that the investment in a variety of languages for theological education is an essential prerequisite for achieving *unity in diversity* in world

Christianity. All churches are challenged to develop a balance between the need for becoming open to the challenges of the globalized world and the need for vital interaction with and inculturation in the local cultures in their own context. All churches are challenged to become 'glocal' in their own identity and in their capacities for dialogue. The appropriate means to assist in this process is theological education. But becoming 'glocal' necessarily entails the development of a counter-balance to one-sided dependency on English language in theological education. The plea of Edinburgh 1910 to develop concepts of theological education in vernacular languages is not yet sufficiently answered and fulfilled.

We therefore *recommend* that deliberate efforts be taken to strengthen non-Anglo-Saxon teaching resources, curriculum developments, and theological publications for theological education. The multi-lingual plurality of human communities and Christian churches will be strengthened and respected the more theological education is not restricted to a mono-lingual setting, but takes place in languages which are close to the communities the churches serve.

Endnotes

[1] The 97-page longer version of this report is available in print from ETE office and also can be found, along with supporting background articles at: www.oikoumene.org/en/resources/documents/wcc-programmes/education-and-ecumenical-formation/ecumenical-theological-education-ete/edinburgh-2010-international-study-group-on-theological-education.html

[2] As this summary report is not a comprehensive treatment of theological education; only selected references will be offered for other resources and research.

[3] The commitment to education prior to 1910 is outlined in Brian Stanley, *The World Missionary Conference: Edinburgh 1910* (Grand Rapids, MI: Eerdmans, 2009) 199.

[4] Edinburgh World Missionary Conference, Edinburgh 1910, *Report of Commission III: Education in Relation to the Christianisation of National Life* (Edinburgh & London: Oliphant, Anderson and Ferrier, 1910), 371-2; see also David Kerr and Kenneth Ross (eds), *Edinburgh 2010: Mission Then and Now* (Oxford: Regnum, 2009) 85-118.

[5] Edinburgh 1910, *Education*, 373.

[6] Christine, Lienemann-Perrin, *Training for a Relevant Ministry: A Study of the Contribution of the Theological Education Fund* (Madras & Geneva: Christian Literature Society & PTE/WCC, 1981); Charles Ranson, 'The Theological Education Fund', *International Review of Mission* 47/4 (1958), 432-38.

[7] Mission Theological Advisory Group, *Presence and Prophecy, A Heart for Mission in Theological Education* (London: Church House Publishing, 2002); Bernhard Ott, *Beyond Fragmentation: Integrating Mission and Theological Education* (Oxford: Regnum, 2002); Max Stackhouse, *Apologia: Contextualization, Globalization, and Mission in Theological Education* (Grand Rapids, MI: Eerdmans, 1988); Peter F. Penner (ed.), *Theological Education as Mission* (Neufeld Verlag, 2005); Daniel Aleshire, *Earthen Vessels: Hopeful Reflections on the Work and Future of Theological Schools* (Grand Rapids, MI: Eerdmans, 2008); Dietrich Werner, 'Guest Editorial: Theological Education in Mission', *International Review of Mission* 388 (April, 2009), 2-10; Vidar

Leif Haanes, 'Theological Education and Mission', in Tormond Engelsviken, *et al* (eds), *Mission to the World: Communicating the Gospel in the Twenty-first Century* (Oxford: Regnum, 2008), 391-404.

[8] Ecumenical Theological Education, 'Message of the Oslo Conference on Theological Education 1996', in John Pobee (ed.), *Towards Viable Theological Education* (Geneva: WCC Publications, 1997), 1-6.

[9] Mark Laing, 'Recovering Missional Ecclesiology in Theological Education', *International Review of Mission* 388 (April 2009), 11-24.

[10] David Bosch, 'Theological Education in Missionary Perspective', *Missiology* X/1 (January 1982), 17-19; see also Michael McCoy, 'Restoring Mission to the Heart of Theological Education, A South African Perspective' available at www.oikoumene.org/fileadmin/files/wcc-main/documents/p5/ete/Michael McCoy, accessed 8/9/09.

[11] See also Mission Theological Advisory Group, *Presence and Prophecy.*

[12] McCoy, 'Restoring Mission', 1.

[13] World Council of Churches, Ecumenical Theological Education, 'Magna Charta on Ecumenical Formation in Theological Education', *Ministerial Formation* 110 (April 2008), 82-88. Available at www.oikoumene.org.

[14] 'Patterns of Ministry: Theological Education in a Changing World' which was presented at the World Council of Churches Assembly in Uppsala 1968 marks the watershed in developments toward diversified ministry and theological education. See Steven Mackie, *Patterns of Ministry: Theological Education in a Changing World* (London: Collins, 1969).

[15] Ross Kinsler, *Diversified Theological Education: Equipping all God's People* (Pasadena, CA: William Carey, 2008).

[16] Kinsler, *Diversified Theological Education*, 8-9.

[17] www.globalconnections.co.uk; http://trainforchrist.org/public/; http://new.gbgm-umc.org/umw/; www.worldevangelicals.org/resources/2005_02.pdf.

[18] Robert Brynjolfson & Jonathan Lewis (eds), *Integral Mission Training: Design and Evaluation* (Pasadena, CA: William Carey, 2006), x.

[19] See Glory E. Dhamaraj, 'Lay Women, Mission Practices, and Theological Thought', paper presented at the Queen's Foundation, March 2009, and submitted to Edinburgh 2010 Study Group 6.

[20] See www.nccindia.in/affiliates/christianorganization.htm.

[21]See www.lib.berkeley.edu/SSEAL/SoutheastAsia/seaphil.html

[22] Lydia Johnson & Joan Alleluia Filemoni-Tofaeno (eds), *Weavings: Women Doing Theology in Oceania* (Suva: SPATS/USP, 2003).

[23] See: www.eatwot.org.

[24] www.anglicancommunion.org/acns/news.cfm/2009/3/3/ACNS4584

[25] The following is from Dietrich Werner, 'Edinburgh 2010 Process and Theological Education: The Legacy of the World Mission Conference and the Vision for ETE in the Twenty-first Century', paper presented at the Queen's Foundation, March 2009, and submitted to Edinburgh 2010 Study Group 6. See ETE website on Edinburgh 2010 theological education study process.

[26] Today, in many situations in the South, Christians live and practice their faith in a context similar to that of Christians before Christianity was accepted by Constantine and given a respectable status as a state religion. In these situations in the South, Christians are a minority with no political clout, no social status compared to other religious communities. In some circumstances they are despised and persecuted with charges that

they belong to a foreign religion and culture (such as the challenges that Christians face in Indonesia, India, Pakistan, Egypt, and Nigeria). Some of these Christian communities came into being through Western missionary activity during the colonial era and enjoyed special status during the Western colonial time, but then had to adjust to the new reality of having no privilege or position. Therefore they need to rethink their practice of Christianity with a mindset and spirit of pre-Constantinian Christianity.

[27] Timothy P. Weber, 'The Seminaries and the Churches: Looking for New Relationships', *Theological Education* 44:1 (2008), 65-92, at 80.

[28] Francois Swanepoel, 'Lecture for the Joint Conference of Theological Societies', Stellenbosch University, June 2009.

[29] UNESCO, CONFINTEA VI, Belem, Brazil, May 2009.

[30] Herbert Zorn, *Viability in Context: A Study of the Financial Viability of Theological Education in the Third World. Seedbed or Sheltered Garden*? (London: TEF, 1975). See also Yeow Choo Lak, 'The Financial Viability of Theological Formation', in Pobee, *Towards Viable Theological Education*, 94-102.

[31] 'The Way of Dialogue', Appendix 6 of the Lambeth Conference 1998, available at www.anglicancommunion.org/the-holy-land/info/lambeth1.cfm.

THEME SEVEN
CHRISTIAN COMMUNITIES IN CONTEMPORARY CONTEXTS

Preface

The 'Christian Communities in Contemporary Contexts' study group reformulated the questions suggested for study (see Appendix II) and focused on the following themes and key questions:

i. Poverty, suffering and marginalized communities: How do adjectives of Christian community such as 'discipling', 'healing', 'witnessing', and 'contextual' become lived realities in today's world?
ii. Globalization and the reproduction of hierarchies: What is involved in being the church in the cities and mega-cities of today?
iii. Christianity and socio-political action: How can the local church be an agent of the kingdom of God and a source of healing and reconciliation?
iv. Identity, gender and power: What is the true identity (the 'core DNA') of the church? How does it manifest itself in different denominations and cultures?
v. The interface of migration, diaspora and ethnicity: what are the tensions between homogenous and multi-ethnic churches? How is church life in diaspora communities shaped?
vi. HIV/AIDS, church and mission: Does Christian mission bear some responsibility for the spread of the virus? How can mission contribute to the struggle to stop the pandemic? What other forms of ill-health call for particular attention from practitioners of Christian mission?

The following report, which is organised around these questions, has input from three levels: First, the study group comprised 15-20 core members drawn from all continents and diverse Christian traditions, Catholic and Protestant. It comprises *inter alia*, Dr Afe Adogame, University of Edinburgh (convener), Dr Philomena Mwaura, Kenyatta University, Nairobi (co-convener) and the central organising committee made up of Erica Dunmow (Urban Mission Development Project, UK), and Janice McLean (Jamaica/USA) and Anderson Jeremiah (India) both doctoral students at the University of Edinburgh, who have drawn up this report. The report drew from the expertise and benefited from the input of participants at two successful consultations held in Edinburgh on 5 December 2008 and 12-13 June 2009. In investigating the themes/questions we sought to incorporate views of academics, researchers, church leaders, religious NGOs, and policy makers. Such a multidimensional perspective was necessary for critical thinking about how mission is articulated and practised in contemporary contexts and in seeking new directions for engagement in Christian mission in the twenty-first century.

The one-day workshop held in December 2008 comprised twenty participants drawn mainly from the church leadership of immigrant/diaspora communities in the UK. Papers and discussions at this seminar focused on 'challenges in urban mission', 'understanding the impact of power dynamics' and 'gender and youth'. The second, much larger, consultation was a two-day international conference held in June 2009. Thirty-five participants were drawn from Africa, North America, Asia and Europe; with a paper presented in absentia on behalf of a contributor from Australia. The conference had its focus on the themes of 'church and reconciliation', 'gender and identity', 'church and poverty', 'media representation and Pentecostalism', 'conducting mission in Edinburgh', 'church and society' and 'mission in diaspora'. The events attracted Christians from a wide range of churches – Evangelical, Pentecostal, Protestant and Catholic. Papers presented are available on the Edinburgh 2010 website.

Second, the report had input from the UK Urban Mission (*Jesus in the City (JITC)*). The JITC Executive agreed with Edinburgh 2010 to link in to the study process via Study Group 7. The JITC listened to discussion on these issues at a number of events around the UK in 2009 and heard 'bubbles of enthusiasm for urban mission' in order to feed in the UK experience to Group 7. The fourteen events were organised in cooperation with a range of Protestant denominations and in two cases with Catholic organisations and dioceses. In order to relate the themes and questions to UK urban mission practitioners, Erica Dunmow, Urban Mission Development Advisor (on behalf of the JITC Executive) undertook some work on interpreting them and linking them to examples of the practical issues faced in the UK urban mission context.

Third, the report further benefited from the proceedings of the Eastern Africa Conference held in Nairobi from 26-28 May 2009. The East African team identified with the themes of Study Group 7 and drew its forty-six participants from Protestant and Evangelical churches and mission societies, church leaders, theologians, scholars, clergy and lay people from East Africa. The process entailed a critical evaluation of the what, how and why of the way Christian missions have been carried out in Eastern Africa; and endeavoured to understand what lessons may be learnt for enhanced missiological enterprise in the twenty-first century. The conference was also to highlight how such missiological themes can be woven together with praxis in contemporary East Africa. The conference was inclusive in terms of Christian traditions, regions, gender, age, disability, youth, academics and mission practitioners. A report of the event is available on the Edinburgh 2010 website.

1 Church and Society

1.1 Poverty, suffering and marginalized communities

How do adjectives of Christian community – such as 'discipling', 'healing', 'witnessing', 'contextual' – become lived realities in today's world? How does the contemporary church faithfully engage with issues of success, wealth, empowerment, poverty, disempowerment and exploitation that mark the lives of many who live within rural/urban contexts?

With an estimated 1.3 billion in the ranks of the poor worldwide, the United Nations target is to lift 650 million people out of ranks of 'abject poverty' – with an income of less than a dollar a day. It has been estimated that 40 billion USD is needed annually to achieve the international goals related to poverty eradication. This is less than what people in Europe spend on cigarettes and one tenth of the value of world trade in illegal drugs. Issues of poverty, suffering and marginalized communities were recurring themes and were treated as interrelated, integrated but not as disparate entities. Although poverty and suffering are often to be associated with marginalized groups or communities, a crucially important task is how to define poverty in the first instance. Festus Olatunde of Mountain of Fire and Miracle Ministries International, Edinburgh,[1] defined poverty 'as hunger, lack of shelter, being sick with no access to treatment, not having a job, powerlessness, a state of being without, association with hardship, spiritual lack, fear for the future – living one day at a time'. Two causes of poverty were differentiated as general and personal causes of poverty. The former includes high cost of living, changing economy, lack of education attainment, lack of asset and support, large family structure, selfishness and corruption, sin and lack of knowing God, and physical and spiritual war (1 Sam 2:18-20, Jer 49:12,13,27). Personal causes of poverty were identified as ignorance, laziness, unfaithfulness, disobedience, pride, curses, and lack of investment mentality. The consequences of poverty include homelessness, hunger, diseases, sexual exploitation, AIDS, profitless labour, drug trafficking, lack of education, disability and untimely death.

Poverty is indeed a complex, relative concept that conveys different meanings in different contexts. For instance, we can distinguish between generational and situational poverty based on patterns, just as there are cultural differences in poverty. Thus an interrogation of poverty needs to be cross-cultural in orientation and outlook. Poverty as a multifaceted state of deprivation cannot be wholly divorced from its socio-cultural context. It also creates marginalization and social exclusion, referring to relational dimensions, which bring with it inferior access of people to what they need, resulting in low mobility, low security, inferior opportunities for participation in social life and collective decision-making.

Two popular lenses through which poverty can be viewed are in terms of materiality and spirituality – that is, being deficient in material or spiritual terms. Although the indices for measuring these may be problematic, they nevertheless suggest that material and spiritual poverty could have grave, unintended consequences for advancing or stultifying Christian mission and growth. Our global societies and churches are now characterized by huge inequalities, a widening gap between the rich and the poor, social-economic injustices and class disparities. How has and will the church respond to these circumstances both within and outside the church context? Power structures are crucial to an understanding of marginalization, a tendency in which certain groups become more susceptible to poverty and suffering than others. Ostensibly, lack of education and unemployment can result in poverty and suffering. The poor in their respective societies are vulnerable to suffering and diseases; just as Christians in minority situations are vulnerable in the societies in which they find themselves.

How can we understand power dynamics in the particular context of the slums in Bombay, Nairobi, Lagos, Rio de Janeiro, and so on? The oppression of the Kakure Kirishitan in Japan[2] and of Dalit Christians in India is a problem that comes not only from outside, but also from within the Christian communities. The caste system in India tends to be reflected in the congregations. Sometimes, it is extremely difficult to cross frontiers and boundaries even within the context of the church. Anderson Jeremiah discussed how in many cases access to resources is linked to power dynamics.[3] For many within the Dalit community in Bombay (India), their access to resources in the churches has been prevented due to the perpetuation of a hierarchy in the churches that mirrors what is present within the society. As a result, the Christian ministry has become privatized with the rich having more access to pastoral care because they contribute more economic resources to the church, ultimately producing a fragmented community. So although church numbers have grown, this has coincided with an increase in the number of people begging outside the church premises. This singular example therefore throws down a challenge to how we can understand the Christian message in light of growing unemployment and growing slums.

A biblical view of poverty is essential if the world church is to fulfil its responsibilities to the poor and the marginalized. A biblical classification of the causes of poverty is instructive here: *oppression and fraud* (Prov 14:31; 22:7; 28:15); *misfortune, persecution, or judgment* (Job 1:12-19; Ps 109:16; Isa 47:9; Lam 5:3); *laziness and neglect* (Prov 10:4; 13:4; 19:15); and *the culture of poverty* (Prov 10:15). Poverty breeds poverty, and the cycle is not easily broken. People who grow up in an impoverished culture usually lack the nutrition and the education that would enable them to be successful in the future. An individual who grows up in a culture of poverty is destined for a life of poverty unless something rather dramatic takes place.

Jesus' solidarity with the poor, the deprived and marginalized cannot be overemphasised. Female leaders in African churches, for instance, do perceive Jesus as friend, as brother, as father and as redeemer. In different denominations, theologies are developing which emphasise this concern from their respective angles. From the perspective of the Pentecostals, Amos Yong emphasises that Paul is concerned about the foolish, the low, and the despised (1 Cor 1:27-28), and about God's power as manifest in and perfected through suffering and weakness (2 Cor 11:16-33 and 12:7-10). He suggests that

> the gift of the Spirit is not only not held back from but explicitly extended to those who were most oppressed and marginalized in the ancient world: women and slaves (Acts 2:17-18). In each of these cases, the 'weak' and the oppressed are not only recipients of divine favour, but are also, precisely through endowment of the gifts of the Spirit, instruments of God's activity in and for the world.[4]

Thus, the primary task of the church is being with the poor and marginalized. The question of agency is pertinent. Christians may find themselves in positions of power or being given powerful positions, but how are they utilizing that power and to whose advantage? The organisational structures of the church have become obstacles in dealing with poverty, oppression, injustice and issues of marginalization. Absence of clearly defined objective(s) in the church produces somewhat ambiguous roles and functions that are unachievable. Ecclesiastical hierarchies have turned out to be autocratic in their functioning, thus resulting in the misuse of power and resources, self-centeredness and misappropriation of official machinery for personal benefits.

Current socio-economic realities starkly indicate that hardly any secular government the world over has the wherewithal, resources or will to shoulder the entire responsibility for caring for its poor, the suffering, the oppressed and marginalized. Where the government is not doing much in this direction, and where in fact the oppression or injustice is coming from the government itself, then Christians must exercise their 'prophetic' voice and speak out against abuse and misuse of power. The world church has the great potential to offer unique solutions to poverty both in terms of alleviation and eradication. Ideally, the church should be in the vanguard of providing help to the poor, but it has in many respects become insensitive and complacent, thus neglecting her responsibility. Poverty is as much a psychological and spiritual issue as it is an economic problem, and it is in this realm that the church can be most effective. Although spiritual salvation is not the sole answer, the church is better equipped to meet the psychological and spiritual needs of poverty-stricken people.

The church can provide some panacea through capital investment, generating funds to help those in need, and appropriating their gifts and abilities to help those caught in the web of poverty. Christians should reach out to those in poverty by supporting ministries working in this area. Such an outreach provides churches with a mechanism to meet the physical needs of the poor as well as a context to meet their spiritual needs. Social action and evangelism often work hand in hand and thus this kind of social involvement can also provide opportunities for evangelism.

The world church must take urgent, concrete actions to alleviate poverty, suffering and marginalization in different local-global contexts. Such actions must include the following: the forging of a global alliance by the world church, in partnership with the governments, to make poverty eradication a central goal of humanity; empowering the poor; ending discrimination against women/girls, supporting women, and tapping their tremendous potential; enabling access of the poor to capital and other productive resources so as to gain productive self employment. Other actions are to provide enlightenment campaigns on reducing the proportions of hunger and malnutrition; encouraging implementation of comprehensive programmes to promote good health; encouraging quality basic education, as well as secondary and higher education, vocational training, and skill acquisition throughout life; developing social services with more social investments in partnership with governments and agencies; encouraging good governance and effective administration as prerequisites to effectively fight poverty; praying consistently to wipe out poverty.

Erica Dunmow[5] addressed in the UK the question of how we can make sure that the people born into the poorest neighbourhoods are seen as leaders, not just for their locality but also for the wider church. In this regard it is important to examine the nature of the incarnation; past efforts and possible reasons for failure; and signs of change in the twenty-first century – learning from the non-Western world. Ann Morisy[6] and David Stevens[7] both spoke about the contribution that individual Christians can make to the wellbeing of their communities by their attitudes to life. As the National Estate Churches Network Manchester conference put it, we have to: 'empower people to look outside the box' and 'raise their eyes beyond their surroundings'.[8] The Evangelical Fellowship of the Anglican Communion made reference to the parable of the Good Samaritan as a key discipling model saying that 'it will involve us…crossing boundaries of faith, culture and race'.[9] This cross-cultural mission works in many directions.

The church compounds marginalization in its leadership selection and training processes. Vocations seem more easily recognised from white and/or middle class people and congregations, which means that many of our urban church leaders are effectively engaged in cross-cultural mission. The mainstream churches are gradually becoming aware of the need to grow leaders from within the indigenous working class population, especially where churches serve those communities.

The notion that mission needs to be an integrated process including practical action, proclamation and community or civic engagement, which is best done together with other churches, is gaining much greater ground in the UK through initiatives such as HOPE 08 and the earlier United We Stand process of the Evangelical Alliance UK. This includes congregations that might previously have concentrated on personal piety and individual conversion now realising that 'Jesus was proactive and reactive: we need to stop being just reactive. [So] we need to be more prophetic, speaking out to get agendas and rules changed…we need to find out whose voice is heard and talk to them'.[10]

1.2 Mission, marginalization and conflict management

The East African consultation[11] highlighted mission concerns for East Africa and posed crucial lessons from the history of mission. As it aptly demonstrated, various lessons may be learnt by reading through history. First, the importance of memory: an analysis of contemporary problems in Eastern Africa indicates that these are related to the nineteenth century Christian missions. The chief challenges faced by African peoples are associated with alienation – from their land, their cultures, their worldviews, and from themselves. Christian missions played a role in this alienation. For example, part of the cause of the 2007-2008 post-election violence in Kenya was the quest for land, much of which was illegally appropriated by the church in the name of mission. Another example may be given of how Christian missions stigmatized and marginalized African cultural, religious, educational, social and political systems.[12] This has consequently resulted in hypocrisy and confusion as Africans seek to be 'Christian'. Christian mission in the twenty-first century must contribute to redressing some of these historical injustices committed in the process of evangelization.

Second, while the church in Eastern Africa has actively demonstrated love and concern for people, at another level the church has been a source of marginalization of its own body thereby creating centres and margins. At the global level, North-South differences continue to hamper Christian mission, while at the local level the mainline churches marginalize Pentecostal and indigenous churches. Within churches, stratification along class, race, ethnicity, gender, age, abilities continue unabated. Edinburgh 2010 must grapple with questions of justice, equity and representation. While we appreciate the limitations of Edinburgh 2010 with regard to the number of people who can be physically present, there is need to ensure equitable representation of people from the global South (Africans included), women, children, youth, disabled, African independent Pentecostal and indigenous churches, People Living With HIV/AIDS (PLWHA), indigenous peoples, and so on.

The church in East Africa has been instrumental in the proclamation of the good news of our Lord Jesus Christ. Over the period between 1990 and 2002 in Kenya for example, the church united with other religions and together pushed for democratic changes, thereby bringing an end to an era of serious human rights abuses. This clearly demonstrated the power of religious unity. However, on many occasions the church has been guilty of conformity where it has allowed itself to be led rather than to lead. Often the church has been reactionary rather than proactive. In Uganda, ecumenical cooperation has been threatened by sectarianism. We appreciate the major role played by the church in Eastern Africa in the context of conflict management and peace-building. However, we acknowledge that the church has often been a source of, or party to, conflict. Conflict and violence among and even within churches has marred the image and integrity of the church, thereby eroding its authority. Without being democratic in its structures, the church cannot hope to address lack of democracy and conflict in the secular sphere. European/American missionaries to Africa adopted a model of church management that is centralized and imperialistic. Unfortunately, this model continues to hamper inclusive participation in mission. There is need to shift to a cyclical communitarian model where God is at the centre and every one is seen as part of mission work to the glory of God.

1.3 Globalization and the reproduction of hierarchies

What is involved in being the church in the cities and mega-cities of today? Globalization impacts on the church and the reproduction of hierarchies. Such interrogation is particularly important when issues of power are considered. What happens when the church continues to perpetuate the power structures that marginalize the marginalized? How does one reconcile this reality with the liberating message of the gospel? Who are the people within world Christianity who influence what happens? What are the avenues that provide those at the grassroots an opportunity to speak and be heard?

The impact of European colonialism continues to be felt and requires a more detailed analysis. Frieder Ludwig and Israel Akanji's contributions shed light on contemporary forms of international relations between Western countries, Liberia and Nigeria respectively.[13] They showed the use and impact of the modern phenomenon of multimedia communication. Internet videos have been used to foster relations between contexts through particular representations of events, and the publication of cartoons in Denmark rapidly sparked violence in Nigeria. As the 2010 project is already well aware, increased global interconnectedness has to be taken seriously; it is both a resource and also a threat.

Ministry in an urban context is dynamic and can take a variety of dimensions. In the British context, Lawrie Hudson and Tom Kisitu of the Edinburgh City Mission (ECM) provide valuable models of ministry in an urban context that the world church can learn from.[14] They explained that the ECM is totally committed to the concept of sharing the gospel message through their several areas of ministry, which include community mission, counselling ministry, workplace outreach, cultural mission, New Age outreach, street work, street evangelism, student outreach and creative mission:

> **West Pilton Christian Centre** coordinated by Tom Kisitu has a drop-in centre with a cafe, a Freedom in Christ course and a fellowship time. The centre creates an environment that allows people to relax and chat. These people come to the Centre from hectic lives mostly due to alcohol and drugs issues. This goes on in the midst of their apparent poverty.

Basics Bank is a ministry which operates in both West Pilton and in Pilrig Street (Edinburgh). Their clients are people who have fallen on hard times and cannot afford to buy food. Basic Banks engage with them for an initial eight weeks during which they are supplied with some basic food and toiletries on a weekly basis. When the clients visit they get a chance to sit down and have a cup of tea/coffee with staff listening to them and trying to provide guidance where possible but also sharing the gospel when given the opportunity.

The Underbelly is on a Friday night in the Cowgate area and is a ministry to the club goers.

Streetwork is an ongoing ministry to students at Edinburgh University. Missionary Paul James-Griffiths can be seen outside the library offering hot drinks and engaging in conversations about Jesus, and people become Christians through this ministry. Street evangelism involves distribution of literature, drama presentation, and other activities. Another aspect of street evangelism is the Care Van. The ECM and Bethany Christian Trust are in partnership with Edinburgh churches 'touching' lives, sharing God's care and compassion to homeless people through provision of food, clothing and blankets.

There is also the **Community Outreach** and other programmes. As Lawrie Hudson remarked:

> it is of paramount importance that along with providing all the different types of help, we take every opportunity to share the message of Jesus. We have a saying in the mission that we do not want to send people to hell with a full belly. Feeding is part of our ministry but providing food for the soul is more important long term. As Christians: 'Together we can make a difference' touching lives in Edinburgh.

In another vein, city centre ministry has been summed up by the Methodist City Centre Network, which specialises in this area of mission, as demonstrating 'the love of God as seen in Christ, for all who live, work and spend time in the city centre'.[15] One of the most interesting questions raised was 'What does "community" mean in the city centre?'[16] Morisy talked of the flows in and out of city centres and how the church in that setting can be a place of encounter with the separate flows and a place of bringing those flows into connection with each other.[17] This can be especially challenging in providing various sorts of worship that feed the spirituality of those different groups and still enables them to feel part of the wider body of Christ.[18] One of the most challenging flows is obviously that of the migration of people, but more hidden and just as powerful is the flow of money.

City centre ministry often involves having a place at the civic table – through local regeneration partnerships or cross-sectoral Local Strategic or Community Planning Partnerships. Also, just as in matters of theology the churches do not speak with one voice, so their engagement with civic and secular structures is not uniform. Civic and secular authorities want a 'one-stop' place of conversation, but we are doing a disservice to the complexity of our understandings of mission if we let one strand in the church hold the ring. The trick is to find a way of being connected in our differences. The Evangelical Fellowship of the Anglican Communion held an urban mission workshop which produced a set of priorities for the church in the twenty-first century.[19] They remarked that the churches 'must seek the welfare of our cities and this will involve holistic, incarnational mission'.[20]

The movement of people around British cities means that some historic churches no longer have a large congregation and are looking to creative ways of enabling the buildings to be held in trust for the local community. The challenge raised, at the London Urban Theology Project, by a lay Christian working as an architect with an interest in this area, was when to decide to do this. She considered when churches should create a resource such as social housing on the site, and when to pass on the resource to perhaps a newer denomination.[21] The response from those newer churches is that more constructive conversation with the property authorities of the historic denominations on this would be helpful to avoid the new denominations being simply left with the problem buildings of the historic churches.[22] This again reflects one of the advantages of doing mission in a joined up way.

Churches are in danger of replicating the hierarchies of society in the way that they select and train leaders. Jesus' action was counter to this: relatively uneducated men were given the instruction to 'follow me', a phrase usually used by rabbis to call people to a process of intensive textual training. But even in the gospels the tension around leadership is there from start to finish. Simon Peter, a relatively poor fisherman, the first-called, fishing in the shallows by hand, is challenged for leadership by James and John, richer men whose father has hired crew for their boat (Mark 1:16-20). Right up to the Last Supper Jesus has to tell them that hierarchy is not what his style of ministry is about (Luke 22:24-30). Maybe the fact that Peter is finally given the shepherd's role (not a Pharisee's or a judge's one) is because Jesus knows his gut instinct will be to look out for poor people, yet Peter himself cannot quite believe it (John 21:15-21).

2 Christianity and Socio-Political Action

How can the local church be an agent of the kingdom of God and a source of healing and reconciliation? Does Christian mission bear some responsibility for the spread of the HIV/AIDS virus? How can mission contribute to the struggle to stop the pandemic? What other forms of ill-health call for particular attention from practitioners of Christian mission?

2.1 Church and reconciliation

We need to understand how the local church can be an agent of the kingdom of God and a source of healing and reconciliation. How do we get on with issues of our own traditions and religious values when it comes to reconciliation? We need to address issues of traumas and embark on social action to try to prevent future problems. We reflected on issues of partnerships which involve personal encounters that are spiritual in nature. We need to encourage interfaith and intra-faith conversations in order to strengthen communal identity and facilitate reconciliation. The strengthening of commonalities would help to deemphasise religious boundaries.

Social cohesion is a current buzz-word within the UK government circles at the moment and 'faith communities'[23] are seen as providers of the 'bridging social capital' that is expected to help create neighbourhoods in which individuals from diverse backgrounds feel comfortable with each other. Engagement across communities does not mean hiding our faith: participants at one meeting declared: 'we are a value-based Christian organisation and we are not going to hide this in working with government'.[24] In the past, churches most involved in civic engagement and social action often let this become separated from faith-sharing and discipleship – a process sometimes called 'mission creep' which they are now beginning to mend.

2.2 Divided churches and social reconciliation

If churches themselves are divided, how can we aim for reconciliation in the wider community when we have not healed ourselves? An event in Wales tackled this struggle with internal tensions. The group looking at this theme presented two cases where living the reality of healing in the community was – by the process of a breadth of denominations working together – modelling healing and reconciliation in action. The group explored the need for internal reconciliation in the body of Christ. Matters of women in leadership and the place of gay and lesbian people are deeply divisive for some traditions and between traditions in the UK and globally. Mission could not simply be put on hold until these issues were resolved, as service to the community is an imperative. Churches have to find a way of acknowledging their brokenness and disagreements, and then seeking the common, 'kingdom' ground to enable them to serve together despite the differences.

The Urban Mission Forum in the autumn of 2008 took as its theme 'Youth at Risk in the City'. It was held at a point when the extent of the current recession was less obvious. The discussions highlighted the need for the church to counter negative stereotypes, especially those of young people. One person called the church 'an agent of counter-cultural mission to the community'.[25] Several spoke of how the churches needed to 'focus on the factors feeding violent gang behaviour rather than the factors feeding gang membership'. Some felt that the church needed to critique society as a whole as there was a danger of 'dysfunctional children being taught by dysfunctional adults'.[26] Joe Aldred, reporting on some churches' response to youth violence, remarked how important it is not to assume that gang members are 'morally deficient': such responses, he maintained, plus calls for punitive measures to respond to drug dealers, lack 'both compassion and understanding'. He stressed that the 'church must move away from [such responses] if it is to be "salt and light" and constructive peacemakers [*sic*] in our communities'.[27] The group also called for a theology of childhood – do we see young people as God does and treat them accordingly?

The churches need to take pre-emptive action with secular and other decision-makers as well as engaging in service provision. Speaking out against unjust structures is also good news for poor people. In September 2007 a group of African pastors in Glasgow brought together the mainstream denominations to model a powerful, holistic piece of mission action where whole-hearted proclamation of the gospel was fully integrated with political action.[28] But socio-political action by churches is fraught even when the desired outcome is clear and consensual. People at the Yorkshire & Humber event spoke of the need for 'training on project development, organisational development, business skills and planning'[29] if church-based social action is to be effective and credible with secular authorities.

2.3 HIV/AIDS, church and mission

Whilst many religious groups may have avoided addressing HIV/AIDS when it first became a development issue in the 1980s and early 1990s, there has more recently been a stronger engagement from Christian Faith-Based Organisations (FBOs) in the prevention of HIV and care of people living with AIDS. The past reticence to work in this field largely stemmed from denial of HIV/AIDS being a problem, and from silence driven by the perception that transmission was through immoral acts and illegal behaviour. There has been recognition more recently amongst both FBOs and donor agencies that FBOs are themselves well placed to inform, educate, motivate and support behaviour change within communities and advocate at national, regional and international forums on behalf of those people affected by HIV/AIDS. Certainly running education campaigns and supporting individuals to minimize their 'risk' behaviour have had some success. However, greater success has been recorded when interventions happen at the local level as this is tailored to the very particular circumstances of the target community and individuals. Within some countries, faith-based and mission organisations have assumed an important role in educating and supporting local communities in reducing HIV transmission.

Matthew Clarke demonstrated how FBOs are preventing HIV/AIDS in developing countries. He illustrated with *Yayasan Kesehatan Bethesda* (Bethesda Health Foundation – YKB), a Christian FBO that works with church groups, rural communities, people living with HIV and street children in New Papua.[30] It was set up by nine churches (different denominations) as a means to distribute medical supplies to Christian communities all over Papua. While medical supplies were once their sole purpose, the main focus is now health training. HIV became a priority because it was noted that seventy percent of people living with HIV in Papua were Christian church attendees and the churches did not know how to address the issues or help their people. YKB responded to this through setting up a sexual health programme run through church leaders. The role that YKB have assumed of providing reliable and relevant information on the transmission of HIV is very important. Church leaders are taught about HIV/AIDS and are given a range of resources and ongoing training and evaluation sessions. This FBO's ability to successfully engage with its community around issues of sexuality and sexual practice provides important lessons for other FBOs seeking to reduce HIV transmission through sustained behaviour change.

Based on the success story of the YKB, Matthew Clarke identified eight characteristics for successful approaches to HIV/AIDS care and prevention programmes: acknowledging disconnection between religious teaching and human behaviours; training religious leaders in HIV/AIDS transmission; understanding that HIV/AIDS interventions require long-term commitment; starting interventions where the community are; integrating HIV/AIDS interventions into social and community development activities; addressing all modes of transmission; advocating for better national programmes; and working with other FBOs and secular organisations.

HIV/AIDS in the UK context is largely seen as associated with sexual behaviour which the church has problems with: same-sex relationships and prostitution, or drug use. Few churches have ministries with sex workers – the Assemblies of God, some of the independent charismatic churches and Catholic missions tend to be the exceptions. Having the attitude that Christians are supposed to deal with their difficulties through faith and prayer alone can make dealing with mental illness and aberrant behaviours very difficult.

3 Youth, Gender and Identity

What is the true identity (the 'core DNA') of the church? How does it manifest itself in different denominations and cultures?

The diversity that exists when we consider issues of gender, youth and identity is crucial. The world church seems to lack stamina in fulfilling the needs and desires of youth. The church urgently needs to understand their language, and speak to them 'where they are' – an incarnational model. We need to acknowledge the manner in which various societies, both the home and the host contexts are undergoing change as a result of immigration. We also need to consider the intergenerational dynamics that emerge and the 'age wars' that may result – giving attention to certain age groups while neglecting others. The first generation of immigrants is concerned about identity issues. What are the exceptions? The second generation are more open in terms of engaging with the host society. Is this always the case? We now witness gender role reversal in terms of economic (breadwinner) roles and religious roles. How are the traditional gender roles re-asserted within new religious landscapes? What are the emerging female roles in church? Is there a glass ceiling? Does this apply to all women or just some? How is this difference articulated?

Janice McLean remarked in her presentation on 'the challenge of context: the case of women and youth' that specific attention needs to be given to the experiences of women and youth within our contemporary communities.[31] First, demographically, females constitute the majority of the world church membership. Second, in many ways the youth can be seen as constituting the frontlines of social and cultural change. Both women and the youth can challenge the contemporary church in terms of its relevance, leadership, capacity to empower or disempower, social and cultural capital and the dynamic between home and church.

We are now witnessing the changing dynamics of community and shifting identities in home countries and diaspora ethnically and religiously. Living and working in the diaspora entails the reconstruction of power within the family unit. Koreans in diaspora are becoming Christian specifically within the US. Why is this occurring? What is the felt need that becoming a Christian provides? Is this seen in other ethnic groups as well? Different identities are meeting certain needs – what are the contexts that foster this negotiation? What is the negotiation process like? What changes and what remains the same?

The key factor that has often been used to identify whether a group of Christians are operating as a church is whether and how a group expresses its commemoration of the Lord's Supper. Urban congregations are often small and some meet in houses rather than formal church buildings. They can sit light to some of the liturgical regulations of their churches in order to express their fellowship together, and have for over twenty years developed creative liturgy and alternative forms of being church. These are now being experimented with in other settings through the 'fresh expressions'[32] and 'church without walls'[33] movements. An urban youth worker in the Elim Pentecostal church agreed that for his young people their Wednesday meeting was church and his leadership would accept that. He felt that sharing cake and juice together at the close of a meeting was a valid 'communion'.[34] Higher church ecclesiology finds that harder to deal with.

The difference in worship style, between the incoming African-Caribbean Christians and the indigenous white British worshippers, was one of the factors leading to the setting up of the new Black Majority Church denominations in the UK in the 1960s and 70s. Similar factors affect the more recent immigrant Christians to the UK from Nigeria, Ghana, Zimbabwe, and other countries in sub-Saharan Africa, who often prefer to worship in their own language and style, whilst still wishing to retain their Anglican, Catholic or Methodist identities.

The other key element of the DNA of being church is community mission engagement – what the Anglican Evangelical Fellowship event called 'a fierce commitment to staying in our urban areas'.[35] We should have a 'mission-shaped church not a church-shaped mission', they said.[36] This is a slightly vexed issue at the moment in the UK where proposed changes in the law mean that churches have to prove that their community engagement is part of their religious function and therefore consistent with their religious charitable aims and objects. As one person at the National Estates Churches event in London put it: 'It's really important to retain Christian distinctiveness and not become a social/community work "clone"'. This means 'being prepared to be open about the place of prayer and spirituality in the life of a project and its staff'.[37] Those churches that have previously shied away from social action 'must repent of our sins of proclaiming a truncated privatised gospel in our cities, based on selective texts and not taking the whole of Biblical revelation seriously'.[38]

4 Mission, Migration, Diaspora and Ethnicity

4.1 Understanding mission

What is mission? Why do and how to do Christian mission? The East African consultation described Christian mission as purpose-driven and God-centred. Its success is not based on material measure but on whether God is glorified. As an agent of mission, the church in any place or time is manifested in the following activities: proactive engagement in empowering not disempowering; peace building, healing and reconciling – not causing conflict, injuring and segregating; loving and being all-inclusive and not marginalizing; proclamation of the good news of our Lord Jesus Christ; and presence – in situations of persecution the 'ministry of presence' is part of mission. However, specific situations define the specifics of mission. For Eastern Africa, a region largely characterized by poverty, disease, and ignorance amidst enormous resources, the mission of the church has no alternative but to direct its engagement and proclamation towards redressing this anomaly. Beyond mission at home, the church in Eastern Africa has to go out to all corners of the earth to make disciples as per the great commission. In this the church has to identify the various mission fields in order to discern the engagement, proclamation and presence required of it. With globalization, mission fields are complex and so deep analysis of each situation is required.

The immense success of Christian mission is not only evident in the huge number of Christians in Eastern Africa but also in the strong convictions and faith among many Christians manifested in religious practice. However, celebration of success necessarily requires honest appraisal of mistakes made and opportunities lost. We cannot afford to lose the opportunity presented to us by 2010 to repent of those moments when we made mistakes, remembering that genuine repentance calls for reparation and reconciliation. We take this moment to look back at our understanding of mission, why and how we have carried out this mission in order to discern in humility what we need to buttress, correct and improve in future mission. Critical evaluation will indicate that there is change in context and therefore the need to change the content and text of mission.

Given the complexity of mission fields, there is need for multifaceted and multidisciplinary approaches to mission. This is necessary for effective identification of the needs of specific field areas and the resources required for each. For example, post Christian fields in Europe and America require African, Asian and Latin American missionaries and therefore there is need to open spaces for missionaries to Europe and North America.

History attests to the need to acknowledge and appreciate people's cultures and the lay foundation for mission in order to be effective. Within the East African context it is necessary to consider communal values and therefore do mission from the grassroots experiences. Further, it is essential to understand cultural dynamics in evangelizing a community. The basic Christian values of justice and love remain the guiding values of mission in whatever time or place. Interpreted in the context of mission in contemporary Eastern Africa, these values translate into: sharing, compassion, integrity (no compromise of God's mission), equity as opposed to charity, humility, respect for the human person, and building community beginning with family values.

4.2 Mission and diaspora

What is church life like in diaspora communities? What is the interface between migration, diaspora and ethnicity? How is cross-cultural expectation for mission articulated within contemporary church communities? The distinction between homogenous and multi-ethnic churches may always exist; moreover this history may also cause resistance to the project of inclusion. To what extent is the picture of the global church today characterized by reverse mission dynamics? Do we have homogenous local churches but multi-ethnic societies?

4.3 Immigrant churches, reverse mission

Who speaks for whom in the Western and non-Western world? How is the global church in its relationship engaging with the shift not only in the demographics within world Christianity but also the power, financial and missional shifts? In several majority churches in the diaspora, the financial resources, and administrative structure comes from the host country and not from the Western context. What effect do these developments have on the interaction within and growth of the world church?

Sadiri Joy Tira and Enoch Wan studied Filipino experience in mission in diaspora communities. They expressed the importance of advocacy for workers abused and persecuted away from home, and the need of pastoral care for their families in the Philippines. However, they also believe that

> The Filipino experience in diaspora missions also illustrates the providential grace of God in spite of the painful past of colonization of the Philippines by Western

> powers and sorrowful financial state of contemporary Filipino society. Hence, the sovereignty of God is evidently shown in the scattering of Filipinos globally for a purpose. It is diaspora mission in action – those being scattered have become gatherers for the Kingdom in many nations.[39]

As Andrew Walls points out, today is an 'Ephesian moment' in church history. We come together from different backgrounds, with different cultural and religious heritages. Yet there is one centre. Only together, not on our own, can we attain the whole measure of the fullness of Christ. It is within this plurality of voices that the gospel displays power.[40] Church membership in Europe is declining as compared to Africa, Asia, and Latin America. The West tends to be paternalistic ecclesiastically. To achieve a full world church, there is the need to create room and listen to Christians from the Two-Thirds World. There is much that can be gained and shared mutually. Elijah Obinna raised questions about the concept of reverse mission, highlighting ways in which the secularization of the West was linked to the modernization of the society and the seeming growth of an ideology that views religion to be irrelevant.[41] Within contemporary world Christianity, Africa, Asia and Latin America are no longer on the periphery. There needs to be a redefinition of the concept of mission to include both sending and receiving. With regard to the issue of partnership, there needs to be greater interrogation of what exactly this means to both parties. Rebecca Catto's focus on 'reverse mission dynamics' highlights some difficulties associated with the terminology 'reverse mission':[42] Who are the new missionaries ministering to? What are some of the implications associated with Britain being perceived as a mission field? How are the relationships between the non-Western and Western Christians changing as a result of this activity?

4.4 Ethnicity – the tension between homogenous and multi-ethnic churches

The UK denominations respond differently to the issue of the relationship between homogenous and multi-ethnic churches, depending upon their ecclesiologies. The Catholic and Methodist Churches tend to work on a chaplaincy model. The former appoint priests from overseas who can provide mother-tongue masses for the incomers. In the latter, Ghanaian ministers in the UK act as chaplains to Ghanaian fellowships which meet monthly for services whilst the Ghanaians worship in mainstream Methodist churches for the rest of the time. The Episcopal Church in Scotland has a Kenyan-born priest acting as a link person to the African pastors in that setting. The hope is that the changing attitudes on race in white British culture will mean that the newer ethnic minority diaspora people will be more warmly welcomed into the historic church congregations than the earlier Afro-Caribbean incomers were, and that the chaplaincies will be a staging post to integration rather than the beginning of separate denominations. But that process may take a long while. Welsh-language churches still existed in London until very recently. It is also not clear that white British people are as accepting of minority ethnic incomers as denominational leaders nationally assume.[43] Anecdotal evidence from black Christians suggests that white people still show considerable unease with black people and racism, even if not intentional, still occurs, especially outside the more ethnically diverse metropolitan areas.[44]

Some of the new diaspora African and Black Majority Churches (BMCs) are playing a different role in the Christian community from that of the older African-Caribbean denominations. In London they are a very big presence and the Redeemed Christian Church of God, a Nigerian-led church, is the fastest growing in the UK, currently planting many churches.[45] The extent to which African groups and BMCs can engage with the historic churches depends greatly on whether they have the confidence to engage, and on whether the host churches are open and ready to listen and engage in conversation.

There are diaspora congregations meeting in many historic church premises. In most cases not much link is built between them and their host. Perhaps it is because this largely black (African) presence is seen as parallel to indigenous mission and activity locally, even where the congregation may have members from earlier migrations. This is part of the 'passive' racism of the historic churches still to be tackled. The Evangelical Fellowship of the Anglican Communion event said that 'the church must learn to listen and give a voice to those who mainstream society wants to ignore',[46] and suggested this can be modelled by consciously inviting them to mainstream church activity. There are some very good examples where congregations do come together for major festivals and link with community projects, but this is not so in the majority of cases. The lack of paid or full-time pastors and the structure of these diaspora congregations does make this process harder. So it is not always about a lack of wish for positive engagement on the part of the host community. Assumptions can be made by white churches about differences in ecclesiology and attitudes.

Street Pastors is a ministry spreading across the UK, where older Christians walk the streets of city centres at night to be a responsible presence and offer practical support to young people coming out of clubs and pubs, often the worse for alcohol and drug consumption.[47] Revd Les Isaacs, a black church pastor set up the organisation, and BMCs are often in the lead in developing it. This model, and similar ones, has been widely adopted by integrated teams across the denominations and is a good example of joint action by homogeneous and multi-ethnic congregations – again coming out of a common, and obvious, mission imperative.

There is a very complex interrelationship of poverty, class and race affecting how and whether black (African) Christians engage with the Christian community as a whole, and whether congregations are remaining relatively homogenous, or becoming more truly the body of Christ in terms of racial diversity. This means that generalisations are almost meaningless. But it is incumbent upon the historic churches to examine their practice. Churches 'who find themselves with possibilities of partnerships… should proactively and creatively move from passive accommodation of each other to active collaboration'.[48] In the run up to the 2009 local and European elections in the UK, all the denominations spoke out against the racism and the rise of the British National Party, and the need for the churches to provide 'opposition to extremism'[49] was endorsed at the Yorkshire and Humber event at that time. A mixed group of white and black Christians at the *Adfywio'n Trefi-Urban Refreshment* event in Wales talked of the need for white people to overcome their 'suspicion of the stranger' and asserted that the host churches need to 'accommodate difference and give welcome'.[50] They suggested that the idea that we all have multiple identities was a helpful way forward.

4.5 Church life in diaspora communities

An asylum-seeking Catholic spoke powerfully at the Welsh urban mission event about how his faith has supported him spiritually in coping with the traumas not only in his own country, but also the dehumanising aspect of being an asylum-seeker in the UK. Churches, often absorbed in the practical side of immigration procedures, might also consider the pastoral aspects of supporting traumatised people. One Catholic religious group in Wales has developed a ministry providing spiritual direction and retreats for asylum seekers. A social worker, dealing mostly with migration issues, spoke at the same Welsh event about how her faith was a factor in encouraging her to engage in this demanding area of work. Like homelessness, work with asylum seekers is one mission area where the churches are almost united in their wish to respond and able to work very effectively together to address the issues. The church must not rest on its laurels in this, but it is in contrast to the often less supportive secular NGO sector.[51]

5 Conclusion

Power, identity and community came out as key issues in our study group, as did the question of the nature and texture of mission. It was quite clear that working to improve people's, not just Christians', contexts is the priority in the contemporary world, rather than conversion. Thus, one thread of our discussion demonstrated the significance of 'context'. There are Christian ideals of unity and equality, but these become challenged in context. Religious, historical, ethnic and political, along with socio-economic, factors all interact. Christians are human too and affected by pre-existing structures such as the caste system. There are very real problems of injustice, inequality, life and death, which Christians have to engage with and try to mitigate, if not solve, and this is really difficult when Christians are also tied up with the problem. Nonetheless, there is hope, through communication and non-violent action based upon conviction and love.

The centre of gravity of Christianity is shifting southwards – in Europe, church membership is stagnating or declining, in Africa, Asia and Latin

America it is rapidly increasing. At the Edinburgh 1910 conference, mission was still very much seen as a Western enterprise. Today we realise that mission cannot be a one-way road – not only from North to South or from West to East, but that it is much more multi-dimensional, from 'everywhere to everywhere'. Concepts such as 'mission in reverse' or 'mission and migration' are therefore vitally important. We realised in our conversations that we come from different backgrounds. Some papers introduced us into the practical experiences of pastors, others offered analytical case studies. We became more and more aware that both dimensions are needed. Westerners are part of the process of migration; in fact, the most scattered people are Westerners. However, Christianity cannot be a one-way-traffic religion.[52] We learned about many missionary movements – from Seoul (Korea) to Bogota (Columbia) to Charlotte (USA), or from Nigeria to Europe, or from the Philippines to Canada, or from South Korea to the UK. Transnational migration often includes multiple destinations – from Asia to Latin America and then to the USA, or from Africa to the USA and then to Europe – and new and fascinating approaches are coming out of this. These immigrant congregations not only give a sense of identity or provide 'a home away from home'; they are also constantly adapting themselves and their mission to new situations. They operate in very different contexts and provide unique insights into intercultural theology. Christianity is a migrating religion and important theologies are coming out of immigrant congregations.

Immigrant Christian congregations are vulnerable, and vulnerability can be also experienced by Christians in minority situations, such as the Kakure Kirishitan in Japan and of Dalit Christians in India. The response of some mainline denominations in the West to African, Asian or Latin American immigrant congregations has been fairly problematic. Sometimes rather loose ecumenical networks are formed: African choirs sing hymns while Europeans preach. There is a problematic compartmentalization – often accompanied by an all too easy categorization: Pentecostals, for instance, are frequently portrayed as apolitical, as uninterested in social problems. And it is true that sometimes they do focus on individual well-being and preach a kind of prosperity gospel. As Abel Ugba demonstrated, the old Weberian thesis of the relationship between capitalism and Protestantism can be applied to African Pentecostals in Ireland:[53] 'If you are something and you can prove it, then you are in power'. Some African Pentecostal pastors who drive big Mercedes cars would refer to Jesus who rode a donkey which was, as they say, the most expensive means of transport available at that time. But we also got to know that the realities in Pentecostalism are different and that much more is going on. We learned about the interactions of Pentecostalism and politics in Zambia[54] and of the many social activities by the Redeemed Christian Church of God as well as of African female-led churches in Nigeria.[55]

It was emphasised in our discussions that we need a theology of empowerment of the poor and marginalized and to avoid the problem of paternalism. In contrast to the 'mainline denominations', which still struggle to get away from the 'helper syndrome': the widespread notion that we are there 'for the other' and that we already have figured out what is good for her/him. The concept of a 'holistic mission' now needs to the applied. Poverty alleviation, combating illnesses and epidemics (such as HIV/AIDS) and participation in Truth and Reconciliation processes are part of this process. These are multi-dimensional and global phenomena that cannot be addressed by local congregations alone. The church is situated in a global context and global alliances must be forged. The problem of Truth and Reconciliation Commissions is, for instance, that they are usually confined to victims and perpetrators from one particular country and do not include the international supporters of dictatorial regimes. (Charles Taylor in Liberia, for example, was supported by one particular group of US-American evangelicals.[56]) In this context, it was also stressed that it is important to analyse the role of the media, and especially the Western media. How do they portray conflicts in other parts of the world? Are the categorizations with which they work all too easy? It is good to remember in this age of globalization that mission societies were among the first global players. There is Christian experience in international networking and in crossing boundaries.

If Christ's mission is to be fulfilled by the churches as well as possible, Christians need to be generous and cooperative with each other. Churches must realise that our mission has been inadequate in the past and so we must work prayerfully, aware of our disparate failings, in the Holy Spirit's strength, to discover together what it is that God wants of us. Churches which are centred upon Jesus, which make a statement about welcoming strangers, and which live by Jesus' statement by reaching out in relation to others, followers of Jesus or not, will be best placed to fulfil Christ's mission in whatever context they are based, in this twenty-first century as always. Our key question and challenge is: 'How can we work together better for God's purposes? We cannot grasp the fullness of God's plan, and we have tendency to become myopic in our understanding of our Christian identity. Our group collectively felt that any discussion on identity needs to be more than just 'identity of fear'; it should also hold God's vision for and our understanding of the world together.

Endnotes

[1] Festus Olatunde, 'War Against Poverty – A Challenge for Christianity'. Paper presented at the Study Group 7 consultation, Edinburgh, 12-13 June 2009.
[2] Kirk Sandvig, 'Who Are Kakure Kirishitan? Issues of Communal Identity within Hidden Christians of Japan'. Paper presented at the Study Group 7 consultation, Edinburgh, 12-13 June 2009.
[3] Anderson Jeremiah, 'Dalit Christians in South India'. Paper presented at the Study Group 7 consultation, Edinburgh, 12-13 June 2009.
[4] Amos Yong, 'Poured Out on All Flesh', *PentecoStudies* 6/1 (2007), 16-46.

[5] Erica Dunmow, 'The Challenge of Indigenous Leadership in the UK Urban Mission Context'. Paper presented at the Study Group 7 consultation, Edinburgh, 12-13 June 2009.
[6] Ann Morisy, Community Theologian, Methodist City Centre Network Conference, Swanick, November 2008.
[7] David Stevens, Leader Corrymeela Community, Churches Community Alliance Meeting, Belfast, November 2008.
[8] National Estate Churches Network, day conference, Manchester, October 2008.
[9] Evangelical Fellowship of the Anglican Communion, Pre-Lambeth Urban Workshop, June 2008.
[10] National Estate Churches Network, day conference, Manchester, October 2008.
[11] 'Christian Communities in Contemporary Contexts', Carmelite Center Karen, Nairobi, 26-28 May 2009. Statement and report available on the Edinburgh 2010 website, www.edinburgh2010.org.
[12] Some forms of Christianity in Africa continue to denigrate African culture even as others try to inculturate the Gospel in the African context.
[13] Frieder Ludwig, 'Religion and Reconciliation Processes in the African Diaspora'; Israel Akanji, 'The Local Church as an Agent of Healing and Reconciliation in the Face of Religious Conflict'. Papers presented at the Study Group 7 consultation, Edinburgh, 12-13 June 2009.
[14] Lawrie Hudson & Tom Kisitu, 'Touching Lives in Edinburgh', Paper presented at the Study Group 7 consultation, Edinburgh, 12-13 June 2009.
[15] Methodist City Centre Network spring meeting, Darlington, February 2009.
[16] Yorkshire and the Humber Urban Mission Network, Sheffield, March 2009.
[17] Ann Morisy, Methodist City Centre Network Conference, Swanick, November 2008.
[18] Methodist City Centre Network spring meeting, Darlington, February 2009.
[19] *Anglican Ten Commandments for Urban Mission*, Evangelical Fellowship of the Anglican Communion, Pre-Lambeth Urban Workshop, June 2008.
[20] Evangelical Fellowship of the Anglican Communion, Pre-Lambeth Urban Workshop, June 2008.
[21] London Urban Theology Project, Westbourne Park, London, December 2008.
[22] Conversation between Erica Dunmow and pastors in the West Yorkshire African Caribbean Churches Council, 2007.
[23] This is the term that the UK statutory bodes use to encompass followers of all the major world religions, calling each religion – its authorities and followers - a 'faith community'.
[24] National Estate Churches Network, day conference, Manchester, October 2008.
[25] Urban Mission Forum, *Youth at Risk in the City*, London, October 2008.
[26] Urban Mission Forum, *Youth at Risk in the City*, London, October 2008.
[27] Joe Aldred, Sophie Hebden & Keith Hebden, *Who is My Neighbour? A Church Response to Social Disorder Linked to Gangs, Drugs, Guns and Knives* (London : Churches Together in England, 2008). Available at http://cte.churchinsight.com/.
[28] In September 2007 an informal grouping of African pastors held a Saturday afternoon event in George Square, Glasgow, marking the 200th centenary of the abolition of slave trading. Performances by a very wide variety of Christian musicians (Black rappers, a Korean classical choir and a white hillbilly group – all singing Christian material) were interspersed with short addresses by the leaders of all the major denominations talking of how the church had campaigned against slavery because freedom for captives was

part of Jesus' message of salvation. They also urged people to sign a petition being taken around the Square to ask the Scottish Executive to change regulations affecting current trafficked people.

[29] Yorkshire and the Humber Urban Mission Network, Sheffield, March 2009.

[30] Matthew Clarke & Juliette Lumbers, 'Churches and Condoms: How Christian Faith-Based Organisations are Preventing HIV/AIDS in Developing Countries'. Paper presented at the Edinburgh 2010 Study Group 7 conference, Edinburgh, 2009.

[31] Janice McLean, 'The Challenge of Context: The Case of Women and Youth'. Paper presented at the Study Group 7 consultation, Edinburgh, 12-13 June 2009.

[32] 'Fresh expressions' is an initiative of the Church of England and the Methodist Church which encourages new forms of church for a fast changing world, working with Christians from a variety of denominations and traditions. The initiative has resulted in hundreds of new congregations being formed alongside more traditional churches. See www.freshexpressions.org.uk/.

[33] 'Church without walls' is a term more commonly used in Scotland to refer to new forms of ecclesiology, which results from an initiative of the Church of Scotland.

[34] Private communication with Erica Dunmow after Scripture Union Scotland event.

[35] Evangelical Fellowship of the Anglican Communion, Pre-Lambeth Urban Workshop, June 2008.

[36] Yorkshire and the Humber Urban Mission Network, Sheffield, March 2009. 'Mission-shaped church' is an important Church of England policy from the early twenty-first century. See Graham Cray (ed.), *Mission-shaped Church: Church Planting and Fresh Expressions of Church in a Changing Context* (London: Church House Publishing, 2004). Available at www.cofe.anglican.org/.

[37] National Estate Churches Network, day conference, London, October 2008.

[38] Evangelical Fellowship of the Anglican Communion, Pre-Lambeth Urban Workshop, June 2008.

[39] Sadiri Joy Tira & Enoch Wan, 'The Filipino Experience in Diaspora Missions: A Case Study of Christian Communities in Contemporary Contexts'. Paper presented at the Study Group 7 consultation, Edinburgh, 12-13 June 2009.

[40] Andrew Walls, *The Cross-cultural Process in Christian History: Studies in the Transmission and Appropriation of Faith* (Maryknoll, NY: Orbis Books, 2002), 72-81.

[41] Elijah Obinna, 'The Power and Challenges of Urban Mission'. Paper presented at the Study Group 7 consultation, Edinburgh, 12-13 June 2009.

[42] Rebecca Catto, 'Reverse Mission Dynamics'. Paper presented at the Study Group 7 consultation, Edinburgh, 12-13 June 2009.

[43] The Catholic Association for Racial Justice is the only denominationally specific body remaining that is looking at this issue. The other denominations in the UK have subsumed their race relations' specialists into more general equalities teams, on the basis that racism has been effectively tackled.

[44] Bishop Delroy Hall of Church of God of Prophecy at the Annual Reporting meeting of the Urban Mission Development Project, June 2009, which looked at the issue of 'The Contribution of Black Christians to the Christian Community in the Twenty-first Century'.

[45] Kingsway International Christian Centre, London. See www.kicc.org.uk/.

[46] Evangelical Fellowship of the Anglican Communion, Pre-Lambeth Urban Workshop, June 2008.

[47] See www.streetpastors.co.uk/.

[48] Methodist City Centre Network Spring meeting, Darlington, February 09.
[49] Yorkshire and the Humber Urban Mission Network, Sheffield, March 2009.
[50] Adfywio'n Trefi – Urban Refreshment – a day of conversation and prayer about mission in the twenty-first century, Newport, Wales, June 2009.
[51] Chloe Clements, Scottish Churches Parliamentary Office, talking of evidence from research undertaken by her organisation. Private conversation with Erica Dunmow, August 2009.
[52] Kosuke Koyama, 'Christianity Suffers from Teacher Complex', in Gerald H. Anderson & Thomas F. Stransky (eds), *Mission Trends No. 2* (Grand Rapids, MI: Wm B. Eerdmans, 1975), 70-75, at 73.
[53] Abel Ugba, 'Between God, Ethnicity and Politics: African Pentecostals in Contemporary Ireland'. Paper presented at the Study Group 7 consultation, Edinburgh, 12-13 June 2009.
[54] Naar Mfundisi, 'Zambian Pentecostalism: A Study of History, Theology and Politics'. Paper presented at the Study Group 7 consultation, Edinburgh, 12-13 June 2009.
[55] Bolaji O. Bateye, 'The Interplay of Gender, Identity and Power in African Female-led Churches: London and Nigeria'. Paper presented at the Study Group 7 consultation, Edinburgh, 12-13 June 2009.
[56] Harold D. Hunter, 'Pentecostal Social Engagement: Excerpts from around the World', Paper presented at the Study Group 7 consultation, Edinburgh, 12-13 June 2009.

Theme Eight
Mission and Unity – Ecclesiology and Mission

Preface

The genesis of this chapter is to be found in a text submitted by the Commission for World Mission and Evangelism (CWME) of the World Council of Churches, which is a product of the collaboration of its Working Group on Mission and Ecclesiology. It was drafted by the Revd Dr. László Gonda, Debrecen Reformed Theological University, Hungary; Revd Dr Jooseop Keum (Presbyterian, South Korea), on the staff of the World Council of Churches; and Revd Dr Ron Wallace, Presbyterian Church in Canada – all members of the CWME.[1] Further to their work, revisions and additions were contributed by Kyriaki Avtzi (Greece) of the Conference of European Churches, Professor Dr Paul Isaak (Namibia) of the Ecumenical Institute at Bossey, Revd Dr Darrell Jackson (UK) of the Nova Research Centre, Professor Dimitra Koukoura (Greece) of Thessaloniki University, Revd Dr Raymond Pfister (France) of Ichthus 21, and Mr Hemming Meinecke (Germany), student of theology, Lausanne. Collectively, these authors represent Pentecostal, Evangelical, Orthodox, and Protestant perspectives. The authors took particular account of the document produced for Edinburgh 2010 on mission and unity by the Roman Catholic Institut Africain des Sciences de la Mission, Kinshasa, as well as other submissions too numerous to mention.[2] The final text is submitted by the co-convenors, Kyriaki Avtzi and László Gonda and the moderating co-convener, Darrell Jackson.

1 Introduction

'Edinburgh 1910 was one of the great landmarks in the history of the Church'.[3] Indeed, it was not only a landmark of the worldwide missionary movement, 'it was crucial for the ecumenical movement as a whole.'[4] Evangelicals meeting in Lausanne in 1974 considered it 'the most historic conference on evangelism and mission of [the] century.'[5] In Edinburgh a decisive attempt was made for a global gathering in order to facilitate cooperation across denominational barriers. That the organisers of the Edinburgh conference were able to understand it as a world conference was a reflection of the fact that the missionary endeavour had already by that point become a global activity not merely of, or by, European or American missionaries. The Mar Thoma Evangelistic Association (1885) and the Indian Missionary Society (1903) are early examples of the growing role of indigenous missionary agencies. The decision to emphasise denominational cooperation built on the experiences of earlier conferences such as those held in Liverpool (1860), London (Centenary Missions Conference, 1888), New York (Ecumenical Missionary Conference,

1900), Shanghai (Missionary Conference, 1907), and the Indian Decennial Missionary Conferences (especially the fourth, held in Madras in 1902).

Reflections on the question of the unity of the Christian church in mission were an important agenda item at Edinburgh 1910. The theme of Commission VIII of the conference was 'Co-operation and the Promotion of Unity.' This Commission gave impetus to the founding of the International Missionary Council (IMC) in 1921, which merged with the World Council of Churches (WCC) in New Delhi, 1961. By this, the first permanent organ was created in the history of the church with the intention of worldwide assistance for the activities of Christian organisations of different denominational allegiance.

2 The Journey towards Mission in Unity

The issues of mission and unity have always been intertwined throughout the history of the modern Ecumenical movement, of which the World Missionary Conference in Edinburgh 1910 has become the symbolic beginning. It is remarkable that the issue of mission and unity was the very concern out of which Edinburgh 1910 was born. The parallelisms, competitions, conflicts and divisions on what was then called 'the mission field' gravely undermined the credibility of the witness of the love of Christ. This was painfully felt by those committing their lives to mission in different contexts. Although attempts were made to settle these conflicts on local and regional levels (through 'comity agreements' and regional missionary conferences), it was still felt that there was a need for Christian mission to be harmonized globally. Intercultural situations on the mission field also led to unprecedented personal experiences of loyalty, even friendship, among Christians that transcended denominational and organisational divides. This, and the generally optimistic mood at the turn of the century, led to the fulfilment of William Carey's 'pleasing dream' of a world missionary conference.

2.1 Edinburgh 1910: An ecumenical turning point

It is well known that Edinburgh 1910 was a conference of missionary societies and not of churches. Nevertheless, the experience of very different missionary organisations from various denominational backgrounds working together was a source of optimism for the future of ecumenical cooperation. The issues of doctrinal and structural differences between churches were not addressed systematically in Edinburgh 1910. John R. Mott, Joseph H. Oldham and other leaders of the conference agreed to avoid all the areas of theological conflict. However, Commission VIII did address the theoretical issues of the unity of mission. Although Edinburgh 1910 did not offer a systematic elaboration of the relationship between mission and unity, nevertheless the relevance of it was felt and addressed in a surprisingly illuminating way, and the importance of this issue was expressed clearly. As the Report of Commission VIII puts it: '...for the achievement of the ultimate and highest end of all missionary work – the establishment in these non-Christian lands of Christ's one Church – real unity must be attained'.[6] The Commission report stirred the conference to make a unanimous decision establishing a Continuation Committee to continue the journey of seeking unity in mission. At the national level, missionary agencies and churches started to form National Missionary Councils or Councils of Churches as a domestic vehicle for seeking unity. The Continuation Committee and the National Missionary Councils formed the IMC at Lake Mohonk, 1921.

The civilizational optimism of the nineteenth century came to an abrupt and disillusioning end when the so-called 'Christian' European powers entered into two unprecedentedly brutal and devastating world wars. The painful consequences of these wars accelerated the disintegration of the colonial system and brought into question the Christian quality of Western civilization. This growing disillusionment could also be felt at the two World Missionary Conferences between the wars. At Jerusalem 1928, the issue of emerging younger churches became an important part of the agenda. The paternalistic, Western model of mission was challenged and the relationship between the churches in the home base and the younger churches made its way onto the agenda of mission. Mission and the visible unity of the church became a burning question. As the movements of Life and Work (Stockholm, 1925) and Faith and Order (Lausanne, 1927) emerged, and then later merged to form the WCC (Amsterdam, 1948), the quest for the visible unity of the church became the agenda of the Ecumenical movement *par excellence*.

In the meantime, however, an inner fermentation within the missionary movement led to a growing uncertainty about the mission of the church. The exposure of the interrelatedness of colonial structures and Christian mission and – among others – the philosophical consequences of the two wars and of the Holocaust raised the question of whether it was possible to speak about authentic Christian mission at all. On the other hand, in spite of positive developments at the regional level (including the National Councils of Churches), separations and divisions among the churches continued to undermine the credibility of mission to a considerable extent.

2.2 Missio Dei

It was the rediscovery and reinterpretation of the ancient trinitarian concept of the *missio Dei,* at the 1952 Willingen conference of the IMC, which facilitated a way out of the conceptual crisis facing mission. The concept of *missio Dei* became a frame of reference for defining mission. According to this understanding, God's mission is directly related to the world and the church is defined as the instrument – a privileged instrument – of God's mission of redemption and the recreation of humanity and the cosmos. This theological paradigm shift in the interpretation of what mission is has far-reaching ecclesiological consequences. It makes impossible the separation of mission and church.[7] If the church is defined by mission, then the unity of the church and mission are deeply interrelated (John 17:21), not just technically – disunity being a scandal for those looking at the church from 'outside' – but also theologically. The church as the sign of the kingdom of God should also be structurally congruent with the nature of God's kingdom, characterized by divine love. As the 1952 Willingen Report puts it:

> The missionary movement of which we are a part has its source in the Triune God Himself. Out of the depths of His love for us, the Father has sent forth His own beloved Son to reconcile all things (*ta panta*) to Himself, that we and all men might, through the Spirit, be made one in Him with the Father in that perfect love which is the very nature of God.[8]

This understanding led the IMC and the WCC to make a decision to merge, the consequence of which was the formation of the Commission on World Mission and Evangelism within the structure of the WCC.[9] The IMC brought with it to the ranks of the WCC the representation of missionary organisations (known today as 'affiliated bodies') as well as churches involved in mission. But more than that, the structure of the WCC became congruent with its theology of the church. However, certain developments since New Delhi show that, although the structural integration of the missionary movement was achieved, there remain several open questions and challenges regarding the theological and practical issues of mission and unity. The integration was problematic for a number of Evangelical mission agencies who withdrew their support for the merger or strongly criticised it from outside, with the Lausanne Congress on World Evangelization (LCWE) claiming in 1974 that out of Edinburgh flowed 'two major streams' – Evangelical and Ecumenical – 'of the modern missionary movement'.[10]

2.3 Contemporary context: Mission in unity redefined

One such development is related to the well known debates in the 1960s and 1970s, especially around the concept of salvation and the role of evangelism (at the WCC assemblies at Uppsala, 1968, and Bangkok, 1973). This led to a growing distance between the WCC and the LCWE (Lausanne Congress, 1974). The LCWE, together with the World Evangelical Alliance's Mission Commission, represents a significant alternative approach to issues of unity in mission in the light of an increase in the numbers worldwide of Evangelical Christians. The sad reality remains, however, that there are parallel global Christian structures and that there is still much distrust and animosity between them. This legacy weighs heavily upon those in the current generation as they search for the visible unity of the church.

There is, at the same time, an ever-growing diversity of all kinds of interdenominational cooperation in mission. A growing communication in the area of mission can be recognised overarching denominational borders in Evangelical and Pentecostal/Charismatic circles. The Global Christian Forum,[11] a new way of ecumenical encounter, represents another new challenge to reflect on. In the meantime, within the framework of the CWME, Roman Catholic, Orthodox, Protestant, Anglican, Evangelical and Pentecostal Christians work together closely in reflecting on relevant issues of Christian mission. At the Conference on World Mission and Evangelism held in Athens, 2005, the full participation of these ecclesial families was made visible.

It can be concluded that much has been achieved regarding mission and unity since Edinburgh 1910. The integration in New Delhi in 1961 demonstrates that the inseparability of the quest for the unity of the church and of its missionary nature can also lead to far-reaching, 'visible' structural consequences. The same is expressed by positive examples of united and uniting churches all over the world. The missionary nature of the church and the deep interrelatedness of this with unity has achieved a wide theological consensus. 'There is a growing awareness among the churches today of the inextricable relationship between Christian unity and missionary calling, between ecumenism and evangelization. "Evangelization is the test of our ecumenical vocation"'.[12] This understanding is affirmed, too, in the study document on ecclesiology issued by the WCC's Faith and Order Commission:

> Mission thus belongs to the very being of the Church. This is a central implication of affirming the apostolicity of the Church, which is inseparable from the other three attributes of the Church – unity, holiness and catholicity. All four attributes relate both to the nature of God's own being and to the practical demands of authentic mission. If in the life of the Church, any of them is impaired, the Church's mission is compromised.[13]

The Lausanne Covenant states that 'the church's visible unity in truth is God's purpose' and adds that 'Evangelism also summons us to unity, because our oneness strengthens our witness'.[14] The LCWE's Manila Manifesto, 1989, affirmed the 'need for churches to cooperate in evangelism and social action, repudiating competition and avoiding duplication'.[15] The Manila Congress Reports described practical achievements in this field and noted that 'left to ourselves, we isolate, insulate, exclude, and put "self" in first place'.[16]

The separate existence of the WCC and of the World Evangelical Alliance (WEA) and LCWE represent painful experiences of divisions and disunity present in the life of the world church, which hinder churches in putting the missionary nature of the church into practice. However, a deep conviction is expressed repeatedly that however hopeless it appears to be, the high goal of the visible unity of all God's people cannot be given up. One hundred years after Edinburgh 1910, the Christian churches still have much for which to ask forgiveness and much work to do for the reconciliation and healing of relationships, being 'called to unity, for the sake of mission'.[17]

3 The Present Context of Mission and Church

The ethos of the Edinburgh 1910 World Missionary Conference was shaped by the spirituality of the Student Volunteer Movement for Foreign Missions with the watchword, 'the evangelization of the world in this generation'. This watchword reflected the optimistic air of that time, and it illustrates the prevailing understanding of mission. This was characterized by a concept of geographical dichotomy: the Christian North/West was to evangelize the non-Christian South/East. An identification of mission and evangelism was taken for granted: mission was predominantly understood as the proclamation of the gospel of Jesus Christ and as converting non-believers to faith in him, in order to 'win over the souls in darkness'. There was still a prevailing optimism that the Western Christian civilization had both the mandate and the means to convert the majority of the population of the globe to Christianity within a foreseeable period of time. The question of unity was predominantly looked upon as a strategic question; joining forces, avoiding duplication in the investment of human and financial resources, and good coordination of missionary activity would, it was hoped, help accelerate the geographical progress of the Christian religion in the then 'unreached territories'. However, as demonstrated above, unity was also seen as a theologically undergirded precondition for the credibility of the proclamation of the gospel: divisions must be overcome to be able to give an authentic witness of Jesus Christ as the head of the one body.

3.1 Promising developments

The situation of Christianity has fundamentally changed during the past century, since Edinburgh 1910. In a sense, the dream of the participants of the conference has come true: Christianity is a world religion today with followers – although with differing density – all over the planet. The Christian faith has permeated almost all the cultures of the earth. While the Edinburgh 1910 Conference was dominated by white, male, Western Protestants, the churches today show an endlessly colourful picture: women and men from almost all nations and regions are represented in a rich variety of ecclesial structures, worshipping in many languages and in multiple forms of liturgies shaped by a wide spectrum of local cultures.

One hundred years after the first large-scale attempt to bring Christians together in order to express their unity, there are functioning and stable global structures to safeguard, promote and reflect on the unity of churches. The Commission on World Mission and Evangelism of the WCC stands in institutional continuity with the Edinburgh 1910 Conference and exists to facilitate the quest for unity in mission as an integral part of the WCC; the most comprehensive representative global body of 349 Orthodox, Anglican, Protestant, Evangelical and non-Western churches. In the framework of the CWME, churches and mission agencies have a structure to seek ways of expressing and strengthening unity in mission. The LCWE is rooted in the call for world evangelization issued by Edinburgh 1910 and its 1974 Lausanne Congress has been described by mission historians as one of the great missionary conferences, exercising a 'maturity of judgement', particularly in the drafting of its Lausanne Covenant.[18] The Lausanne and Manila Congresses on World Evangelization have been complemented by four additional global mission conferences (Pattaya in 1980, Singapore in 1987, Pattaya in 2004, and Malaysia in 2006) and are to be followed by a third Congress in Cape Town in 2010.[19]

While Edinburgh 1910 was a predominantly Protestant event, Orthodox churches have also become an integral part of the modern Ecumenical movement. The Patriarchal and Synodical Encyclical of the Ecumenical Patriarchate in 1920 had encouraged 'rapprochement between the various Christian Churches [...] for the preparation and advancement of that blessed union which will be completed in the future in accordance with the will of God'.[20] The World Fellowship of Christian Youth, *Syndesmos*, has recognised from its foundation in 1953 that 'missionary activity is an indispensable element in the fullness of ecclesial life: we are not fully Christian if we shun our missionary responsibilities'.[21] The Orthodox role in the common quest for the visible unity of the churches accelerated in pace following the creation of the Orthodox Mission Studies and Relations desk in WCC in 1970, and its close collaboration with CWME. Although there are still obstacles hindering eucharistic communion of Orthodox and Protestant churches, it is significant that the last Conference on World Mission and Evangelism was held in a country with an Orthodox majority (Athens, 2005). Orthodox churches are not only present in the ecumenical gatherings, but they shape the mission theology and practice in the ecumenical dialogue, as well.

At the Edinburgh 1910 Conference, no official representatives of the Roman Catholic Church were present[22] and there was little cooperation, at the time, between Roman Catholic and Protestant missionary activities. Since the Second Vatican Council (1962–1965), the attitude of the Roman Catholic Church towards mission and unity has changed fundamentally. *Lumen Gentium*, 'On the Dogmatic Constitution of the Church', in 1964 and the Decree *Ad Gentes*, 'On the Mission Activity of the Church', in 1965, both identified the mission of the church with the nature of the church. Although there are still doctrinal and structural differences, there are promising signs that express a serious quest for unity. Expressions of this have included the International Anglican – Roman Catholic Commission for Unity and Mission (IARCCUM), established in 2001, which published its report *Growing Together in Unity and Mission* in 2007,[23] a non-authoritative declaration but still a significant manual for fostering discussion and reflection on the theme. In 2001 the Catholic Bishops' Conference of Europe (CCEE) and the Conference of European Churches signed the *Charta Oecumenica*, offering guidelines for the growing cooperation among the churches in Europe, and committing each party to 'discuss[ing] plans for evangelisation with other churches'.[24] There is an active and integral participation of Roman Catholic members in CWME and the Roman Catholic Church has officially been involved in preparations for the Edinburgh centenary celebration, as a member of the Edinburgh 2010 General Council. Collaboration with Roman Catholic mission actors continues to grow dramatically.

3.2 The changing landscape of global Christianity today

One hundred years after Edinburgh 1910, we recognise the ever-changing landscape of world Christianity. There are several elements in these changes that could not have been foreseen by the participants of the first World Missionary Conference. In the optimistic sphere of the early twentieth century, the confidence of Western Christian civilization in its own cultural superiority had not yet been challenged in a fundamental way. However, as a result of radical secularization, active followers of the Christian religion have become a stagnating or shrinking minority in the Western/Northern world. Mainline, established, historical churches are struggling with decreased membership, financial difficulties, and sometimes with a grave identity crisis. On the other hand, the end of the Christendom era offers a new opportunity for the churches in the West to find new ways of authentic discipleship, which can be expressed by terms like diaspora, prophetic witness, advocacy for the disadvantaged, evangelism in humble solidarity, and so on. At the same time – as convincingly demonstrated by authors like Andrew F. Walls – the Christian churches in the global South/East are experiencing a constant – sometimes even explosive – numerical growth. As Walls puts it: 'The fact remains that, by a huge reversal of the position in 1910, the majority of Christians now live in Africa, Asia, Latin America or the Pacific, and that the proportion is rising.'[25] The geographic dichotomy of Christian and non-Christian worlds is not sustainable any more – as was already noted at the Tambaram meeting of the IMC in 1938 – and this phenomenon also has far-reaching missionary consequences. While Edinburgh 1910 was still thinking about mission as 'one-way traffic' from the Christian West to the non-Christian South/East, today we experience the reality of mission 'from everywhere to everywhere.' New mission concepts arise and the diverse expressions of Christian faith that are deeply rooted in the cultures of the global South, and have contributed to the development of a truly global Christianity.

Another phenomenon that needs special attention is the emergence of a strong Pentecostal/charismatic movement during the last century. While the Pentecostal/ charismatic form of Christianity was present as an existing, though marginal, phenomenon in world Christianity at the beginning of the twentieth century, this community of Christianity has become the second largest one (after the Roman Catholic Church) today. The exponentially growing Pentecostal/charismatic communities show a strong missionary fervour. They are able to reach out to underprivileged communities in the global South, and their missionary activity often results in mass people's movements. The Pentecostal/charismatic experience of the Christian faith is embodied both as a diversity of denominations and as movements within the traditional, established churches. The charismatic experience creates, therefore, a new sense of belonging together for Christians from very different ecclesial affiliations (a spectrum from the Roman Catholic to, for example, un-institutionalized youth churches). Another important emerging phenomenon is the direct missionary activity of Pentecostal/charismatic communities from the global South within the global South itself, as well as in the West. At the same time the rapid expansion of these movements raises questions for some about the criteria for authentic expressions of the Christian faith.

At its origins, experiences of the Spirit within Pentecostalism had more of an ecumenical character, as witnessed by an early vision for Christian unity supported by a number of Pentecostal leaders from various countries.[26] Despite this fact, a strong concern for missions and evangelism led to tensions with leaders from established church traditions who felt that such initiatives were unwanted intrusions. From a Pentecostal/charismatic perspective, few leaders from other churches have grasped its significance as a movement for Christian unity whilst, in their practice, Pentecostals/charismatics have tended to favour unity as a grass-roots phenomenon over its more institutional forms.

The new landscape of world Christianity is even more colourful when the very diverse world of the non-Western Christian churches is taken into account. African- and Asian-initiated churches, the Christ *Bhakti* movement in India, the home churches and cultural Christians in China – these and others are challenging traditional ecclesiological and missiological concepts, even as they make a new approach to ecumenical dialogue necessary. At the same time, new forms of Christianity are emerging in the West. Non-denominational communities, the so-called 'emergent church', 'mega-churches', networks of 'house churches', approaches like the Alpha-course, the Neocatechumenate movement, and Cursillo are all expressions of a search for a renewed understanding and experience of Christianity. And forms of an anonymous 'cathedral Christianity,' reviving pilgrimage experiences (El Camino de Santiago de Compostela), the Taizé Community, and the presence of Christianity in 'cyberspace' are other examples of new, sometimes experimental forms of living as followers of Jesus Christ in the postmodern context of global Western civilization. Adding another layer of complication to this multicoloured picture are the alarming signs of intolerant Christian fundamentalism and even extremist voices. The Western context is made even more diverse by the presence of strong migrant and non-Western church communities. While the traditional churches are often dwindling, vibrant African, Asian and Latin-American congregations are emerging, especially in urban areas.

These new forms of Christianity – in the global South and in the North – challenge traditional concepts of the unity of the church. Ecumenical dialogue and cooperation must handle questions around the lack of established structure, the absence of creeds and doctrinal systems, and radically new liturgical expressions. The emergence of these new expressions of Christianity has led to an unprecedented growth in the number of Christian denominations. This increasing diversity of world Christianity is an important challenge when seeking unity today and is further complicated by the fact that Pentecostal and Evangelical expressions of Christianity are frequently trans-denominational in nature.

A century after the first World Missionary Conference, the context of Christian mission and of the search for the visible unity of the church has changed fundamentally. Much has been achieved toward the realisation of the vision of the participants of Edinburgh 1910; however, there are still many steps ahead on the common pilgrimage towards a visible unity of the church. And the fact that the percentage of world population identified as Christian has not changed since the beginning of the twentieth century (thirty-three percent) reminds us that the goal formulated in the watchword of Edinburgh 1910 has not yet been achieved: the whole world has not been evangelized – not in their generation, and not in ours.

4 Biblical and Theological Foundations of Mission in Unity

4.1 The triune God's mission

The theological foundation of mission in unity is built on the *koinonia* of the triune God. Mission is based on the infinite love of God, who created out of nothing the whole of creation and humankind in his image and likeness, so as to make us part-takers of this ineffable love.[27] The Father sent the Son (John 16:5) to fulfil the plan of the Divine Economy. The Word of God became incarnate, born fully human by the Holy Spirit (Nicene Creed). This inner communion of the Holy Trinity is the ultimate source of the unity of the church and the aim of God's mission: to invite every human being to experience fellowship with God and with one another according to the inner unity of the One God in three Persons (John 17:21) in the eschatological hope of the restoration of the whole created world. The aim of God's mission is uniting all things in God as new creation so that God may be all in all (Eph 4:6).[28]

The mission of Jesus Christ is to proclaim the kingdom of God to the world. The salvific work of Christ starts with the *kerygma* of *metanoia* because the kingdom of God is no longer an expectation, but has come near. In this way, the world may believe and gratefully accept reconciliation with God and one another, and be saved. Jesus Christ, through his obedience to the Father, is led to the ultimate in humility: he undergoes insults, suffers on the cross, dies a human death, and offers new life to sinful human beings. At Pentecost, the mission of Jesus Christ is carried forward by the sending of the Holy Spirit, which derives from the Father and is sent by the Son to the world for the salvation of all.

After the resurrection, the disciples received the 'great commission'. This is to call all nations to be disciples of Christ, baptising them in the name of the Father and of the Son and of the Holy Spirit, reassuring them that he will be with them always, even unto the end of the world (Matt 28:19-20, see also John 20:21, Mark 16:15). Teaching all the nations means to spread the good news of the Risen Christ and salvation over death to all humanity, a gift offered by the incarnated Lord regardless of race, sex, culture, social status, or tradition. It is the task of the church to bring this good news to the ends of the earth.

This mission is being fulfilled by the first disciples of Christ and by their disciples throughout the centuries as they give witness to the gospel through preaching, teaching, and the good deeds of Christian communities in solidarity with the suffering people of God. This 'imperative commission' is to be fulfilled in Christ's way (John 13:16; John 17:21). So the mission of the church is to witness to the salvation of all, and to offer prophetic witness (*martyria*). The church is thus called to exist as the Body of Christ and as a community of those who believe in Christ, living as reconciled and reconciling fellowship (*koinonia*), as a sign of the kingdom of God that has come near but that is still to come in its full consummation.

4.2 Mission in kenotic love

This witness determines our ethos as Christians, doing mission in Christ's way: kenotic love; humility; co-suffering with the those who suffer; offering healing of the whole person, giving rather than taking; respecting cultural, ethnic and social diversities and especially the dignity of each human being as if he or she was Christ himself. The disciples are sent into the world by the Son, as he was sent by the Father (John 17:18). Those who are baptised in Christ and are clothed in him act within the world like yeast. Their lives are an actual mission in Christ's way. Those having experienced the love and wonders of God spontaneously share their treasure with others no matter who they are. This treasure is the experience of the triune God, who is affirmed to be a continuous sharing of love. Therefore, a community of believers cannot be conceived without the sharing of love, in Christ's way and in specific ways according to the needs of each cultural and social context. This experience of love determines the mission of the church, which cannot be understood without an opening to the other – not aiming to oppress, subordinate, underestimate or pity, but wishing to share with another the richness that was offered.[29]

Thus, the mission to the world in *koinonia* becomes a testimony to Christ himself. The church, as the body of Christ rejoices in constantly receiving God's love as a free but costly gift and worshipping the triune God in liturgy and in life. For this to be realised, it is necessary for the communities in mission to be in continuous repentance, and to be constantly nurtured by the grace of God. This is manifested in the sacramental life of the church and in a vigilant spirit, which abolishes every threat of egoism, arrogance and self-contentment. Such a witness becomes the expression of our visible unity, which is realised through our deeds. Our common work for peace, justice, reconciliation, and love for the poor, in a humble spirit of ceaseless *metanoia*, is all done for the glory of the triune God (Matt 5:16), who first loved humankind. 'Thus the missionary opening-up of the church to the world is not an optional activity, but, on the contrary, a fundamental condition for her catholicity'.[30]

Although invisible unity as the work of God already exists, visible unity is the work of humans, living in love and, despite different ecclesiologies, being able to cooperate in the common call for mission, through the grace of God. If the commandment to love extends even to our enemies, then love and understanding should be considered as a given among those who confess the same triune God, as his co-operators in God's mission. Diversity as such is a gift in the church, uniting people of all kinds of backgrounds, cultures and identities and it enriches ecclesial life, being congruent with God's creational intentions. However, diversity may also lead to divisions, to discrimination, to intolerance, to animosity and even to violence. Mission may create more diversity which is welcome, but it also may lead to tensions and to the emergence of church-dividing differences. Unity in mission should be a unity in diversity, but, in the same time, must avoid creating divisions. Unity and diversity, enrichment and division are examples of the dualities that are likely to remain a central focus in discussions concerning structured unity in the practice of mission and evangelization.

4.3 Church as missionary by its very nature

A theology that starts from the participation of the church in God's mission cannot fail to point out that the church came into being through the mission of Jesus Christ. Therefore, from a missiological perspective, the church has not always existed historically but, both theologically – as shown above – and empirically, has come into being as a result of mission. It is not possible therefore to separate the church from mission in either its theological or its historical origin. Nor is it possible to separate church and mission in terms of their purpose. The church came into being as a result of the purpose of God to bring salvation to the world. The missionary intention of God is the *raison d'être* of the church, and its goal is to fulfil God's missionary purpose. The relationship is even more intimate than that: the Spirit of Christ who empowers the church in mission is also the life of the church. Jesus Christ breathed the Holy Spirit into the church at the same time as he sent the church into the world (John 20:19-23).[31] In this sense, mission theologians often quote from Emile Brunner, 'the Church exists by mission as a fire exists by burning'.[32] Unless the church is participating in God's mission, the church in history will expire. From a mission perspective, therefore, it is impossible to separate the nature and mission of the church. The church is 'missionary by its very nature'.[33] Even more emphatically, Pentecostalism throughout the past century has asserted that a church which is not missionary-minded has given up being a church altogether: 'Une église qui n'est pas missionnaire est démissionnaire'.[34]

5 Ecumenical Evangelism

The prayer of Jesus Christ, 'May they all be one…so that the world may believe,' invites Christians and the church in history to live out a 'double wrestling'[35] between evangelism and unity, as the Edinburgh 1910 World Missionary Conference aimed to do. The goal of Edinburgh 1910 was the evangelization of the world within the present generation. In order to achieve this urgent task, the participants prayed together for the unity of Christians, missions and churches. Edinburgh 1910 reached a common conclusion that the division of Christians is a scandal and an obstacle to the witness of the church.

The modern Ecumenical movement has been directly rooted in this double wrestling of Edinburgh 1910, seeking evangelism through overcoming the disunity of Christian families. After a century of ecumenical endeavour inheriting and developing the ethos of Edinburgh 1910, it is time for the worldwide Christian families to reflect together on our journey of evangelism in unity during the last century, and to envision ecumenical evangelism for the new century, on the historic occasion of the Edinburgh centenary celebration in 2010. There is a growing awareness among Christians and churches today that *common witness* to the life and teaching of Jesus Christ is an authentic way of participating in God's mission. Is evangelism still something we are unable to do together across different denominational backgrounds in spite of Jesus' prayer?

5.1 Holistic salvation and unity

Evangelism has been defined as 'the proclamation of the good news accompanied by an invitation to turn away from false absolutes and to turn to the living God, to follow Jesus Christ as one's only Saviour and Lord, to join the community of his Church and to live under the prompting of the Holy Spirit and take the ethics of the kingdom of God as one's guide'.[36] Evangelism, while not excluding the different dimensions of mission, mainly focuses on the explicit and intentional proclamation of the gospel, including the invitation to personal conversion to a new life in Christ and to discipleship.[37]

The ultimate goal of evangelism is bringing about the salvation of the whole world through witnessing to Jesus Christ. Therefore, 'the only valid theological method for evangelism is conscious participation in the whole of human life and its problems… evangelism is a question not of apologetics but of life'.[38] 'The teaching of Jesus on the kingdom of God is a clear reference to God's loving lordship over all human history'.[39] As God does not give us a partial salvation, we cannot limit evangelism only to the spiritual realm. Rather, we must acknowledge that evangelism proclaims good news for every part of our life, society and creation. Jesus prayed for the unity of all. He did not pray exclusively for unity for Christians and their churches. He prayed also for the unity of human community and society, and for our relationship with creation, which are also, therefore, important parts of our ecumenical evangelism.

5.2 Understanding of evangelism

Evangelism is proclaiming the good news of the kingdom of God. It is not expanding one's own dominion. It is sharing the news of salvation through the crucifixion and resurrection of Jesus Christ. It is not overwhelming others with our own experience. Therefore, evangelism should not be regarded as simply the expansion of Christendom, but as witnessing to the sacrificial love of God. The nature of this love is the servanthood of Christ, who was sent as the Lamb of God for the world. 'The self-emptying of the servant who lived among the people, sharing in their hopes and sufferings, giving his life on the cross for all humanity – this was Christ's way of proclaiming the good news, and as disciples we are summoned to follow the same way.'[40]

This *kenotic* understanding of evangelism does not merely shape our methods, but is the very nature and essence of our faith in Christ. Jesus became our Christ not through power or money but through his *kenosis* (Phil 2:7). We believe in God who 'made himself nothing.' Therefore, we, the disciples who have been sent by Christ to proclaim his good news, have to follow in his footsteps by witnessing to his humility and humbleness in our own practice of evangelism. Edinburgh 1910 was organised at the height of triumphalism of the Western missionary movement. However, evangelism in the twenty-first century has to overcome this image of 'winners' and 'conquerors' through evangelism in humility.

As the subject of mission is the triune God, we are the servants of God, who gives us the mission of proclaiming the good news to all suffering humanity and creation longing for new hope in their lives. Ecumenical evangelism is not conquering or winning against the others. Rather, it is a humble invitation to the 'feast in the kingdom of God.' The people of God are not conquerors, but humble servants called to invite all God's people to his banquet in the 'garden of life.'

5.3 Proselytism and freedom of religion

We are living in the highly competitive environment of the free market which is reinforcing many churches and para-church movements in their perception of mission as the effort to attract and recruit new 'customers,' while retaining the old ones. They evaluate the success of their mission in terms of growth, of numbers of converts or of newly planted churches. Unfortunately, very often their 'new members' already belonged to other churches. Thus *proselytism* (as competition and 'sheep-stealing') is one of the sharp contemporary issues facing the churches.[41]

'Proselytism' is used to mean the encouragement of Christians who already belong to a church to change their denominational allegiance, through ways and means that 'contradict the spirit of Christian love, violate the freedom of the human person and diminish trust in the Christian witness of the Church'.[42]

On the other hand, it is important for Christians to embrace and act upon the imperative of religious freedom. 'Religious freedom will not be respected by the state if it is not respected by Christians or, even worse, if Christians attempt to recruit the state in repressing religious freedom'.[43] Freedom of choice is the centre of freedom of religion. Institutions cannot own persons. The concept of ownership can lead to the abuse of religious power. Personal choice is the heart of religious freedom. It is not compatible with subjugating or manipulating persons to join another religious structure.

5.4 Towards common witness

The churches are called to identify ways of witnessing in unity, of partnership and cooperation, and of responsible relationships in evangelism. In order to reach such a mutually enriching missionary ethos, the churches must

- repent of past failures and reflect more self-critically on their ways of relating to one another and their methods of evangelizing;
- renounce all forms of denominational competition and rivalry and the temptation to proselytize members of other Christian traditions;
- avoid establishing parallel ecclesial structures, but rather stimulate, help and cooperate with the existing local churches in their evangelistic work;
- condemn any manipulation of humanitarian assistance to individual Christians or churches to induce people into changing their denominational allegiance or to further the missionary goals of one church at the expense of another;
- help people who are in process of changing their church allegiance to discern whether they are being guided by worthy or unworthy motives;
- learn to 'speak the truth in love' to one another when they consider others to be proselytizing or engaging in dishonest practices in evangelism.[44]

In order to overcome the scandal of proselytism, we are called to practise common witness as an act of ecumenical evangelism. *Common witness* is the 'witness that the churches, even while separated, bear together, especially through joint efforts, by manifesting whatever divine gifts of truth and life they already share and experience in common'.[45] In order to do this together, it is extremely important to develop a process of reconciliation between churches through the healing of wounds and memories. Mutual recognition of baptism (as expressed in the WCC's *Baptism, Eucharist and Ministry* text[46]) can be the foundation for Christian unity and common witness.[47] More recently, Lausanne has given attention to the creedal formulation of 'one, holy, catholic, and apostolic Church' as the basis for understanding common participation in the one *missio Dei.*[48]

As new contexts call for new initiatives in proclaiming the gospel in unity, churches in partnership in mission must commit themselves to

- deepened understanding of what it means to be church in today's world, and acceptance and celebration of their interrelatedness in the one body of Christ (cf. 1 Cor 12:12);
- deepened conviction that it is God's mission in which the churches share as God's co-workers, not their own;
- efforts to come to a greater common understanding and vision of their missionary role in contemporary society;
- reaching out together in Christ's way to new frontiers of mission – listening, accompanying, walking with, resourcing, receiving from one another;
- renewed determination to manifest together 'the one hope of [their] calling' (Eph 4:4) in order to
- share more fully in the plan of salvation for the reconciliation and gathering up of all peoples and all things in Christ (cf. Eph 1:9-10).[49]

5.5 Creative tension between evangelism and prophetic witness

The ecumenical debate on evangelism has reminded us that we cannot allow a false dichotomy to be created as we play out truth and unity, prophetic witness for the values of the kingdom of God, and the vocation for the unity of the church. Therefore, ecumenical evangelism does not mean unity at any price, but is about costly unity for prophetic witness.[50]

There is a long debate about holistic salvation and social justice and reconciliation.[51] Its relevance for the understanding of ecumenical evangelism in a context of grave global injustices and inequalities should not be overlooked. As the WCC mission conference at Melbourne in 1980 stated: 'In a world of large-scale robbery and genocide, Christian evangelism can be honest and authentic only if it stands clearly against these injustices which are diametrically opposed to the kingdom of God and looks for response in an act of faith which issues in commitment.'[52] Therefore, ecumenical evangelism does not seek cheap unity through diminishing either evangelistic zeal or the passion for justice and peace. Rather, it seeks to firmly hold together both, to be truly holistic in carrying out God's mission today.

In a similar vein the LCWE's Manila Congress made reference to the Good News touching 'people in their individual situations of pain, suffering and oppression' which 'if it is transforming… will be empowering.'[53] In affirming the Lausanne Covenant's holistic treatment of evangelism and social justice, Manila offered an extended treatment of social concern and evangelism with reference to disability, oppression, poverty, refugees, and state-sponsored violence.[54]

The theme of Edinburgh 2010, the centenary celebration and study process, is '*Witnessing to Christ Today*.' From an Ecumenical point of view, '*common*' should be added to the theme, because one of the most important legacies of Edinburgh 1910 has been '*mission and evangelism in unity.*' This refers to the search for ways of witnessing together in unity and cooperation – despite differing ecclesiologies and missiologies – within the context of the burning challenges facing churches everywhere today, 'so that the world may believe,' avoiding any form of confessional rivalry or competition. This does not imply an unrealistic super-church ecclesiology; neither does it deny the intrinsic relationship between mission and ecclesiology.[55] Seeking unity and evangelism together is not an impossible task. Indeed, it is one of the most authentic ways of participating in God's glorious mission.

6 God's Mission of Healing and Reconciliation

Since the late 1980s, mission has been increasingly connected with healing and reconciliation. Furthermore, the language of healing and reconciliation has come to the fore in many different contexts, and has caught the imagination of people both inside and outside the churches. This is certainly also an invitation to the church in this broken world to promote the concept of healing and reconciliation through both words and deeds.

6.1 Unity and diversity: The role of the Holy Spirit

Just as the world in general and the church in particular are a colourful and not a monochromic reality, the encounter of diversity is not meant to be synonymous with the experience of brokenness and fragmentation. Humanity, as God's creation, is blessed with a great variety of diverse and complementary gifts that are expressed in a multiplicity of cultural and historical contexts. It is God's design that such diversity does not lead to separation and division, to opposition and hostility, but to interdependence and harmony.

When considering the ministry of the Holy Spirit as a ministry of unity, it is essential to see the work of the Spirit as equipping the church to experience unity in diversity both proactively and constructively The Spirit becomes the Helper who transforms the problem of difference into the promise of difference.[56] The Spirit is also the Teacher who provides both the dynamic context and the resources needed for people to explore differences in a safe, positive, nurturing environment. Individuals from a variety of backgrounds, and with ideas and concepts that are new to their experience, need an appropriate educational framework in which to understand each other and move beyond simple tolerance to the embrace and celebration of the rich dimensions of diversity contained within each individual and community.

The ministry of unity is a ministry of conciliation (Latin *conciliare*, to bring together), which refers more generally to the process of bringing various different parties into relationships of mutual benefit and enrichment, in order to live in a model of unity in diversity. Reconciliation refers more specifically to the healing of broken relationships and the resolving of conflicts and wrongs of the past, in both cases promoting peace, justice and solidarity.

6.2 Healing a broken world

The church, as a community of believers, brings a message of healing to a broken world longing for hope to replace despair. In order to be God's instrument of healing for others, the church needs first to be a recipient of God's healing power and grace. The healing ministry of the church will find its credibility rooted in a demonstration of *resurrection of life*, that is, restored wholeness and unity within. However, the history of the church is, sad to say, also a story of divisions, separations and crises that have often harmed the *living organism* it is called to be by severely disconnecting its members from each other. It has often produced congregations that failed to serve the needs of the community. It is essential for the church to acknowledge its brokenness and repent of its present shortcomings. A return to good health within the body of Christ needs to be seen as an integral part of the church's mission. A range of significant strategies and initiatives needs to be taken in order to ensure that responding to the Spirit's work will allow such recovery and restoration to take place radically and/or gradually.

From the very beginning of the church, Christians have grappled with the issue of what it means to be human in light of the gospel. This in many cases deeply challenges the social structures that demean human beings. It sets its face resolutely against all that disgraces or destroys human beings created by God in God's own image. In a world where views of humanity veer between confident optimism and utter cynicism, Christians believe that human beings, the family, the local communities, societies and cultures all have the potential for creativity, responsibility and goodness that comes from being made by God, and yet being deeply affected by sin and brokenness. Sin denies the worth and dignity of human beings, disrupts community, and hampers the flow of love and justice. Sin must be faced, confessed, forgiven and healed; for Christians believe in costly reconciliation and love, not an easy and unreal optimism.

While the worth and dignity of the human person have been under threat throughout history the current context in which human beings live presents a number of pressing challenges. The Christian gospel is a significant contributing force to the quest for justice, peace and reconciliation in general and among nations in particular.[57] Its basic thrust is to experience a Spirit-empowered work of re-creation that replaces hostility with proximity, thus enabling a new kind of relationship both with the Creator and creation. The book of Revelation paints the vision of a renewed creation described in terms of 'new heaven and new earth' (21:1). In summary, the sin and brokenness of our world is a reality which cannot be ignored nor minimized. It results in the alienation of humanity from God and from the person, the family, the church, communities, nations, and creation, and leads to structural injustice, too. To put it differently, the sin of human beings contributes to, and belongs within, a wider context: the disorder and evil which affect the whole of creation. Paul expresses this graphically when he writes that 'the whole creation has been groaning' (Rom 8:22). This cry for help needs healing and reconciliation.

6.3 Called to be healing and reconciling communities

The Bible is full of stories of reconciliation from which we can draw our own stories of healing and reconciliation. The Old Testament addresses the estrangement between God and God's people, and also God's work for the healing, reconciliation and restoration of a relationship with the God of life and justice that was broken. Similarly, in the New Testament, Paul is greatly concerned that those whom Christ has reconciled in his body should not be divided, and that community life should be the first expression of God's plan to reconcile all things. He envisages the unity of not only Jew and Gentile, but also of slave and free, male and female, in Christ (Gal 3:28).

Where does the church get its inspiration to respond to the call to become healing and reconciling communities? The answer is found in the healing ministry of Jesus which provides a model for the church to explore today. Healing includes the transformation of life made possible by crossing cultural and religious boundaries.[58] In this connection it becomes important for the church to realise that its calling is a response to the gifts of healing, which equip it and enable it to fulfil that role.[59] The healing ministry of Jesus has always been an integral part of his mission. A closer look at the experience of various churches will show a consistent link between salvation and healing. A rediscovery of the work of Holy Spirit for healing, and reconciliation – at the heart of today's Ecumenical mission theology – has significant ecumenical implications.

In summary, over the past years, reconciliation has become the emerging new paradigm that defines the mission of the church in today's 'global village'. Catholic, Orthodox, Protestant and Pentecostal voices from all over the world are increasingly speaking one and the same language.[60] As witnessed by various international conferences during the last five years,[61] a spirituality of reconciliation is called for in order to face the challenges brought about by the damaging effects of cultural and religious clashes, and of economic and political boundaries. The Athens 2005 report contains a statement on mission as reconciliation 'in the power of the Spirit' in the context of a broken world. Truth, memory, justice and forgiveness are understood as four essential aspects, needed within both the church and society at large, to enable the dynamics of the reconciliation and healing process.[62]

Healing and reconciliation as the restoration of right relations with God is the source of healing and reconciliation with oneself, with people of our own faith and other faiths, and with the whole of creation. It is time for the worldwide Christian family to heal the pain of our divisions, because unity through healing and reconciliation is an integral part of God's mission.

7 Conclusion

The World Missionary Conference held at Edinburgh in 1910 marks the beginning of the modern Ecumenical movement and remains an important inspiration to many within the modern Evangelical mission movement. The primary basis for the concerns expressed around the issues of mission and unity at Edinburgh 1910 was strategic. Problems related to the lack of unity were hindering the conference's goal of 'the evangelization of the world in this generation'. During the century that has passed since Edinburgh 1910, the world, and especially the Christian world, has undergone incredible changes. The centre of world Christianity has shifted from the global North to the global South. There has been an explosion of new ecclesial communities and of new forms of Christian expression around the world that the participants at Edinburgh 1910 could not have imagined.

Ongoing reflection on issues of mission and unity continues to lead to a deeper understanding of the *missio Dei.* The church is called to participate in this and thereby demonstrates that the relation of unity and mission has acquired a more than strategic importance. Mission is increasingly seen as being a matter of the very essence of the church. Therefore, the inextricable link between unity and mission becomes more important than ever. Significant steps have been taken towards the goal of Christian unity over the last century, but there have also been many setbacks along the way. While recognising the intransigent nature of the many sources of their division, churches need to recommit themselves both to the ongoing struggle to overcome their divisions and also to engage in 'common witness' whenever and wherever it is possible to do so. The growing consensus among theologians from many ecclesial traditions that the mission of the church in the twenty-first century must be a mission of healing and of reconciliation is presented as an approach to mission that can both express the unity that is already present in the churches' mission and also prepare the way for a greater unity to come.

Endnotes

[1] World Council of Churches, Working group of the Commission on World Mission and Evangelism, 'Towards Common Witness to Christ Today: Mission and the Visible Unity of the Church' (September 2009).

[2] The results of the 'Mission Today' joint project of the World Alliance of Reformed Churches and the Lutheran World Federation were too late to be taken into account in this report but will be included in the report of the Edinburgh 2010 conference, June 2010. This study looks at mission and unity as experienced today by small, ecumenical groups of Christians in test locations in Argentina, Cameroon and The Netherlands.

[3] K.S. Latourette, 'Ecumenical Bearings of the Missionary Movement and the International Missionary Council', in R. Rouse and Stephen C. Neill, (eds), *A History of the Ecumenical Movement 1517-1948* (Philadelphia: The Westminster Press, 1967), 355. Cf. also D. Claydon (ed.), *A New Vision, a New Heart, A Renewed Call: Volume*

One. Lausanne Occasional Papers from the 2004 Forum for World Evangelization Hosted by the Lausanne Committee for World Evangelization in Pattaya, Thailand (Pasadena: William Carey Library, 2005), vii.

[4] Latourette, 'Ecumenical Bearings…', 355.

[5] J.D. Douglas (ed.), *Let the Earth Hear His Voice: International Congress on World Evangelization Lausanne, Switzerland.* (Minneapolis, MN: World Wide Publications, 1975), 26.

[6] World Missionary Conference, Edinburgh 1910, *Report of Commission VIII: Co-operation and the Promotion of Unity.* (Edinburgh & London: Oliphant, Anderson & Ferrier, 1910), 5.

[7] Already in 1910, in his opening address, the Archbishop of Canterbury claimed that the very nature of church is mission. Cf. 'The Central Place of Missions in the Life of the Church', in World Missionary Conference, Edinburgh 1910, *Volume IX: The History and Records of the Conference* (Edinburgh & London: Oliphant, Anderson & Ferrier, 1910), 146-51. Cf. also, 'the pilgrim church is missionary by its very nature', Vatican II, *Ad Gentes* 'Decree on the Mission Activity of the Church' (1965), §9. Available at www.vatican.va.

[8] N. Goodall (ed.), *Missions under the Cross. Addresses Delivered at the Enlarged Meeting of the International Missionary Council at Willingen, Germany, 1952; with Statements Issued by the Meeting* (London: Edinburgh House Press, 1953), 189.

[9] In the General Assembly of the IMC at New Delhi, 1961, the integration was decided upon by all members of the constituency of the IMC, with the exception of only one of the member councils from 37 countries. 'The Minutes of the Assembly of the IMC at New Delhi, India, 17-18 November 1961', in *The New Delhi Report. Third Assembly of the WCC.* (London: SCM Press, 1962), §7.

[10] Douglas, *Let the Earth Hear His Voice*, 26. Cf. also T. Yates, *Christian Mission in the Twentieth Century.* (Cambridge: Cambridge University Press, 1994), 155-158. Yates describes the two streams as 'conciliar' and 'evangelical', 199.

[11] See www.globalchristianforum.org.

[12] World Council of Churches, 'Mission and Evangelism: An Ecumenical Affirmation' (hereafter: EA), in J. Matthey (ed.), *'You Are the Light of the World' Statements on Mission by the World Council of Churches 1980-2005* (Geneva: WCC, 2005), 1-38, at 5. Available at www.oikoume.org.

[13] WCC Commission on Faith and Order, *The Nature and Mission of the Church* (Faith and Order Paper, 198; Geneva: WCC, 2005), 10. Available at www.oikoumene.org.

[14] Douglas, *Let the Earth Hear His Voice*, 5. The Lausanne Covenant (LC) is available at www.lausanne.org. Three papers addressing unity and mission were presented at the Lausanne Congress 1974.

[15] J.D. Douglas (ed.), *Proclaim Christ Until He Comes: Calling the Whole Church to Take the Whole Gospel to the Whole World* (Minneapolis, MN: World Wide Publications, 1990), 27. The Manila Manifesto (MM) is available at www.lausanne.org.

[16] Bill O'Brien, 'Cooperation in Mission', in Douglas, *Proclaim Christ Until He Comes*, 204-207, at 204.

[17] J.S. Stromberg, 'Ecumenical Affirmation on Mission and Evangelism: A Review', *International Review of Mission (IRM)* 90/358 (July 2001), 243-52, at 249.

[18] Yates, *Christian Mission*, 200.

[19] See www.lausanne.org/cape-town-2010.

[20] Cf. Although there was no Orthodox participant, the *Encyclical of the Ecumenical Patriarchate, 1920* proposed to the churches to make efforts at cooperation and proselytism. See, Michael Kinnamon & Brian E. Cope (eds), *The Ecumenical Movement: An Anthology of Key Texts and Voices* (Geneva: WCC Publications, 1997), 11-14.
[21] 'Resolutions reached by the Working Group at the Sevres Conference, 7th-12th April 1953', *Syndesmos News* 1 (June 1953).
[22] Cf. Although there was no official Roman Catholic representation, there was a message of greeting from Bishop Geremina Bonomelli of Cremona. See, Brian Stanley, *The World Missionary Conference, Edinburgh 1910* (Grand Rapids, MI: Eerdmans, 2009), 11-12.
[23] IARCCUM, *Growing Together in Unity and Mission* (London: SPCK, 2007).
[24] *Charta Oecumenica* (Geneva: Conference of European Churches, 2001), Ch.II, para 2. Available at www.cec-kek.org/.
[25] Andrew F. Walls, 'The Great Commission 1910-2010', 6. Paper submitted to Edinburgh 2010, and available at www.edinburgh2010.org.
[26] Allan Anderson, *An Introduction to Pentecostalism* (Cambridge: CUP, 2004), 249.
[27] Cf. Commission on World Mission and Evangelism, 'Mission and Evangelism in Unity Today' (hereafter: MEUT), §10-13, in Matthey, *'You Are the Light of the World...'* 59-89. Available at www.oikoumene.org.
[28] MEUT §15.
[29] EA §23.
[30] Athanasios N. Papathanasiou, 'Is Mission a Consequence of the Catholicity of the Church? An Orthodox Perspective', *IRM* 90/359 (October 2001), 409-416.
[31] See Kirsteen Kim, 'Mission Theology of the Church', keynote paper presented at the Joint Consultation on Mission and Ecclesiology of the Faith and Order Commission and of the Commission on World Mission and Evangelism, Berekfürdő, 4-9 March 2009, forthcoming in *IRM* in 2010.
[32] Emil Brunner, *The Word and the World* (London: Student Mission Movement Press, 1931), 108.
[33] Vatican II, *Ad Gentes*, §9; cf. David J. Bosch, *Transforming Mission: Paradigm Shifts in Theology of Mission* (Maryknoll, NY: Orbis Books, 1991), 372; cf. EA, §3.
[34] Raymond Pfister, 'Pratiques missionaires penticôtistes et œcuménisme'. Available at www.pfister.ws.
[35] Shoki K. Coe coined this term in articulating his notion of contextualization in theological education, see, *The Human and the Holy: Asian Perspectives in Christian Theology*, edited by Emerito P. Nacpil and Douglas J. Elwood (Quezon City: New Day, 1978), iii.
[36] Jacques Matthey, 'Evangelism, Still the Enduring Test of Our Ecumenical and Missionary Calling', *IRM*, 96/382-383 (2007), 355.
[37] MEUT, §7. Cf. also Article 4 'The Nature of Evangelism' in the *Lausanne Covenant* which defines evangelism as proclamation and persuasion leading to reconciliation with God, a life of discipleship, incorporation into the church, and service to the world.
[38] Emilio Castro, 'Evangelism', in Nicholas Lossky *et al*, eds., *Dictionary of the Ecumenical Movement*, (Geneva: WCC, 1991), 400.
[39] EA, §14.
[40] EA, §4.
[41] MEUT, §27.

[42] MEUT, §71.
[43] Evangelicals and Catholics Together, 'Christian Mission in the Third Millenium,' 1994. Available at www.firstthings.com.
[44] MEUT, §73.
[45] Thomas F. Best & Günther Gassmann (eds), *On the Way to Fuller Koinonia: Official Report of the Fifth World Conference on Faith and Order, Santiago de Compostela, 1993* (Geneva: WCC, 1994), 254.
[46] WCC, *Baptism, Eucharist and Ministry* (Faith and Order Paper No. 111, the 'Lima Text'; Geneva: WCC, 1982).
[47] WCC Central Committee, 'Towards Common Witness: A Call to Adopt Responsible Relationships in Mission and to Renounce Proselytism' (1997) §2, par.3. Published in Matthey, *'You Are the Light of the World'*, 39-58. Available at www.oikoumene.org.
[48] *The Whole Church: Reflections of the Lausanne Theology Working Group*, Panama, 26th-30th January 2009, (Panama: LCWE, 2009).
[49] WCC, *Towards Common Witness...*, 52-53.
[50] Dietrich Werner, 'Evangelism from a WCC Perspective: A Recollection of an Important Ecumenical Memory, and the Unfolding of a Holistic Mission', *IRM* 96/382-383 (July/October 2007), 183-203.
[51] Particularly at the World Mission Conference in Bangkok, 1972/3 (Section II, Salvation and Social Justice) and Melbourne, 1980 (Section IV, Christ – Crucified and risen – Challenges Human Power).
[52] CWME, *Your Kingdom Come: Report on the World Conference on Mission and Evangelism, Melbourne, Australia, 12-25, May 1980* (Geneva: WCC, 1980), 218.
[53] J.D. Douglas, *Proclaim Christ Until He Comes*, 296.
[54] CWME, *Your Kingdom Come*, 289-300.
[55] MEUT, §7.
[56] See, Commission for World Mission and Evangelism, 'Mission as Ministry of Reconciliation' (2005), §22-27. Published in Matthey, *'You Are the Light of the World'*, 90-126. Available at www.oikoumene.org,
[57] Joanna Udal, 'Reconciliation Among Nations: The Role of the Church – Common Understanding and Vision,' *The Ecumenical Review*, 49 (January 1997), 61-77.
[58] Turid Karlssen Seim, *The Double Message: Patterns of Gender in Luke-Acts* (Edinburgh: T&T Clark, 1994), 57.
[59] World Council of Churches, study group on healing, 'The Healing Mission of the Church', §54. Published in Matthey, *'You Are the Light of the World'*, 127-62. Available at www.oikoumene.org.
[60] Petros Vassiliadis, 'Reconciliation As a Pneumatological Mission Paradigm: Some Preliminary Reflections by an Orthodox,' *IRM* 94/372 (January 2005), 30-42.
[61] E.g. International conferences of the International Association of Mission Studies (IAMS) in Malaysia, 2004, and in Hungary, 2008 – www.missionstudies.org.
[62] Jacques Matthey (ed.), *Come Holy Spirit, Heal and Reconcile! Called in Christ to be Reconciling and Healing Communities. Report of the WCC Conference on World Mission and Evangelism, Athens, Greece, May 9-16*, 2005. (Geneva: WCC, 2008).

Theme Nine

Mission Spirituality and Authentic Discipleship

Preface

The saying goes that 'hindsight is 20/20' (or, it is easy to be knowledgeable after the events). For our purposes, perhaps a more appropriate saying would be 'hindsight is 2010', for Edinburgh 2010 is in many ways about looking back and seeing with clarity things that could not possibly have been envisioned a century ago. But Edinburgh 2010 is not just about looking back; it is also about looking around us now and looking forward to the future, and it is with this in mind that this chapter on mission spirituality and authentic discipleship commences.

Looking back at the World Missionary Conference in 1910, it has been observed that 'notable absent groups were the Orthodox, Roman Catholic, Pentecostals and most Evangelical churches and organisations; Africans and South American Christians were not present either.'[1] For the purposes of this study on mission spirituality and authentic discipleship, a concentrated effort has been made to seek out and include voices from these particular perspectives. Hence, whilst attention will be paid to the experience of the early church and Christians throughout the ages, the bulk of the space in this study will be dedicated to addressing insights gained from newer Christian movements, particularly among those mentioned above.

Study Group 9 was led by conveners Dr Wonsuk Ma (South Korea, Pentecostal), Director of the Oxford Centre for Mission Studies (OCMS) and Dr Cathy Ross (New Zealand, Anglican), Manager of the Crowther Centre for Mission Education at the Church Mission Society (CMS) in Oxford and JV Taylor Fellow in Missiology at Regent's Park College and Wycliffe Hall, Oxford. The core group, which was based in Oxford and met regularly, also included Dr Thomas Harvey (USA, Presbyterian) of OCMS and Naomi Rose (USA, Anglican) of CMS. The group organised an international consultation on the theme in Seoul, South Korea on 22-24 March 2009, which was hosted by Youngnak Presbyterian Church.

This summary is intended to serve as a collection of samples. Most of the studies used for this summary were presented at the Study Group 9 consultation held in Seoul. Since then, several more studies have been added to this primary group of studies. The authors are well aware that many important traditions and regions are not included in this summary due to the limited nature of the process. The final published volume of Study Group 9 will include more studies representing a wider spectrum of church traditions and regions.

1 Some Words and Thoughts about Mission Spirituality

The term 'mission spirituality' has only been articulated as such relatively recently and has come to mean different things to different people. For the purposes of this present study, it is important to say what is meant by 'mission spirituality' in this document.

Mission spirituality is specifically concerned with what is necessary for the Christian to engage in mission. It examines the sources from which mission arises. 'It suggests that Christian mission begins with the spiritual activity of discerning the spirits (according to the revelation of Jesus Christ) in order to discover the movement of the Spirit of God in the world and join with it.'[2] For help with understanding mission spirituality for this paper, we turned to biblical precedent and to mission scholars and practitioners from a variety of cultural contexts, such as C. Rene Padilla,[3] David Bosch,[4] Gustavo Gutiérrez,[5] Samuel Rayan,[6] Juan Esquerda Bifet[7] and Christopher Duraisingh.[8]

Padilla, seeing Acts 1:8 as a promise, not a commandment, asserts, 'The same Spirit that makes possible life in Christ on both the personal and community levels is the Spirit that empowers and guides the church so that this life is shared…Christian spirituality is, therefore missionary spirituality'.[9] This will be important to bear in mind as throughout this essay, one will see that some contributors will have used 'Christian spirituality' and 'mission spirituality' interchangeably, and taken mission spirituality as a 'given'; or assumed it as a natural part of the Christian life. Also, it will be seen that mission spirituality is not a term that is used universally or with the same amount of familiarity as other theological terms that have made their way into vernacular.

So it could be said that mission spirituality is essentially Christian spirituality lived in and fuelled by awareness of the *missio Dei*, and that, mission spirituality results in tangible mission practice in the world. Yet, as will be demonstrated, it is more than awareness that prompts global mission, which brings us to the key question for this study. At the heart of this study on mission spirituality and authentic discipleship is the desire to begin to answer the query: 'What motivates and sustains mission?' It was a question put to the diverse group of participants for this consultation and their answers, coupled with internal and external observations of mission past and present, should lead us to some helpful conclusions.

2 What Motivates and Sustains Mission? Churches and Mission Movements

Historically and currently, motives for mission have run the gamut from love of God to fear of God, to compassion, to guilt, to eschatological urgency. The more honest amongst us have also added a desire for power, control or even money to the list of possible motivations for mission.

The question of what motivates mission is an important one, not only because according to Scripture, our motivations matter to God (see Jer 12:3; 17:10, Ps 44:21, 1 Sam 16:7; Matt 15:8; 2 Cor 13:3, Phil 1:15-17), but because our motivations for mission have ramifications for mission sustainability. If for example, our mission is motivated by eschatological expectations of an imminent second-coming of Christ and a 'rapture' of believers in Christ only, this cannot help but affect our set of mission priorities, and it may very well be a motivation that lessens in its fervour with the passage of more and more time.

As aforementioned, one of the aims of this study was to ask this question, 'What motivates and sustains mission?' of Christians whose voices were not heard in 1910. What follows next is a survey of some of their perspectives pertaining to how their mission understanding, activity and motivation have evolved in the past century.

We will observe both accomplishments and challenges within such varying churches and movements as African Instituted Churches, China's Back to Jerusalem movement, the Russian Orthodox Church and a variety of Asian contexts, including Roman Catholicism in India and Pentecostalism in Korea. Four regional and one collaborative reflections have also been included. We will also comment specifically on the relationship between mission sustainability and authentic discipleship. From all of this, we then make some recommendations for future generations.

2.1 African Instituted Churches

African Instituted Churches (AICs) have experienced incredible growth in the last several decades, with more than 50 million members globally. The OAIC (Organisation of AICs) understands its mission as originating in founding visions. In his paper, 'Doing Mission at the Margins of Society: Harnessing the Resources of Local Visions', OAIC senior leader Nicta Lubaale Makiika says specifically that the rediscovered Jesus Christ healer as well as the Holy Spirit who was dwelling among them

> ...what the people of faith hear God telling them to do (often through the leadership and guidance of a prophet or preacher), what they believe about the world around them, and how they understand their call to live out their faith in the particular society they belong to.[10]

The original founding visions came out of a time of crisis in the lives of Africans when they were faced with a threefold challenge: cultural, political and spiritual domination. At the same time people were beginning to read the Bible for themselves in their own mother tongues and discovering Jesus and the Holy Spirit afresh. In his paper, Makiika says specifically that the rediscovered Jesus Christ healer as well as the Holy Spirit who was dwelling among them.

Though not a homogenous group by any means, most AICs view themselves to be engaging in mission from the margins. Marginality is understood as 'being on the sidelines of dominant movements and activities in society' and as 'doing mission in a way that challenges the established understanding of mission'.[11] It is this second category of marginality that the Holy Spirit is understood to break down the barriers between the resource-rich and the resource-poor. This understanding of mission has enabled and empowered the AICs to engage in mission in a holistic way.

There is a focus on community in the AIC mission approach. The African worldview integrates the physical and the spiritual so they focus on the role of the Holy Spirit in the lives of individuals and communities. Prayer is a major part of mission at the grassroots, as is community building. The AIC 'communities of the Spirit' have modelled a counter-cultural approach to the Western models on offer and enabled support for those in the communities who suffered HIV/AIDS, unemployment and homelessness, to name a just a few of the needs being addressed.

AIC members develop their understanding of mission through 'listening to the voice of the Spirit and reading the Scriptures in situations in which they are placed.'[12] This reading of the Scriptures in context has led to social action and engagement. In one community, praying over the issue of the increasing number of orphans in their midst directly led the women to start a ministry caring for the orphans and children in need in that community.

For the AICs it is prayer, the inspiration of the Holy Spirit and the reading of the Scriptures in community that sustains and motivates them in mission. The current challenge is for present day missioners to dream dreams and see visions for their own generation. This will require a process of training and remobilising to enable 'the missioners to read the word, listen to the Holy Spirit and scan the environment they are operating in.'[13] Sociological tools such as Participatory Learning and Action (PLA) programmes have been used to help them see and analyse the social realities of the communities around them. When used alongside the Scriptures, African Christians begin to realise the place of the Bible in social transformation. The founding visions are also a resource for the AICs and the wider church. Being on the margins is also a good place to be forced to rely on God for one's ongoing Christian sustenance. The question, arises, how can AICs, which have become more popular, continue to identify with a marginalized stance? Perhaps if other global church structures and movements made a conscious effort to also identify with the marginalized, this would shore up the AIC commitment to remain true to this stance.

As communities and voices on the margins, AICs can be overlooked or not taken seriously. Their spirituality, which depends on being empowered and enabled by the Holy Spirit with visions, dreams and prophecies, challenges the dominant model of civic education 'which hardly recognises the motivation of the Holy Spirit to speak to power'.[14] At the same time, this very spirituality can cause AICs to slip back into cultural prejudice and values. For example, some may claim that the Holy Spirit has told them not to talk about HIV/AIDS while others may claim that this condition is entirely demonic, warranting exorcism.

Inadequate theological training is seen as a problem. Theology is sometimes carelessly borrowed with little attempt made to integrate it into an AIC context. Lack of a carefully worked out theology is considered 'a significant constraint on contemporary AIC mission.'[15] AICs also have a tendency to remain separatist, which therefore limits their effective involvement. Patriarchal models of leadership are still prevalent.

The AICs developed in a context of challenge and resistance and it may be that they need to recapture some of this early sense of marginalization and resourcefulness once again, in which case their solidarity with the marginalized could be their unique offering to the wider church.

2.2 Back to Jerusalem Movement

The Back to Jerusalem movement is helpfully summarised and evaluated by Kim Kwong Chan in his study: 'Mission Movement of the Christian Community in Mainland China: The Back to Jerusalem Movement'.[16]

Chan looks at the origins and missiological ramifications of the Back to Jerusalem mission movement. This movement arose in the mid-twentieth century and has more recently been taken up as a mission cause by some house church leaders in China and Western missionary groups. Chan documents how the movement arose from visions of a pilgrimage west to evangelize the Middle East and culminate in Jerusalem. This mission quest was to fulfil the final leg of world evangelism; a mandate that was the unique burden and honour of Chinese Christians to bring the gospel 'back to Jerusalem'.

Chan's essay tells not only the history of this movement but its spiritual, theological and ethical dynamics. His article is a cautionary tale exposing the difficulties such visions encounter when they bump up against harsh reality. These dreams and visions of reaching Jerusalem led to remote Kashgar but not beyond. There, the small churches founded remain, but the mandate to go on to the Middle East or Jerusalem remained unfulfilled. Thus, more recently their vision has been taken up by a new generation of Christian converts. Some have ventured into Middle Eastern countries such as Iraq, but with no cross-cultural training and no knowledge of Arabic their ability to effectively share the gospel is difficult at best. For example, Chan points to one group of itinerant pig herders who had much missionary zeal, but were without a 'profession for gaining acceptance in the Muslim world'.[17]

Moreover, Chan's article brings to the fore the dearth of reflection by Western mission organisations that have uncritically championed the Back to Jerusalem movement. The fact that it is 'cheaper' to send Chinese Christian labourers to the mission field and the assumption that given their years of persecution in China they will be better able to handle persecution in Muslim countries, when added to the economic motives of poor Chinese Christian peasants and labourers to leave China, raise all sorts of ethical, moral and economic issues that have not been fully sorted out. All this, however, should serve as an ongoing reminder that in the end, despite all the academic and spiritual reflection on mission, mission is messy, and that despite all best or poorly laid plans, mission takes place and has all sorts of positive and negative unintended consequences.

Chan recognises that the Back to Jerusalem Movement, generated as it was by visions and a special mission mandate to the Christians of China, has done much to motivate mission both in China and abroad. Nonetheless, one also senses Chan's concern that that motivation leads to a mission emphasis and practice that is in many ways spiritually and ethically malformed. That said, one senses in Chan's essay a deep appreciation for Chinese enthusiasm for and willingness to sacrifice in mission. Further, he recognises the good unintended consequences of these movements and expresses appreciation for how this has impressed and heartened Christians in the West. Nonetheless, as Chan notes,

> (T)he dubious motives of many… mission candidates within the current Chinese social trend of migration to overseas, the clandestine style of operation lacking accountability and transparency on financial and administrative matters and the ethical issues with the law both in China and in the mission field, all these factors cast doubt on the idea that the Back to Jerusalem will bear strong influence on the development of global Christianity.[18]

Regarding the Back to Jerusalem movement, we have raised critical questions surrounding a trajectory in mission that seeks to utilize global Christians to complete the work that Western missionaries no longer can. On the one hand, the Back to Jerusalem movement is but one of many indigenous Christian missionary movements that have taken up the mission mandate; nonetheless, as noted above it runs the risk of repeating many errors that have been committed by missions and missionaries in the past as well as raising a raft of new issues not easily resolved. Whether one feels that the Back to Jerusalem movement signals the completion of the great missionary enterprise or is mere missionary folly, bringing out the worst characteristics of missions in the occident and the orient, it represents the fecund energy that lies at the heart of global Christian mission that has now moved well beyond the bounds of the Western missionary endeavours of the past two centuries.

2.3 CMS Africa

Regarding African mission in general, it is helpful to consider reflections from Serah Wambua of CMS Africa, a mission agency recently weaned from its parent body in February, 2009. CMS Africa is convinced that God's intentions for Africa are found in Isaiah 65:20:

> Never again will there be an infant who lives for a few days
> Or an old man who does not live out his years;
> He who dies at a hundred will be thought a mere youth;

He who fails to reach a hundred will be considered accursed.

CMS Africa celebrates the tremendous church growth in Africa but is challenged by what it identifies as a lack of discipleship. In its view, the missionary church failed to address this and the current church is failing as well.

> The African indigenous church movement largely grew out of this failure by the church to address pertinent issues rooted in the African culture and religion. African cultural practices such as polygamy, witch doctrine, the place of ancestral spirits, clan and communal responsibility left African Christians hanging and the result has been Christians torn between the two worlds.[19]

CMS Africa forms part of a wider Africa Working Group, which is convinced that a paradigm shift is necessary for the church in Africa to make any difference. They believe that the mission of the church is for social and cultural transformation and that the church is 'the single most important indigenous sustainable institution with members in virtually every area of society.'[20] Integral mission is their call and challenge to the African church so that African Christians do not experience a kind of schizophrenia but rather an integrated Christian lifestyle, or mission spirituality. Accordingly, a group of trainers in Africa has developed the Samaritan Strategy – an advanced, holistic discipleship training programme to be used all over Africa. Churches that have received this training are indeed making a noticeable difference to their contexts:

> They are effectively and practically addressing issues like the HIV and AIDS pandemic, responding to conflict with biblical peacemaking principles; and effectively engaging in social, political, business and environmental concerns using their local recourses. Not surprisingly, they are also more effective in their evangelistic outreach.[21]

Business as Mission (BAM) is a programme being used in several African countries. BAM is about establishing real businesses and not an excuse to enter into a community for evangelistic purposes. BAM is seen as the entry point for poverty reduction and it 'is empowering and inspiring businessmen in Africa to create jobs and make wealth strategically dealing with the poverty challenge.'[22] This approach also capitalises on Africa's extraordinary resources in terms of people and natural resources. CMS Africa's challenging of the dominant worldview is an example to the wider church, especially in those contexts where the state church takes on the colour and hue of the society around it so it is virtually indistinguishable from it.

CMS Africa firmly believes that more effective Christian discipleship is needed for the church in Africa to grow and develop. They believe that the church is God's agent for transformation and so as the church is challenged and changed so will Africa be changed. CMS Africa is committed to working at retaining the best of the African worldview that is not at odds with the gospel and challenging that which is. This ongoing study of the Scriptures inspired by the leading of the Holy Spirit to transform the African worldview is what motivates and sustains them in their mission.

2.4 Immigrant church example

The Grace Korean Church in Southern California is a first-generation Korean immigrant church. Although the formal affiliation of this fast growing church is Presbyterian, its theology and ethos are more Pentecostal.[23]

The church's understanding of mission has been deeply influenced by the vision of its founder, Kwang-shin Kim. Mission is understood as the proclamation of the gospel and the establishment of strong local congregations in challenging places. Other areas of engagement support these goals, such as martial arts programmes among Muslim youth, community development programmes in Africa, and general education in Latin America. The single goal of the church's mission has been the presence of dynamic local missionary congregations. However, recently the church made a change in its mission thinking. The recently dedicated Vision Centre includes a Prayer Centre for Nations where intercessory prayers will be offered continuously. This implies the church's continuing priority toward the spiritual aspect of mission, but also the expansion of its mission scope to include its own neighbours and its host country, the United States.

Kim was radically converted after seeing a vision of a weeping Jesus (weeping, he presumed, for lost lives). This led him to establish a church of 'award-winning' members who would win souls. The unique immigrant context of the founder and the members has been another motivation; the motif of 'sojourning' or 'pilgrimage' is often highlighted in Kim's sermons.

Another source of motivation is a sense of historic mission opportunity, which motivated Kim and the church to launch an 'all-out' mission effort to the former Soviet areas, including massive celebrations of new believers with several hundreds of Grace Church members who were flown in by a chartered jumbo jet. The church also has a mission-oriented understanding of ecclesiology. The paradigm is reinforced repeatedly that the real heroes are missionaries, and the primary reason for the church's existence is to support their work. They also employ military language to express their 'all-out' commitment to mission. The large banner in the church lobby reads: 'Mission is Prayer, Mission is War, and Mission is Martyrdom'. Mission has priority in finance, the pastor's schedule, church programmes, and so on. One also senses a commitment to the 'democratization of mission.' There is a distinct expectation in the church that every member is to give to mission. Moreover, an average member is expected to visit a mission field at least once a year, often with his or her family at their own expense and also contribute to missionary work through finances, time or whatever is needed. Any lay leader of the church is also expected to be 'commissioned by the pastor' to be a missionary and to prepare to go as a missionary in the near future. Finally, a belief in the supernatural intervention of the Holy Spirit, particularly in a mission setting, through miracles, divine healing, miraculous provision and protection, fuels their mission activity.

Like Yoido Full Gospel Church in Seoul (see section 2.6 below), Grace Church in the United States employs various forms of worship that contribute to the orientation and reinforcement of the church's mission commitment. They include preaching, prayer, teaching, testimony and intercessory prayers for missionaries and mission fields. Passionate presentations of God's missionary call on individuals and the church have been made by Kim and now his successor Kee-Hong Han. Sacrificial giving to mission projects and to mission support was exemplified by Kim himself when he offered his own personal resources. The church has repeatedly reported that over fifty percent of its gross income has been committed to mission each year, and sometimes over sixty percent. The true picture, however, is not that of planned spending, but that of spontaneous and often emergency contributions toward urgent needs in mission fields. This 'mission without proper plan' demonstrates the church's openness to and preparedness for any surprise development.

Grace Church has a discipleship programme called the Tres Dias. This modified Catholic retreat is intended for participants to experience lavish, genuine Christian love from their hosts, who are mature church members. The programme has been extremely effective for individual conversion and spiritual renewal. This is where, in the context of high Christian commitment, the ultimate calling of God upon his people is presented – the proclamation and sharing of God's love for the lost world. Through this programme, seeds for Christian missionary commitment are planted and this results in an unusually high level of participation in mission.

2.5 Russian Orthodox Church

The Russian Orthodox Church (ROC) provides a particularly interesting example of mission spirituality because, as Orthodox educator Valentin Kozhuharov states, the ROC did not really express an intentional interest in mission as an activity or as a field of study until quite recently.[24]

At the end of the 1980s, as major changes took place within Russia, churches struggled to regain their properties and buildings. Simultaneously, they began to restore their teaching activity, social ministry and worship structures. The Missionary Department of ROC was established at the end of 1995, thus initiating a new, more concentrated stage in ROC missionary practice and missionary theology.

The ROC had not up until this time used the term 'mission' as such but rather understood such activity as ecclesiastical discipline, ecclesiastical tasks and witnessing. In this context mission was understood as forming and strengthening God's people. In 2005 further work was done towards developing an understanding of mission and the document *Concept 2005* states that 'the mission of the Orthodox church aims at the salvation of every human being'.[25] The document affirms 'all the faithful children of the Orthodox church should take the path of Orthodox Christian witnessing'.[26] By 2007, the understanding of mission was further nuanced:

> The Orthodox mission aims at teaching the peoples to be enlightened in the truths of the faith, at educating people to enable them to live a Christ-like life, and mainly at passing on the experience of communion with God through a personal participation of the believers in the sacramental life of the Eucharistic community.[27]

We see here twin emphases on participation in the Eucharist and participation in a healthy Orthodox community as essential parts of mission. Another important aspect of mission for the ROC is the re-evangelization or re-Christianisation of large parts of the Russian territories that lost their faith under Communism. *Concept 2005* (April 2007 version) notes this as a new focus:

> For the last 800 years, the Russian Orthodox Church has never been exposed to the necessity of apostolic preaching on areas and territories where millions of people, through the violence of the atheistic communist regimes of the past decades, have lost their faith and tradition and have acquired other types of culture and history. Now we have faced the paradoxical situation where Russia needs a second Christianisation of the peoples living on the vast Russian territories.[28]

For the ROC, mission is very much focused on their current context of dealing with the legacy of atheistic communism and attracting believers back into the Orthodox Christian community.

The ROC understands mission as enabling people to live a Christ-like life by participating in the eucharistic community. There is no distinction between internal and external mission as mission is about coming closer to the world, sanctifying and renewing it. Ten main 'directions of missionary service' are defined in *Concept 2005:*

1) Missionary service of lay people
2) Missionary commissioning
3) Missionary parish
4) Missionary worship and services
5) Organisation of missionary schools
6) Mobile mission
7) Establishing of missionary camps and stations
8) Mission amongst young people
9) Mission amongst the immigrants in Siberia and Russia's Far East
10) Characteristics and qualities of the modern missionary[29]

More recently the mission of reconciliation has been added to this list.

Special attention is now also being paid to young people in an attempt to attract them back to the church. Mobile mission carried out in the form of missionary pilgrimages by train covering distances of more than 15,000 km to Siberia and Russia's Far East are novel ways of engaging in mission. This involves building and transporting a car-temple – a trailer truck and a temple (or sanctuary) built within. Other forms of mobile mission are missionary camps and field stations, which involve building hundreds of new churches, chapels and educational centres, as well as bringing and leaving priests in Russia's territories in the east. Through this method, thousands have converted to Orthodoxy – including Russians and other ethnic groups.[30]

In 2007 the mission and ministry of lay people was also developed – especially that of women who have four main areas of mission engagement:

1) Founding charitable organisations and bodies to serve those in need
2) Missionary ministry in hospitals
3) Missionary and teaching ministry in social homes, mainly children's homes, nursing homes and boarding schools
4) Missionary ministry in prisons for women[31]

ROC believers need to be nurtured and strengthened through building eucharistic communities to be spread to the ends of the earth. Missionary bishops, missionary priests and missionary lay people all bear responsibility for this.

Perhaps, in addition to the emphasis on being a healthy Christian community, the unique contribution that the ROC offers to the wider Christian community is that Eucharist is the mission of the church and that 'it is this most intimate and holy act of communion with God that makes believers wish the same intimate and holy communion for every human being. Communion means unity.'[32] The Eucharist is understood as the mission of the church as it represents the meeting point of God and his people and as it is an eschatological celebration of the forthcoming kingdom. So real unity is to be found not in ecumenical gatherings, nor even in common actions and witness but in the Eucharist, this eschatological celebration which foreshadows the coming of the kingdom.

For the ROC, their mission engagement is not only practised within a specific community, but it is also sustained by that eucharistic community, supported by catechising and teaching. It also requires love 'towards God and neighbour, and towards all the creation, since the Orthodox affirmation of sanctification of nature through sanctification of man lies in the foundation of the Christian understanding of the salvific mission of Christ.'[33] However, the ROC faces some challenges in her ongoing mission engagement – she needs to interact with the world more and to cooperate with other Christian churches. This would not only enhance her mission but also the mission engagement of other churches as they learn from the ROC approach to mission.

The ROC is aware of the challenges facing it in its missionary task today, including a loss of cultural identity and an increase of socio-economic hardship since the collapse of communism. There is also an attempt to divinise science and intentional 'informational violence' has been expressed against Orthodoxy. An increasing plurality of religions and worldviews also poses a challenge for the ROC.

2.6 Pentecostal church: Korea

The example of Yoido Full Gospel Church (YFGC), Seoul, Korea, the largest single congregation in the world, was studied by Young-hoon Lee, the current senior pastor of the church.[34] The YFGC can be described as 'classical Pentecostal' or denominational Pentecostal. However, the theology and spiritual ethos of David Yonggi Cho, its founder, reveals a contextualized version of classical Pentecostalism.

For the church, evangelism is the foremost form of mission engagement. The growth of the congregation to 750,000 attendees in its fifty-year history attests to the full mobilization of the whole church in sharing Christ's 'good news' at home and beyond. Cho regularly conducts mass evangelistic crusades in many parts of the world. Church growth is also a priority. Cho has been responsible for the birth of more than five hundred churches throughout Korea, some quite large. Yoido's Church Growth International programme has promoted active church growth, which has influenced the increase of large or mega-churches. In addition to evangelism and church growth, there is an emphasis on caring for the needy at home and abroad. The church now operates two international NGOs and is constructing a cardiac hospital in North Korea. Yoido members also engage with various social issues. The most conspicuous platform for this is the *Kukmin Daily Newspaper*, which has a national circulation.

Cho espouses a holistic view of the gospel and Christian mission, encompassing the whole spectrum of human life: physical, material and spiritual. The term 'mission' is used in conjunction with the expansion of God's kingdom, visibly expressed in the presence of local congregations. Several things surface as key elements in Cho's motivation for mission. The first is his encounter with God. His experience on his 'deathbed' resulted in a radical conversion and coincided with healing from a severe case of tuberculosis. This is where his theology of a 'good God' began. The second is human suffering, which formed the context of his life-long ministry. This includes poverty after the Korean War, social disorder, injustice, insufficient health care, and rampant corruption, among other factors. His first congregation represented the marginalized and 'disinherited', who might have otherwise resorted to Shamanism, alcoholism, and social crime. The third is his sense of empowerment through the Holy Spirit. His conversion experience and subsequent theological education orientated him around the empowering work of the Holy Spirit. He often admonishes his congregation to 'receive the baptism in the Holy Spirit' which opens a floodgate of spiritual gifts. This missiology of empowerment has been demonstrated in his use of female lay leaders to organise and lead cell groups.

The growth of the church in number and in influence also motivated the church to expand its missionary engagement. The establishment and maintenance of a national daily newspaper, for instance, requires resources that only a church of this strength can afford.

For Yoido Full Gospel Church, it seems that things commonly known as spiritual disciplines sustain their mission. Worship appears to be the backbone. A church bulletin lists at least twelve worship services per week in the main sanctuary. However, a countless number of group worship services are organised by groups specific in age, gender, vocation, language, and special needs. The centre of worship is preaching. Cho's message can be summed up as a message of hope, as he emphasises God's goodness, although deep spirituality also includes the element of suffering in human life.

Prayer is the most significant spiritual practice of the church, and this is where the church draws most from the traditional spirituality of the Korean church. Fasting prayer, congregational unison prayer and supplication for specific needs are characteristics of the church's prayer life. Every day the church holds an overnight prayer meeting and dawn prayer meetings. Its international fasting prayer mountain is crowded with people who dedicate a period of several days, a week or even forty days for fasting and prayer.

Sharing of narratives is a typical part of Pentecostal tradition. Stories of mission engagement are shared at almost every opportunity in church life: formal worship service, the weekly church newspaper, the monthly magazine, and also through cell group meetings. The transformation of human life through mission engagement is a regular feature of Sunday worship services through a video presentation. The church holds a full-scale weeklong annual mission conference and all of its missionaries participate with their families and sometimes with choirs from various countries. The event not only promotes mission but also provides every member with an opportunity to pledge their monetary contribution to mission. Giving is another unique part of the spirituality of Korean Christianity, and the members of the church have been generous in their sacrificial giving. Unique to the church is that most of the mission funding is generated through individual giving outside of the church's budget.

2.7 Reformed church example

This example is taken from the Youngnak Presbyterian Church, Seoul, Korea, another high-profile Korean church. According to Chul-shin Lee, Senior Pastor of Youngnak Church, Kyung-chik Han, the founder, has been considered as a 'model pastor' of Korea.[35] He was born and grew up during the Japanese occupation of Korea, and his encounter with God's reality includes a miraculous healing of tuberculosis. After studying in the United States, his pastoral ministry began under the careful watch of Japanese authorities and soon he was forced out of ministry. Until liberation, he cared for orphans and widows in North Korea. After liberation, he was subjected to communist persecution, including imprisonment. After he fled to South Korea, he established the Youngnak Church and influenced Korean Christianity in many areas.

Han's vision and that of the church was for the evangelization of the nation. The link between patriotism and Christianity is noteworthy, as both Japanese and Communist authorities viewed Christianity as their ideological enemy. Han viewed Christianity as the answer to the nation's survival and identity. He and the church were responsible for the establishment of over six hundred new congregations. Han initiated several nation-wide evangelistic initiatives such as 'Three Million to Christ' and 'Five Million to Christ' campaigns. Han and the church have had a special interest in evangelism in the military, in which every Korean man is required to serve.

The provision of a good education with a Christian foundation has been the vision of Han and Youngnak Church. They established a number of educational institutions and supported many secondary schools and universities. Many prominent leaders in politics, education, economics, social sectors and Christianity have been graduates of such schools. Currently the church operates nine schools. Scarcity of education for Koreans during the Japanese period and the communist rule must have motivated Han's dedication to education. Han's own education was provided by dedicated Christians who also shared a passion for the nation. This later developed into the notion that a good Christian should have a good love of nation.

Social service is another area of the church's mission engagement. Care for the neglected began in the early days of Han's ministry in North Korea. The church established facilities for orphans, the disabled, widows and the elderly. The mission mandate has been understood by the church to include the demonstration of God's love, in addition to the proclamation of the good news. Further, restoration of social and church life in North Korea has been unique in the Youngnak's mission. Han, himself a North Korean refugee, attracted similar refugees to begin his church. Naturally, the church has had a deep commitment to the restoration of Christianity in North Korea, where it has been suppressed by the communist regime. Han, the recipient of the 1992 Templeton Freedom Award, donated the award fund to the church's North Korean mission. Since then, various mission initiatives have been used to bring the gospel and God's love to North Korea, including relief and welfare projects. Currently the church operates a large ministry to recent North Korean refugees to assist them to settle in the South Korean social environment.

What has been observed of the mission discipleship in Yoido Full Gospel Church is also found at the Youngnak Church. Yet another ministry should be noted and that is its commitment to pray for the divided nation with families separated by fortified borders. This focused prayer indicates that the hope of reunification may be a sustaining force. The gradual disappearance of the generation who experienced war has brought a new urgency to see the divided nation united.

2.8 Roman Catholic Church in Asia

'Expressions like "mission, evangelization, and conversion" so vital to the Christian faith, are greatly misunderstood in many Asian countries (like India),' according to Executive Secretary for the Office of Ecumenical and Intereligious Affairs for Federation of Asian Bishops' Conferences, Sister Clemens Mendoca, working in Pune.[36] One way of approaching mission in India is to engage in a 'triple dialogue'[37] with the poor, people of other religions as well as people from all walks of life. In India, harmony is considered to be a core value and this triple dialogue calls for the church to 'stretch our capacities for relationships that are more inclusive'.[38]

The Roman Catholic Church in Asia tries to listen actively to its context and also recommends a four-pronged dialogue. Subjects for dialogue include life (living together as neighbours), action (collaborating with others), experience/testimony (sharing of spiritual riches) and theological exchange (deepening an understanding of respective religious heritages). The Roman Catholic Church in Asia sees mission as striving towards the fullness of life and the intent of this mission of dialogue is to lead to greater understanding along the path of love. Mendoca reports that listening and receiving leads to a deeper relationship and a 'civilisation of love'.[39] She acknowledges that for the wider church to take this dialogue approach would require a paradigm shift that many would not be eager to undertake.

Rather than attempting to follow in the footsteps of Western mission, the Roman Catholic Church in Asia is learning to re-read Scripture in their own context. They have discovered that Western creedal formulae are for the most part meaningless in their context and that more work needs to be done to make Jesus relevant so that their mission engagement can be sustained.

3 What Motivates and Sustains Mission? Regional and Collaborative Insights

3.1 Indian indigenous Christianity

David Emmanuel Singh, Research Tutor of OCMS, asserts that approaches to mission in India must become more suited to the cultural context. He turns to the spirituality of Sadhu Sunder Singh and Narayana Vamana Tilak to bring to light fresh paradigms by which to consider mission spirituality and discipleship.[40] Singh argues persuasively that it is only by looking at the great diversity of India's rich spiritual tradition that mission and discipleship can break out of the spiritual and missiological confines that have limited Christian witness to only certain castes and worldviews. He turns to these two critical converts to Christianity whose embrace of the rich spiritual traditions of India could, if tapped, energize and transform mission today. Were mission to embrace the 'direct, personal, devotional and sacrificial faith focused on the living guru-sanyasi 'teacher-renouncer' Jesus'[41] emulated by Sadhu Singh and Narayana Tilak, Singh argues that Christian mission could begin to shed its Western vestments and present itself transformed in a manner receptive and conducive to Indian spiritual traditions, devotion and desire.

For Sadhu Singh and Tilak, it was the 'direct experience of Jesus' that transformed not only the life of the disciples, but their own lives. It was this direct 'experience' of the risen Jesus which was the warp and woof of their spirituality that in turn shaped how they viewed discipleship. Both Sadhu Singh and Tilak had a spiritual encounter that they describe as a vision that utterly changed their lives. The result was that they literally became followers of the guru Jesus. In their view, through spiritual vision the Transcendent God was able to relate with his creatures through Jesus. Moreover this spiritual experience of Jesus was in turn mediated through parental modes of relation. Thus, Jesus as father required the 'need to maintain reverence' whereas 'Jesus as the mother' fulfilled their deepest aspiration for actual friendship, intimacy, and loving communion.[42] Accordingly, Singh argues that emphases upon experiential encounter, familial imagery and spiritual intimacy lead to a view of mission and discipleship that is needed to 'tone down the polemical approach that characterised much of... missionary work up until now'. Thus, mission spirituality and discipleship would be seen as 'the path of devotion to Jesus' as opposed to the establishment of Christian churches and institutions or polemical debates surrounding Scripture and the nature of God.

David Singh laments that the examples of Sadhu Sunder Singh and Narayana Vamana Tilak have not done more to motivate mission or define its mandate. Indeed, Singh argues that, given these early examples, Indian Christians ought to walk in their path and adopt their attitude and engagement with Indian society so that missions, Christians and the church might become more attractive to the great diversity of Indian ethnic people groups of various religious backgrounds. By moving from an institutional and polemical model of Christianity and Christian mission to one that is based on discipleship and enlightenment while engaging people personally, devotionally and sacrificially, Singh believes that a mission more reflective and formed by the Indian context could be realised.

David Singh argues for a mission spirituality and discipleship that was once embodied in the life and witness of Sadhu Sunder Singh and Narayana Vamana Tilak, but has since been neglected much to the detriment of mission reflection and practice in India. Were this to be embraced it would represent a definite shift in missional thought, word and deed in India itself. Further, it would probably run into severe tension as it calls into question the established church in North and South India which might feel threatened by approaches that question the roots of their own faith, mission work, institutions and theological convictions. Nonetheless, as Singh points out, without change, Christianity in

India will be stuck in the same narrow channels and not be able to begin to reach out in ways that resonate with traditional Indian perspectives of spirituality and discipleship.

3.2 Korean spirituality

One study that Group 9 received was dedicated to taking a close look at Korean Christianity as an example of an emerging missionary church or spirituality within the global South. The growth of Christianity and mission engagement in Korea in recent years is certainly remarkable. Shin Ahn, professor of religious studies at Seoul National University, has provided further insight into the relationship between Korean spirituality, social engagement and Christian mission in his paper 'Korean Spirituality: Christian Presence among World Religions'.[43]

Ahn maintains that the unique alchemy of Korean Confucianism and Shamanism has given rise to a mission spirituality and discipleship that transcends the borders of 'religion' proper. Given its emphasis on a moral and social righteousness founded upon essential relationships, Korea's Confucian moorings provided the framework for Christian emphases on social justice and liberation while the spiritual emphasis of Shamanism has served as a precursor to a Christian spirituality deeply connected with the harmony of body, mind and spirit. [44] Thus, for Ahn mission spirituality and discipleship in Korean Christianity draw deeply from the philosophical and spiritual roots of Korean culture.

For Ahn, the nature of mission lies in its appeal to the spiritual and philosophical concerns that arise out of Confucianism and Shamanism. Thus, from a Confucian standpoint, Christian mission has had significant impact in Korea due to its engagement with the cultivation of virtue through moral education along with its concern for social righteousness particularly in terms of liberation and social justice. This embrace, however, is not without complication. As Ahn notes, given that Confucianism recognises no distinction between moral education, social justice, citizenship and identity, Christians have often sought to impose a Christian worldview and faith upon a society where they still represent a minority of the population, even if active and powerful. Nonetheless, Ahn notes that Koreans are appreciative that for Christianity authentic discipleship includes an emphasis upon human political liberation as well as a willingness to share in and help relieve those suffering hardship and injustice. This owes much to a spirituality that seeks to cultivate moral and ethical character both individually and socially. For Ahn, this is complemented by Christian spirituality that has the power to bring about wholeness, healing and personal transformation. This spirituality not only brings harmony to body, mind and spirit, it is turned to as sign and seal of the visible blessing of material and economic well-being. Thus, mission spirituality in the Korean context has its physical and tangible expression in healing power as well as material and economic development, all of which are seen as blessing bestowed by the power of the Holy Spirit.

Ahn holds that the concern for liberation, moral and ethical individuals and society motivates Christian Korean mission. In turn these goals are energized and informed by traditional Korean spirituality, and this has now taken on Korean forms such as dawn prayer and praying from spiritually discerned prayer mountains. This has served as well to define the holistic and transformational mandate of Korean missions that hold together concern for education, democracy, human rights, moral and ethical individuals and society as well as political and spiritual liberation. At the same time, Koreans have been spiritually formed by their unique forms of prayer, devotion and discipline.

No one can doubt the impact of Korean mission activity globally. Ahn's essay provides insight into the sort of implications the Korean experience and view of mission will have as mission enters a new century. Certainly the spiritual emphasis on prayer, healing, and social and ethical transformation resonate with trends within global Christianity and the mission work of Christians outside the West. Although missionaries arising out of more staid and traditional understandings of mission spirituality and discipleship will find some of these aspects disturbing, nonetheless, Korean emphasis upon holism and ministry resonates with Christians in the 'majority world' who share their concern for holistic transformation.

In conversation at the consultation held in Seoul, Shin Ahn pointed out that, following the explosive growth of the megachurch movement, there has been a subsequent diminishing of Sunday school attendance. Adding to that, he said that young Korean Christians now see Christian education as oppressive, whereas for the previous generation, Christianity was a liberator. He cited as a further challenge the relatively low number of ordained women. Korean Christians, he said, also face the challenge of migration; there are an estimated one million foreign workers in South Korea. Speaking candidly, he further noted that atheism is on the rise and that there is some inter-denominational tension.

3.3 Philippine and Mexican Christian spirituality and culture

For each of the contexts that we have explored, there are other places and situations that would resonate with the thoughts expressed. For example, like India, the Philippines has never seen Christianity flourish the way it has elsewhere. Some have stated that this is partly because Western missionaries had no fundamental understanding of the fatalistic *bahala na* worldview espoused by Filipinos. Filipino missiologist Tereso Casino has suggested that perhaps a parallel can be drawn between *bahala na* and 'Thy will be done.'[45] This is just one example.

Similarly linking spirituality and culture, regarding the aboriginal church in Mexico, Mario Perez Perez proposes a renewed profile of the priest as disciple-missionary, who draws from and is nurtured by all the richness of his indigenous ancestral culture as well as Christian tradition. [46] These two examples call upon Christians in mission to consider, and embrace the existing spiritualities already inherent within a culture and in a sense, to recognize that God is already at work within these cultural contexts.

3.4 Ecumenical spirituality

The Commission on World Mission and Evangelism of the World Council of Churches contributed a paper on 'Mission Spirituality and Discipleship' prepared by their working group on Transformative Spirituality and Mission.[47] They point out the importance of the disciple's authentic gospel lifestyle as we traverse as pilgrims and migrants through the mission landscapes of these troubled times.

The reflections start by acknowledging the ways in which contemporary borders, boundaries and barriers shape our life in mission and discipleship today. Then the group take a biblical approach, turning to Acts 10 to understand how the early church dealt with the issue of borders, and how their encounter with each other in the Spirit led them to cross over various barriers in order to move into a new spirit of reconciliation. Then the group addresses how the church, as a pilgrim people or a migrant in this world, is called to overcome contemporary barriers. Finally, the reflections look at how we travel as authentic disciples and identify elements of a healthy spirituality, one that can help us cross over the barriers of our contemporary world in order to become a church which participates in God's transforming mission at the borderlands.

In its conclusion, the reflection affirms that the world in 2010 looks different to the world in 1910, but still it is a world characterized by borders, barriers and boundaries, a world rich in diversity and yet filled with inequalities. We can rejoice, like Peter, that God has a transformative encounter in store for us as individual disciples and for the church if we are willing to step outside our comfort zones. In the story from Acts we see that transformation takes place when we meet each other at the boundary and cross over the borders that humanity has turned into barriers. The metaphor of the church as a migrant calls the church to participate in God's mission by travelling to the borderlines. And how should we, as part of the church, walk on this journey to the borderlines as authentic disciples? What can sustain us in difficult times? It is the vision that this is precisely Christ's way and when we cross over to this way we will meet him and be sustained by him to be bridges and blessing amongst our neighbours. In the 'crossing over' we meet each other and a bridge is built; the impenetrable spot is penetrated and we too, like Peter and Cornelius, can experience in 2010 a spiritual transformation made possible by the transforming power of God's Holy Spirit.

4 Conclusions and Recommendations

As we see it, Edinburgh 2010 calls us to celebrate what God has done and is doing in global mission, to admit to mistakes that have been made, and to look to the future.

For Western mission thinkers and practitioners, it may be tempting to look at developments such as the Back to Jerusalem movement or the mega-church movement in Korea, and advise, 'Do as we say, not as we've done.' And yet, the Western church has by no means 'arrived' in terms of determining what motivates and sustains mission. We must continue to work together globally, to listen and receive from each other.

At this point in mission history, it is probably a given that what is called for in our time is a mission spirituality that recognises that God is already working, has been working within all cultures, revealing Godself. And yet, having observed recent mission history in Asia and Africa, it becomes necessary to reiterate this point. If we officially recognised and articulated this years ago, we could have perhaps made greater strides toward effective mission in places like India and the Philippines, for example.

As we strive toward a mission spirituality that embraces the contributions of a diversity of cultural spiritualities, we have seen that some of our terms may need to change. Instead of discipleship, we may, as the Orthodox do, need to talk about a path to holiness or a path of devotion, as Indian spirituality espouses. Instead of mission, we may need to speak of a path of love, of dialogue or of ecclesiastical or community duty.

Regardless of what we call it, we have certainly seen that authentic discipleship is crucial to sustain effective mission. Mission spirituality cannot exist without authentic discipleship--a discipleship, a path, that specifically addresses mission and that necessitates mission as an integral part of the path.

What should an authentic discipleship path look like? What sort of spirituality will it embrace? This will of course in some ways vary from culture to culture, and yet, we can glean some seeds of commonality. We have seen that discipleship should be holistic. Categories (sacred and secular, physical and spiritual, religious and ordinary) and compartmentalizing do not seem to work in the long term; they do not make for sustainable mission. To speak about spirituality is to speak about living a life oriented toward the fulfilment of God's purposes for all creation. Rene Padilla has made the following point:

> Christian spirituality is a gift and a task. It requires communion with God (contemplation) as well as action in the world (praxis). When these two elements are separated, both the life and the mission of the church are deeply affected. Contemplation without action is an escape from concrete reality; action without contemplation is activism lacking a transcendent meaning. True spirituality requires a missionary contemplation and a contemplative mission.[48]

Alongside this we recognise and make the distinction that mission is for everyone; authentic missional discipleship cannot exist without acknowledging this as fundamental. Christian spirituality is mission spirituality.

We commend a discipleship that embraces diverse Christian spiritual practices, not merely tolerating but actively seeking to understand and incorporate them. We call for a renewed discipleship that expects the unexpected in a spirit of humility and reconciliation. We have seen over and over, since the early church, that God's Holy Spirit is actively involved in reconciliation and bringing nations, tribes and cultures together. At the same time, this spirituality should be Christ-centred and biblically grounded.

With all these worldviews working together, we must of course practice discernment. Therefore we must embark on a path of discipleship that calls us to be inclusive, yet authentic with each other. In a world that is aware of the temptation of corruption, we need to be accountable and transparent with each other. We must commit to a discipleship that recognises that God is fundamentally concerned with 'the least of these'. This kind of discipleship most certainly has personal and community dimensions. This is not a path to be walked alone by oneself, or even in just one set-apart community. It crosses the boundaries in today's world.

If this sounds too idealistic, then perhaps our ears are too jaded. Or perhaps we are not teaching the values of reconciliation, accountability and transparency early enough. Scott Todd, senior ministry advisor at Compassion International, has suggested that we be more proactive with cultivating mission spirituality and discipleship in children and young people. With regard to spirituality, Todd points out that Jesus himself held that those who follow him must become like children.[49] Perhaps, if we followed his advice, we would see a more sustainable mission for the future, particularly in countries like DR Congo, where youth comprise a majority of the population.[50]

Regardless of whether we are talking about children or adults, new followers of Jesus or seasoned Christians, it is becoming increasingly clear that there is much to learn with respect to mission spirituality and authentic discipleship. No matter who we are, our vision needs to be broadened. Hindsight may be 2010, but as long as we continue to listen to the voices of God's children from all over the globe, the future may become ever clearer as well.

Endnotes

[1] From 'Anglican Communion Official Website', www.anglicancommunion.org/ministry/mission/events/edinburgh_2010/index.cfm.

[2] Kirsteen Kim, 'Mission Spirituality', *Religion in Geschichte und Gegenwart* 4th edn (Tübingen: Mohr Siebeck, 2007).

[3] C. Rene Padilla. 'Spirituality in the Life and Mission of the Church' (2009), paper submitted to Edinburgh 2010 Study Group 9.

[4] David J. Bosch, *A Spirituality of the Road* (Eugene, OR: Wipf & Stock, 2001).
[5] Gustavo Gutiérrez, *We Drink from Our Own Wells: The Spiritual Journey of a People* (20th Anniversary edition; Maryknoll, NY: Orbis Books, 2003).
[6] Samuel Rayan, *Come, Holy Spirit* (Delhi: Media House, 1998); *Renew the Face of the Earth* (Delhi: Media House, 1998).
[7] Christopher Duraisingh, 'Encountering Difference in a Plural World: A Pentecost Paradigm for Mission', in Ian T. Douglas (ed.), *Waging Reconciliation: God's Mission in a Time of Globalization and Crisis* (New York: Church Publishing, 2002), 171-212.
[8] Juan Esquerda Bifet, *Spirituality for a Missionary Church* (Rome: Urbania University Press, 1994), 47-49, 54-56.
[9] Padilla, 'Spirituality in the Life and Mission of the Church', 3.
[10] Nicta Lubaale Makiika, 'Doing Mission at the Margins of Society: Harnessing the Resources of Local Visions', in Wonsuk Ma & Cathy Ross (eds), *Mission Spirituality and Authentic Discipleship* (Seoul, 2009), 37-44, at 38. Available at www.edinburgh2010.org
[11] Makiika, 'Doing Mission at the Margins of Society, 37.
[12] Makiika, 'Doing Mission at the Margins of Society, 40.
[13] Makiika, 'Doing Mission at the Margins of Society, 43.
[14] Makiika, 'Doing Mission at the Margins of Society, 43.
[15] Makiika, 'Doing Mission at the Margins of Society, 41.
[16] Kim-kwong Chan. 'Mission Movement of the Christian Community in Mainland China: The Back to Jerusalem Movement', in Wonsuk Ma & Cathy Ross (eds), *Mission Spirituality and Authentic Discipleship* (Seoul, 2009), 67-82. Available at www.edinburgh2010.org.
[17] Chan. 'Mission Movement of the Christian Community in Mainland China', 75.
[18] Chan. 'Mission Movement of the Christian Community in Mainland China', 78.
[19] Serah Wambua, 'Mission Spirituality and Authentic Discipleship: An African Reflection', in Wonsuk Ma & Cathy Ross (eds), *Mission Spirituality and Authentic Discipleship* (Seoul, 2009), 45-54, at 49. Available at www.edinburgh2010.org
[20] Wambua, 'Mission Spirituality and Authentic Discipleship', 48.
[21] Wambua, 'Mission Spirituality and Authentic Discipleship', 49.
[22] Wambua, 'Mission Spirituality and Authentic Discipleship', 51.
[23] Wonsuk Ma, 'Grace Korean Church: Mission from a New Margin' (2009), paper submitted to Edinburgh 2010 Study Group 9.
[24] Valentin Kozhuharov, 'Mission in an Orthodox Christian Context: Witnessing Christ as Pastoral Responsibility', in Wonsuk Ma & Cathy Ross (eds), *Mission Spirituality and Authentic Discipleship* (Seoul, 2009), 15-26. Available at www.edinburgh2010.org.
[25] Kozhuharov, 'Mission in an Orthodox Christian Context', 17. *Concept 2005* is the shortened title for *Concept of the Missionary Activity of the ROC for 2005-2010*.
[26] Kozhuharov, 'Mission in an Orthodox Christian Context', 17.
[27] Kozhuharov, 'Mission in an Orthodox Christian Context', 20.
[28] Kozhuharov, 'Mission in an Orthodox Christian Context', 23.
[29] Kozhuharov, 'Mission in an Orthodox Christian Context', 18.
[30] Kozhuharov, 'Mission in an Orthodox Christian Context', 25, footnote 12.
[31] Kozhuharov, 'Mission in an Orthodox Christian Context', 23.
[32] Kozhuharov, 'Mission in an Orthodox Christian Context', 24.
[33] Kozhuharov, 'Mission in an Orthodox Christian Context', 24.

[34] Young-hoon Lee, 'The Spirit and Mission: Mission Engagements of the Yoido Full Gospel Church'(2009), paper submitted to Edinburgh 2010 Study Group 9, available at www.edinburgh2010.org.
[35] Chul-shin Lee, 'Spirituality and Christian Mission: The Journey of Youngnak Presbyterian Church, Seoul, Korea', in Wonsuk Ma & Cathy Ross (eds), *Mission Spirituality and Authentic Discipleship* (Seoul, 2009), 97-101. Available at www.edinburgh2010.org.
[36] Clemens Mendoca, 'Mission According to the Catholic Church in Asia: A New Way of Being Church', in Wonsuk Ma & Cathy Ross (eds), *Mission Spirituality and Authentic Discipleship* (Seoul, 2009), 27-36, at 28. Available at www.edinburgh2010.org.
[37] Mendoca, 'Mission According to the Catholic Church in Asia', 5.
[38] Mendoca, 'Mission According to the Catholic Church in Asia', 5.
[39] Mendoca, 'Mission According to the Catholic Church in Asia', 4.
[40] David Emmanuel Singh. 'Sadhu Sunder Singh and Narayana Vamana Tilak: Some Lessons for Mission Thinking/Practice in India', in Wonsuk Ma & Cathy Ross (eds), *Mission Spirituality and Authentic Discipleship* (Seoul, 2009), 55-66. Available at www.edinburgh2010.org.
[41] Singh. 'Sadhu Sunder Singh and Narayana Vamana Tilak', 57.
[42] Singh. 'Sadhu Sunder Singh and Narayana Vamana Tilak', 59.
[43] Shin Ahn, 'Korean Spirituality: Christian Presence Among World Religions' (2009), 1. Paper submitted to Edinburgh 2010 Study Group 9, available at www.edinburgh2010.org.
[44] Ahn, 'Korean Spirituality'.
[45] Tereso C. Casino. 'Mission in the Context of Filipino Folk Spirituality: *Bahala na* as a Case in Point', in Wonsuk Ma & Cathy Ross (eds), *Mission Spirituality and Authentic Discipleship* (Seoul, 2009), 83-96, at 85. Available at www.edinburgh2010.org.
[46] Mario Perez Perez, 'The Indigenous Priest in the Aboriginal Church'(2009), paper submitted to Edinburgh 2010 Study Group 9, available at www.edinburgh2010.org.
[47] World Council of Churches, Commission for World Mission and Evangelism, 'Mission Spirituality and Discipleship: Beyond and Through Contemporary Boundaries', paper prepared by the Working Group on Transformative Spirituality and Mission to contribute to the Edinburgh 2009 study process and available at www.edinburgh2010.org. The paper was based on the reflections of two meetings of the group in Manila in 2008 and in Geneva in 2009.
[48] Padilla, 'Spirituality in the Life and Mission of the Church', 1.
[49] Scott C. Todd. 'Spiritual Formation and Discipleship in Childhood', in Wonsuk Ma & Cathy Ross (eds), *Mission Spirituality and Authentic Discipleship* (Seoul, 2009), 103-116. Available at www.edinburgh2010.org.
[50] Rosauro Lopez, from Cochabamba, also asserts this in 'A Mission for and from the Youth' (2009), paper submitted to Edinburgh 2010 Study Group 9, available at www.edinburgh2010.org. This reflective paper proposes to consider youth not as receivers of mission but as missionary agents, challenging current church procedures and structures.

TRANSVERSALS

WOMEN AND MISSION, BIBLE AND MISSION

In addition to the nine study themes, seven transversal topics were defined by the International Council in 2005-2006. These are:

1) Women and mission
2) Youth and mission
3) Healing and reconciliation
4) Bible and mission – mission in the Bible
5) Contextualization, inculturation and dialogue of worldviews
6) Subaltern voices
7) Ecological perspectives on mission

The transversals are important themes which are intended to run like a thread across all the main study themes offering complementary and critical perspectives. The transversals were not developed by means of core groups as were the main study themes but a number of different bodies have come forward wishing to contribute the them. Representatives of many of these are invited to give input at the conference. Two bodies have submitted short papers on particular themes for this publication – 1 Women and Mission and 4 Bible and Mission – and these are included here.

1 'Who Is Not at the Table?'
Women's Perspectives of Holistic Mission as Mutually Inclusive·

Lord, yet even the dogs eat crumbs that fall from their masters' table (Matt 15:27).

1.1 Introduction

In attempting to provide a women's perspective on mission as a transversal for the Edinburgh 2010 publication, this article uses an ecofeminist theological approach to explore how, through three selected women's consultations on mission (1992, 2003, 2008), women view mission and Christian spirituality as a response to God's mission. This is done by firstly, raising the still existing realities of women's exclusion from and their suggestions for the churches' understanding of mission in two women's mission consultations (1992, 2003). Exclusion of women is used here in relative terms of evaluating the involvement of women at different levels of leadership and decision-making processes of churches in general against the usually higher women's church membership numbers in comparison to that of men, who nevertheless are an

· Compiled and edited by Dr Fulata L. Moyo, World Council of Churches Programme Executive for Women in Church and Society and current Coordinator of the inter-faith Circle of Concerned African Women Theologians (www.thecirclecawt.org).

overall majority in leadership positions and decision-making processes. Compared to the state of women's exclusion towards the 1910 mission conference, we can celebrate more inclusion in this twenty-first century, and some churches can celebrate even more inclusion than others. However, when we compare the great numbers of women in church membership versus their position in leadership and decision-making processes, we can still talk in terms of women's exclusion in that manner.[1]

Secondly, it is done by sharing some aspects of mission that came from a contextual bible study of the above biblical story from the last women's consultation on mission (2008). The weaving of the women's voice and vision through these three meetings is done from a personal perspective using the 'beads and thread' of the compiler/editor's African experience of the Christian missionary enterprise that mainly 'missionised' us into a Christianity that was clad in Western culture. For us to be both African and Christian at the same time without suffering any identity crisis, we now have to go through processes of inculturation (mutual dialogue) of the Christian gospel and African culture for a more meaningful and holistic spirituality. Since this topic is only a transversal topic for Edinburgh 2010, and not a main theme, engagement with the topic in this article is limited to the topic of exclusion and does not include critique of ecofeminist theological theory.

1.2 Who is at the table?

Part of the Anglican prayer of humble access, in memory of the Syrophoenician woman who challenged Jesus for her inclusion, says:

> We do not presume to come to this your table merciful Lord, trusting in our own righteousness, but in your manifold and great mercies. We are not worthy so much as to gather the crumbs under your table. But you are the same Lord whose nature is always to have mercy.[2]

As God's people, who adhere to the Christian faith, our sense of being acceptable before God does not depend on what we have merited. It is rather based on God's gratuitous mercy expressed through God's self-giving mission in Jesus, the human-God: It is the sharing of his life of love, humility and sacrifice so as to bring fullness of life – the restoration of right relationship with God, within the human race, whatever our differences, as well as with the rest of creation. Inspired and challenged by God's Spirit and self-giving, the Church responds by embarking on a journey of living God's love and seeking ways of sharing it with others as its mission. This exploration of being and living as the expression of God's love, modelled after Jesus' radical pursuit for holistic transformation of his community and inspired by the Holy Spirit, can be understood as Christian spirituality.

An ecofeminist perspective puts forward the women's struggle for a transformed community, where there is fairness and mutual inclusion of all:

men, women of all ages, abilities, races, classes and whatever else distinguishes them from the others, and also with the rest of creation as ecology.[3] This advocacy and praxis for the process of transformation of the whole community is rooted in the acknowledgement of the reality of the connectedness of oppression that usually the feminine principles in society suffer. This ecofeminist quest for transformation, therefore, is also a quest to acknowledge the intrinsic connectedness between sexuality and spirituality especially in women's experiences as bodied-beings.

As an attempt to reclaim the feminine as an important part of being *imago Dei* (the image of God), ecofeminist spirituality acknowledges the reality of women's holistic being as embodied, interconnected and interdependent with each other as well as with the rest of creation, the living *Adama*.[4] Embodied spirituality is, therefore, conceived in Elizabeth S. Tapia's (2006) definition,[5] as a lived experience in contemplation and praxis of being interconnected and interdependent, challenged to contribute to the balance, blossoming, the healing and wholeness of the life of the human race, and of the rest of creation, inspired and embraced by God's Spirit. The ecofeminist affirmation of spirituality for transformation provides the tracing thread through the issues of concern raised by the two women-in-mission consultations and also the choice of contextual bible study as a theological resource and methodology that helps facilitate a process of reflection and action for transformation in mission.

1.3 Mission as working with

At the meeting of women-in-mission in 1992,[6] the criteria for the evaluation of mission priorities, in keeping with stage in the life of the conciliar ecumenical movement, were primarily about helping Christians make God's option for the poor, defenceless, abused, forgotten and the bored. This included the question of whether they help the Christians to empathise with the concerns of others, accept their issues and their structures as vehicles of involvement, and the wider question of whether particular situations are the best for facilitating processes of discernment with others of the signs of the times, and moving with history towards the fulfilment of the new humanity.

The general androgynous perspective taken by the churches seems to forget to include the women's experiences of exclusion as an unfortunate reality that puts them (women) and their experiences at the centre of those to be prioritised by all the three criteria above. This was affirmed by sentiments articulated by Mercy Amba Oduyoye, the then deputy general secretary of WCC. She made the following observation as articulating women's insights about mission: 'Traditional imperialistic and colonial models have little appeal to women, so whether they travel from Canada to work with Africans in Africa or stay in Egypt to work with garbage collectors in Cairo, the approach is working with rather than working for.'[7]

Looking at the impact of the Western missionary enterprise among the Chewa women in central Malawi, Isabel Phiri argues that before the coming of

Dutch Reformed Church missionaries in the 1870s, the matrilineal system gave greater freedom and dignity, 'essential elements of personhood'[8] to women, which were diminished by the influence of Christian settlers. The missionaries who came to 'evangelize' (doing mission *to*) the Chewa imposed certain aspects of their Western culture with a biased understanding that the existing African indigenous cultural practices were a necessarily evil and therefore they needed to be transformed by replacing them with their Western beliefs and practices. These included the Western patrilineal family systems and their biases towards male church leadership. This was contrary to the matrilineal Chewa people's realities where women exerted considerable influence as priestesses and prophetesses in their community through initiation rites as well as rainmaking shrines.

According to the 1992 women-in-mission consultation, mission has to be a communication of love in action. Influenced by their reflection on the story of Peter and Cornelius (Acts 10), women agreed that mission should be guided by mutuality and should be allowed to make a positive impact on all involved. As working *with*, the mission of the churches should be 'set in motion where one is or in collaboration with people where one goes'.[9] They concluded by spelling out three aspects stressed by women's approaches to mission. These were: partnership, interdependence and solidarity. They affirmed the fact that women see their involvement in mission as God's will, which is different from the will of the human authorities that rule the churches. Like everyone else involved in mission, they are commissioned by the Holy Spirit.

The three aspects they raise can be emphasised as still relevant in today's search for transformative mission. We still need to work with each other in partnership, as interdependent on each other, journeying in solidarity with each other. This consultation, however, did not explore sufficiently the still-existing models of mission involvement that have been attributed to women according the gender roles accepted by the churches. The women-in-mission consultation in 2004 built on the above raised issues but also explored the meaning of mission within the reality of diversity.

1.4 Mission in diverse historicity: the challenge for contextualization

At the 2003 consultation,[10] women recognised the diverse contextual understanding of mission as expressed through their different ecclesiologies. Acknowledging the rich and wide spectrum of ministries in which women are engaged, they also pointed out that much of women's involvement in mission is as a gift of love, given in a voluntary capacity. Sometimes all this voluntarism goes without even being recognised by the church authorities. Women still carry out their labour of love as an expression of their spirituality, knowing that it is their deep response to a God who accepts them and values their significant contribution in working towards transformative communities.

Aruna Gnanadason summaries major questions this consultation wrestled with into the following two: (i) Within the context of globalization with its homogenising tendency, how can the integrity of the particularity of the diverse traditions and their understanding of mission be maintained? (ii) How can the healing and reconciliation role of the Church be defined amidst different expressions of violence against women, children and other minority groups?[11] There was a call to women to find new ways of reconciling themselves with their past histories but then to move into new realms of reflection in response to the new and existing challenges. In Musa Dube's words: 'We must always insist on new spaces for cultivating new contextual and international readings and writings, which are both decolonising and depatriarchising'.[12]

Digging into the historical missionary enterprise, these women raised concerns regarding how certain tasks were relegated to women, which sometimes seemed to be extensions of 'house-wifely' roles. Such roles usually belong to the private and are therefore not usually appreciated. Unfortunately, when it comes to the women's experiences of church and mission, this is still the existing concern in this twenty-first century. There is still a need to raise gender awareness for a more just and inclusive mission.

1.5 Using the CBS methodology for transforming and inclusive mission

The third consultation (2008) was on women's perspectives on mission and theological education.[13] It gathered twenty-eight women from the eight regions of the World Council of Churches. They came from twenty-two denominations, including Orthodox, Catholic and Protestant, and included indigenous women, young women, sexual minorities, and women with disability. The consultation used the Contextual Bible Study (CBS) methodology so as to ground each day's reflections in the Bible as an important source of mission and spirituality.

The Contextual Bible Study as a methodology allows for the process of 'see', 'judge' and 'act'. It is a brainchild of liberation theology. It is a community-based process of awareness raising, sometimes using biblical texts that are difficult to deal with, and leading to transformation. It is an interactive study of the biblical texts where the context of the reader and the context of the Bible get into a dialogue guided by the questions asked by the facilitator, in order to raise awareness for transformation in a particular area of concern within the community that has requested for such a process. To ensure that the process of praxis for transformation takes place, the last questions always call for participants to develop action plans. The questions asked are usually: What will you do now in response to this bible study? Are there available resources to do what you want to do?

This enriching process of CBS at the 2008 consultation was facilitated and developed by Sarojini Nadar,[14] and the following section is based on that process. According the CBS of Mark 7:24-30 (cf. Matt 15:21-28), the following five theological aspects of mission came out. The negative aspects call for transformation, while the positive ones continue enhancing the Christian spirituality towards fullness of life.

(i) Mission as holistic development: bread and healing

Women affirmed that food is a basic need that provides security through nourishment. Its benefits go beyond the physical to the intellectual and the spiritual, in that having education on an empty stomach is not very rewarding and unless one is voluntarily fasting, spirituality with an empty stomach does not really evoke much genuine praise to God. Jesus' equating healing and food is deeply indicative of the fact that it is basic to human development and therefore holistic mission has to be inclusive of these two, apart from other equally important aspects. We have to rethink mission holistically as not just physical sustenance but also as holistic healing and wholeness, and vice-versa.

(ii) Mission as crumbs or abundance? Questions of justice and human dignity

By responding, 'Sir, even the dogs under the table eat the children's crumbs' one could argue that the Syro-Phoenican woman was buying into her own oppression. Or was she subtly using his expression of an existing bias so as to challenge Jesus towards his own transformation? Coming to today's realities, there are still a significant number of women trying to understand the meaning of the churches' mission wondering at who deserves bread and who can only get crumbs between men and women.

With the impact of neo-liberal economic globalization, all some people end up getting is crumbs. For example, while in the more affluent contexts in the North, HIV and AIDS has become a chronic disease with the availability of good health care and medical treatment, in the global South, especially in the Sub-Saharan Africa, less than ten percent of those who are HIV positive can access medical treatment. For the majority being HIV positive means a death sentence; needless to say that the majority of these are women. In the Sub-Saharan Africa, where rates of infection are highest,[15] a majority of these women are married women whose marriage certificates have become their death certificates as victims of their husbands' irresponsible and sinful involvement with multiple sexual partners. Increasing numbers of women from the global South are trapped as victims of human trafficking in their desperate search for a better-than-survival life.

When we explore women's participation in the ministries of the church, it seems that there are times when crumbs are enough. We can even ask whether the theology of survival is the only theology we can muster up in terms of mission. Is valourizing survival a way to ease our consciousness? We need to re-evaluate whether food as development is simply for survival or for fullness of life (John 10:10).

(iii) Mission as an exclusive enterprise

Going back to the Anglican prayer, the many Christians who use that prayer sometimes have no capacity to connect it to their own experiences in response to women, people of different races, differing sexual orientation, foreigners, or people with disability, just to mention a few. The Syro-Phoenician woman's experience shows how intrinsically oppression by sexism is linked to racism, classism, religious exclusion and all the other related *isms* we can think of.

According to an affirmation of Faith and Order study document, all human beings are created in God's image and Jesus Christ is the perfect realisation of true humanity. Yet 'sin denies the worth and dignity of human beings, disrupts community and hampers the flow of love and justice. Sin must be faced, confessed, forgiven and healed'.[16] Women-in-mission, therefore, challenges us to acknowledge our ecclesiological practices of exclusion as sin, confess and repent, and accept God's forgiveness and healing. With such a new perspective, we have to develop holistic approaches to addressing injustice as inter-linked and therefore work out ways of uprooting the dangerous causes for genuine transformation.

(iv) Mission as critical (reverse mission)

Mark 7:29 records Jesus as saying: 'For saying that, you may go – the demon has left your daughter'. 'That' in Jesus' sentence refers to the woman's challenge to him. Jesus acknowledges the challenge that even makes him change his mind and provides healing. The woman's subtle challenge as 'the excluded other' provides the radical truth that leads to Jesus' social conversion experience.

When it comes to our Christian understanding of spirituality, a significant number of Christians either lack critical consciousness to ask the critical questions or they deliberately 'leave their brains at the door of the church' so as to uncritically hear what their ears itch to hear (2 Tim 4:3-4). We need to allow God's Spirit to inspire and guide us as we continuously ask the critical questions. For example, in another biblical text (Mark 12:41-44) we usually do not ask why this widow became so poor that the two coins she put in the offering basket were her last ones. Those justice-seeking people who dare to ask such critical questions risk suffering even more marginalization and derogatory remarks. For example, according to Sarojini Nadar, sharing her own experience: 'When I build shelters for abused women, they call me a saint, when I ask why women are battered they call me a feminist'.[17]

(v) Hierarchies of grace in mission?

Before he could heal the woman, Jesus argues that he was sent to the lost sheep of Israel (Matt 15:24). There are times when the mission of the church seems to benefit only the privileged few. In cases where such happens, we need to raise awareness for a more inclusive mission. We need to challenge the powers that control the flow of mission to only certain aspects of life. In the face of ecological degradation, the mission of the church should extend to include our call to protect each other as God's creation. We have to topple hierarchies of grace. Mission should never be exclusive just as God's grace can never be confined only to a privileged few.

In our biblical story, the woman challenges Jesus. Ironically this challenging woman is a mirror of the Jesus we have come to know in the gospels. He prophetically challenges power, including that of religious institutions, and he pays highly for that. According to Megan Mckenna, the Christian proclamation of Jesus' death as primarily for our salvation is to present only half a theology and to forget that he also died because his beliefs and teachings were dangerous to those who benefited from the status quo.[18] He was a dangerous man to the systems of power, a threat to the establishment and therefore he had to be got rid of.

1.6 The way forward: a suggestion

The above three women-in-mission gatherings show that unfortunately while there has been some transformation towards a more inclusive church in mission, women are still a majority of those who are excluded and marginalized. The church-in-mission has been a beacon of hope in so many situations throughout the history of the church. The World Council of Churches was born as a response to the deprivation caused by the Second World War. The prophetic mission of the church in South Africa contributed significantly to the collapse of the apartheid system. Throughout the history of the church, women have created solidarities for survival through women's movements as churches within the institutional churches yet until the church becomes authentically the body of Christ, comprising of men and women, such arrangements are only a reflection of how imperfect the church still is. As suggested above, where such exclusion is still practiced with clear implications of hampering the 'flow of love and justice', this sin of exclusion should be confessed and repented from. After accepting forgiveness and healing, new ways of relating should be built on the understanding that we are all in God's image.

To ensure that the Church's mission is inclusive and just, we might need to clearly articulate a theology of our interdependence and interconnectedness. Not only are we from the one living *Adama*, the God whose mission we are carrying out is a relational God and opts for the marginalized and excluded. God taking an option for the poor and marginalized means that God is actually taking an option *against* poverty and marginalization.

We also need to redefine our prophetic model in our responsive spirituality for transformation. Are we 'catalysts' for change or are we 'ferments'? If it is God's mission we are engaged in by our spiritual response, then we cannot be agents of transformation unless we ourselves are allowing God's Spirit to change us from our own imperfections. Paul's example should be our challenge as we engage in mission: "be imitators of me as I imitate Christ." (1 Cor 11:1)

2 Bible Societies in Mission*

Passion for the Word, compassion for the people[19]

2.1 Beginnings

The Bible Society movement traces its beginnings to the founding of the British and Foreign Bible Society (BFBS) in 1804.[20] BFBS was part of the Evangelical movement in Britain (1780-1850) that saw an expansion of Christian mission hitherto unknown in the history of the Protestant church. The name itself reflected the missionary mood of the time. Here was a remarkable convergence in these beginnings—the Bible and mission went hand in hand. The concern to reach people not yet reached with the Word of God was paramount.

From its beginning the Bible Society movement had bible translation and engagement at the heart of its mission. But without the missionary movement the Bible Societies might have limited their work to providing Scriptures to those who spoke English and the other European languages. Full use was made of the communication channels provided by the *Pax Britannica*, while funding was sought from churches and the Christian public, aided by a strong volunteer movement. The early nineteenth century technology of the printing press was another vital factor.

2.2 Growth and significance

The Bible Societies grew slowly over the next one hundred years, with BFBS, the American Bible Society, the Netherlands Bible Society, and the National Bible Society of Scotland (now the Scottish Bible Society) taking the major role. In 1946, however, thirteen Bible Societies came together to form the United Bible Societies (UBS). Today there are 147 member societies, working in over two hundred countries. In the twentieth century other, non-UBS, bible translation agencies emerged, such as Wycliffe Bible Translators International (WBTI) and the Institute for Bible Translation. The graph shows the increase in the last two hundred years of the number of languages with part or all of the Bible. It points to the key role of bible agencies in promoting mission and reaching new audiences with the Word of God.

UBS was formed as 'a World Fellowship of Bible Societies, united for consultation, mutual support and action in their common task of achieving the widest possible effective distribution of the Holy Scriptures'.[21] In successive World Assemblies since then[22], the Fellowship has sought to understand itself and its mission in the changing world. For the Bible Societies each piece of Scripture distributed to people represented the possibility of a life-giving encounter with the Lord Jesus Christ. In their golden jubilee in 1996 there was an act of thanksgiving that 'the distribution of Scriptures had helped in the

· Section contributed by Fergus Macdonald, Former UBS General Secretary and Bill Mitchell, Former UBS Americas Area Translation Coordinator.

forming and nurturing of new churches, and in meeting the needs of specific audiences, such as the newly-literate, children, youth, and the blind'.[23] The Bible Society movement has been summed up as 'popular, translating, ecumenical, and efficient' and that had 'a unique missiological significance'.[24]

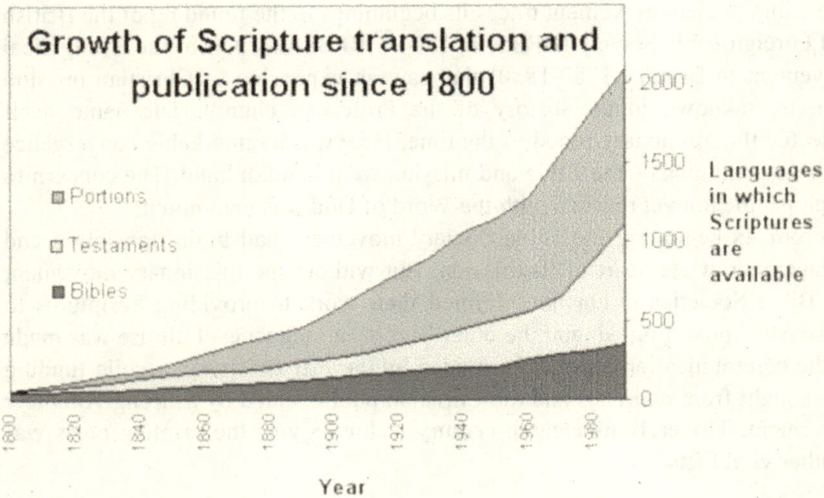

2.3 Into the new millennium

In 2000 the Midrand Assembly specifically added 'Scripture engagement' to the task of distribution of the Scriptures. Societies would now seek 'the widest possible, effective and *meaningful* distribution of the Holy Scriptures and of *helping people interact with the Word of God*'.[25] Distribution of Bibles remained a fundamental need in so many parts of the world, yet it was also recognised that more needed to be done in order to reach new audiences with the Word of God and to enable people in their specific contexts and cultures to interact with it meaningfully.

The 2000 Assembly also officially adopted what had been the practice for some considerable time: 'The Bible Societies seek to carry out their task *in partnership and cooperation with all Christian churches and with church related organisations*'. The role of UBS in serving all the churches was underlined. The African setting of this Assembly also brought into sharp focus a theme from the previous gathering—the need for Scripture use in the context of holistic programmes.

The Newport Assembly (2004) again stressed service to all churches and Scripture engagement. In an increasingly media-saturated age the Bible as 'more than a book'[26] came to the fore, and with it matters of orality, the Bible as story—indeed that grand narrative which gives meaning and direction to life, contextualized translations, and appropriate media for different audiences.

The 'Newport Declaration' stated that 'translation remains at the heart of our task'. In addition to providing further translations as needed,[27] service to the churches means preparation of confessional, literary and liturgical translations. New audiences and their reading and hearing tendencies call for new products to be developed. Cultures are in constant change. The paradox of Christianity is that to be faithful to the gospel is not just to repeat it—we constantly have to translate it. To be faithful to the Word is to be faithful to the Word that speaks to people *where* and *when* they are.

Bible translation today takes place in a world where difference and diversity are increasingly recognised and encouraged, where the centre of gravity of the church is no longer in the 'West', where the predominance of one culture over others is no longer accepted, and where cultural polycentrism is a fact of our time. Lamin Sanneh has observed that 'there is a radical pluralism associated with vernacular translation wherein all languages and cultures are in principle equal in expressing the Word of God'.[28] This affirmation of identity through bible translation is, in itself, good news. UBS consultant Dr Elsa Tamez speaks of the enrichment that comes 'when the final readers/hearers are empowered in their own language, culture and context'. She adds 'we could say, personalizing the biblical text, that it rejoices in empowering its translator and also the readers of the translation'.[29]

2.4 Bible and mission—reflections from practice

It is the practice of mission in diverse global contexts that shows the many facets of 'Bible and Mission', as the following examples indicate.

Witness in a postmodern world. In the dystopia that is the postmodern England, BFBS sums up its mission as 'making the Bible heard', where the Bible is 'available, accessible and credible'. Bible Society initiatives therefore aim to connect different narratives—cultural, personal and biblical—with the aim of transforming culture through the Word using media, arts, politics and education.[30]

Response to crisis and human need. The bible agencies have always been aware of the great comfort and support that the Word of God can bring in times of trouble, whether war, famine, disease or natural disaster. They continue to respond to those situations of human need and suffering with appropriate Scriptures.

The need for appropriate bible-based material to fight AIDS led to a joint effort by Norwegian Church Aid and the UBS to create this kind of material. In many African countries the church network is among the best developed in the country, with which Bible Societies in some forty countries partner in this programme.[31] This *Good Samaritan* programme was featured along with similar holistic projects from other bible agencies in a 2007 consultation on 'Bible Engagement in the context of HIV and AIDS in Africa', sponsored by the Forum of Bible Agencies International (FOBAI).

Serving the churches. In May 2007 Benedict XVI reminded Latin American bishops meeting in Brazil in their Fifth Continental Conference that 'we must base our missionary commitment and our whole life on the rock of the Word of God'.[32] Among the conference's conclusions is the decision that all pastoral ministry should be based on and inspired by the Bible.[33] The 2008 Synod of Bishops which met in Rome echoed this decision in their '55 propositions'.[34] The Brazil conference recommended the recovery of the *Lectio divina* throughout the church.[35] UBS has partnered with CELAM to develop *Lectio divina* materials, related training programmes and special editions of the Bible.

Orthodox churches, for their part, have a rich tradition of imaginative reflection on Scripture, a liturgical practice and an iconographic tradition which are permeated with Scriptural texts, and a deep sense of the Bible as the foundation and cornerstone of spirituality and Christian life. The primary focus for encounter with Holy Scripture is the services of the Church, above all the Divine Liturgy. Bible agencies not only serve these churches by keeping church texts in print, they are also involved with them in modern language translation projects (e.g. Arabic, Greek), both of the Bible and of lectionaries.

New media. In the late twentieth century a fundamental cultural shift was brought about by major changes in media. The world is being redefined by the internet and the new global language is digital—a major challenge for traditionally print-based organisations. The recognition of the Bible as 'more than a book' has led Bible agencies into varied internet and social networking initiatives. In many Latin American countries over fifty percent of the population is under age 25.[36] The web-based *Lectionautas* programme for young people and *Discipulitos* for children have been developed by UBS and CELAM.[37]

2.5 Engaging with the Scriptures

From the inception of the Bible Society movement its motivation was mission. Although originally formed to meet the need for affordable Bibles in the Welsh language, the vision of BFBS was global: 'If for Wales, why not for the world?'[38] The reason for stipulating that the Scriptures it published and distributed be 'without note or comment'[39] was a desire to achieve as broad a coalition as possible.

Basic elements

While the UBS family continues to publish the Scriptures without doctrinal or prescriptive comment, in the last fifty years it has moved towards providing non-sectarian 'helps for readers'. A key catalyst in this development was Eugene A. Nida's article on 'Marginal Helps for the Reader' which argued that such helps are 'the means by which we permit the text to speak for itself in some degree equivalent to the manner in which it spoke to those who first received it'.[40]

The Chiang Mai Assembly (1980) affirmed that helps need to focus on the horizon of the reader as well as on the horizon of the text. In 1992 the UBS approved 'Guidelines for Study Bibles', designed to encourage the development of Study Bibles whose helps would enable readers to better understand and apply practically the meaning of the biblical text. Anticipating the action of the Midrand Assembly incorporating Scripture engagement into the UBS purpose statement, a report of the UBS General Secretary to the UBS Executive Committee in May 2000, entitled 'From First to Twenty-first: The Bible Societies and Scripture Engagement,' contended that the need for greater Bible Society involvement in Scripture engagement was inherent in the nature of the Bible as *story*, inviting readers to enter the narrative, thus becoming involved in it and responding to it.

A significant follow-on from Midrand was the publication in 2003 of a *UBS Background Paper* which defined 'Scripture engagement' as 'a concept that emphasises making the Scriptures discoverable, accessible, and relevant'. It went on to explain that this involves: first, 'making the Bible recoverable and discoverable as sacred Scripture', and, second, 'making Scripture accessible as the place of life-enhancing and life-transforming encounter'.[41]

The debate continues, not only in the UBS family, but also in the Forum of Bible Agencies International (FOBAI).[42] The network's Scripture Engagement Development Group, reporting to the annual meeting of the Forum in April 2007, offered a tentative definition:

> Scripture Engagement describes the intersection of three elements…: a *process* by which individuals and communities gain access to the Word of God (in the most appropriate language(s) and media), an ongoing set of *meaningful individual and group encounters* with God through his Word, and an intended *outcome* – people becoming followers of Jesus in the expectation that this will lead to their transformation as individuals and communities.[43]

Some examples

The debate has stimulated many new Scripture programmes which encourage readers, listeners and viewers to engage with the Bible. The *Good Samaritan* initiative in Africa has been highlighted earlier, as also the *Lectionautas* and *Discipulitos* in Latin America. Scripture engagement programmes are also being produced for Westerners. Space permits reference to only two of these. The *Essential 100 Challenge* produced by Scripture Union in the USA guides participants through a hundred carefully selected Bible passages – fifty from the Old Testament and fifty from the New – that can easily be read in ten minutes or less. A Barna report indicates that the programme led to significantly increased interaction with the Bible by church members across confessions (Catholic and Protestant) and churchmanship (liberal and conservative). In July 2009, Mark Brown of the Bible Society in New Zealand, initiated a Bible Page on the social networking site *Facebook* which within two months had 350,000 fans.[44]

The recognition that some two-thirds of the world's population lives in an oral context has led to major initiatives in Bible storying.[45] At the same time, in the world of academic biblical studies the rediscovery of orality in the Scriptures is leading to important contributions on 'performance' in the communication of the Scriptures in both the first century and the twenty-first.[46]

A common feature of these initiatives is that they take seriously their respective target audiences. Those preparing such programmes have listened carefully to what the people they are anxious to see engaging with the Scriptures are thinking, saying and doing. They have asked: What are their ideals? And their felt needs? Against this background of audience research FOBAI is now seeking to identify the key factors influencing Scripture engagement.

Key factors

At FOBAI's annual meeting held in Fort Worth in April 2007, the Scripture Engagement Development Group presented a paper on 'Key Factors in Scripture Engagement'. The paper highlighted sixteen key factors which the larger gathering was invited to prioritise. This resulted in the following seven key factors being identified as the most important:

i. Being constantly open and responsive ourselves to God's Word. Scripture engagement is not something we 'professionalise' and do to other people, but a mutual process in which we are life-long learners together.
ii. Finding authentic and practical connecting points – points of felt need between Word and world that will enable hearers to find ways in which Scripture answers the questions raised in and by the hearers' context and reality.
iii. Considering the centrality of the church and its processes for understanding, using and disseminating the Word of God across geographic space, across cultural space and across time (from generation to generation).
iv. Identifying factors in providing access to the Word of God and evaluating how adequate/effective that access actually is.
v. Developing our theology of Scripture in an early twenty-first century context.
vi. Considering the factors that are shaping people's understanding of Scripture today.
vii. Taking seriously the reality of God's mysterious, supernatural activity in Scripture engagement and consequently the crucial role of prayer.

In October 2009 FOBAI sponsored an international consultation on Scripture engagement in Melaka, Malaysia. Details of the new models of

Scripture engagement that emerged there will be fed into the Edinburgh 2010 consultation in June 2010.

2.6 An emerging missiology?

The ministry of the UBS and other bible agencies is one of facilitating the impact of the gospel in all aspects of life by providing the Scriptures—evangelization is seen in the broadest terms as the gospel, in the Scriptures, addressing and renewing all areas of life, personal, interpersonal, social, political, for the sake of Christ. While affirming the movement of human history towards a divine consummation, it is a missiology motivated fundamentally by an eschatology that stresses the presence of the kingdom of God, the in-breaking and inauguration of this kingdom and its salvation in human history now.

Endnotes

[1] For tabulated research findings, see Constance F. Parvey (ed.), *The Community of Women and Men* (Geneva: WCC Publications, 1993), 2-154.
[2] Anglican Councils in Malawi and Zambia, *Ukaristia 1976 The Eucharist* (Chichewa/English: Limbe: AGLC Press, 1981), 18.
[3] Ivone Gebara, *Longing for Running Water: Ecofeminism and Liberation* (Minneapolis, MN: Fortress Press, 1999), 76. Gebara argues that, as a reaction against the destructive duality carried out by patriarchal systems, ecofeminism works with a holistic (unified) understanding of life wherea each being and each vital process is absolutely interdependent. According to Gebara, therefore, there are two linked aspects in the feminist perspective: women's struggle for freedom, self-determination and equality contextually expressed in each culture and the feminine as the oppressed reality of every human life and all biological systems.
[4] *Adama* as mother earth is a Hebrew female noun captured in the creation story of Genesis 2:7. According to Brigitte Kahl, *Adama* appears in a kind of motherly position as she provides the matter from which Adam is formed. For a more detailed discussion, see Brigitte Kahl, 'Fratricide and Ecocide: Genesis 2-4', in World Council of Churches, Unit III, *Working on Theology of Life: A Dossier* (Geneva: WCC, 1997), 38-44.
[5] Elizabeth Tapia, 'Our Spirituality as Interdependent to Creation', paper presented at the WARC/CWM consultation 'Living the Accra Confession in our Theology, Mission and Spirituality', Kuala Lumpur, 2006.
[6] This consultation organized by World Council of Churches Commission on World Mission and Evangelism was held in partnership with the Ecumenical Association of Third World Theologians (EATWOT) in Nairobi, Kenya, January 1992.
[7] Mercy Amba Oduyoye, 'Guest Editorial', *International Review of Mission* 81/322 (April 1992), 173-74.
[8] Isabel Phiri, *Women, Presbyterianism and Patriarchy*, (Blantyre: CLAIM, 1997), 44.
[9] Mercy Amba Oduyoye, 'Guest Editorial', 174.
[10] World Council of Churches consultation on 'Women in Mission', Ecumenical Institute, Bossey, Switzerland, June 2003.
[11] Aruna Gnanadason, 'Guest Editorial', *International Review of Mission* 95/368 (January 2004), 5-8.

[12] Musa Dube, *Postcolonial Feminist Interpretation of the Bible* (St Louis, Missouri: Chalice Press, 2000), 116.
[13] 'Towards Edinburgh 2010: Women's Perspectives on Mission and Theological Education in the 21st Century', Ecumenical Institute, Bossey, Switzerland, 24-28 November 2008.
[14] Sarojini Nadar, 'Mission Bible Study: Mark 7:24-30', presentation at the 'Towards Edinburgh 2010: Women's Perspectives on Mission and Theological Education in the 21st Century', Ecumenical Institute, Bossey, Switzerland, 24-28 November 2008. Available at www.oikoumene.org. Dr Sarojini Nadar is Senior Lecturer in Biblical Studies and Coordinator of the Gender, Religion and Theology Department, School of Religion and Theology, University of KwaZulu-Natal, South Africa. For detailed notes and resources on CBS, visit the Ujamaa website: www.ukzn.ac.za/sorat/ujamaa/ resources.htm.
[15] In sub-Saharan Africa, some of the percentages of those who are HIV positive are as follows: Botswana is 23.9%, Lesotho is 23.2% and Swaziland is 26.1%. 71% of deaths of those in the age group of 15-49 years in South Africa are caused by AIDS-related complications. For more detail, see www.avert.org/aafrica.htm.
[16] WCC Faith and Order, *Christian Perspectives on Theological Anthropology: A faith and Order Study Document*, (Faith and Order Paper no. 199; Geneva: WCC publications, 2005), 11. Available at www.oikoumene.org.
[17] Sarojini Nadar, 'Mission Bible Study: Mark 7:24-30'. Nadar's example is inspired by the Brazilian Bishop, Helder Camara who once lamented, 'When I called for the role of the Church to be with the poor, I am called a saint; when I'm asked to do something about the causes of poverty, I am called a communist'. For details, visit, http://onlinecatholics.acu.edu.au/issue65/commessay1.html
[18] Mckenna, Megan, *On Your Mark: Reading Mark in the Shadow of the Cross* (Maryknoll, NY: Orbis Books, 2006).
[19] Ole Christian Kvarme , Plenary speaker, UBS World Assembly, Mississauga 1996.
[20] The first regional Bible Society in Germany (the Von Canstein Bible Institute) was founded in Halle in 1710, almost a century before BFBS. The BFBS differed from its earlier German counterpart by subsidising the price of its Scriptures to make them affordable to the poor, and by embarking on a global mission. The Von Canstein Bible Society was one of the 34 regional Bible Societies that came together in 1948 to form the German Bible Society which became a key partner in the UBS fellowship.
[21] UBS By-Laws.
[22] 1972, Addis Ababa; 1980, Chiang Mai, Thailand; 1988, Budapest; 1996, Mississauga, Canada; 2000, Midrand, South Africa; 2004, Newport, Wales.
[23] *Mississauga Document* (Reading: UBS, 1996), 4.
[24] Samuel Escobar, 'The United Bible Societies and World Mission', *International Bulletin of Missionary Research* 30/2 (April 2006), 77-81, at 81.
[25] Our italics.
[26] Earlier a feature of the 1996 Mississauga discussions.
[27] E.g. those languages with as yet no Scripture, those without a complete New Testament or Bible, those existing translations in need of revision.
[28] Lamin Sanneh, *Translating the Message: The Missionary Impact on Culture* (2nd edition; Maryknoll, NY: Orbis Books, 2009), 251.

[29] 'Challenges of Multiculturalism to Bible Translation'. Paper presented in the 'Symposium on Translation, Identity and Heterogeneity: Cross-Cultural Discourse in Postmodernity' in the University of San Marcos, Lima, Peru, 7-9 December 2007.
[30] www.biblesociety.org.uk.
[31] www.ubs-goodsamaritan.org.
[32] Benedict XVI, Inaugural Address, Latin American Bishops' Conference (CELAM) V, Brazil, May 2007. Available at www.vatican.va
[33] CELAM, *Documento Conclusivo: Aparecida, 13-21 de mayo de 2007* (Bogota: Conferencia Episcopal Latinoamericana, 2007), §248.
[34] Proposition 30.
[35] '…this prayerful reading of the Word leads us to meet Jesus, the Master; to understand the mystery of Jesus, the Messiah; to commune with Jesus, the Son of God; and to bear witness to Jesus, the Lord of the Universe.' *Documento Conclusivo*, §249.
[36] In Honduras 42 percent are under age 15.
[37] www.lectionautas.com; www.discipulitos.com. To date some 10,000 young people have taken part in training programmes and are developing groups in their parishes.
[38] These words are attributed to Joseph Hughes, a founder who was to become one of the first Secretaries of the BFBS. See W. Canton, *A History of the BFBS*, 5 vols. (London, 1908) and D. Burke, 'Text and Context: The Relevance and Viability of the Bible Society Movement's Fundamental Principle – "Without Doctrinal Note and Comment" - Past, Present and Future', *United Bible Societies Bulletin* 194/195 (2002).
[39] Article 1 of the BFBS *Laws and Regulations*.
[40] Eugene A. Nida, 'Marginal Helps for the Reader', *Bible Translator*, 9/1 (1958).
[41] P. Noss (ed.), *UBS Background Paper on Scripture Engagement* (Reading: United Bible Societies, 2003).
[42] The Forum of Bible Agencies International is a network involving the UBS, Wycliffe Bible Translators International, OneBook, The Jesus Film Project, Lutheran Bible Translators, the Institute for Bible Translation and around twenty additional agencies. It was formed in 1990 to minimise competition and encourage cooperation in Bible work.
[43] Italics original.
[44] www.facebook.com/TheBible
[45] See, for instance, Lausanne Committee for World Evangelization, *Making Disciples of Oral Learners* (Lausanne Occasional Paper 54; LCWE, 2004), available at www.lausanne.org.
[46] David Rhoads, 'Performance Criticism: An Emerging Methodology in Biblical Studies', *SBL Forum* (2005), available at www.sbl-site.org.

APPENDIX I
THE 2010 MISSION THEMES

Essential to the work of the Edinburgh 1910 Conference, and of abiding value, were the findings of the eight think-tanks or 'commissions'. These have inspired the idea of a new round of collaborative reflection – but focused on the themes identified as being key to mission in the twenty-first century. A small but widely representative consultation held in Edinburgh in June 2005 identified key themes and these were further developed in subsequent rounds of email discussion.

Following are the suggested titles for each thematic study, an outline of the subject matter and key questions to be addressed. The suggestions provided should be regarded as provisional – a starting point from which each Mission Theme will develop its particular approach. On each of the Mission Themes the aim would be to gather, evaluate and share models and stories of good practice.

The nine mission themes are as follows:

1. Foundations for mission
2. Christian mission among other faiths
3. Mission and postmodernity
4. Mission and power
5. Forms of missionary engagement
6. Theological education and formation
7. Christian communities in contemporary contexts
8. Mission and unity – ecclesiology and mission
9. Mission spirituality and authentic discipleship

1 Foundations for Mission

The task of this study group will be to explore how a Trinitarian understanding of God as Father, Son and Holy Spirit relates to the theory and practice of mission; how the confession that God has a missionary identity impacts Christian witness; how a discernment of the Trinitarian God's inner relationships and love impacts ecclesiology, community life and society. The meaning of salvation will be considered in its biblical witness and in relation to freedom from every form of slavery in every context and culture. The group will consider the interfaces between the Trinity, mission, salvation, ecclesiology and scripture.

Key issues and questions

1. The relation of the Trinitarian nature of God to our understanding of Christian mission.
2. The relation of Christology to mission theology and practice.

3. The relation of the work of the Holy Spirit to mission theology and practice.
4. How does our understanding of the mission of the triune God affect our ecclesiology and church practice?
5. What do we mean by salvation, present and future? What is its link to conversion, baptism and participation in the sacramental life of the church?
6. How does our understanding of salvation affect the way we do mission?
7. How does mission engagement affect our biblical hermeneutics and vice-versa?

2 Christian Mission among Other Faiths

This study group will investigate ways of witnessing to Christ while acknowledging the religious plurality of a world experiencing a resurgence of religious belief and an escalation of conflict. It will explore the theological meaning of religious plurality reflecting on how it bears on Christian soteriology and missiology and address questions of conversion, proselytisation, dialogue and encounter. It will be invited to explore issues such as religious fundamentalism, persecution, 'secret' and 'churchless' believers and the continuing growth of many different forms of religious conviction. Studies undertaken under this theme will as much as possible be conducted together with or in consultation with representatives of other faiths.

Key issues and questions

1. Developing our theological understanding of the presence of non-Christian religions in the world.
2. The nature of the Christian proclamation to people of other Faiths and how we understand salvation in relation to those of other Faiths.
3. What is the meaning of "world evangelisation" today?
4. How do we bear witness to the uniqueness of Jesus in a multi-religious world?
5. How does a pneumatology defined within a Trinitarian framework affect our understanding of the significance of other religions and the nature of our mission?
6. How do we understand the activity of spirits, as understood within traditions in which they play a prominent role?
7. What is the significance of New Age and other religious movements for Christian mission?
8. How do we understand syncretism?
9. How does the mission activity of other Faiths affect Christian mission?

3 Mission and Postmodernity

The study group will be asked to take on the issues raised by the new phenomena of postmodernity and their significance for mission. This will involve an investigation of twenty-first century thought structures, religious beliefs and practices as well as ethical principles in our world of information technology. It will also require consideration of the influence of post-colonialism, economic structures, internationalism and engagement (or disengagement) with institutions and particularly with institutional religion. The group will discern commonalties and particularities in postmodern developments in different regions of the world

Key issues and questions

1. What do we mean by postmodernity/ies, and in what contexts do we see its/their influence?
2. What is the relationship between postmodernity, globalization, and neo-colonialism?
3. How does postmodernity affect understanding of the basis of Christian faith, and hence of Christian mission; particularly in and from Europe?
4. What are the promises and potentials of postmodernity/ies for new understandings of mission?
5. What is the relationship between believing and belonging, both with regard to Christian discipleship and to the agencies of mission?
6. How do we understand and engage with postmodern patterns of community, including virtual communities on the Internet?
7. What have been the effects of postmodernity on Christian mission in Europe and in other regions? What is similar from region to region? How is postmodernity perceived by churches in the South? How will present and foreseeable developments affect churches and their mission in all regions? What response needs to be made?
8. How do we tell the biblical story to those who embrace postmodern relativism and are suspicious of all metanarratives?

4. Mission and Power

The study group will recognise that mission is practised in a world shaped by various forms of power: spiritual, political, military, financial and international; raising issues of culture change, human rights, ecological sustainability and inequalities in the production, distribution and consumption of resources. It will consider tensions and asymmetries resulting from the exercise of power and how these affect the sharing and communication of the Gospel message and life. It will assess the function of both power and weakness in our understanding and practice of Christian mission.

Key issues and questions

1. Power within the church; power between churches; power between mission bodies and churches. Can mission be a form of manipulation? What strategies are needed to guard against exploitation?
2. Power between church and state: in the different contexts in which we find ourselves how can Christians ensure that their relationship to the state does not compromise loyalty to their faith? Is state protection for missionaries justifiable?
3. Idolatry of the market: how does the 'idolatry' of the modern market economy affect Christian faith and mission?
4. Internalisation of power structures: how can we guard against unexamined presuppositions, blinkered thinking, cultural conditioning and adverse spiritual powers? How can we be remade in God's image?
5. Reconstruction of power: can political reconstruction foster democratic processes? How does structural and political violence affect the witness of the Gospel?
6. Creative power: is there a positive and creative use of power in mission? How can missions avoid being subverted by the human will to power? What is the role of vulnerability in mission?
7. Indigenous peoples: how can we proclaim the Gospel without destroying indigenous cultures?

5. Forms of Missionary Engagement

The study group is invited to recognise and consider the huge variety of groups, organisations, trends, methods and new expressions of church life involved in mission today. It will seek to discern where initiative lies in today's missionary movements. It will be forward-looking in assessing patterns, initiatives and developments as they emerge and considering their implications for the future. It will treat issues of mission strategy, diversity and cooperation and identify problems of conflict and misuse of resources.

Key issues and questions

1. The primary role of the local church in mission: what does it take for the local church to become the primary missional agent through the priesthood of all believers? How is the local church related to the universal responsibility of Christian mission?
2. What forms of cooperation are appropriate to mission today? How may reciprocal partnerships best be developed?
3. What forms does "mission in poverty" / "mission without power" take?

4. In what ways can those in centres of power receive the gift of the Gospel from missionaries who come from the disempowered peripheries?
5. What are the implications of recent developments in cross-cultural mission: South-South, South-North? What is the future and role of the Western missionary movement? What is the future and role of the missionary movement in and from the South?
6. The role of media in evangelization.
7. How do we formulate mission strategy that is biblically based, theologically informed and ecclesiologically responsible, yet concrete and operational?

6. Theological Education and Formation

The study group is to examine the connection between the catechetical and missional mandates of the church. It will consider how to strengthen the missional aspects of the training and formation of every member of the church, as well as the ordained and lay leaders. Included in the study will be educational methodologies, theological study, character development, spiritual formation and the contemporary context. The group will further examine the relation between academy and society, clergy and laity, local and global issues, resources, relevance and gifts.

Key issues and questions

1. How can every member of the people of God be motivated and empowered for mission?
2. How can formation of mission spirituality become integrated into theological training programmes?
3. How can the study of missiology become an integral part of the theological curriculum? How can mission perspectives be integrated into every theological discipline?
4. The role of accreditation in relation to mission and ministry.
5. How can churches best develop relevant curricula for local contexts?
6. Specific training for cross-cultural ministries and for those involved in reconciliation ministry.
7. Catalysts for theological training and formation where theological institutions are lacking.

7. Christian Communities in Contemporary Contexts

This study group will focus on the variety of Christian communities as they draw on different traditions and engage with specific contexts. It will take cognisance of such issues as urbanisation, immigrant communities, migrant workers, affluence, poverty and virtual worlds. It will note underlying forms of

Christian expression including such concepts as world view, language, customs, traditions, inculturation, transformation, etc. It will examine ways in which churches can become holistic healing and reconciling communities, expressing both the welcoming and the transforming character of Christ's gospel. It will explore what is involved in deep-level conversion.

Key issues and questions

1. How do adjectives of Christian community such as *discipling, healing, witnessing, contextual* become lived realities in today's world?
2. What is involved in being the church in the cities and mega-cities of today?
3. How can the local church be an agent of the kingdom of God and a source of healing and reconciliation?
4. What is the true identity (the "core DNA") of the church? How does it manifest itself in different denominations and cultures?
5. Ethnicity – the tension between homogenous and multi-ethnic churches.
6. Church life in Diaspora communities.
7. HIV/AIDS – does Christian mission bear some responsibility for the spread of the virus? How can mission contribute to the struggle to stop the pandemic?
8. What other forms of ill-health call for particular attention from practitioners of Christian mission?

8. Mission and Unity – Ecclesiology and Mission

The 1910 Edinburgh Conference is considered the starting point of the contemporary ecumenical movement, due to its insistence on the importance of unity and cooperation in worldwide mission. Today, there is a need to revisit the intimate relationship as well as underlying tensions between a focus on mission and a focus on church unity. This track will deal with various interpretations of the link between ecclesiology study mission in theological and practical terms. Interface with the work on the history of mission and ecumenism in the last century (in particular as to the evaluation of "integration" in 1961) will be key for this area.

Key issues and questions

1. The mission agencies of 1910 preferred to avoid ecclesiological discussion. Why has ecclesiology come to prominence in the contemporary discussion of mission and unity?
2. In the new landscape of world Christianity, What and where are the new or emerging missionary movements, missional ecclesiologies, and ecumenical missiologies?
3. Where are the biblical, theological, and contextual resources for a satisfactory discussion of 'mission, unity, and ecclesiology'?

4. What are the missiological and ecumenical implications of baptism, Eucharist, apostolicity, and ordination?
5. What are the ecclesiological and ecumenical implications of mission focused on healing and reconciliation?
6. Are evangelistic witness and prophetic witness compatible with the search for visible church unity?
7. What and where are the models of evangelistic witness undertaken ecumenically?
8. How might the coming century be one in which a journey towards one common commemoration in 2110 is charted and undertaken together by churches and mission agencies?

9. Mission Spirituality and Authentic Discipleship

The study group on mission spirituality will seek to articulate a motivation and dynamic for mission that is rooted in the Kingdom of God. It will draw on the experience of the early church, of Christians from all ages, as well as that of new Christian movements, and of the many new churches in the South. It will seek to understand mission in relation to such concepts as new creation, spiritual gifts, renewal, reconstruction, identity, service and holism. It will explore the role of the Spirit and of the church as signs and portents of the goal of all endeavour in the glory of God.

Key issues and questions

1. What shape does Christian mission take when it has the Kingdom of God as its ultimate horizon?
2. What is the proper place of the natural order in mission spirituality?
3. Prophetic witness: challenging the "principalities and powers" of human institutions with "signs and wonders" and God-given spiritual authority.
4. Love of enemies; reconciliation and healing through the power of the Cross, and witness through self-emptying, humility, and sacrifice.
5. How can we form new and creative relationships with Christians of all traditions, given our diverse understandings of mission, both locally and at international level? How can we form new and creative relationships with fellow human beings beyond the church?
6. How can we be faithful to our Christian confession while being open, adventurous and discerning in encounter with representatives of other religions?

APPENDIX II

CONVENERS OF THE EDINBURGH 2010 STUDY GROUPS

1. Foundations for Mission

Canon Janice Price, Church of England
Revd Dr Deenabandhu Manchala, World Council of Churches, Switzerland

2. Christian Mission among Other Faiths

Dr Lalsangkima Pachuau, Asbury Theological Seminary, USA
Dr Niki Papageorgiou, Aristotle University of Thessaloniki, Greece

3. Mission and Postmodernities

Andrew Kirk, formerly Dean of the School of Mission, Birmingham, UK
Dr Kajsa Ahlstrand, University of Uppsala, Sweden

4. Mission and Power

Dr Jonathan Bonk, Overseas Ministries Study Centre, USA
Lori Ransom, Presbyterian Church in Canada

5. Forms of Missionary Engagement

Canon Mark Oxbrow, Church Mission Society, UK
Dr Genevieve James, University of South Africa (UNISA)

6. Theological Education and Formation

Dr Dietrich Werner, Ecumenical Institute Bossey, Switzerland
Dr Namsoon Kang, Brite Divinity School, Texas Christian University, USA

7. Christian Communities in Contemporary Contexts

Dr Afe Adogame, University of Edinburgh, UK
Dr Philomena Mwaura, Kenyatta University, Kenya
in close association with Erica Dunmow of the JITC UK Urban Mission Congress Executive

8. Mission and Unity – Ecclesiology and Mission

Revd Darrell Jackson (Moderator), Redcliffe College, UK
Ms Kyriaki Avtzi, Churches in Dialogue, Council of European Churches
Rev. Dr Laszlo Gonda, Debrecen Reformed Theological University, Hungary, and Commission for World Mission and Evangelism, World Council of Churches

9. Mission Spirituality and Authentic Discipleship

Dr Wonsuk Ma, Oxford Centre for Mission Studies, UK
Dr Cathy Ross, Church Mission Society, UK

INDEX

BIBLIOGRAPHY

A New Covenant: Towards the Constitutional Recognition and Protection of Aboriginal Self-Government in Canada, www.presbyterian.ca/ministry/justice/healing/newcovenant

Abimbola, W., *Ifá Will Mend Our Broken World: Thoughts on Yoruba Religion and Culture in Africa and the Diaspora* (Roxbury, MA: Aim Books, 2003)

Acts and Proceedings of The Presbyterian Church in Canada, Toronto, 1992

Acts and Proceedings of The Presbyterian Church in Canada, Toronto, 1994

Addicott, E., *Body Matters: A Guide to Partnership in Christian Mission* (Edmonds, WA: Interdev Partnership Associates, 2005)

Adogame, Afe, 'The Rhetoric of Reverse Mission: African Christianity and the Changing Dynamics of Religious Expansion in Europe', outline of a lecture presented at the conference, 'South Moving North: Revised Mission and its Implications', Protestant Landelijk Dienstencentrum, Utrecht, 26 September 2007

Aghamkar, P., 'A Christian *Diwali*: Contextualizing Witness as Celebration with the Hindu Community', paper submitted to Study Group 2, Edinburgh 2010 (2009), available at www.edinburgh2010.org

Ahn, Shin 'Korean Spirituality: Christian Presence Among World Religions' (2009), paper submitted to Edinburgh 2010 Study Group 9, available at www.edinburgh2010.org

Aldred, Joe, Sophie Hebden & Keith Hebden, *Who is My Neighbour? A Church Response to Social Disorder Linked to Gangs, Drugs, Guns and Knives* (London: Churches Together in England, 2008). Available at http://cte.churchinsight.com/

Aleshire, Daniel, *Earthen Vessels: Hopeful Reflections on the Work and Future of Theological Schools* (Grand Rapids, MI: Eerdmans, 2008)

Allen, Roland, *Missionary Methods: St. Paul's or Ours?* (London: World Dominion Press, 1956 [1912]

Anderson, Allan, *An Introduction to Pentecostalism* (Cambridge: CUP, 2004)

Anderson, Gerald H., 'A Moratorium on Missionaries?', *Christian Century* 16 (January 1974)

Anderson, J.N.D., *Christianity and Comparative Religion* (Downers Grove, IL: InterVarsity Press 1970)

Anglican Councils in Malawi and Zambia, *Ukaristia 1976 The Eucharist* (Chichewa/English: Limbe: AGLC Press, 1981)

Antone, E., *In Search of Voice: A Collaborative Investigation on Learning Experiences of all Onyota'a:ka* (Toronto, ON: Unpublished Thesis, University of Toronto, 1997)

_____ 'A Citizenship Dilemma: Aboriginal Peoples and Identity Questions', in Karsten Mundel & Daniel Schugurensky (eds), *Lifelong Citizenship*

Learning, Participatory Democracy and Social Change (Toronto: Transformative Learning Centre, OISE/University of Toronto, 2004)

Ariarajah, Wesley, *Hindus and Christians: A Century of Protestant Thoughts* (Grand Rapids, MI: Wm B. Eerdmans, 1991)

Asamoah-Gyadu, J. Kwabena, 'Listening with African Ears – Reflections on the 2005 World Mission Conference in Athens', *International Review of Mission* 94/374 (July 2005), 343-353

_____ '"Get on the Internet!" Says the LORD': Religion, Cyberspace and Christianity in Contemporary Africa', *Studies in World Christianity* 13 (Dec 2007), 225-242

Azumah, John, 'Christian Mission and Islam', position paper submitted to Study Group 2, Edinburgh 2010 (2009), 2-3, available at www.edinburgh2010.org

Barbour, C.M., 'Seeking Justice and Shalom in the City', *International Review of Mission* 73/291 (1984), 303-309

Barna, George, *Transforming Your Children into Spiritual Champions* (Ventura, CA: Regal Publications, 2003)

Barrett, David B., 'Christian World Communions: Five Overviews of Global Christianity, AD 1800-2025', *International Bulletin of Missionary Research* 33/1 (January 2009), 25-32

_____ *et al.*, 'Missiometrics 2008: Reality Checks for Christian World Communions', *International Bulletin of Missionary Research* 32 (2008), 27-30

Barton, Mukti, *Scripture as Empowerment for Liberation and Justice: The Experience of Christian and Muslim women in Bangladesh* (Bristol: University of Bristol, 1999)

Bateye, Bolaji O., 'The Interplay of Gender, Identity and Power in African Female-led Churches: London and Nigeria'. Paper presented at the Study Group 7 consultation, Edinburgh, 12-13 June 2009

Bauman, Z., *Postmodernity and its Discontents* (Cambridge: Polity Press, 1997)

Bediako, Gillian M., '"All Believers Are Primalists Underneath": Towards a New Appreciation of Old Testament Religion as Primal Religion', a lecture at Calvin College, Grand Rapids, MI (July 2007)

Benedict XVI, Inaugural Address, Latin American Bishops' Conference (CELAM) V, Brazil, May 2007. Available at www.vatican.va

Bertens, Hans, *The Idea of the Postmodern: A History* (London: Routledge, 1995)

Best, Thomas F. & Günther Gassmann (eds), *On the Way to Fuller Koinonia: Official Report of the Fifth World Conference on Faith and Order, Santiago de Compostela, 1993* (Geneva: WCC, 1994)

Bevans, Stephen B., *Models of Contextual Theology* (2nd edition; Maryknoll, NY: Orbis Books, 2002)

_____ & Roger P. Schoeder, *Constants in Context: A Theology of Mission for Today* (Maryknoll, NY: Orbis, 2001)

Bifet, Juan Esquerda, *Spirituality for a Missionary Church* (Rome: Urbania University Press, 1994)

Boff, Leonardo, *Trinity and Society* (Tunbridge Wells: Burns & Oates, 1988)

Bolger, Ryan, *et al.* (eds), 'The Local Church in Mission: Becoming a Missional Congregation in the Twenty-first Century Global Context' (Lausanne Occasional Paper 40), in David Claydon (ed.), *A New Vision, A New Heart, A Renewed Call*, Volume I (Pasadena: William Carey Library, 2004), 565-606. Available at www.lausanne.org

Bonk, Jonathan, *Missions and Money: Affluence as a Missionary Problem ... Revisited* (Revised and expanded edition; New York: Orbis Books, 2006)

Bosch, David J., *Transforming Mission. Paradigm Shifts in Theology of Mission* (Maryknoll, NY: Orbis Books, 1991)

_____ *A Spirituality of the Road* (Eugene, OR: Wipf & Stock, 2001)

_____ 'Theological Education in Missionary Perspective', *Missiology* X/1 (January 1982), 17-19

_____ 'The Structure of Mission: An Exposition of Matthew 28:16-20, in Wilbert R. Shenk (ed.), *Exploring Church Growth* (Grand Rapids, MI: Eerdmans, 1983), 218-48

_____ 'The Vulnerability of Mission', in J.A. Scherer & S.B. Bevans (eds), *New Directions in Mission and Evangelization 2: Theological Foundations* (Maryknoll, NY: Orbis Books, 1994), 73-86

Bradman, O., & R.A. Beckstrom, *The Starfish and the Spider* (London: Penguin Group, 2006)

Brewster, Dan, 'The 4/14 Window: Child Ministries and Mission Strategies', in Phyllis Kilbourn (ed.), *Children in Crisis: A New Commitment* (Monrovia, CA: MARC 1996), 125-139

Bria, Ion, *Go Forth in Peace: Orthodox Perspectives on Mission* (Geneva: WCC, 1986)

_____ *Liturgy After the Liturgy: Mission and Witness from an Orthodox Perspective* (Geneva: WCC, 1996)

British Council of Churches, *The Forgotten Trinity* (London: The British Council of Churches, 1981-91)

Brown, Peter, *The Rise of Western Christendom: Triumph and Diversity, A.D. 200–1000* (Oxford: Blackwell, 2003)

Brown, Raymond E., *An Introduction to the New Testament* (New York: Doubleday, 1997)

Brueggemann, Walter, *The Covenanted Self: Explorations in Law and Covenant* (Minneapolis, MN: Augsburg Fortress, 1999)

_____ (ed.), *Hope for the World: Mission in a Global Context* (Louisville: Westminster John Knox Press, 2001)

Brunner, Emil, *The Word and the World* (London: Student Mission Movement Press, 1931)

Brynjolfson, Robert, 'From Synthesis to Synergy: The Iguassu Think Tanks', in W.D. Taylor (ed.), *Global Missiology for the 21st Century: The Iguassu Dialogue* (Grand Rapids, MI: Baker Academic, 2000), 477-88

_____ & Jonathan Lewis (eds), *Integral Mission Training: Design and Evaluation* (Pasadena: William Carey, 2006)

Bunt, Gary, *iMuslims: Rewiring the House of Islam* (Chapel Hill: University of North Carolina Press, 2009)

Burke, D., 'Text and Context: The Relevance and Viability of the Bible Society Movement's Fundamental Principle – "Without Doctrinal Note and Comment" – Past, Present and Future.' *United Bible Societies Bulletin* 194/195 (2002)

Burrows, William B. (ed.), *Redemption and Dialogue: Reading* Redemptoris Missio *and Dialogue and Proclamation* (Maryknoll, NY: Orbis Books, 1994)

Butler, P., *Well Connected: Releasing Power, Restoring Hope through Kingdom Partnerships* (Milton Keynes, UK: Authentic Media, 2005)

Cahoone, Lawrence (ed.), *From Modernism to Postmodernism: An Anthology* (Oxford: Blackwell, 1996)

Canton, W., *A History of the BFBS*, 5 vols. (London, 1908)

Casino, Tereso C., 'Mission in the Context of Filipino Folk Spirituality: *Bahala na* as a Case in Point', in Wonsuk Ma & Cathy Ross (eds), *Mission Spirituality and Authentic Discipleship* (Seoul, 2009), 83-96. Available at www.edinburgh2010.org

Castro, Emilio, 'Evangelism', in Nicholas Lossky *et al*, eds., *Dictionary of the Ecumenical Movement*, (Geneva: WCC, 1991), 400

Catto, Rebecca, 'Non-Western Christian Missionaries in England: Has Mission Been Reversed?' in S. Spencer (ed.), *Mission and Migration* (Sheffield: Cliff College Publishing, 2008), 109-118

_____ 'Reverse Mission Dynamics'. Paper presented at the Study Group 7 consultation, Edinburgh, 12-13 June 2009

CELAM, *Documento Conclusivo: Aparecida, 13-21 de mayo de 2007* (Bogota: Conferencia Episcopal Latinoamericana, 2007)

Chamorro, G., *Auf dem Weg zur Vollkommenheit. Theologie des Wortes unter den Guaraní in Süd-Amerika* (Exegese in unserer Zeit, 11), (Münster: LIT Verlag, 2003)

Chan, Kim-kwong, 'Mission Movement of the Christian Community in Mainland China: The Back to Jerusalem Movement', in Wonsuk Ma & Cathy Ross (eds), *Mission Spirituality and Authentic Discipleship* (Seoul, 2009), 67-82. Available at www.edinburgh2010.org

Clark, Lynn Scofield & Stewart M. Hoover, 'At the Intersection of Media, Culture, and Religion: A Bibliographic Essay', in Stewart M. Hoover and Knut Lundby (eds), *Rethinking Media, Religion, and Culture* (Thousand Oaks, CA: Sage Publications, 1997)

Clarke, Matthew & Juliette Lumbers, 'Churches and Condoms: How Christian Faith-Based Organisations are Preventing HIV/AIDS in Developing Countries'. Paper presented at the Edinburgh 2010 Study Group 7 conference, Edinburgh, 2009

Claydon, D. (ed.), *A New Vision, a New Heart, A Renewed Call: Volume One. Lausanne Occasional Papers from the 2004 Forum for World*

Evangelization Hosted by the Lausanne Committee for World Evangelization in Pattaya, Thailand (Pasadena: William Carey Library, 2005)

Conference of European Churches, *Charta Oecumenica* (Geneva: Conference of European Churches, 2001). Available at www.cec-kek.org

Congregation for the Doctrine of the Faith, *Dominus Iesus* 'Declaration on the Unicity and Salvific Universality of Jesus Christ and the Church' (2000), available at www.vatican.va

Cooper, M.T., 'Colonialism, Neo-colonialism and Forgotten Missiological Lessons', *Global Missiology* 1 (2005), 1-14

Council for Christian Unity of the General Synod of the Church of England, *Porvoo Common Statement* 1992 (London, 1993), available at www.porvoochurches.org/statements/en.htm

Cox, Harvey, *Fire From Heaven: The Rise of Pentecostalism and the Reshaping of Religion in the Twenty-first Century* (London: Cassell, 1996)

Cray, Graham (ed.), *Mission-shaped Church: Church Planting and Fresh Expressions of Church in a Changing Context* (London: Church House Publishing, 2004). Available at www.cofe.anglican.org

Davie, Grace, *Religion in Britain since 1945: Believing Without Belonging* (Oxford: Blackwell, 1994)

_____ *Europe the Exceptional Case: Parameters of Faith in the Modern World* (London: Darton, Longman and Todd, 2002)

_____ 'Religion in Europe in the 21st Century: The Factors to Take into Account', in *Religion in Late Modernity: Essays in Honour of Pål Repstad* (Trondheim: Tapir Academic Press, 2007), 37-53

Dawkins, Richard, *River out of Eden* (London: Weidenfeld and Nicolson, 1995)

de Beer, Stephan, 'Contesting Inner-city Space: Global Trends, Local Exclusion/s and an Alternative Christian Spatial Praxis', *Missionalia* 36/2-3, 180-206

de Klerk, B.J., 'Worship, Prayers and Poverty', *Ecumenical Review* 57/3 (July 2005), 342-357

de Wit, H., L. Jonker and D. Schipani (eds) *The Eyes of the Other. Intercultural Reading of the Bible* (Amsterdam: Institute of Mennonite Studies, Vrije Universiteit, 2004)

Dedji, Valentin, *Reconstruction and Renewal in African Christian Theology* (Nairobi: Acton, 2003)

del Prado, Consuelo, 'I Sense God in Another Way', in Elsa Tamez (ed.), *Through Her Eyes: Women's Theology from Latin America* (Maryknoll, NY: Orbis, 1989)

Dhamaraj, Glory E., 'Lay Women, Mission Practices, and Theological Thought', paper presented at the Queen's Foundation, March 2009, and submitted to Edinburgh 2010 Study Group 6

Douglas, J.D. (ed.), *Let the Earth Hear His Voice: International Congress on World Evangelization Lausanne, Switzerland.* (Minneapolis, MN: World Wide Publications, 1975)

_____ *Proclaim Christ Until He Comes: Calling the Whole Church to Take the Whole Gospel to the Whole World* (Minneapolis, MN: World Wide Publications, 1990)

Drane, John, *Jesus and the Gods of the New Age: Communicating Christ in Today's Spiritual Supermarket* (Oxford: Lion Publishing, 2001)

Dube, Musa W., *Postcolonial Feminist Interpretation of the Bible* (St Louis, Missouri: Chalice Press, 2000)

_____ 'Reading for Decolonization (John 4.1-42)', in R.S. Sugirtharajah (ed.), *Voices from the Margin: Interpreting the Bible in the Third World* (3rd edition; Maryknoll, NY: Orbis, 2006), 297-318

Duncan, Graham A., 'Towards Partnership in Mission: The Church of Scotland's World Mission Council Policy, 1929–2006', *Missionalia* 35/1 (April 2007), 54-79

Dunmow, Erica, 'The Challenge of Indigenous Leadership in the UK Urban Mission Context'. Paper presented at the Study Group 7 consultation, Edinburgh, 12-13 June 2009

Duraisingh, Christopher, 'Encountering Difference in a Plural World: A Pentecost Paradigm for Mission', in Ian T. Douglas (ed.), *Waging Reconciliation: God's Mission in a Time of Globalization and Crisis* (New York: Church Publishing, 2002), 171-212

Eagleton, Terry, *The Illusions of Postmodernism* (Oxford: Blackwell, 1996)

Ecumenical Theological Education, 'Message of the Oslo Conference on Theological Education 1996', in John Pobee (ed.), *Towards Viable Theological Education* (Geneva: WCC Publications, 1997), 1-6

Elmer, D., *Cross-cultural Servanthood: Serving the World in Christlike Humility* (Downer's Grove, IL: InterVarsity Press, 2006)

Escobar, Samuel, *A Time for Mission* (Leicester: IVP, 2003)

_____ 'The United Bible Societies and World Mission', *International Bulletin of Missionary Research* 30/2 (April 2006), 77-81

European Evangelical Alliance, 'The Foreigner in Our Midst' (2007), available at www.europeanea.org

European Evangelical Missionary Alliance, 'Receiving Mission Workers to Europe: What Every Church Should know', available at www.europeanema.org.

Evangelicals and Catholics Together, 'Christian Mission in the Third Millenium,' 1994. Available at www.firstthings.com

Evangelical Lutheran Church in America, *Called to Common Mission* (1998), available at www.elca.org

Falconer, A.D., 'The Future of Protestantism: Ecumenism and the Mainline Denominations', in A.E. McGrath & D.C. Marks (eds), *The Blackwell Companion to Protestantism* (Oxford: Blackwell, 2004), 405-420

Fiddes, Paul, *Participation in God* (London: Darton, Longman & Todd, 2000)

Field, David, 'Journey Beyond The Gate: The Reign of God and the Response Ability of the Globalised Middle Class', *Journal of Theology for Southern Africa* 123 (November 2005)

Francois, C., 'Systemics and Cybernetics in a Historical Perspective' in *Systems Research and Behavioral Science* 16 (1999), 203-219

Friesen, J. Stanley, *Missionary Responses to Tribal Religions at Edinburgh, 1910* (New York: Peter Lang, 1996)

Gebara, Ivone, *Longing for Running Water: Ecofeminism and Liberation*, (Minneapolis: Fortress Press, 1999)

Gibbs, Eddie & Ryan K. Bolger, *Emerging Churches. Creating Christian Community in Postmodern Culture*, (Grand Rapids, MI: Baker Academic, 2006)

Giles, Thomas S., *Christian History*, XI/35, 3

Gnanadason, Aruna, 'Guest Editorial', *International Review of Mission* 95/368 (January 2004), 5-8.

Gnanakan, Ken, *God's World, A Theology of the Environment* (London: SPCK, 1999)

Goodall, N. (ed.), *Missions under the Cross. Addresses Delivered at the Enlarged Meeting of the International Missionary Council at Willingen, Germany, 1952; with Statements Issued by the Meeting* (London: Edinburgh House Press, 1953)

Gorman, Lyn & David McLean, *Media and Society in the Twentieth Century* (Oxford: Blackwell Publishing, 2003), 221.

Graham, E., *The Mush Hole: Life at Two Indian Residential Schools* (Waterloo, ON: Heffle Publishing, 1997)

Greener, Susan, *Celebrating Children* (Carlisle, UK: Paternoster Press, 2003)

Guder, Darrell L., *The Continuing Conversion of the Church* (Grand Rapids, MI: Wm B. Eerdmans, 2000)

Gutiérrez, Gustavo, *A Theology of Liberation: History, Politics and Liberation* (Maryknoll, NY: Orbis Books, 1988)

_____ *We Drink from Our Own Wells: The Spiritual Journey of a People* (20th Anniversary edition; Maryknoll, NY: Orbis Books, 2003)

Haanes, Vidar Leif, 'Theological Education and Mission', in Tormond Engelsviken, *et al.* (eds), *Mission to the World: Communicating the Gospel in the Twenty-first Century* (Oxford: Regnum, 2008), 391-404

Hanciles, Jehu J., 'Migration and Mission: The Religious Significance of the North-South Divide', in Andrew Walls & Cathy Ross (eds.), *Mission in the Twenty-first Century: Exploring the Five Marks of Global Mission* (London: Darton, Longman and Todd, 2008), 118-29

Harries, Jim, 'An 'Impact Model' of Language, and Mission and Development in East Africa'(2009), paper presented to Edinburgh 2010 Study Group 3 and available at www.edinburgh2010.org

Henriksen, Jan-Olav, 'Multifaceted Christianity and the Postmodern Religious Condition: Reflections on its Challenges to Churches in the Northern Hemisphere' (2009), paper presented to Edinburgh 2010 Study Group 3 and available at www.edinburgh2010.org

Herbst, Michael, 'Plural Mission and Missionary Plural in a Post-Socialist Context: The Example of a Post-*Volkskirche*, East German

Region'(2009), paper presented to Edinburgh 2010 Study Group 3 and available at www.edinburgh2010.org

Hick, John & Paul F. Knitter (eds), *The Myth of Christian Uniqueness: Toward a Pluralistic Theology of Religions* (Maryknoll, NY: Orbis Books, 1987)

Hirsch, Alan, *The Forgotten Ways* (Grand Rapids, MI: Baker Publishing House, 2006)

Hjarvard, Stig, 'The Mediatization of Religion: A Theory of the Media as Agents of Religious Change', *Northern Lights* 6 (2008)

Hocking, William Ernest (ed.), *Rethinking Missions: A Laymen's Inquiry after One Hundred Years* (New York and London: Harper & Brothers Publishers, 1932)

Hoeckman, Remi Emiel, O.P., 'Christian Mission. God Moving to All Men, Transcending All Boundaries', in *Angelicum* 58/3 (1981), 312-322

Hudson, Lawrie & Tom Kisitu, 'Touching Lives in Edinburgh', paper presented at the Study Group 7 consultation, Edinburgh, 12-13 June 2009

Hunter, George G., *The Celtic Way of Evangelism* (Nashville: Abingdon Press, 2000)

Hunter, Harold D., 'Pentecostal Social Engagement: Excerpts from around the World', Paper presented at the Study Group 7 consultation, Edinburgh, 12-13 June 2009

International Anglican-Roman Catholic Commission for Unity and Mission, *Growing Together in Unity and Mission* (London: SPCK, 2007)

Irarrazabal, Diego, 'Convergences and Divergences between Catholics and Pentecostals', paper submitted to Edinburgh 2010 Study Group 9, available at www.edinburgh2010.org

Jameson, Frederic, *Postmodernism, or, the Cultural Logic of Late Capitalism* (Durham: Duke University Press, 1991)

Jathanna, O.V., *The Decisiveness of the Christ-event and the Universality of Christianity in a World of Religious Plurality* (Frankfurt: Peter Lang, 1981)

Jayaraj, Daniel, 'Mission Reports from South India and Their Impact on the Western Mind: The Tranquebar Mission of the Eighteenth Century', in Dana L. Robert (ed.) *Converting Colonialism* (Michigan: Eerdmans, 2008)

Jenkins, Philip, *The Next Christendom: The Coming of the Global Christianity* (New York/Oxford, Oxford University Press, 2001)

Jeremiah, Anderson, 'Dalit Christians in South India'. Paper presented at the Study Group 7 consultation, Edinburgh, 12-13 June 2009

John Paul II, *Redemptoris Missio*, 'On the Permanent Validity of the Church's Missionary Mandate' (1990), available at www.vatican.va

Johnson, Elizabeth A., *She Who Is: The Mystery of God in Feminist Theological Discourse* (New York: Crossroad, 2000)

Johnson, Lydia & Joan Alleluia Filemoni-Tofaeno (eds), *Weavings: Women Doing Theology in Oceania* (Suva: SPATS/USP, 2003)

Jones, Andrew, 'The Virtual Church – Keeping It Real' (2009), http://tallskinnykiwi.typepad.com/tallskinnykiwi/2009/07/the-virtual-church-keeping-it-real.html

Jørgensen, Knud, *Åpen kanal – Misjon og medier* (Oslo: Luther Forlag, 1987)

Kahl, Brigitte, 'Fratricide and Ecocide: Genesis 2-4', in World Council of Churches, Unit III, *Working on Theology of Life: A Dossier* (Geneva: WCC, 1997), 38-44

Kalu, Ogbu (ed.) *African Christianity: An African Story* (Pretoria: University of Pretoria, 2005)

Kärkäinen, Veli-Matti, *An Introduction to the Theology of Religions* (Downers Grove, IL: IVP, 2003)

_____ 'Theologies of Religions. A Position Paper', paper submitted to Study Group 2, Edinburgh 2010 (2009), available at www.edinburgh2010.org

Kerr, David & Kenneth Ross (eds), *Edinburgh 2010: Mission Then and Now* (Oxford: Regnum, 2009)

Kettle, David, 'The Gospel of Hope in a Postmodern Setting' (2009), paper presented to Edinburgh 2010 Study Group 3 and available at www.edinburgh2010.org

Khodr, Georges, 'Christianity in a Pluralistic World – The Economy of the Holy Spirit', *Ecumenical Review* 23 (1971), 118-128

Kim, Hun, 'Receiving Mission: Reflection on Reversed Phenomena in Mission by Migrant Workers from Global Churches to the Western Society', paper submitted to Edinburgh 2010, study group 5, 2009

Kim, Kirsteen, *Mission in the Spirit: The Holy Spirit in Indian Christian Theologies* (New Delhi: ISPCK 2003)

_____ *The Holy Spirit in the World. A Global Conversation* (Maryknoll: Orbis, 2007)

_____ 'Ethereal Christianity: Reading Korean Mega-Church Websites', *Studies in World Christianity* 13 (Dec 2007), 208-224

_____ 'Mission Spirituality', *Religion in Geschichte und Gegenwart* 4th edn (Tübingen: Mohr Siebeck, 2007).

_____ 'Mission Theology of the Church', keynote paper presented at the Joint Consultation on Mission and Ecclesiology of the Faith and Order Commission and of the Commission on World Mission and Evangelism, Berekfürdő, 4-9 March 2009, forthcoming in *International Review of Mission* in 2010

Kinnamon, Michael & Brian E. Cope (eds), *The Ecumenical Movement: An Anthology of Key Texts and Voices* (Geneva: WCC Publications, 1997)

Kinsler, Ross, *Diversified Theological Education: Equipping all God's People* (Pasadena: William Carey, 2008)

Kirk, J. Andrew, *What is Mission? Theological Explorations* (London: Darton, Longman and Todd, 1999)

_____ *Mission under Scrutiny: Confronting Current Challenges* (London: Darton, Longman and Todd, 2006)

_____ *The Future of Reason, Science and Faith:Following Modernity and Postmodernity* (Basingstoke: Ashgate Publishing, 2007)

_____ 'The Post-Modern Condition and the Churches' (Co)Mission' (2009), paper presented to Edinburgh 2010 Study Group 3 and available at www.edinburgh2010.org

_____ & Kevin J. Vanhoozer (eds), *To Stake a Claim: Mission and the Western Crisis of Knowledge* (Maryknoll, NY: Orbis Books, 1999)

Knitter, Paul F., *Jesus and the Other Names: Christian Mission and Global Responsibility* (Maryknoll, NY: Orbis Books, 1996)

_____ 'Mission and Dialogue', *Missiology: An International Review*, 33 (2005), 199-210

Knockwood, I., *Out of the Depths: The Experiences of Mi'kmaw Children at the Indian Residential School at Shubenacadie, Nova Scotia* (Lockeport: Roseway, 1992)

Kollman, P.V., *The Evangelisation of Slaves: And Catholic Origins in Eastern Africa* (Maryknoll, NY: Orbis Books, 2005)

Koyama, Kosuke, 'Christianity Suffers from Teacher Complex', in Gerald H. Anderson & Thomas F. Stransky (eds), *Mission Trends No. 2* (Grand Rapids, MI: Wm B. Eerdmans, 1975), 70-75

Kozhuharov, Valentin, 'Mission in an Orthodox Christian Context: Witnessing Christ as Pastoral Responsibility', in Wonsuk Ma & Cathy Ross (eds), *Mission Spirituality and Authentic Discipleship* (Seoul, 2009), 15-26. Available at www.edinburgh2010.org

Kraemer, Hendrik, *The Christian Message in the Non-Christian World* (London: International Missionary Council, 1938)

Laing, Mark, 'Recovering Missional Ecclesiology in Theological Education', *International Review of Mission* 388 (April 2009) 11-24

Lambeth Conference 1998, 'The Way of Dialogue', Appendix 6 of the Lambeth Conference 1998, available at www.anglicancommunion.org

Langmead, Ross, 'Transformed Relationships: Reconciliation as the Central Model for Mission', *Mission Studies* 25/1 (2008), 5-20

Larkin Jr., William J. & Joel F. Williams (eds) *Mission in the New Testament. An Evangelical Approach* (Maryknoll, NY: Orbis, 1998)

Latourette, K.S. 'Ecumenical Bearings of the Missionary Movement and the International Missionary Council', in R. Rouse and Stephen C. Neill (eds), *A History of the Ecumenical Movement 1517-1948* (Philadelphia: The Westminster Press, 1967)

Lausanne Committee for World Evangelization, *The Lausanne Covenant* (1974) available at www.lausanne.org

_____ *The Manila Manifesto* (1989), available at www.lausanne.org

_____ *Making Disciples of Oral Learners* (Lausanne Occasional Paper 54; LCWE, 2004), available at www.lausanne.org

_____ *The Whole Church: Reflections of the Lausanne Theology Working Group*, Panama, 26th-30th January 2009 (Panama: LCWE, 2009), available at www.lausanne.org

Lederleitner, M., 'Is it possible to adhere to Western ethical and cultural standards regarding financial accountability without fostering neo-colonialism in this next era of global mission partnerships? Thoughts and reflections for broader dialogue', paper submitted to Edinburgh 2010 study group 5, 2009

Lee, Chul-shin, 'Spirituality and Christian Mission: The Journey of Youngnak Presbyterian Church, Seoul, Korea', in Wonsuk Ma & Cathy Ross (eds), *Mission Spirituality and Authentic Discipleship* (Seoul, 2009), 97-101. Available at www.edinburgh2010.org

_____ 'Dr Kyung-Chik Han's Early Life and Ministry: A Model for Korean Church Leadership', in Wonsuk Ma & Cathy Ross (eds), *Mission Spirituality and Authentic Discipleship* (Seoul, 2009), 117-121. Available at www.edinburgh2010.org

Lee, Young-hoon, 'The Spirit and Mission: Mission Engagements of the Yoido Full Gospel Church' (2009), paper submitted to Edinburgh 2010 Study Group 9, available at www.edinburgh2010.org

Legrand, Lucien, *Mission in the Bible: Unity and Plurality* (Maryknoll, NY: Orbis, 1990)

Li, Jieren, 'Multi-identity of the Chinese Christianity in Post-Olympic China: From Pre-modernity towards Postmodernity'(2009), paper presented to Edinburgh 2010 Study Group 3 and available at www.edinburgh2010.org

Lienemann-Perrin, Christine, *Training for a Relevant Ministry: A Study of the Contribution of the Theological Education Fund* (Madras & Geneva: Christian Literature Society & PTE/WCC, 1981)

Lipnack, J., & J. Stamps, *Virtual Teams: People Working across Boundaries with Technology* (New York: John Wiley & Sons, 2000)

Lopez, Rosauro, 'A Mission for and from the Youth' (2009), paper submitted to Edinburgh 2010 Study Group 9, available at www.edinburgh2010.org

Ludwig, Frieder, 'Religion and Reconciliation Processes in the African Diaspora'; Israel Akanji, 'The Local Church as an Agent of Healing and Reconciliation in the Face of Religious Conflict'. Papers presented at the Study Group 7 consultation, Edinburgh, 12-13 June 2009

Lyon, David, *Postmodernity* (Buckingham: Open University Press, 1994)

Lyotard, François, *The Postmodern Condition: A Report on Knowledge* (Minneapolis, MN: University of Minnesota Press, 1984)

Ma, Wonsuk, 'In Jesus Name… Power Encounter from an Asian Pentecostal Perspective', in *Principalities and Powers: Biblical Reflections in the Asian Context* (Manila: OMF Lit., 2007)

_____ 'Grace Korean Church: Mission from a New Margin' (2009), paper submitted to Edinburgh 2010 Study Group 9, available at www.edinburgh2010.org

Mackie, Steven, *Patterns of Ministry: Theological Education in a Changing World* (London: Collins, 1969)

Madsen, Ole Skjerbaek, 'The Church's Encounter with New Spiritualities', a position paper for Study Group 2, Edinburgh 2010 (2009), available at www.edinburgh2010.org

Magesa, Laurenti, *Anatomy of Inculturation: Transforming the Church in Africa* (Maryknoll, NY: Orbis, 2004)

Makiika, Nicta Lubaale, 'Doing Mission at the Margins of Society: Harnessing the Resources of Local Visions', in Wonsuk Ma & Cathy Ross (eds), *Mission Spirituality and Authentic Discipleship* (Seoul, 2009), 37-44. Available at www.edinburgh2010.org

Manohar, Christina, *Spirit Christology: An Indian Christian Perspective* (Delhi: ISPCK, 2009)

Matthey, Jacques, 'Evangelism, Still the Enduring Test of Our Ecumenical and Missionary Calling', *International Review of Mission* 96/382-383 (2007)

_____ (ed.), *Come Holy Spirit, Heal and Reconcile! Called in Christ to be Reconciling and Healing Communities. Report of the WCC Conference on World Mission and Evangelism, Athens, Greece, May 9-16*, 2005 (Geneva: WCC, 2008)

McLean, Janice, 'The Challenge of Context: The Case of Women and Youth'. Paper presented at the Study Group 7 consultation, Edinburgh, 12-13 June 2009

McCoy, Michael, 'Restoring Mission to the Heart of Theological Education, A South African Perspective', available at www.oikoumene.org

McDonald, J., 'The Schools that Failed', The Edmonton Journal, G1–G32 (June 1991)

McGrath, Alister, 'A Particularist View: A Post-Enlightenment Approach', in John Hick, *et al.* (eds), *More than One Way? Four Views on Salvation in a Pluralistic World* (Grand Rapids, MI: Zondervan Publishing House, 1995), 65-70

_____ 'Evangelism and Apologetics' (2009), position paper submitted to Study Group 2, Edinburgh 2010, available at www.edinburgh2010.org

Mckenna, Megan, *On Your Mark: Reading Mark in the Shadow of the Cross* (Maryknoll, NY: Orbis Books, 2006)

McLaren, Brian, *Everything Must Change* (Nashville, TN: Thomas Nelson, 2007)

McVitty, S.R., 'The Story of Seventy Years of Progress', *The Missionary Bulletin* XVI/ 2 (1920), 160-208

Meier, Paul D., *Christian Child Rearing and Personality Development* (2nd ed., Grand Rapids, MI: Baker Publishing Group, 1995)

Mendoca, Clemens, 'Mission According to the Catholic Church in Asia: A New Way of Being Church', in Wonsuk Ma & Cathy Ross (eds), *Mission Spirituality and Authentic Discipleship* (Seoul, 2009), 27-36. Available at www.edinburgh2010.org

Mfundisi, Naar, 'Zambian Pentecostalism: A Study of History, Theology and Politics'. Paper presented at the Study Group 7 consultation, Edinburgh, 12-13 June 2009

Michiels, Robrecht, 'The Self-understanding of the Church after Vatican II', *Louvain Studies* 14 (1989), 83-107

Míguez, Néstor, 'Reading John 4 in the Interface Between Ordinary and Scholarly Interpretation', in H. de Wit, L. Jonker and D. Schipani (eds)

The Eyes of the other. Intercultural Reading of the Bible (Amsterdam: Institute of Mennonite Studies, Vrije Universiteit, 2004), 334-47

Miller, Harold F., 'Closure for an African Century,' *Occasional Papers* 26 (An oral version of the paper was presented to the annual Mennonite retreat at Limuru, Kenya, December 1998) accessed online at: mcc.org/respub/occasional/26closure.html on 27 Aug 2009

Miller, J.R., *Shingwauk's Vision: A History of Native Residential Schools* (Toronto: University of Toronto Press, 2000)

Milloy, John, *A National Crime: The Canadian Government and the Residential School System, 1879-1986* (Winnipeg: University of Manitoba Press, 1999)

Minatrea, Milfred, *Shaped by God's Heart: The Passion and Practices of Missional Churches* (San Francisco: John Wiley, 2004)

Mission Theological Advisory Group, *Presence and Prophecy, A Heart for Mission in Theological Education* (London: Church House Publishing, 2002)

Moltmann, J., *Theology of Hope* (London: SCM Press, 1969)

Morales, Moises. 'The Dream of Unity in Bolivia', paper submitted to Edinburgh 2010 Study Group 9, available at www.edinburgh2010.org

Moreno, Calixto Salvatierra. 'Catholic and Pentecostal Proclamation of the Gospel: Knowledge, Appraisal and Mission Guidelines', paper submitted to Edinburgh 2010 Study Group 9, available at www.edinburgh2010.org

Myers, Bryant L., 'State of the World's Children: Critical Challenge to Christian Mission', *International Bulletin of Missionary Research* 18/3 (1994), 98-102

Nacpil, Emerito P. & Douglas J. Elwood, *The Human and the Holy: Asian Perspectives in Christian Theology* (Quezon City: New Day, 1978)

Nadar, Sarojini, 'Mission Bible Study: Mark 7:24-30', presentation at the 'Towards Edinburgh 2010: Women's Perspectives on Mission and Theological Education in the 21st Century', Ecumenical Institute, Bossey, Switzerland, 24-28 November 2008. Available at www.oikoumene.org.

Neill, S., G. Anderson, J. Goodwin (eds), *Concise Dictionary of the Christian World Mission* (Cambridge: Lutterworth Press, 1970)

Netland, Harold A., 'Christian Mission among Other Faiths: The Evangelical Tradition', position paper submitted to Study Group 2, Edinburgh 2010 (2009), available at www.edinburgh2010.org

Newbigin, Lesslie, *The Relevance of Trinitarian Doctrine for Today's Mission* (London: Edinburgh House Press, 1963)

_____ *The Open Secret* (Grand Rapids, MI: Wm B. Eerdmans, 1978)

_____ *Foolishness to the Greeks* (Grand Rapids, MI: Wm B. Eerdmans, 1986)

_____ *The Gospel in a Pluralist Society* (Grand Rapids, MI: Wm B. Eerdmans, 1989)

Nida, Eugene A., 'Marginal Helps for the Reader', *Bible Translator*, 9/1 (1958)

Nissen, Johannes, *New Testament and Mission: Historical and Hermeneutical Perspectives* (Frankfurt: Peter Lang, 1999)

Nordic Institute for Missiological and Ecumenical Research (NIME), papers of the 2007 Study Days on 'Mission and Postmodernities', *Swedish Missionary Themes*, 95/4 (2007). Available at www.missionsresearch.org

Noss, P. (ed.), *UBS Background Paper on Scripture Engagement* (Reading: United Bible Societies, 2003)

O'Brien, Bill, 'Cooperation in Mission', in J.D. Douglas, *Proclaim Christ Until He Comes: Calling the Whole Church to Take the Whole Gospel to the Whole World* (Minneapolis, MN: World Wide Publications, 1990), 204-207

O'Day, Gail R., 'John', in Carol A. Newsom and Sharon H. Ringe (eds) *Women's Bible Commentary* (Expanded edition; Louisville: Westminster John Knox Press, 1998), 383-85

Obinna, Elijah, 'The Power and Challenges of Urban Mission'. Paper presented at the Study Group 7 consultation, Edinburgh, 12-13 June 2009

Oduyoye, Mercy Amba, 'Guest Editorial', *International Review of Mission* 81/322 (April 1992), 173-74

Okoye, James Chukwuma, *Israel and the Nations: A Mission Theology of the Old Testament* (Maryknoll, NY: Orbis, 2006)

Okure, Teresa, *The Johannine Approach to Mission: A Contextual Study of John 4.1-42* (Tübingen: J.C.B. Mohr, 1988)

Olatunde, Festus, 'War Against Poverty – A Challenge for Christianity'. Paper presented at the Study Group 7 consultation, Edinburgh, 12-13 June 2009

Ott, Bernhard, *Beyond Fragmentation: Integrating Mission and Theological Education* (Oxford: Regnum, 2002)

Padilla, C. Rene, 'Spirituality in the Life and Mission of the Church' (2009), paper submitted to Edinburgh 2010 Study Group 9, available at www.edinburgh2010.org

Papathanasiou, Athanasios N., 'Is Mission a Consequence of the Catholicity of the Church? An Orthodox Perspective', *International Review of Mission* 90/359 (October 2001), 409-416

Parratt, John, *An Introduction to Third World Theologies* (Cambridge: Cambridge University Press, 2004)

Parvey, Constance F., *The Community of Women and Men* (Geneva: WCC Publications, 1993)

Peel, J.D.Y., *Religious Encounter and the Making of the Yoruba* (Indiana: Indiana University Press, 2000)

Penner, Peter F. (ed.), *Theological Education as Mission* (Neufeld Verlag, 2005)

Perez, Mario Perez, 'The Indigenous Priest in the Aboriginal Church' (2009), paper submitted to Edinburgh 2010 Study Group 9, available at www.edinburgh2010.org

Pfister, Raymond, 'Pratiques missionaires penticôtistes et œcuménisme'. Available at www.pfister.ws

Phan, Peter C., *In Our Own Tongues* (Maryknoll, NY: Orbis, 2003)

Philip, T.V., *Edinburgh to Salvador: Twentieth Century Ecumenical Missiology* (Delhi: ISPCK, 1999)

Phiri, Isabel, *Women, Presbyterianism and Patriarchy* (Blantyre: CLAIM, 1997)

Pieris, Aloysius, *An Asian Theology of Liberation* (Edinburgh: T & T Clark, 1988)

_____ *God's Reign for God's Poor: A Return to the Jesus Formula* (Kelaniya: Tulana Research Centre, 1999)

Pinnock, Clark H., *A Wideness in God's Mercy: The Finality of Jesus Christ in a World of Religions* (Grand Rapids, MI: Zondervan, 1992)

Pontifical Council for Inter-Religious Dialogue and the Congregation for the Evangelization of Peoples, 'Dialogue and Proclamation', in William B. Burrows (ed.), *Redemption and Dialogue: Reading* Redemptoris Missio *and Dialogue and Proclamation* (Maryknoll, NY: Orbis Books, 1994), 93-118

Porter, Andrew, *Religion verses Empire? British Protestant Missionaries and Overseas Expansion, 1700-1914* (Manchester: Manchester University Press, 2004)

Pries, S.L., *Die Transnationalisierung der sozialen Welt. Sozialräume jenseits von Nationalgesellschaften* (Frankfurt: Suhrkamp Verlag, 2009)

Prill, T., *Global Mission on Our Doorstep. Forced Migration and the Future of the Church* (Münster: Monsenstein & Vannerstadt, no year)

Pulford, Cedric, *Eating Uganda: From Christianity to Conquest* (Woodford Halse, Northants, UK: Ituri Publications, 1999)

Rajkumar, Peniel Jesudason Rufus, 'Making a Difference Together: Prospects for Ecumenism in the Twenty-first Century', *Ecumenical Review*, 60/3 (2008), 239-253

Randeria, S. & A. Eckert (eds), *Vom Imperialismus zum Empire. Nicht-westliche Perspektiven auf Globalisierung* (Frankfurt: Suhrkamp Verlag, 2009)

Ranson, Charles, 'The Theological Education Fund', *International Review of Mission* 47/4 (1958), 432-38.

Ratcliff, Don 'Children's Religion and Spirituality Research', www.childfaith.net/books.htm

Rayan, Samuel, *Come, Holy Spirit* (Delhi: Media House, 1998); *Renew the Face of the Earth* (Delhi: Media House, 1998)

Reim, R., *Power and Vulnerability: Reflections on Mark 9* (Nottingham, Grove Books, 1994)

'Report cum Statement of the Consultation at the United Theological College, Bangalore, India, 2009. Towards Edinburgh 2010. A Consultation on "Christian Mission among others Faiths"'. Papers available at www.edinburgh2010.org

Report of the Royal Commission on Aboriginal Peoples (Ottawa: Canada Communications Group Publishing, 1996)

Ress, Mary Judith, *Ecofeminism in Latin America* (Maryknoll, NY: Orbis, 2006)

Rhoads, David, 'Performance Criticism: An Emerging Methodology in Biblical Studies', *SBL Forum* (2005), available at www.sbl-site.org

Richardson, Cathy & Bill Nelson, 'A Change of Residence: Government Schools and Foster Homes as Sites of Forced Aboriginal Assimilation – A paper Designed to Provoke Thought and Systemic Change', *First People's Child and Family Review*, 3/2 (Special Issue, 2007)

Rickett, D., *Building Strategic Relationships* (Minneapolis, MN: Stem Press, 2008)

Ricoeur, Paul, *Hermeneutics and the Human Sciences. Essays on Language, Action and Interpretation* (Edited and translated by John B. Thompson; Cambridge: Cambridge University Press and Paris: Editions de la Maison des Sciences de l'Homme, 1981)

Rieger, J., 'Theology and Mission between Neo-colonialism and Postcolonialism', *Mission Studies* 21/2 (2004), 201-227

Robert, Marie-Hélène, Jacques Matthey et Catherine Vialle (eds), *Figures bibliques de la Mission. Exégèse et théologie de la mission, approches catholiques et protestantes* (Paris: Le Cerf, 2010)

Robinson, J.A.T., *The Body: A Study in Pauline Theology* (London: SCM, 1952)

Roembke, L., *Building Credible Multicultural Teams* (Pasadena, CA: William Carey Library, 2000)

Rowell, J., *To Give or Not to Give? Rethinking Dependency, Restoring Generosity, and Redefining Sustainability* (Milton Keynes, UK: Authentic Media, 2006)

Samartha, Stanley J., *Between Two Cultures: Ecumenical Ministry in a Pluralist World* (Geneva: WCC, 1996)

_____ *One Christ – Many Religions: Toward a Revised Christology* (Maryknoll, NY: Orbis Books, 1992)

Sandvig, Kirk, 'Who Are Kakure Kirishitan? Issues of Communal Identity within Hidden Christians of Japan'. Paper presented at the Study Group 7 consultation, Edinburgh, 12-13 June 2009

Sanneh, Lamin, *Translating the Message: The Missionary Impact on Culture* (2nd edition; Maryknoll: Orbis Books, 2009)

Saul, John Ralston, *A Fair Country: Telling Truths about Canada* (Toronto: Viking Canada, 2008)

Sawyerr, Harry, *Creative Evangelism: Towards a New Christian Encounter with Africa* (London: Lutterworth Press, 1968)

Schabel, E.J., *Paul the Missionary: Realities, Strategies and Methods* (Nottingham: Apollos, 2008)

Scherer, James A., *Gospel, Church, & Kingdom: Comparative Studies in World Mission Theology* (Minneapolis, MN: Augsburg Publishing House, 1987)

Schillebeeckx, Edward, *The Understanding of Faith: Interpretation and Criticism* (London: Sheed and Ward, 1974)

Schreiter, Robert, 'The Theology of Reconcilation and Peacemaking', in Howard Mellor & Timothy Yates (eds), *Mission, Violence and Reconcilation* (Sheffield: Cliff College, 2004), 11-28

Schultze, Quentin J., 'Evangelicals' Uneasy Alliance With the Media', in Daniel A. Stout & Judith M. Buddenbaum (eds) *Religion and Mass Media: Audiences and Adaptions* (Thousand Oaks, CA: SAGE Publications, 1996)

Schwartz, G., *When Charity Destroys Dignity: Overcoming Unhealthy Dependency in the Christian Movement* (Bloomington, IN: Author House, 2006)

Sebastian, J. Jayakiran, 'Interrogating *Missio Dei*: From the Mission of God Towards Appreciating Our Mission to God in India Today' (2009), paper presented to Edinburgh 2010 Study Group 3 and available at www.edinburgh2010.org

Seim, Turid Karlssen, *The Double Message: Patterns of Gender in Luke-Acts* (Edinburgh: T&T Clark, 1994)

Senior, Donald & Carroll Stuhlmueller, *The Biblical Foundations for Mission* (Maryknoll, NY: Orbis, 1983)

Shults, F. Leron, 'Reforming Ecclesiology in Emerging Churches', in *Theology Today* 65 (2009), 425- 438

Sim, Stuart (ed.), *Postmodern Thought* (Duxford: Icon Books, 1998)

Sims, David, 'Bibliography on The Child and American Evangelicalism', Houston Child Theology Consultation, 2004, see http://childfaith.net/theology/simsbibliography.pdf

Singh, David Emmanuel, 'Sadhu Sunder Singh and Narayana Vamana Tilak: Some Lessons for Mission Thinking/Practice in India', in Wonsuk Ma & Cathy Ross (eds), *Mission Spirituality and Authentic Discipleship* (Seoul, 2009), 55-66. Available at www.edinburgh2010.org

Singlehurst, L., *Sowing, Reaping, Keeping* (Leicester: Crossway Books, 1995)

Smith, David, *Mission after Christendom* (London: Darton, Longman and Todd, 2003)

Smith, D.B., *Sacred Feathers: The Reverend Peter Jones (Kahkeweaquonaby) and the Mississauga Indians* (Toronto: University of Toronto Press, 1999)

So, Damon, *Jesus' Revelation of his Father: A Narrative-Conceptual Study of the Trinity with Special Reference to Karl Barth* (Milton Keynes: Paternoster, 2006)

Soelle, D., *The Window of Vulnerability* (Minneapolis: Fortress Press, 1990)

Søgaard, Viggo, *Media in Church and Mission: Communicating the Gospel* (Pasadena, CA: William Carey Library, 1993)

Solivan, Samuel, *The Spirit, Pathos and Liberation: Toward an Hispanic Pentecostal Theology* (Sheffield: Sheffield Academic Press, 1998)

Stackhouse, Max, *Apologia: Contextualization, Globalization, and Mission in Theological Education* (Grand Rapids, MI: Eerdmans, 1988)

Stanley, Brian, *The World Missionary Conference, Edinburgh 1910* (Grand Rapids, MI: Wm B. Eerdmans, 2009)

Stott, John R.W. *Christian Mission in the Modern World* (Downers Grove: IVP, 1975)

Stott, John, *Authentic Christianity* (Downer's Grove, IL: InterVarsity Press, 1995)

Stout, Madeleine Dion & Gregory Kipling, *Aboriginal People, Resilience and the Residential School Legacy* (Ottawa: Aboriginal Healing Foundation, 2003)

Stromberg, J.S., 'Ecumenical Affirmation on Mission and Evangelism: A Review', *International Review of Mission* 90/358 (July 2001), 243-52

Swanepoel, Francois, 'Lecture for the Joint Conference of Theological Societies', Stellenbosch University, June 2009.

Syndesmos, 'Resolutions reached by the Working Group at the Sevres Conference, 7th-12th April 1953', *Syndesmos News* 1 (June 1953)

Talusan, Lucille, 'Childlike Faith Transforms Indonesian Village', *Christian World News*, December 11, 2007, www.cbn.com/CBNnews/214912.aspx

Tamez, Elsa, 'Challenges of Multiculturalism to Bible Translation'. Paper presented in the 'Symposium on Translation, Identity and Heterogeneity: Cross-Cultural Discourse in Postmodernity' in the University of San Marcos, Lima, Peru, 7-9 December 2007.

Tamil Nadu Women's Forum, *Unheard Voices: Dalit Women*—An Alternative Report for the 15th-19th Periodic Report on India submitted by the Government of Republic of India for the 70th Session of Committee on the Elimination of Racial Discrimination, Geneva, Switzerland (January 2007)

Tan, Kang-San, 'Who Is in the Driver's Seat? A Critique of Mission Partnership Models between Western Missions and East Asian Mission Movements', *Encounters Mission Ezine*, 24, article 3, available at www.redcliffe.org

Tapia, Elizabeth, 'Our Spirituality as Interdependent to Creation', paper presented at the WARC/CWM consultation 'Living the Accra Confession in our Theology, Mission and Spirituality', Kuala Lumpur, 2006

Tennent, Timothy C., *Christianity at the Religious Roundtable: Evangelicalism in Conversation with Hinduism, Buddhism, and Islam* (Grand Rapids, MI: Baker Academic, 2002)

_____ *Theology in the Context of World Christianity* (Grand Rapids, MI: Zondervan, 2007)

Thelle, Notto R., 'Mission to Buddhists?', position submitted to Study Group 2, Edinburgh 2010 (2009), 9, available at www.edinburgh2010.org

Thiessen, Terrance L., *Who Can Be Saved? Reassessing Salvation in Christ and World Religions* (Downers Grove & Leicester: Inter-Varsity Press, 2004)

Thomas, Joe M., 'Continuity, Discontinuity, and the Finality of Christ: A Theological Essay on the Thought of Lesslie Newbigin and Hendrik Kraemer', *Dharma Deepika: A South Asian Journal of Missiological Research* 29/1 (Jan-Jun, 2009)

Thomas, Norman E., *Classic Texts in Mission & World Christianity* (Maryknoll, NY: Orbis, 1995)

Thompson, John B., *The Media and Modernity* (Stanford, CA: Stanford University Press, 1995)

Thornton, John K., *The Kongolese Saint Anthony: Dona Beatriz Kimpa Vita and the Antonian Movement, 1684-1706* (Cambridge: CUP, 1998)

Tira, Sadiri Joy & Enoch Wan, 'The Filipino Experience in Diaspora Missions: A Case Study of Christian Communities in Contemporary Contexts'. Paper presented at the Study Group 7 consultation, Edinburgh, 12-13 June 2009

Todd, Scott C., 'Spiritual Formation and Discipleship in Childhood', in Wonsuk Ma & Cathy Ross (eds), *Mission Spirituality and Authentic Discipleship* (Seoul, 2009), 103-116. Available at www.edinburgh2010.org

Turner, Harold W., 'The Religious Reactions of Primal Societies to Higher Cultures: A New Field in the History of Religions', A lecture at the Centre for the Study of New Religious Movements in Primal Religions, Birmingham, United Kingdom, 1986

Ucko, Hans, 'Christian Mission among Other Faiths', paper submitted to Study Group 2, Edinburgh 2010 (2009), available at www.edinburgh2010.org

Udal, Joanna, 'Reconciliation Among Nations: The Role of the Church – Common Understanding and Vision,' *The Ecumenical Review*, 49 (January 1997), 61-77

Ugba, Abel, 'Between God, Ethnicity and Politics: African Pentecostals in Contemporary Ireland'. Paper presented at the Study Group 7 consultation, Edinburgh, 12-13 June 2009

United Bible Societies, *Mississauga Document* (Reading: UBS, 1996)

United Mission to Nepal, *Fifty Years in God's Hand* (Kathmandu: UMN, 2003)

Vandana, *Waters of Fire* (Bangalore: Asia Trading Corporation, 1989)

Vargas, M., 'A Neopentecostal Experience of Bolivian Aimara people' (2009), paper submitted to Study Group 2, Edinburgh 2010, available at www.edinburgh2010.org

Vassiliadis, Petros, *Eucharist and Witness: Orthodox Perspectives on the Unity and Mission of the Church* (Brookline, MA: Holy Cross Orthodox Press, 1998)

_____ 'Reconciliation As a Pneumatological Mission Paradigm: Some Preliminary Reflections by an Orthodox,' *International Review of Mission* 94/372 (January 2005), 30-42

_____ Niki Papageorgiou, George Kondortha & Nikos Dimitriadis, 'Mission among Other Faiths: An Orthodox Perspective', a position paper submitted to Study Group 2, Edinburgh 2010 (2009), available at www.edinburgh2010.org

Vatican II, *Lumen Gentium* 'Dogmatic Constitution on the Church' (1963), available at www.vatican.va

_____ *Ad Gentes* 'Decree on the Mission Activity of the Church' (1965), available at www.vatican.va

Volf, Miroslav, 'Being as God Is: Trinity and Generosity', in Miroslav Volf & Michael Welker, *God's Life in Trinity* (Minneapolis, MN: Fortress Press 2006), 3-12

von Sinner, Rudolf, 'Trust and *Convivencia*', *The Ecumenical Review*, 57/3 (July 2005), 322-41

Vatican, Secretariat for Non-Christians, 'The Attitude of the Church Towards the Followers of Other Religions: Reflections and Orientations on Dialogue and Missions', *AAS* 75 (1984), 816-828

Vatican II, *Ad Gentes: Decree on the Mission Activity of the Church* (1965). Available at www.vatican.va

Wade, A., 'Resistance Knowledges: Therapy with Aboriginal Persons Who Have Experienced Violence', *Canadian Western Geographical Series* 31 (1995), 167-206

Währisch-Oblau, Claudia, 'From Reverse Mission to Common Mission … We Hope', *International Review of Mission* 89/353 (July 2000), 467-483.

Walldorf, Friedemann, 'Searching for the Soul(s) of Europe: Missiological Models in the Ecumenical Debate on Mission in Postmodern Europe'(2009), paper presented to Edinburgh 2010 Study Group 3 and available at www.edinburgh2010.org

Walls, Andrew F., 'Primal Religious Traditions in Today's World', in *The Missionary Movement in Christian History: Studies in the Transmission of Faith* (Maryknoll, NY: Orbis Books, 1996), 119-39

_____ *The Cross-cultural Process in Christian History: Studies in the Transmission and Appropriation of Faith* (Maryknoll, NY: Orbis Books / Edinburgh: T and T Clark, 2002)

_____ 'The Great Commission 1910-2010'. Paper submitted to Edinburgh 2010, and available at www.edinburgh2010.org.

Wambua, Serah, 'Mission Spirituality and Authentic Discipleship: An African Reflection', in Wonsuk Ma & Cathy Ross (eds), *Mission Spirituality and Authentic Discipleship* (Seoul, 2009), 117-121, 45-54. Available at www.edinburgh2010.org

Warmback, A.E., 'The Journey Continues: Oikotheology and Urban Ministry', *Missionalia* 36/2-3, 165-179

Weber, Timothy P., 'The Seminaries and the Churches: Looking for New Relationships', *Theological Education* 44/1 (2008), 65-92

Werner, Dietrich, 'Evangelism from a WCC Perspective: A Recollection of an Important Ecumenical Memory, and the Unfolding of a Holistic Mission', *International Review of Mission* 96/382-383 (Jul-Oct 2007), 183-203.

_____ 'Edinburgh 2010 Process and Theological Education: The Legacy of the World Mission Conference and the Vision for ETE in the Twenty-first

Century', paper presented at the Queen's Foundation, March 2009, and submitted to Edinburgh 2010 Study Group 6

_____ 'Guest Editorial: Theological Education in Mission', *International Review of Mission* 388 (April 2009), 2-10

West, Gerald, *Contextual Bible Study Methods* (Pietermaritzburg: Cluster Publications, 1992)

Wild-Wood, Emma, 'St Apolo of Europe or What's in a Luganda Name?' *Church History* 77 (2008), 105-127

Wink, Walter, *Engaging the Powers. Discernment and Resistance in a World of Domination* (Minneapolis, MN: Fortress Press, 1984)

Wood, R., 'What Is it like to be a Partnership Facilitator?' in *Mission Frontiers: Bulletin of the US Center for World Missions* (Sept-Dec 1999)

World Council of Churches, *The New Delhi Report. Third Assembly of the WCC* (London: SCM Press, 1962)

_____ *The San Antonio Report* (Geneva: World Council of Churches, 1990)

_____ 'Mission and Evangelism: An Ecumenical Affirmation' (1982), in Jacques Matthey (ed.), *'You Are the Light of the World' Statements on Mission by the World Council of Churches 1980-2005* (Geneva: WCC, 2005), 1-38. Available at www.oikoume.org

_____ 'Religious Plurality and Christian Self-understanding', preparatory document for the Porto Alegre Assembly, 2006

_____ 'Toward a Code of Conduct on Conversion' (draft), available at www.oikoumene.org (accessed 5 Aug 2009)

_____ Central Committee, 'Towards Common Witness: A Call to Adopt Responsible Relationships in Mission and to Renounce Proselytism' (1997), in Jacques Matthey (ed.), *'You Are the Light of the World' Statements on Mission by the World Council of Churches 1980-2005* (Geneva: WCC, 2005), 39-58. Available at www.oikoumene.org

_____ Commission on Faith and Order, *Baptism, Eucharist and Ministry* (Faith and Order Paper No. 111, the 'Lima Text'; Geneva: WCC, 1982). Available at www.oikoumene.org

_____ Commission on Faith and Order, *The Nature and Mission of the Church* (Faith and Order Paper, 198; Geneva: WCC, 2005). Available at www.oikoumene.org

_____ Commission on Faith and Order, *Christian Perspectives on Theological Anthropology* (Faith and Order Paper 199; Geneva: WCC publications, 2005). Available at www.oikoumene.org

_____ Commission on World Mission and Evangelism, *Your Kingdom Come: Mission Perspectives*. Report on the World Conference on Mission and Evangelism, Melbourne, Australia, 12-25 May 1980 (Geneva: WCC, 1980)

_____ Commission on World Mission and Evangelism, 'Mission and Evangelism in Unity Today', in Jacques Matthey (ed.), *'You Are the Light of the World' Statements on Mission by the World Council of*

Churches 1980-2005 (Geneva: WCC, 2005), 59-89. Available at www.oikoumene.org

_____ Commission for World Mission and Evangelism, 'Mission as Ministry of Reconciliation' (2005), in Jacques Matthey (ed.), *'You Are the Light of the World': Statements on Mission by the World Council of Churches* (Geneva: WCC Publications, 2005), 90-126. Available at www.oikoumene.org

_____ Commission on World Mission and Evangelism working group, 'Towards Common Witness to Christ Today: Mission and the Visible Unity of the Church' (September 2009). Available at www.edinburgh2010.org

_____ Commission for World Mission and Evangelism working group, 'Mission Spirituality and Discipleship: Beyond and Through Contemporary Boundaries' (September 2009). Available at www.edinburgh2010.org

_____ Study group on healing, 'The Healing Mission of the Church' (2005), in Jacques Matthey (ed.), *'You Are the Light of the World': Statements on Mission by the World Council of Churches* (Geneva: WCC Publications, 2005), 127-62. Available at www.oikoumene.org

_____ Ecumenical Theological Education, 'Magna Charta on Ecumenical Formation in Theological Education', *Ministerial Formation* 110 (April 2008), 82-88, available at www.oikoumene.org

World Missionary Conference, Edinburgh 1910, *Report of Commission III: Education in Relation to the Christianisation of National Life* (Edinburgh & London: Oliphant, Anderson and Ferrier, 1910)

_____ *Report of Commission IV: The Missionary Message in Relation to Non-Christian Religions* (Edinburgh and London: Oliphant, Anderson, & Ferrier, 1910)

_____ *Report of Commission VIII: Co-operation and the Promotion of Unity.* (Edinburgh & London: Oliphant, Anderson & Ferrier, 1910)

_____ *Volume IX: The History and Records of the Conference* (Edinburgh & London: Oliphant, Anderson and Ferrier, 1910)

Wright, Christopher J.H., *The Mission of God: Unlocking the Bible's Grand Narrative* (Downers Grove, IL: IVP Academic, 2006)

Yannoulatos, Anastasios, 'Orthodoxy and Mission', *SVSQ* 8 (1964), 139ff

_____ 'Problems and Prospects of Interreligious Dialogue: An Eastern Orthodox Perspective', *Ecumenical Review* 52/3 (July 2000), 351ff

Yates, Timothy, *Christian Mission in the Twentieth Century* (Cambridge: Cambridge University Press, 1994)

Yeow, Choo Lak, 'The Financial Viability of Theological Formation', in John Pobee (ed.), *Towards Viable Theological Education* (Geneva: WCC Publications, 1997), 94-102

Yong, Amos, *Discerning the Spirit(s): A Pentecostal-Charismatic Contribution to Christian Theology of Religions* (Sheffield: Sheffield Academic Press, 2000)

_____ '"As the Spirit Gives Utterance": Pentecost, Intra-Christian Ecumenism and the Wider *Oikumene*', *International Review of Mission* 92/366 (Apr 2003), 299-314

_____ 'Poured Out on All Flesh', *PentecoStudies* 6/1 (2007), 16-46

Zaprometova, Olga, 'Bitter and Sweet Tears: Exploring the Spirituality of the Eastern Church Fathers in the Light of Post-modern Pentecostalism in Russia' (2009), paper presented to Edinburgh 2010 Study Group 3 and available at www.edinburgh2010.org

Zizioulas, John, *Being as Communion: Studies in Personhood and the Church* (London: Darton, Longman & Todd, 1985)

Zorn, Herbert, *Viability in Context: A Study of the Financial Viability of Theological Education in the Third World. Seedbed or Sheltered Garden?* (London: TEF, 1975)

REGNUM EDINBURGH CENTENARY SERIES

David A. Kerr, Kenneth R. Ross (Eds)
Mission Then and Now
2009 / 978-1-870345-73-6 / 343pp (paperback)
2009 / 978-1-870345-76-7 / 343pp (hardback)

No one can hope to fully understand the modern Christian missionary movement without engaging substantially with the World Missionary Conference, held at Edinburgh in 1910. This book is the first to systematically examine the eight Commissions which reported to Edinburgh 1910 and gave the conference much of its substance and enduring value. It will deepen and extend the reflection being stimulated by the upcoming centenary and will kindle the missionary imagination for 2010 and beyond.

Daryl M. Balia, Kirsteen Kim (Eds)
Witnessing to Christ Today
2010 / 978-1-870345-77-4 / 301pp (hardback)

This volume, the second in the Edinburgh 2010 series, includes reports of the nine main study groups working on different themes for the celebration of the centenary of the World Missionary Conference, Edinburgh 1910. Their collaborative work brings together perspectives that are as inclusive as possible of contemporary world Christianity and helps readers to grasp what it means in different contexts to be 'witnessing to Christ today'.

Claudia Währisch-Oblau, Fidon Mwombeki (Eds)
Mission Continues
Global Impulses for the 21st Century
2010 / 978-1-870345-82-8 / 271pp (hardback)

In May 2009, 35 theologians from Asia, Africa and Europe met in Wuppertal, Germany, for a consultation on mission theology organized by the United Evangelical Mission: Communion of 35 Churches in Three Continents. The aim was to participate in the 100th anniversary of the Edinburgh conference through a study process and reflect on the challenges for mission in the 21st century. This book brings together these papers written by experienced practitioners from around the world.

Brian Woolnough and Wonsuk Ma (Eds)
Holistic Mission
God's Plan for God's People
2010 / 978-1-870345-85-9 / 268pp (hardback)

Holistic mission, or integral mission, implies God is concerned with the whole person, the whole community, body, mind and spirit. This book discusses the meaning of the holistic gospel, how it has developed, and implications for the church. It takes a global, eclectic approach, with 19 writers, all of whom have much experience in, and commitment to, holistic mission. It addresses critically and honestly one of the most exciting, and challenging, issues facing the church today. To be part of God's plan for God's people, the church must take holistic mission to the world.

Kirsteen Kim and Andrew Anderson (Eds)
Mission Today and Tomorrow
2010 / 978-1-870345-91-0 / 450pp (hardback)

There are moments in our lives when we come to realise that we are participating in the triune God's mission. If we believe the church to be as sign and symbol of the reign of God in the world, then we are called to witness to Christ today by sharing in God's mission of love through the transforming power of the Holy Spirit. We can all participate in God's transforming and reconciling mission of love to the whole creation.

Tormod Engelsviken, Erling Lundeby and Dagfinn Solheim (Eds)
The Church Going Glocal
Mission and Globalisation
2011 / 978-1-870345-93-4 / 262pp (hardback)

The New Testament church is... universal and local at the same time. The universal, one and holy apostolic church appears in local manifestations. Missiologically speaking... the church can take courage as she faces the increasing impact of globalisation on local communities today. Being universal and concrete, the church is geared for the simultaneous challenges of the glocal and local.

Marina Ngurusangzeli Behera (Ed)
Interfaith Relations after One Hundred Years
Christian Mission among Other Faiths
2011 / 978-1-870345-96-5 / 338pp (hardback)

The essays of this book reflect not only the acceptance and celebration of pluralism within India but also by extension an acceptance as well as a need for unity among Indian Christians of different denominations. The essays were presented and studied at a preparatory consultation on Study Theme II: Christian Mission Among Other Faiths at the United Theological College, India July 2009.

Lalsangkima Pachuau and Knud Jørgensen (Eds)
Witnessing to Christ in a Pluralistic Age
Christian Mission among Other Faiths
2011 / 978-1-870345-95-8 / 277pp (hardback)

In a world where plurality of faiths is increasingly becoming a norm of life, insights on the theology of religious plurality are needed to strengthen our understanding of our own faith and the faith of others. Even though religious diversity is not new, we are seeing an upsurge in interest on the theologies of religion among all Christian confessional traditions. It can be claimed that no other issue in Christian mission is more important and more difficult than the theologies of religions.

Beth Snodderly and A Scott Moreau (Eds)
Evangelical Frontier Mission
Perspectives on the Global Progress of the Gospel
2011 / 978-1-870345-98-9 / 312pp (hardback)

This important volume demonstrates that 100 years after the World Missionary Conference in Edinburgh, Evangelism has become truly global. Twenty-first-century Evangelism continues to focus on frontier mission, but significantly, and in the spirit of Edinburgh 1910, it also has re-engaged social action.

Rolv Olsen (Ed)
Mission and Postmodernities
2011 / 978-1-870345-97-2 / 279pp (hardback)

This volume takes on meaning because its authors honestly struggle with and debate how we should relate to postmodernities. Should our response be accommodation, relativizing or counter-culture? How do we strike a balance between listening and understanding, and at the same time exploring how postmodernities influence the interpretation and application of the Bible as the normative story of God's mission in the world?

Cathy Ross (Ed)

Life-Widening Mission

2012 / 978-1-908355-00-3 / 163pp (hardback)

It is clear from the essays collected here that the experience of the 2010 World Mission Conference in Edinburgh was both affirming and frustrating for those taking part - affirming because of its recognition of how the centre of gravity has moved in global Christianity; frustrating because of the relative slowness of so many global Christian bodies to catch up with this and to embody it in the way they do business and in the way they represent themselves. These reflections will - or should - provide plenty of food for thought in the various councils of the Communion in the coming years.

Beate Fagerli, Knud Jørgensen, Rolv Olsen, Kari Storstein Haug and Knut Tveitereid (Eds)

A Learning Missional Church

Reflections from Young Missiologists

2012 / 978-1-908355-01-0 / 218pp (hardback)

Cross-cultural mission has always been a primary learning experience for the church. It pulls us out of a mono-cultural understanding and helps us discover a legitimate theological pluralism which opens up for new perspectives in the Gospel. Translating the Gospel into new languages and cultures is a human and divine means of making us learn new 'incarnations' of the Good News.

Emma Wild-Wood & Peniel Rajkumar (Eds)

Foundations for Mission

2012 / 978-1-908355-12-6 / 309pp (hardback)

This volume provides an important resource for those wishing to gain an overview of significant issues in contemporary missiology whilst understanding how they are applied in particular contexts.

Wonsuk Ma & Kenneth R Ross (Eds)

Mission Spirituality and Authentic Discipleship

2013 / 978-1-908355-24-9 / 248pp (hardback)

This book argues for the primacy of spirituality in the practice of mission. Since God is the primary agent of mission and God works through the power of the Holy Spirit, it is through openness to the Spirit that mission finds its true character and has its authentic impact.

Stephen B Bevans (Ed)

A Century of Catholic Mission

2013 / 978-1-908355-14-0 / 337pp (hardback)

A Century of Catholic Mission surveys the complex and rich history and theology of Roman Catholic Mission in the one hundred years since the 1910 Edinburgh World Mission Conference. Essays written by an international team of Catholic mission scholars focus on Catholic Mission in every region of the world, summarize church teaching on mission before and after the watershed event of the Second Vatican Council, and reflect on a wide variety of theological issues.

Robert Schreiter & Knud Jørgensen (Eds)

Mission as Ministry of Reconcilation

2013 / 978-1-908355-26-3 / 382pp (hardback)

There is hope – even if it is "Hope in a Fragile World", as the concluding chapter of Mission as Ministry of Reconciliation puts it. At the very heart of the gospel of Jesus Christ is a message of hope and reconciliation. Nothing could be more relevant and more necessary in a broken world than this Christian message of hope and reconciliation. ... I would like to congratulate the editors of Mission as Ministry of Reconciliation, for they listened carefully and planned with farsightedness. ... This rich book offers a valuable elucidation of the importance and the understanding of mission as ministry of reconciliation.

Petros Vassiliadis, Editor
Orthodox Perspectives on Mission
2013 / 978-1908355-25-6 / 262pp (hardback)

Orthodox Perspectives on Mission is both a humble tribute to some great Orthodox theologians, who in the past have provided substantial contribution to contemporary missiological and ecumenical discussions, and an Orthodox input to the upcoming 2013 Busan WCC General Assembly. The collected volume is divided into two parts: Part I: The Orthodox Heritage consists of Orthodox missiological contributions of the past, whereas Part II includes all the papers presented in the Plenary of the recent Edinburgh 2010 conference, as well as the short studies and contributions prepared, during the Edinburgh 2010 on going study process.

Pauline Hoggarth, Fergus MacDonald,
Bill Mitchell & Knud Jørgensen, Editors
Bible in Mission
2013 / 978-1908355-42-3 / 317pp (hardback)

To the authors of Bible in Mission, the Bible is the book of life, and mission is life in the Word. This core reality cuts across the diversity of contexts and hermeneutical strategies represented in these essays. The authors are committed to the boundary-crossings that characterize contemporary mission – and each sees the Bible as foundational to the missio Dei, to God's work in the world.

Wonsuk Ma, Veli-Matti Kärkkäinnen
& J Kwabena Asamoah
Pentecostal Mission and Global Christianity
*2014 / 978-1908355-43-0 / 397pp (*hardback)

Although Pentecostalism worldwide represent the most rapidly growing missionary movement in Christian history, only recently scholars from within and outside the movement have begun academic reflection on the mission. This volume represents the coming of age of emerging scholarship of various aspects of the Pentecostal mission, including theological, historical, strategic, and practical aspects.

Afe Adogame, Janice McLean & Anderson Jeremiah, Editors
Engaging the World
Christian Communities in Contemporary Global Societies
*2014 / 978-1908355-21-8 / 235pp (*hardback)

Engaging the World deals with the lived experiences and expressions of Christians in diverse communities across the globe. Christian communities do not live in a vacuum but in complex, diverse social-cultural contexts; within wider communities of different faith and social realities. Power, identity and community are key issues in considering Christian communities in contemporary contexts.

Peniel Jesudason Rufus Rajkumar, Joseph Prabhakar Dayam
& IP Asheervadham, Editors
Mission At and From the Margins
Patterns, Protagonists and Perspectives
*2014 / 978-1908355-13-3 / 283pp (*hardback)

Mission At and From the Margins: Patterns, Protagonists and Perspectives revisits the 'hi-stories' of Mission from the 'bottom up' paying critical attention to people, perspectives and patterns that have often been elided in the construction of mission history. Focusing on the mission story of Christian churches in the South Indian state of Abdhra Pradesh this collection of essays ushers its readers to re-shape their understanding of the landscape of mission history by drawing their attention to the silences and absences within pre-dominant historical accounts.

REGNUM STUDIES IN GLOBAL CHRISTIANITY

David Emmanuel Singh (Ed)
Jesus and the Cross
Reflections of Christians from Islamic Contexts
2008 / 978-1-870345-65-1 / 226pp

The Cross reminds us that the sins of the world are not borne through the exercise of power but through Jesus Christ's submission to the will of the Father. The papers in this volume are organised in three parts: scriptural, contextual and theological. The central question being addressed is: how do Christians living in contexts, where Islam is a majority or minority religion, experience, express or think of the Cross?

Sung-wook Hong
Naming God in Korea
The Case of Protestant Christianity
2008 / 978-1-870345-66-8 / 170pp (hardback)

Since Christianity was introduced to Korea more than a century ago, one of the most controversial issues has been the Korean term for the Christian 'God'. This issue is not merely about naming the Christian God in Korean language, but it relates to the question of theological contextualization - the relationship between the gospel and culture - and the question of Korean Christian identity. This book demonstrates the nature of the gospel in relation to cultures, i.e., the universality of the gospel expressed in all human cultures.

Hubert van Beek (Ed)
Revisioning Christian Unity
The Global Christian Forum
2009 / 978-1-870345-74-3 / 288pp (hardback)

This book contains the records of the Global Christian Forum gathering held in Limuru near Nairobi, Kenya, on 6 – 9 November 2007 as well as the papers presented at that historic event. Also included are a summary of the Global Christian Forum process from its inception until the 2007 gathering and the reports of the evaluation of the process that was carried out in 2008.

Young-hoon Lee
The Holy Spirit Movement in Korea
Its Historical and Theological Development
2009 / 978-1-870345-67-5 / 174pp (hardback)

This book traces the historical and theological development of the Holy Spirit Movement in Korea through six successive periods (from 1900 to the present time). These periods are characterized by repentance and revival (1900-20), persecution and suffering under Japanese occupation (1920-40), confusion and division (1940-60), explosive revival in which the Pentecostal movement played a major role in the rapid growth of Korean churches (1960-80), the movement reaching out to all denominations (1980-2000), and the new context demanding the Holy Spirit movement to open new horizons in its mission engagement (2000-).

Paul Hang-Sik Cho
Eschatology and Ecology
Experiences of the Korean Church
2010 / 978-1-870345-75-0 / 260pp (hardback)

This book raises the question of why Korean people, and Korean Protestant Christians in particular, pay so little attention to ecological issues. The author argues that there is an important connection (or elective affinity) between this lack of attention and the other-worldly eschatology that is so dominant within Korean Protestant Christianity.

Dietrich Werner, David Esterline, Namsoon Kang, Joshva Raja (Eds)
The Handbook of Theological Education in World Christianity
Theological Perspectives, Ecumenical Trends, Regional Surveys
2010 / 978-1-870345-80-0 / 759pp

This major reference work is the first ever comprehensive study of Theological Education in Christianity of its kind. With contributions from over 90 international scholars and church leaders, it aims to be easily accessible across denominational, cultural, educational, and geographic boundaries. The Handbook will aid international dialogue and networking among theological educators, institutions, and agencies.

David Emmanuel Singh & Bernard C Farr (Eds)
Christianity and Education
Shaping of Christian Context in Thinking
2010 / 978-1-870345-81-1 / 374pp

Christianity and Education is a collection of papers published in *Transformation: An International Journal of Holistic Mission Studies* over a period of 15 years. The articles represent a spectrum of Christian thinking addressing issues of institutional development for theological education, theological studies in the context of global mission, contextually aware/informed education, and academies which deliver such education, methodologies and personal reflections.

J.Andrew Kirk
Civilisations in Conflict?
Islam, the West and Christian Faith
2011 / 978-1-870345-87-3 / 205pp

Samuel Huntington's thesis, which argues that there appear to be aspects of Islam that could be on a collision course with the politics and values of Western societies, has provoked much controversy. The purpose of this study is to offer a particular response to Huntington's thesis by making a comparison between the origins of Islam and Christianity.

David Emmanuel Singh (Ed)
Jesus and the Incarnation
Reflections of Christians from Islamic Contexts
2011 / 978-1-870345-90-3 / 245pp

In the dialogues of Christians with Muslims nothing is more fundamental than the Cross, the Incarnation and the Resurrection of Jesus. Building on the *Jesus and the Cross*, this book contains voices of Christians living in various 'Islamic contexts' and reflecting on the Incarnation of Jesus. The aim and hope of these reflections is that the papers weaved around the notion of 'the Word' will not only promote dialogue among Christians on the roles of the Person and the Book but, also, create a positive environment for their conversations with Muslim neighbours.

Ivan M Satyavrata
God Has Not left Himself Without Witness
2011 / 978-1-870345-79-8 / 264pp

Since its earliest inception the Christian Church has had to address the question of what common ground exits between Christian faiths and other religions. This issue is not merely of academic interest but one with critical existential and socio-political consequences. This study presents a case for the revitalization of the fulfillment tradition based on a recovery and assessment of the fulfillment approaches of Indian Christian converts in the pre-independence period.

Bal Krishna Sharma
From this World to the Next
Christian Identity and Funerary Rites in Nepal
2013 / 978-1-908355-08-9 / 238pp

This book explores and analyses funerary rite struggles in a nation where Christianity is a comparatively recent phenomenon, and many families have multi-faith, who go through traumatic experiences at the death of their family members. The author has used an applied theological approach to explore and analyse the findings in order to address the issue of funerary rites with which the Nepalese church is struggling.

J Kwabena Asamoah-Gyada
Contemporary Pentecostal Christianity
Interpretations from an African Context
2013 / 978-1-908355-07-2 / 194pp

Pentecostalism is the fastest growing stream of Christianity in the world. The real evidence for the significance of Pentecostalism lies in the actual churches they have built and the numbers they attract. This work interprets key theological and missiological themes in African Pentecostalism by using material from the live experiences of the movement itself.

David Emmanuel Singh and Bernard C Farr (Eds)
The Bible and Christian Ethics
2013 / 978-1-908355-20-1 / 217pp

This book contains papers from the Oxford Centre for Mission Studies' quarterly journal, Transformation, on the topic of Christian Ethics. Here, Mission Studies is understood in its widest sense to also encompass Christian Ethics. At the very hearts of it lies the Family as the basic unit of society. All the papers together seek to contribute to understanding how Christian thought is shaped in contexts each of which poses its own challenge to Christian living in family and in broader society.

Martin Allaby

Inequality, Corruption and the Church

Challenges & Opportunities in the Global Church

2013 / 978-1-908355-16-4 / 228pp

Why are economic inequalities greatest in the southern countries where most people are Christians? This book teases out the influences that have created this situation, and concludes that Christians could help reduce economic inequalities by opposing corruption. Interviews in the Philippines, Kenya, Zambia and Peru reveal opportunities and challenges for Christians as they face up to corruption.

Paul Alexander and Al Tizon (Eds)

Following Jesus

Journeys in Radical Discipleship – Essays in Honor of Ronald J Sider

2013 / 978-1-908355-27-0 / 228pp

Ronald J. Sider and the organization that he founded, *Evangelicals for Social Action*, are most respected for their pioneering work in the area of evangelical social concern. However, Sider's great contribution to social justice is but a part of a larger vision – namely, biblical discipleship. His works, which span more than four decades, have guided the faithful to be authentic gospel-bearers in ecclesial, cultural and political arenas. This book honors Ron Sider, by bringing together a group of scholar-activists, old and young, to reflect upon the gospel and its radical implications for the 21st century.

Cawley Bolt

Reluctant or Radical Revolutionaries?

Evangelical Missionaries and Afro-Jamaican Character, 1834-1870

2013 / 978-1-908355-18-8 / 287pp

This study is based on extensive research that challenges traditional ways of understanding some evangelical missionaries of nineteenth century Jamaica and calls for revision of those views. It highlights the strength and character of persons facing various challenges of life in their effort to be faithful to the guiding principles of their existence.

Isabel Apawo Phiri & Dietrich Werner (Eds)

Handbook of Theological Education in Africa

2013 / 978-1-908355-45-4 / 1110pp

The *Handbook of Theological Education in Africa* is a wake-up call for African churches to give proper prominence to theological education institutions and their programmes which serve them. It is unique, comprehensive and ambitious in its aim and scope.

Hope Antone, Wati Longchar, Hyunju Bae, Huang Po Ho, Dietrich Werner (Eds)

Asian Handbook for Theological Education and Ecumenism

2013 / 978-1-908355-30-0 / 675pp (hardback)

This impressive and comprehensive book focuses on key resources for teaching Christian unity and common witness in Asian contexts. It is a collection of articles that reflects the ongoing 'double wrestle' with the texts of biblical tradition as well as with contemporary contexts. It signals an investment towards the future of the ecumenical movement in Asia.

Bernhard Reitsma

The God of My Enemy

The Middle East and the Nature of God

2014 / 978-1-908355-50-8 / 206pp

The establishment of the State of Israel in 1948 for the Church in the West has been the starting point of a rediscovery of its own roots. In the Middle East the effect has been exactly the opposite: Christians have become estranged from their Old Testament roots, because they have been expelled from their land exactly because of an appeal to the Old Testament. The concept of Israel changed from a nation in the Bible, with which they could associate, to an economic, political and military power that was against them

REGNUM STUDIES IN MISSION

Kwame Bediako

Theology and Identity

The Impact of Culture upon Christian Thought in the Second Century and in Modern Africa

1992 / 978-1870345-10-1 / 507pp

The author examines the question of Christian identity in the context of the Graeco–Roman culture of the early Roman Empire. He then addresses the modern African predicament of quests for identity and integration.

Christopher Sugden

Seeking the Asian Face of Jesus

The Practice and Theology of Christian Social Witness in Indonesia and India 1974–1996

1997 / 1-870345-26-6 / 496pp

This study focuses on contemporary holistic mission with the poor in India and Indonesia combined with the call to transformation of all life in Christ with micro-credit enterprise schemes. 'The literature on contextual theology now has a new standard to rise to' – Lamin Sanneh (Yale University, USA).

Hwa Yung

Mangoes or Bananas?

The Quest for an Authentic Asian Christian Theology

1997 / 1-870345-25-5 / 274pp

Asian Christian thought remains largely captive to Greek dualism and Enlightenment rationalism because of the overwhelming dominance of Western culture. Authentic contextual Christian theologies will emerge within Asian Christianity with a dual recovery of confidence in culture and the gospel.

Keith E. Eitel

Paradigm Wars

The Southern Baptist International Mission Board Faces the Third Millennium

1999 / 1-870345-12-6 / 140pp

The International Mission Board of the Southern Baptist Convention is the largest denominational mission agency in North America. This volume chronicles the historic and contemporary forces that led to the IMB's recent extensive reorganization, providing the most comprehensive case study to date of a historic mission agency restructuring to continue its mission purpose into the twenty-first century more effectively.

Samuel Jayakumar

Dalit Consciousness and Christian Conversion

Historical Resources for a Contemporary Debate

1999 / 81-7214-497-0 / 434pp

(Published jointly with ISPCK)

The main focus of this historical study is social change and transformation among the Dalit Christian communities in India. Historiography tests the evidence in the light of the conclusions of the modern Dalit liberation theologians.

Vinay Samuel and Christopher Sugden (Eds)

Mission as Transformation

A Theology of the Whole Gospel

1999 / 978-18703455-13-2 / 522pp

This book brings together in one volume twenty five years of biblical reflection on mission practice with the poor from around the world. This volume helps anyone understand how evangelicals, struggling to unite evangelism and social action, found their way in the last twenty five years to the biblical view of mission in which God calls all human beings to love God and their neighbour; never creating a separation between the two.

Christopher Sugden

Gospel, Culture and Transformation

2000 / 1-870345-32-3 / 152pp

A Reprint, with a New Introduction,

of Part Two of Seeking the Asian Face of Jesus

Gospel, Culture and Transformation explores the practice of mission especially in relation to transforming cultures and communities. - 'Transformation is to enable God's vision of society to be actualised in all relationships: social, economic and spiritual, so that God's will may be reflected in human society and his love experienced by all communities, especially the poor.'

Bernhard Ott

Beyond Fragmentation: Integrating Mission and Theological Education

A Critical Assessment of some Recent Developments

in Evangelical Theological Education

2001 / 1-870345-14-9 / 382pp

Beyond Fragmentation is an enquiry into the development of Mission Studies in evangelical theological education in Germany and German-speaking Switzerland between 1960 and 1995. The author undertakes a detailed examination of the paradigm shifts which have taken place in recent years in both the theology of mission and the understanding of theological education.

Gideon Githiga

The Church as the Bulwark against Authoritarianism

Development of Church and State Relations in Kenya, with Particular Reference to the Years after Political Independence 1963-1992

2002 / 1-870345-38-x / 218pp

'All who care for love, peace and unity in Kenyan society will want to read this careful history by Bishop Githiga of how Kenyan Christians, drawing on the Bible, have sought to share the love of God, bring his peace and build up the unity of the nation, often in the face of great difficulties and opposition.' Canon Dr Chris Sugden, Oxford Centre for Mission Studies.

Myung Sung-Hoon, Hong Young-Gi (Eds)

Charis and Charisma

David Yonggi Cho and the Growth of Yoido Full Gospel Church

2003 / 978-1870345-45-3 / 218pp

This book discusses the factors responsible for the growth of the world's largest church. It expounds the role of the Holy Spirit, the leadership, prayer, preaching, cell groups and creativity in promoting church growth. It focuses on God's grace (charis) and inspiring leadership (charisma) as the two essential factors and the book's purpose is to present a model for church growth worldwide.

Samuel Jayakumar

Mission Reader

Historical Models for Wholistic Mission in the Indian Context

2003 / 1-870345-42-8 / 250pp

(Published jointly with ISPCK)

This book is written from an evangelical point of view revalidating and reaffirming the Christian commitment to wholistic mission. The roots of the 'wholistic mission' combining 'evangelism and social concerns' are to be located in the history and tradition of Christian evangelism in the past; and the civilizing purpose of evangelism is compatible with modernity as an instrument in nation building.

Bob Robinson

Christians Meeting Hindus

An Analysis and Theological Critique of the Hindu-Christian Encounter in India

2004 / 987-1870345-39-2 / 392pp

This book focuses on the Hindu-Christian encounter, especially the intentional meeting called dialogue, mainly during the last four decades of the twentieth century, and specifically in India itself.

Gene Early

Leadership Expectations

How Executive Expectations are Created and Used in a Non-Profit Setting

2005 / 1-870345-30-9 / 276pp

The author creates an Expectation Enactment Analysis to study the role of the Chancellor of the University of the Nations-Kona, Hawaii. This study is grounded in the field of managerial work, jobs, and behaviour and draws on symbolic interactionism, role theory, role identity theory and enactment theory. The result is a conceptual framework for developing an understanding of managerial roles.

Tharcisse Gatwa

The Churches and Ethnic Ideology in the Rwandan Crises 1900-1994

2005 / 978-1870345-24-8 / 300pp

(Reprinted 2011)

Since the early years of the twentieth century Christianity has become a new factor in Rwandan society. This book investigates the role Christian churches played in the formulation and development of the racial ideology that culminated in the 1994 genocide.

Julie Ma

Mission Possible

Biblical Strategies for Reaching the Lost

2005 / 978-1870345-37-8 / 142pp

This is a missiology book for the church which liberates missiology from the specialists for the benefit of every believer. It also serves as a textbook that is simple and friendly, and yet solid in biblical interpretation. This book links the biblical teaching to the actual and contemporary missiological settings with examples, making the Bible come alive to the reader.

I. Mark Beaumont

Christology in Dialogue with Muslims

A Critical Analysis of Christian Presentations of Christ for Muslims from the Ninth and Twentieth Centuries

2005 / 978-1870345-46-0 / 227pp

This book analyses Christian presentations of Christ for Muslims in the most creative periods of Christian-Muslim dialogue, the first half of the ninth century and the second half of the twentieth century. In these two periods, Christians made serious attempts to present their faith in Christ in terms that take into account Muslim perceptions of him, with a view to bridging the gap between Muslim and Christian convictions.

Thomas Czövek,

Three Seasons of Charismatic Leadership

A Literary-Critical and Theological Interpretation of the Narrative of Saul, David and Solomon

2006 / 978-1870345-48-4 / 272pp

This book investigates the charismatic leadership of Saul, David and Solomon. It suggests that charismatic leaders emerge in crisis situations in order to resolve the crisis by the charisma granted by God. Czovek argues that Saul proved himself as a charismatic leader as long as he acted resolutely and independently from his mentor Samuel. In the author's eyes, Saul's failure to establish himself as a charismatic leader is caused by his inability to step out from Samuel's shadow.

Richard Burgess

Nigeria's Christian Revolution

The Civil War Revival and Its Pentecostal Progeny (1967-2006)

2008 / 978-1-870345-63-7 / 347pp

This book describes the revival that occurred among the Igbo people of Eastern Nigeria and the new Pentecostal churches it generated, and documents the changes that have occurred as the movement has responded to global flows and local demands. As such, it explores the nature of revivalist and Pentecostal experience, but does so against the backdrop of local socio-political and economic developments, such as decolonisation and civil war, as well as broader processes, such as modernisation and globalisation.

David Emmanuel Singh & Bernard C Farr (Eds)

Christianity and Cultures

Shaping Christian Thinking in Context

2008 / 978-1-870345-69-9 / 271pp

This volume marks an important milestone, the 25th anniversary of the Oxford Centre for Mission Studies (OCMS). The papers here have been exclusively sourced from Transformation, a quarterly journal of OCMS, and seek to provide a tripartite view of

Christianity's engagement with cultures by focusing on the question: how is Christian thinking being formed or reformed through its interaction with the varied contexts it encounters? The subject matters include different strands of theological-missiological thinking, socio-political engagements and forms of family relationships in interaction with the host cultures.

Tormod Engelsviken, Ernst Harbakk, Rolv Olsen, Thor Strandenæs (Eds)
Mission to the World
Communicating the Gospel in the 21st Century: Essays in Honour of Knud Jørgensen
2008 / 978-1-870345-64-4 / 472pp (hardback)

Knud Jørgensen is Director of Areopagos and Associate Professor of Missiology at MF Norwegian School of Theology. This book reflects on the main areas of Jørgensen's commitment to mission. At the same time it focuses on the main frontier of mission, the world, the content of mission, the Gospel, the fact that the Gospel has to be communicated, and the context of contemporary mission in the 21st century.

Al Tizon
Transformation after Lausanne
Radical Evangelical Mission in Global-Local Perspective
2008 / 978-1-870345-68-2 / 281pp

After Lausanne '74, a worldwide network of radical evangelical mission theologians and practitioners use the notion of "Mission as Transformation" to integrate evangelism and social concern together, thus lifting theological voices from the Two Thirds World to places of prominence. This book documents the definitive gatherings, theological tensions, and social forces within and without evangelicalism that led up to Mission as Transformation. And it does so through a global-local grid that points the way toward greater holistic mission in the 21st century.

Bambang Budijanto
Values and Participation
Development in Rural Indonesia
2009 / 978-1-870345-70-4 / 237pp

Socio-religious values and socio-economic development are inter-dependant, inter-related and are constantly changing in the context of macro political structures, economic policy, religious organizations and globalization; and micro influences such as local affinities, identity, politics, leadership and beliefs. The book argues that the comprehensive approach in understanding the socio-religious values of each of the three local Lopait communities in Central Java is essential to accurately describing their respective identity.

Alan R. Johnson
Leadership in a Slum
A Bangkok Case Study
2009 / 978-1-870345-71-2 / 238pp

This book looks at leadership in the social context of a slum in Bangkok from a different perspective than traditional studies which measure well educated Thais on leadership scales derived in the West. Using both systematic data collection and participant observation, it develops a culturally preferred model as well as a set of models based in Thai concepts that reflect on-the-ground realities. It concludes by looking at the implications of the anthropological approach for those who are involved in leadership training in Thai settings and beyond.

Titre Ande

Leadership and Authority

Bula Matari and Life - Community Ecclesiology in Congo

2010 / 978-1-870345-72-9 / 189pp

Christian theology in Africa can make significant development if a critical understanding of the socio-political context in contemporary Africa is taken seriously, particularly as Africa's post-colonial Christian leadership based its understanding and use of authority on the Bula Matari model. This has caused many problems and Titre proposes a Life-Community ecclesiology for liberating authority, here leadership is a function, not a status, and 'apostolic succession' belongs to all people of God.

Frank Kwesi Adams

Odwira and the Gospel

A Study of the Asante Odwira Festival and its Significance for Christianity in Ghana

2010 /978-1-870345-59-0 / 232pp

The study of the Odwira festival is the key to the understanding of Asante religious and political life in Ghana. The book explores the nature of the Odwira festival longitudinally - in pre-colonial, colonial and post-independence Ghana - and examines the Odwira ideology and its implications for understanding the Asante self-identity. Also discussed is how some elements of faith portrayed in the Odwira festival can provide a framework for Christianity to engage with Asante culture at a greater depth.

Bruce Carlton

Strategy Coordinator

Changing the Course of Southern Baptist Missions

2010 / 978-1-870345-78-1 / 273pp

This is an outstanding, one-of-a-kind work addressing the influence of the non-residential missionary/strategy coordinator's role in Southern Baptist missions. This scholarly text examines the twentieth century global missiological currents that influenced the leadership of the International Mission Board, resulting in a new paradigm to assist in taking the gospel to the nations.

Julie Ma & Wonsuk Ma

Mission in the Spirit:

Towards a Pentecostal/Charismatic Missiology

2010 / 978-1-870345-84-2 / 312pp

The book explores the unique contribution of Pentecostal/Charismatic mission from the beginning of the twentieth century. The first part considers the theological basis of Pentecostal/Charismatic mission thinking and practice. Special attention is paid to the Old Testament, which has been regularly overlooked by the modern Pentecostal/Charismatic movements. The second part discusses major mission topics with contributions and challenges unique to Pentecostal/Charismatic mission. The book concludes with a reflection on the future of this powerful missionary movement. As the authors served as Korean missionaries in Asia, often their missionary experiences in Asia are reflected in their discussions.

Allan Anderson, Edmond Tang (Eds)

Asian and Pentecostal

The Charismatic Face of Christianity in Asia

2011 / 978-1870345-94-1 / 500pp

(Revised Edition)

This book provides a thematic discussion and pioneering case studies on the history and development of Pentecostal and Charismatic churches in the countries of South Asia, South East Asia and East Asia.

S. Hun Kim & Wonsuk Ma (Eds)
Korean Diaspora and Christian Mission
2011 / 978-1-870345-89-7 / 301pp (hardback)

As a 'divine conspiracy' for Missio Dei, the global phenomenon of people on the move has shown itself to be invaluable. In 2004 two significant documents concerning Diaspora were introduced, one by the Filipino International Network and the other by the Lausanne Committee for World Evangelization. These have created awareness of the importance of people on the move for Christian mission. Since then, Korean Diaspora has conducted similar research among Korean missions, resulting in this book

Jin Huat Tan
Planting an Indigenous Church
The Case of the Borneo Evangelical Mission
2011 / 978-1-870345-99-6 / 343pp

Dr Jin Huat Tan has written a pioneering study of the origins and development of Malaysia's most significant indigenous church. This is an amazing story of revival, renewal and transformation of the entire region chronicling the powerful effect of it evident to date! What can we learn from this extensive and careful study of the Borneo Revival, so the global Christianity will become ever more dynamic?

Bill Prevette
Child, Church and Compassion
Towards Child Theology in Romania
2012 / 978-1-908355-03-4 / 382pp

Bill Prevett comments that "children are like 'canaries in a mine shaft'; they provide a focal point for discovery and encounter of perilous aspects of our world that are often ignored." True, but miners also carried a lamp to see into the subterranean darkness. This book is such a lamp. It lights up the subterranean world of children and youth in danger of exploitation, and as it does so travels deep into their lives and also into the activities of those who seek to help them.

Samuel Cyuma
Picking up the Pieces
The Church and Conflict Resolution in South Africa and Rwanda
2012 / 978-1-908355-02-7 / 373pp

In the last ten years of the 20th century, the world was twice confronted with unbelievable news from Africa. First, there was the end of Apartheid in South Africa, without bloodshed, due to responsible political and Church leaders. The second was the mass killings in Rwanda, which soon escalated into real genocide. Political and Church leaders had been unable to prevents this crime against humanity. In this book, the question is raised: can we compare the situation in South Africa with that in Rwanda? Can Rwandan leaders draw lessons from the peace process in South Africa?

Peter Rowan
Proclaiming the Peacemaker
The Malaysian Church as an Agent of Reconciliation in a Multicultural Society
2012 / 978-1-908355-05-8 / 268pp

With a history of racial violence and in recent years, low-level ethnic tensions, the themes of peaceful coexistence and social harmony are recurring ones in the discourse of Malaysian society. In such a context, this book looks at the role of the church as a reconciling agent, arguing that a reconciling presence within a divided society necessitates an ethos of peacemaking.

Edward Ontita

Resources and Opportunity

The Architecture of Livelihoods in Rural Kenya

2012 / 978-1-908355-04-1 / 328pp

Poor people in most rural areas of developing countries often improvise resources in unique ways to enable them make a living. Resources and Opportunity takes the view that resources are dynamic and fluid, arguing that villagers co-produce them through redefinition and renaming in everyday practice and use them in diverse ways. The book focuses on ordinary social activities to bring out people's creativity in locating, redesigning and embracing livelihood opportunities in processes.

Kathryn Kraft

Searching for Heaven in the Real World

A Sociological Discussion of Conversion in the Arab World

2012 / 978-1-908355-15-7 / 142pp

Kathryn Kraft explores the breadth of psychological and social issues faced by Arab Muslims after making a decision to adopt a faith in Christ or Christianity, investigating some of the most surprising and significant challenges new believers face.

Wessley Lukose

Contextual Missiology of the Spirit

Pentecostalism in Rajasthan, India

2013 / 978-1-908355-09-6 / 256pp

This book explores the identity, context and features of Pentecostalism in Rajasthan, India as well as the internal and external issues facing Pentecostals. It aims to suggest 'a contextual missiology of the Spirit,' as a new model of contextual missiology from a Pentecostal perspective. It is presented as a glocal, ecumenical, transformational, and public missiology.

Paul M Miller

Evangelical Mission in Co-operation with Catholics

A Study of Evangelical Tensions

2013 / 978-1-908355-17-1 / 291pp

This book brings the first thorough examination of the discussions going on within Evangelicalism about the viability of a good conscience dialogue with Roman Catholics. Those who are interested in evangelical world missions and Roman Catholic views of world missions will find this informative.

Alemayehu Mekonnen

Culture Change in Ethiopia

An Evangelical Perspective

2013 / 978-1-908355-39-3 / 199pp

This book addresses the causes and consequences of culture change in Ethiopia, from Haile Selassie to the present, based on thorough academic research. Although written from an evangelical perspective, this book invites Ethiopians from all religions, ideological, and ethnic backgrounds to reflect on their past, to analyse their present and to engage in unity with diversity to face the future.

Godwin Lekundayo
The Cosmic Christ
Towards Effective Mission Among the Maasai
2013 / 978-1-908355-28- 7 / 259 pp

This book reveals a complex interaction between the Christian gospel brought by western missionaries and the nomadic Massai culture of Tanzania … an important insider's voice courageously questioning the approach to condemn some critical Maasai practices, particularly polygamy, and its missionary consequences. This is a rare study from a Maasai Christian leader.

Philippe Ouedraogo
Female Education and Mission
A Burkina Faso Experience
2014 / 978-1-908355-11-9 / 263pp

This volume is the result of six years research in 'Overcoming Obstacles to Female Education in Burkina Faso'. It narrates how Christians and religious groups can speed up female education and contribute to the socio-economic growth of Burkina Faso. Religious culture and traditions were seen as a problem to female education. However, the evidence from this research shows that Christianity is also part of the solution to a quality female education, thus a key factor of socio economic growth of the country.

Haw Yung
Mangoes or Bananas?
The Quest for an Authentic Asian Christian Theology
(Second Edition)
2014 / 978-1-908355-47-8 / 232pp

Over the past few decades there has been a growing awareness of the need for contextual theologies throughout Asia. But how genuinely contextual are these? Based on the premise that theology and mission are inseparable, the author applies four missiological criteria to representative examples of Protestant Asian writings to assess their adequacy or otherwise as contextual theologies.

Daniel Taichoul Yang
Called Out for Witness
The Missionary Journey of Grace Korean Church
2014 / 978-1-908355-49-2 / 167pp

This book investigates the theological motivation for GKC's missions: Reformed theology, Presbyterian theology, and mission theology. The book also shows the extent of the church's mission engagement by continents. Finally, the book turns its attention to the future with an evaluation of the church's missionary journey.

REGNUM RESOURCES FOR MISSION

Knud Jørgensen
Equipping for Service
Christian Leadership in Church and Society
2012 / 978-1-908355-06-5 / 150pp

This book is written out of decades of experience of leading churches and missions in Ethiopia, Geneva, Norway and Hong Kong. Combining the teaching of Scripture with the insights of contemporary management philosophy, Jørgensen writes in a way which is practical and applicable to anyone in Christian service. "The intention has been to challenge towards a leadership relevant for work in church and mission, and in public and civil society, with special attention to leadership in Church and organisation."

Mary Miller
What does Love have to do with Leadership?
2013 / 978-1-908355-10-2 / 100pp

Leadership is a performing art, not a science. It is the art of influencing others, not just to accomplish something together, but to want to accomplish great things together. Mary Miller captures the art of servant leadership in her powerful book. She understands that servant leaders challenge existing processes without manipulating or overpowering people.

Mary Miller (Ed)
Faces of Holistic Mission
Stories of the OCMS Family
2013 / 978-1-908355-32-4 / 104pp

There is a popular worship song that begins with the refrain, 'look what the Lord has done, look what the Lord has done'. This book does exactly that; it seeks to show what the Lord has done. Fifteen authors from five different continents identify what the Lord has indeed been doing, and continues to do, in their lives. These are their stories.

David Cranston and Ruth Padilla DeBorst (Eds)
Mission as Transformation
Learning from Catalysts
2013 / 978-1-908355-34-8 / 77pp

This book is the product of the first Stott-Bediako Forum, held in 2012 with the title *Portraits of Catalysts*. Its aim was to learn from the stories of Christian leaders whose lives and work have served as catalysts for transformation as each, in his or her particular way, facilitated the intersection between the Good News of Jesus Christ and the context in which they lived, in particular amongst people who are suffering.

Brian Woolnough (Ed)
Good News from Africa
Community Transformation Through the Church
2013 / 978-1-908355-33-1 / 123pp

This book discusses how sustainable, holistic, community development can be, and is being, achieved through the work of the local church. Leading African development practitioners describe different aspects of development through their own experience.

Makonen Getu (Ed)
Transforming Microfinance
A Christian Approach
2013 / 978-1-908355-31-7 / 264pp

"This book highlights the important role that Christian-based organisations bring to the delivery of financial services for the poor. It is times, significant and important and deserves a wide circulation".

Lord Carey of Clifton, former Archbishop of Canterbury

Jonathan Ingleby, Tan Kand San, Tan Loun Ling, (Eds)
Contextualisation & Mission Training
Engaging Asia's Religious Worlds
2013 / 978-1-908355-40-9 / 109pp

Contextualisation & Mission Training, offers "contextual frameworks" and "explorations" in order to enhance deeper engagement with the complexity of Asian social, cultural and religious systems.

On Eagle's Wings
Models in Mentoring
2013 / 978-1-908355-46-1 / 105pp

David Cranston writes unashamedly as a Christian for whom no account of mentoring would be complete without placing it in the biggest context of all – that of the relationship between humans and God.

John Lennox, Professor of Mathematics, University of Oxford
Fellow in Mathematics and Philosophy of Science

GENERAL REGNUM TITLES

Vinay Samuel, Chris Sugden (Eds)
The Church in Response to Human Need
1987 / 1870345045 / xii+268pp

Philip Sampson, Vinay Samuel, Chris Sugden (Eds)
Faith and Modernity
Essays in modernity and post-modernity
1994 / 1870345177 / 352pp

Klaus Fiedler
The Story of Faith Missions
1994 / 0745926878 / 428pp

Douglas Peterson
Not by Might nor by Power
A Pentecostal Theology of Social Concern in Latin America
1996 / 1870345207 / xvi+260pp

David Gitari
In Season and Out of Season
Sermons to a Nation
1996 / 1870345118 / 155pp

David. W. Virtue
A Vision of Hope
The Story of Samuel Habib
1996 / 1870345169 / xiv+137pp

Everett A Wilson
Strategy of the Spirit

J.Philip Hogan and the Growth of the Assemblies of God Worldwide, 1960 - 1990
1997 /1870345231/214

Murray Dempster, Byron Klaus, Douglas Petersen (Eds)
The Globalization of Pentecostalism
A Religion Made to Travel
1999 / 1870345290 / xvii+406pp

Peter Johnson, Chris Sugden (Eds)
Markets, Fair Trade and the Kingdom of God
Essays to Celebrate Traidcraft's 21st Birthday
2001 / 1870345193 / xii+155pp

Robert Hillman, Coral Chamberlain, Linda Harding
Healing & Wholeness
Reflections on the Healing Ministry
2002 / 978-1- 870345-35- 4 / xvii+283pp

David Bussau, Russell Mask
Christian Microenterprise Development
An Introduction
2003 / 1870345282 / xiii+142pp

David Singh
Sainthood and Revelatory Discourse
An Examination of the Basis for the Authority of Bayan in Mahdawi Islam
2003 / 8172147285 / xxiv+485pp

REGNUM AFRICA TITLES

Kwame Bediako
Jesus in Africa, The Christian Gospel in African History and Experience
(2000) (Theological Reflections from the South series)
SECOND EDITION FORTHCOMING 2013

Mercy Amba Oduyoye
Beads and Strands, Reflections of an African Woman on Christianity in Africa
(Theological Reflections from the South series)
2002 / 1-870345-41-X / 114pp

Kä Mana
Christians and Churches of Africa Envisioning the Future, Salvation in Christ and the Building of a new African Society
(Theological Reflections from the South series)
2002 / 1-870345-27-4 / 119pp

Ype Schaaf
On Their Way Rejoicing, The History and Role of the Bible in Africa
2002 / 1-870345-35-9 / 252pp

E.A.W. Engmann
Kpawo-Kpawo Toi Kpawo – Vol. 1, Adesai, Oboade, Lalai, Ajenui ke Shwemoi
(Folklore of the Ga People)
(Gbotsui Series - Indigenous Sources of Knowledge in Ghanaian Languages)
2009 / 978-9988-1-2296-6 / 70pp

Philip Tetteh Laryea
Yesu Homowo Nuntso (Jesus, Lord of Homowo)
(Nyamedua series in Mother-tongue Theology)
(reprinted 2011) / 1-870345-54-1 / 176pp

E.A.W. Engmann
Kpawo-Kpawo Toi Kpawo – Vol. 2, Kusumii (Folklore of the Ga People)
(Gbotsui Series - Indigenous Sources of Knowledge in Ghanaian Languages)
2012 / 978-9988-1-2294-2, 186pp

Philip T. Laryea
Ephraim Amu: Nationalist, Poet and Theologian (1899–1995)
2012 / 978-9988-1-2293-5, 425pp

Jon P. Kirby
The Power and the Glory, Popular Christianity in Northern Ghana
(Trends in African Christianity Series)
2012 / 978-9988-1-2295-9, 350pp

For the up-to-date listing of the Regnum books visit www.ocms.ac.uk/regnum

Regnum Books International
Regnum is an Imprint of The Oxford Centre for Mission Studies
St. Philip and St. James Church
Woodstock Road
Oxford, OX2 6HR

regnum